CRITICAL
FOR *TRAVEL*

"The *Travelers' Tales* series is �
—Jan Morris,

"For the thoughtful traveler,
There's nothing like them on the market.
—Pico Iyer, author of *Video Night in Kathmandu*

"This is the stuff memories can be duplicated from."
—Karen Krebsbach, *Foreign Service Journal*

"I can't think of a better way to get comfortable with a destination
than by delving into *Travelers' Tales*…before reading a guidebook, before
seeing a travel agent. The series helps visitors refine their interests and
readies them to communicate with the peoples they come in contact
with…."
—Paul Glassman, Society of American Travel Writers

"…*Travelers' Tales* is a valuable addition to any pre-departure reading
list."
—Tony Wheeler, publisher, Lonely Planet Publications

"*Travelers' Tales* delivers something most guidebooks only promise: a real
sense of what a country is all about…."
—Steve Silk, *Hartford Courant*

"These anthologies seem destined to be a success…*Travelers' Tales*
promises to be a useful and enlightening addition to the travel bookshelves. By collecting and organizing such a wide range of literature,
O'Reilly and Habegger are providing a real service for those who
enjoy reading first-person accounts of a destination before seeing it
for themselves."
—Bill Newlin, publisher, Moon Publications

"The *Travelers' Tales* series should become required reading for anyone
visiting a foreign country who wants to truly step off the tourist track
and experience another culture, another place, first hand."
—Nancy Paradis, *St. Petersburg Times*

"Like having been there, done it, seen it. If there's one thing traditional guidebooks lack, it's the really juicy travel information, the personal stories about back alleys and brief encounters. The *Travelers' Tales* series fills this gap with an approach that's all anecdotes, no directions."

—Jim Gullo, *Diversion*

TRAVELERS' TALES

THE ROAD WITHIN

TRUE STORIES OF TRANSFORMATION

TRAVELERS' TALES

THE ROAD WITHIN

TRUE STORIES OF TRANSFORMATION

✦ ✦ ✦

Collected and Edited by

SEAN O'REILLY   JAMES O'REILLY

TIM O'REILLY

Series Editors
JAMES O'REILLY AND LARRY HABEGGER

TRAVELERS' TALES, INC.
SAN FRANCISCO, CALIFORNIA

Distributed by
O'REILLY AND ASSOCIATES, INC.
101 MORRIS STREET
SEBASTOPOL, CALIFORNIA 95472

The traveler has to knock
at every alien door
to come to his own,
and he has to wander
through all the outer worlds
to reach the innermost
shrine at the end.

—Rabindranath Tagore, *Gitanjali*

For our parents,
Sean and Anne O'Reilly,
whose love remains our
deep blessing and compass.

Table of Contents

Preface   *xvii*

Map   *xx*

Part One
THE HIDDEN WORLD

No Distance in the Heart   3
THOM ELKJER
Barcelona

Garden of Paradise   9
NATALIE GOLDBERG
New Mexico

Out of the Depths   19
LYALL WATSON
Indonesia

Call of the Jungle   34
JANIS ROZE
Venezuela

The Green Halo   44
JOHN R. HOWE
Nepal

Passing Through   52
MARIANNE DRESSER
Bodh Gaya

Hearts with Wings   58
PAUL WILLIAM ROBERTS
Cairo

A Man of the World   73
  ANNIE DILLARD
    Beijing

The Old City   78
  RABBI DAVID A. COOPER
    Jerusalem

Beyond the Sky   91
  LAURENS VAN DER POST
    Africa

The Pure Jones of It   94
  PAUL MCHUGH
    Florida

Fire Beneath the Skin   105
  TIM WARD
    Varanasi

                    Part Two
              CHANGING YOUR LIFE

Monk without a Robe   127
  MIKE MCINTYRE
    California

If You Meet the Buddha on the Road   139
  GLADYS MONTGOMERY JONES
    Asia

Homewaters of the Mind   144
  HOLLY MORRIS
    Montana

Paris Angels   150
  GERARD WOZEK
    Paris

Wake Up Call   155
  SCOTT ERICKSON
    Lake Superior, Minnesota

St. Peter's Black Box 163
SEAN O'REILLY
Rome

Luzviminda 167
RICHARD STERLING
Philippines

Gidget Would Go 180
CLAUDIA CAREY-ASTRAKHAN
California

Psalm Journey 186
MARAEL JOHNSON
Italy

Treading Water 191
LARRY HABEGGER
Around the World

The Labyrinth 204
JONAH BLANK
Lucknow, India

Part Three
TRADITIONS AND TEACHERS

The Master 211
MARK SALZMAN
China

The Vomiting Game 220
JAMES HALL
Swaziland

A Taste of *Satori* 232
HUSTON SMITH
Japan

Dreamtime Odyssey 236
DAVID YEADON
Australia

Stone by Stone   244
    JEANINE BARONE
        France

The Great Holy Mystery   249
    WHITE DEER OF AUTUMN (GABRIEL HORN)
        USA

Twist of Faith   254
    RHODA BLECKER
        USA

The Guy at the End of the Bed   262
    JUDY MAYFIELD
        California

Instincts   269
    RICHARD GOODMAN
        France

The Serpent   275
    DENNIS COVINGTON
        Alabama

The Interior Landscape   291
    BARRY LOPEZ
        Alaska

Up Your Nose   294
    REDMOND O'HANLON
        Venezuela

Meera Gazing   299
    MARK SEAL
        Germany

Part Four
THE PROBLEM OF EVIL

Slouching Towards Turin   319
    BILL BUFORD
        Italy

Ground Zero 350
PETER MAASS
Bosnia

Parade of Demons 357
KATIE HICKMAN
Mexico

Sword of Heaven 373
MIKKEL AALAND
Around the World

Part Five
SIMPLE GIFTS

Encounter with a Stranger 387
ANDREW HARVEY
Pondicherry

Prague Interlude 397
DAVID BERLINSKI
Prague

Allah Hit Me 405
JOHN KRICH
Turkey

Everything for God 408
WILLIAM ELLIOTT
Calcutta

The Palais-Royal 415
JULIAN GREEN
Paris

Recommended Reading 419
Index 423
Index of Contributors 425
Acknowledgements 427

Preface

TRAVELERS' TALES

The Road Within is a very different kind of travel book, a venture into the hidden territory of the human spirit and heart. It is a book of transformation, of lessons learned, maps drawn and burned, and blessings bestowed by that great and hard teacher: travel.

Some journeys are destined to alter our lives irrevocably. Many of us have had experiences on the road which have changed our view of the world in ways we have difficulty articulating on our return home. We come back from travel changed, awareness broadened, consciousness clearer—a feeling of being closer to who we really are. Once we have had a taste of this kind of change, we can't get enough of it, or learn too much about the process. In this vein, other peoples' stories can help us understand the dimensions of the inner journey, and help us prepare for and better assimilate our own discoveries.

The ecology and topography of the inner journey is no less real than any other place we encounter "out there" in the world-at-large. If ecology is defined as the relationship that an organism has with its environment, we must understand that the tissue of what we call consciousness is composed of layers of relationships with many aspects of the world, ourselves, and others, which may not be readily apparent. Gary Fontaine notes in *Presence in Strange Lands,* "The impact of our journey to strange lands may be much more than the culture shock produced by encountering a new culture. Our previous vision of reality may become vulnerable—spirits may enter our consciousness. Journeys to strange lands become encounters with ourselves."

In his book *The Longing for Home,* Frederick Buechner puts his finger squarely on a central part of this process: "Whether we are rich or poor, male or female, our stories are all stories of searching. We search for a good self to be and for good work to do. We search to become human in a world that tempts us always to be less than human or looks to us to be more. We search to love and be loved..."

No matter what we are looking for, we need maps or a way of comparing our experiences against those of others. Indeed, the essence of following another's journey is to be shown a map or told a story. But what do you do when the territory consists of more than three dimensions? The stories in *The Road Within* have been collected and edited to provide you with something of a non-linear map of consciousness. Some of the stories are more typical of the travel genre than others, but all are reflective of the many dimensions that constitute the path to self-knowledge. They include the experiences of scientists, writers, students of Buddhism and the martial arts, deep ecologists, and many ordinary travelers from all creeds and no creeds, each in search of the meaning of life.

Each Travelers' Tales book is organized into five simple parts. In *The Road Within* the format has been altered slightly to give a little additional guidance for the reader. For the first section, we've chosen stories to illustrate the "Hidden World" of self and nature. Part II contains stories about "Changing Your Life" and those mystifying, frightening, or plainly strange encounters with other people, places, and ideas that irrevocably alter our lives. In Part III, we've chosen stories by people who are exploring inner boundaries and reaching for wisdom through "Traditions and Teachers." Part IV, "The Problem with Evil," gives witness to the dangers of devolved ecologies of culture and startles us into realizing our personal limitations. The "Simple Gifts" of Part V show us the radiance and sometimes unsettling beauty of life that shines through all difficulties and limitations, self-imposed or otherwise.

This is a guide for the soul, a primer for the journey that is the archetype of all journeys: the road within. Hopefully, this book will help you understand what all the great mystics, visionaries, and saints have always known—that you are closer to your self, the

world, and God than you can possibly imagine, and that wondrous
things await you.

SEAN O'REILLY, JAMES O'REILLY, AND TIM O'REILLY

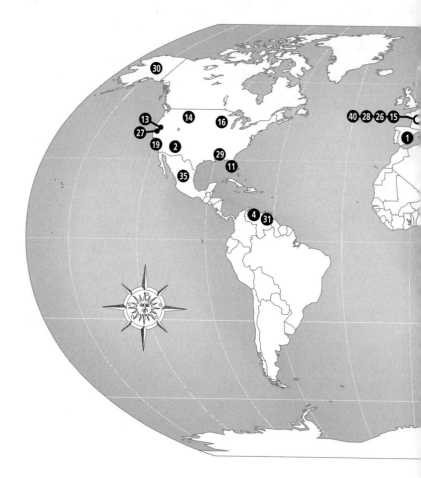

1. No Distance in the Heart - Barcelona
2. Garden of Paradise - New Mexico
3. Out of the Depths - Indonesia
4. Call of the Jungle - Venezuela
5. The Green Halo - Nepal
6. Passing Through - Bodh Gaya, India
7. Hearts with Wings - Cairo
8. A Man of the World - Beijing
9. The Old City - Jerusalem
10. Beyond the Sky - Africa
11. The Pure Jones of It - Florida

12. Fire Beneath the Skin - Varanasi, India
13. Monk without a Robe - California
14. Homewaters of the Mind - Montana
15. Paris Angels - Paris
16. Wake Up Call - Lake Superior
17. St. Peter's Black Box - Rome
18. Luzviminda - Philippines
19. Gidget Would Go - California
20. Psalm Journey - Assisi, Italy
21. The Labyrinth - Lucknow, India
22. The Master - China

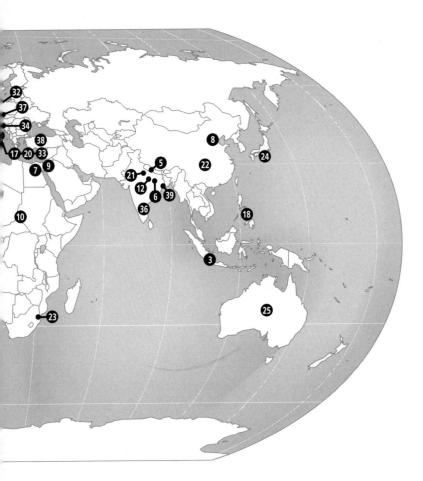

23. The Vomiting Game - Swaziland

24. A Taste of *Satori* - Japan

25. Dreamtime Odyssey - Australia

26. Stone by Stone - France

27. The Guy at the End of the
Bed - California

28. Instincts - France

29. The Serpent - Alabama

30. The Interior Landscape - Alaska

31. Up Your Nose - Venezuela

32. Meera Gazing - Germany

33. Slouching Towards Turin - Italy

34. Ground Zero - Bosnia

35. Parade of Demons - Mexico

36. Encounter with a Stranger -
Pondicherry, India

37. Prague Interlude - Prague

38. Allah Hit Me - Turkey

39. Everything for God - Calcutta

40. The Palais-Royal - Paris

PART ONE

THE HIDDEN WORLD

THOM ELKJER

* * *

No Distance in the Heart

Some knowledge comes from a
place beyond the mind.

THE LITTLE BOY WAS TROTTING AROUND BETWEEN THE BREAK-
FAST tables in the hotel, his arms wide behind him like airplane
wings. His eyes were dark and round, his hair tousled black, his
features unmistakably Catalán. I watched him and reflected that
I might easily have been home, watching my own child fly
about the kitchen. Instead I was in Barcelona, thousands of
miles from the small town in California where my wife was
probably sleeping.

We had moved away from the city a few weeks earlier, to
recover from twin blows: first a miscarriage, then cancer. It
appeared now that we would never have children of our own. I
also sensed a growing gulf between us, which no amount of loving
words or physical tenderness seemed to bridge. It was hard to be
away from her but also, I had to admit, a relief.

In Spanish, I asked the boy where he was flying.

"Cataluña," he answered, and looked down at the floor as if
from a great height. "Can't you see it?" An elderly woman at the
next table played along, telling the boy that it was too far down
for her to see with her old eyes. This brought him up short. He
stopped flying and stared at her, as if seeing something terrible in

her wrinkled skin and snow white hair. A moment later he ran back to his mother's lap and buried his head in her skirts.

The elderly woman spoke across the tables, apologizing to the boy's mother for scaring him. Her companion, in tweed blazer, patted her hand and consoled her. "You couldn't know," he said to her in a polished British accent. "Lord knows we never had children of our own." Now it was my turn to stare. I dropped some money on the table, picked up my newspaper, and left.

Barcelona seems to me a town full of art directors, with everyone dressed in black with splashes of red. This is especially true in the winter, when chill winds blow down the city's wide streets. The uniform seems to be a black overcoat, with a snow-white scarf and dashing red beret. The Catalans are an elegant people, especially walking together in public, but today I had my eye on the children. Many of them, too, were in black with boldly colored hats or mittens. They capered about, their bright eyes flashing and voices ringing in the cool air. I began to want one of them, any one. I would take the child home to my wife, and we would be parents at last. Surely that would knit us back together.

I finished my appointments, had some coffee in the Café de la Opera, and trudged back up Las Ramblas to Plaza de Cataluña for the train back to my hotel, north of the Diagonal. It was morning in California. My wife would be waking up, maybe reading in bed. I would call her and tell about bringing home a kid from Catalonia. We would laugh together as we embellished the plot. I would feel better.

The platform was not too crowded so I wandered to the edge and looked down. The cars of the Barcelona metro ride three or feet above the tracks, on springy undercarriages. The platform is even with the floor of the cars, but there is a wide gap between them. Unlike London, however, there is no warning painted on the platform, or loudspeaker constantly intoning "Mind the gap!" Worst of all, the wall of the platform sloped down toward the tracks, so anything that fell over the edge could wind up on the tracks. An accident waiting to happen, I thought, until a little girl in a pink hooded jacket materialized next to me.

This was not a miniature art director, but an open-faced, curious child in soft, little-girl colors. She was three or four years old, steady on her feet except when she was looking up, as she was right now, at me. Her mother struggled with a clutch of parcels and shopping bags. I smiled at her briefly but she was too harried to return it. Instead she spoke sharply to her daughter to stay close. I had been preparing to pat the girl's pig-tailed head, but I slipped my hand back into my pocket.

The girl and her mother got on the same train I did. We boarded mid-car, and the two of them got the last two available seats. I stood up near the door. We passed Grecia and St. Gervasi stations on our way to Reina Elisenda, and all the while I was thinking, this is the child I want. She merrily explored the train without getting in others' way, she kissed her mother impulsively (the only time I saw the woman smile), and chatted amiably with someone, perhaps a cat or dog, that only she could see. Once she looked up at me and smiled. I smiled back. A delightful child.

After the doors of the car closed at Muntaner station, the woman began to gather her parcels and make sure her daughter had her mittens. I realized they were getting off at Bonanova, a station before me, and thought briefly about getting off with them. I didn't really intend to steal the girl, but I wasn't prepared to lose her so soon, either. Then I remembered my wife, back home in bed. I didn't want to miss her before she left for work. I had to get back to the hotel to make my call.

The train stopped and the doors opened. Everyone who was getting off the train left the car. The woman quickly zipped up her daughter's coat and took her hand to walk her off the train. But as they came to the open doorway, just next to me, the little girl pulled her hand free so she could prove to her mother that she could step across the gap herself. Her mother said "no" and snatched at the girl's hand. Instead she got the sleeve of her daughter's coat, just as the girl began to step out of the train.

Looking down, I saw her hands disappear into the sleeves of her coat as her mother pulled it upward. The girl's foot did not reach the platform. The bell rang to announce that the doors were about to close. At the same moment as her mother, who was stepping onto the platform, I realized that the little girl was sliding out of her coat, through the gap, and down onto the tracks beneath the departing train.

Her mother dropped her parcels and yanked harder on the pink hooded jacket, but it was too late for that. I was already on the floor of the car, thrusting my arm down the gap, aiming for the area underneath the girl's coat. I felt skin, grabbed hard, and managed to get hold of the girl's wrist. She was so light that it took just one long pull to bring her out from beneath the train and into the air. The woman snatched her daughter from my one-handed grip an instant before the train doors closed. Now I was on the train, mother and daughter on the platform. The train pulled away.

Looking back, I saw the woman convulsively clutching her daughter to her chest and stroking her hair. Some people on the platform picked up parcels while others pointed toward the train, shouted and gesticulated, or simply clapped their hands. But it was like watching TV with the sound turned off. The doors and windows of the train were sealed shut. I couldn't hear anything but the sound of the train and the pounding of my own heart.

I suddenly remembered the passengers on the train, and turned around to see how many had witnessed the miracle of the girl's salvation. Not a single person was looking at me. They were all reading, or looking out the window, or talking to each other. For a moment I thought they were all pretending, and that they would suddenly begin to buzz about what had happened. They did not. Finally it dawned on me that the partitions by the door of the train, and the shortness of the girl, had concealed everything. No one on the train knew I had saved her life. It was too fast, and too silent. For them it had never happened.

My heart was still beating high in my chest when I got into my room at the hotel. I took off my coat and sat on the bed, seeing again the scene on the platform as the train pulled away from Bonanova station. I had gotten the girl in my hand all right, but only for a second or two. Now she was gone forever. I would not take her home. She would not knit my marriage back together. Hot tears welled up and spilled out of my eyes. I was wiping them away when the phone rang. I mumbled a greeting.

"Oh, thank God," my wife moaned, and then she was crying too. I pulled myself together and asked her what was wrong. She told me she had just woken from a terrifying dream in which I was trapped by my coat beneath the wheels of a train that was about to leave the station. A little girl had pushed me off the platform and I was lying there, unable to get up. She had woken herself up so she would not see me die.

At that point she began to cry all over again. I was too stunned to reply. Instead I forced myself to listen. She was apologizing for pushing me away after the miscarriage and her cancer. She was so afraid I would leave her, she said, that she was unconsciously trying to get it over with. But now she knew she didn't want me to leave. She wanted me to come home. She wanted everything to be all right again.

When I could speak, I told her what had happened to me in the train. Now it was her turn to be speechless. For a long time we were silent, paying hotel international long-distance phone rates to simply be together. We needed to recover from experiencing a similar shock, at virtually the same time, thousands of miles apart. When we began speaking again, it was to promise that I would come home soon, that she would be waiting, and that we would begin again.

In certain native traditions, a life you save belongs to you forever afterward. Five years after that day in Barcelona, I can still see that girl in my mind's eye. She's eight or nine now, her hair is longer, and she looks more like her mother. I see her running toward me on the Paseo de la Bonanova, her arms swept behind her as if they are wings and she is flying high over Cataluña. Indeed she has been mine since the day I met her, the day I learned there is no separation in love, no distance within the heart.

Thom Elkjer is a novelist and freelance journalist. He and his suitcase live in Mill Valley, California.

And so I look forward to my next journey. I don't know where it will be yet, but I do have a long list. Whenever someone tells me about a great spot that I must check out I say, "I'll have to put that on my list." I just know that no matter where I go in the world, traveling renews my faith in humankind, as well as in myself. It's a journey of remembrance back to my original self, the one who is wholly connected to all beings and nature. It's a journey that rediscovers what's really important, ultimately.

—Barbara Sansone, "Under the Mango Tree"

NATALIE GOLDBERG

✦ ✦ ✦

Garden of Paradise

Listen carefully and you will hear
the strangest things.

BY ACCIDENT, NOT INTENDED, NOT EVEN WANTED, I HAD A DEEP
awakening experience in front of a sixth-grade class I was teaching
in the Northwest Valley in Albuquerque, New Mexico.

I was wearing a white button-down blouse, gray slacks. I had my
hair pulled back with a barrette. I stood near the third row, the
blackboard with a map of the world pulled down was behind me,
and I was 26 years old. I was an ardent atheist—only "lit-er-a-
chure" would save me. I had studied Descartes, Kant, Plato. I believed in reason, rationality. I had been hired in the middle of the
school year; the veteran teacher of eleven years had quit because
she couldn't control this particular group of Hispanic and Indian
kids, and I was next in line to try my fortitude and courage. This
was my first time in a contracted teacher's position. I had received
my teaching certification six months before, in Ann Arbor,
Michigan. I said yes immediately when Mr. Jones, the school district personnel manager, called me. He said the other teacher was
taking a leave of absence to pursue a Ph.D. It wasn't true. She told
me she was beat, exhausted, and she also told me which kids to
watch out for, when I visited the class on her last day of duty. I was-
n't even supposed to teach English, the only thing I knew. I was

supposed to teach social studies, a subject I knew nothing about, but I tried. I was in New Mexico, naïve about the state, its culture and customs.

That morning, three men in suits had appeared at our classroom door. They knocked.

"Yes," I said, "please, class, be still." The class was never still. They did not become still then either, but they were curious. They half sat in their seats.

"We're from Cuba," one of the men said. "We're here to study your school."

"Cuba! Come in. Come in." I ran to the blackboard and stood before the world map.

"Now who can point out Cuba for me?"

Skinny Roberto ran down the aisle between two rows of desks. He pointed his finger to Costa Rica. I adjusted it to Cuba.

"Yes, that's it." I turned to the three men. "How did you pick our school?"

They looked bewildered. One said, "Our principal sent us," and they quickly excused themselves.

The lunch bell rang. The kids ran out the door. I went to the teacher next door.

"Mrs. Martinez, you're not going to believe this. There were three men here from Cuba! Can you imagine? They picked our school."

She looked up from her desk. She was about to pop a Chiclet into her mouth.

"Miss Goldberg, they came from Cuba, New Mexico. Not Havana, Cuba. Cuba's a small town north of here."

"Oh," I said, and backed out of her class. My face turned red.

I sat down at the steel desk in my classroom, opened a drawer, took out a container and scooped strawberry yogurt into my mouth. I rubbed the chest bone over my heart. It was sore. The night before I had been so busy writing a short story about my grandfather's orange bowl that I forgot two eggs I'd left on the stove to boil. Suddenly I smelled something burning and jerked up from my desk and bolted into the kitchen. As I turned the corner

I ran into the refrigerator; the handle hit me hard in the chest. I fell back, staggered, and saw stars. They were the same stars I'd seen the weekend before on a wall painting at the palm reader's.

I had been driving down Highway 25 just outside of Albuquerque when I passed a small adobe house with a huge white sign of a red hand with red lettering, KNOW YOUR FUTURE. I quickly swung into the driveway. I thought to myself, what are you doing? I don't believe in this.

I knocked at the door. A seventeen-year-old Chicano girl answered. I lied and said I was a student, so I could get the two-dollar discount she told me about. I followed her through a dining room, past a brown velvet couch, a television set, and a black velvet painting of a tiger hanging on a yellow wall, and into a back room separated from the rest of the house by a curtain of beads.

Christ, a wood sculpture of his head, was on the wall, and next to it that painting of gold stars on a blue-black background.

I thought, oh, Jesus, I don't believe in this.

She told me to hold out my hand.

I held it out.

"Um, you're very sure of yourself. Your whole way of seeing and understanding is going to change."

Oh, yeah, I thought. "When's this going to happen?"

"Soon."

"How soon?"

"Very, very soon."

I rolled my eyes. I argued with her. That wasn't going to happen. "Anything else?" I asked.

"You're going to go someplace you've never been before. Where you know no one. Into the deep north. You'll do this for the love of a man." She held my hand.

Oh, brother, I thought. I was a strong feminist. I wasn't going to drop everything for a man. "Yeah, when will this happen?" I asked.

"Not for a long while. In the future."

I had had enough. I pulled my hand away. I put it forward again. I started to ask about writing, I pulled it back again.

I paid her the three dollars and left and forgot about it.

When I ran into the refrigerator handle, I remembered the palm reader, the dusty road, the turquoise sky, the rock cliffs behind her house, and the star painting behind her left shoulder.

Stunned, I turned off the stove. The egg shells were burned brown and the pot was black. There was an awful smell in my apartment. I threw the eggs and pot in the garbage.

My chest still hurt. I had fifteen minutes before the kids returned to the class. There were paper planes on the floor, at least fourteen of them. Paper clips, textbooks, pencils, empty Frito-Lay orange-and-red cellophane bags, a whistle, three sweaters, and two pairs of sneakers also were on the floor. The wooden desks with attached chairs were in jagged rows, some turned all the way around and facing each other.

After I finished my yogurt and dumped the container in the wastebasket, I just sat at my desk and waited for the bell to ring.

When it did, the kids charged into the class in jeans and sweat-shirts. It was April. They ran to their seats.

I stood up in the middle of "Please, please, be quiet," and suddenly stopped. The place where my chest was sore—it was opening, opening red and enormous like a great peony, and it was radiating throughout my body. I felt the blood flowing in my hands and legs. I turned and looked out the window. I looked at the smoky appearance of the spring cottonwoods near the parking lot. Any day now they would break into leaf. There was a spindly Russian olive near our window. Suddenly it looked beautiful. Then I had one simple vision: I saw myself wandering in autumn fields and I felt that nothing, nothing else was important. This was a profound feeling, a big feeling. It wasn't a passing, momentary flash. I knew I had to stay true to that one vision.

Some old traditions say that no man is adult until he has become opened to the soul and spirit world, and they say that such an opening is done by a wound in the right place, at the right time, in the right company. A wound allows the spirit or soul to enter.

—Robert Bly, *Iron John: A Book About Men*

Understand, I had no idea what was happening. It wasn't some glorious enlightenment that many of us imagine and wish for. I was frightened. I didn't want it. I just wanted to be a writer and to earn a living keeping this class in front of me quiet. I didn't understand what was going on, and I had no clue about those autumn fields. Just then, there was a fist fight in the corner between Henry and Anita, the toughest girl in the class, and the spectators were enthusiastic. I had signed a contract, my first. I hated my job; I wasn't qualified for it—which, in this case, meant keeping control of everyone but that didn't matter. I was going to get through it. I had two months until the end of school and now something was inside me and I had to stop that fight.

When I got home that night I called a friend.

"Gabrielle, my heart opened in front of the class. Nothing makes sense."

"I don't know what you're talking about," she replied.

She was an intellectual. She, too, had read Kant, Descartes, Henri Bergson, Aristotle.

I hung up. None of my friends wanted to hear about it. They all were like the person I'd been before this afternoon in class: atheists, intellectuals.

At two in the morning, I bolted up in bed, wide awake. I got up and walked into the living room, sat down on the couch and stared at the kitchen clock over the refrigerator in the other room. My mind was totally blank. I just stared. I didn't go back to sleep until five a.m. I had to wake up for school at seven. I was exhausted the whole next day in class.

This waking up and staring in the middle of the night continued for three weeks. It became clear that I should quit my job and go to the mountains. Simultaneous with this clear feeling was another voice in me: "What! Are you crazy? You've signed a contract. If you quit, you won't get another one. The mountains! You're a city girl. You don't know anything about the mountains!"

The kids continued to run around the classroom. I became quite fond of several of them, and I was tired from no sleep and strung out between my heart and my teacher's contract.

Finally on one Monday in school, without plan or thought, I went next door to Mrs. Martinez and asked her to watch the class. I marched down the just-waxed linoleum corridor lined with tan lockers to the principal's office. I have no idea what I said to him as I sat across from him at his large brown desk, because while my mouth, connected with my body, spoke one thing, my busy mind was screaming at me. "What are you doing? You're crazy. You're finished! You'll starve in a gutter." I must have been eloquent, though, because when I was finished, Mr. Peterson, the principal, stood up, gave me a strong handshake, and said, "I understand completely. And if you ever want a job again, just call me."

If you want to identify me, ask me not where I live, or what I like to eat, or how I comb my hair, but ask me what I am living for, in detail, and ask me what I think is keeping me from living fully for the thing I want to live for.

—Thomas Merton

I felt such relief. I flew down the hall back to my class. I was free. This was my last week trying to get the kids in their seats. As a matter of fact, when I entered the class again, after thanking Mrs. Martinez for watching them, I thought, "What the hell. Let them do what they want. They do it anyway." I sat behind my desk the rest of the afternoon, smiling. We all seemed happier and, given freedom, they seemed less unruly.

On Tuesday I took attendance and then lined them up at the door. I didn't have a plan but I was sure one would emerge. I marched them outside and along the weedy road. Just being outside made us all happy. We walked for a quarter of a mile and I saw the Staff of Life sign in the distance. I remembered it was a food coop on five acres of land, with swings and paths and an herb garden. We headed toward it, and for the whole morning the kids gathered in small groups, played, and were content. The coop people were thrilled. They were getting a chance to educate the youth. They ran out intermittently with samples of organic carrots and roasted corn. Anita even said she could definitely taste the difference between organic and non-organic carrots and she liked the organic better, said she was going to ask her mom to buy some.

Each day of that week we did something different. I trusted something inside me, instead of what I thought I should do, and the kids responded. Because I was leaving soon, I didn't feel the restraints of the public school. It was as though that institution was no longer between me and the kids, that massive brick structure had crumbled, a new path had opened, a new way to be together. It wasn't all obvious to me at the time, but it was the beginning of something new.

On Thursday it rained. The kids were dismayed. We wouldn't be able to leave the building.

"Nonsense," I said. "It's not cold out and it's not raining hard. Let's get very still." I waited for them to become still and they did, unlike a few weeks ago. "When we go out and enter the rain, see if you can walk between the drops." I paused. "If we do get wet, don't worry—it's New Mexico!" In one enormous rush, I felt the whole glory of the state. "We'll dry quickly."

I led them to the front door. They were excited and a little nervous. We were breaking a rule: you couldn't get wet by rain, only by swimming in pools, by sprinklers, showers, and never in school. I was happy, fearless. I was taking that girl in Mr. Clemente's class out from behind the desk and into the downpour.

I stood by the door. "I will demonstrate. All of you watch and then you can follow." They stood huddled in the entry way. I stepped out, no raincoat, no umbrella, my palms up and open in supplication to water. I stepped along the sidewalk.

I went up to a bush, picked a twig, turned to face the group and said, "Ahhh, sagebrush smells best in the rain. Come slowly and enter it."

They stepped away from the building like the patients in the movie *King of Hearts,* who had been freed from the insane asylum. They stepped out into the rain gingerly, tenderly, and were delighted.

On Friday, I stood in front of the blackboard. "I have something to tell you." They were all attentive. "Today is the last day of the week and the last day I'll be here." There was an awkward, stunned silence. "Look, I know, this has been a tough year for you.

Let's face it, none of you were dolls. You weren't that well behaved." Alvaro, Roberto, and Eloy smirked. "But this week was a great week." They all nodded. "I want you to remember it. It's important. All of you get in your seats"—they were leaning against bookshelves and sitting on top of desks—"and when you do, I want you to close your eyes and put out your hands." I walked around and placed a Hershey's Kiss in each kid's palm. "Now unwrap it, and all on the same count, when I say yes, put it on your tongue, close your eyes and your mouth, let it melt slowly, and remember this week. Promise to never forget it, no matter what else happens in your life." I switched off the classroom lights.

An infinite universe will always have the capacity to surprise. The Earth moves. And stones fall from heaven. Tonight, Perseids clatter to the Earth like hailstones. They embed themselves in Arctic ice caps. They sprinkle the forests of the Amazon with a fine cometary dust. Meteors clatter at my feet and I dance in the road. "Up, noble soul!" cried Meister Eckhart. "Put on your jumping shoes which are intellect and love." I put on my jumping shoes and go leaping between the hedgerows.

—Chet Raymo, *Honey from Stone: A Naturalist's Search for God*

I felt sad and happy when I left that day. I had begun to redeem something from a long time ago, all that deadness I had felt as a child.

A few days later someone told me to check out the Lama Foundation, a commune that had spiritual retreats, seventeen miles north of Taos. It was started by Ram Dass as a place to further consciousness. His book *Be Here Now*, about his experience in India and his recipes for being in the present, was put together there. I had read it years before when I lived in Ann Arbor and was impressed by it, though I didn't understand it then. The Lama Foundation had an open house every Sunday.

I drove north in my Volkswagen Beetle, made a right at a sawmill and drove down a long, circuitous dirt road that took me up Lama Mountain. There were white and faded pink squares of material hanging from trees along the road—prayer flags, I learned later—and then a wooden sign that said: Park: the rest of the way you go on foot. I parked; I followed the dirt path. About halfway up, a woman six feet tall, barefoot, wearing a long white robe, was coming in the opposite direction.

"What are you doing here?" she asked bluntly.

I looked up. I clasped my hands to my breast. "The Garden of Eden opened up in my heart and I don't know what to do," I blurted out, earnestly.

"You must find a practice to water that garden," she said without missing a beat.

I was so grateful. "You mean you understand?"

"Of course I do," she said.

After that day I drove back to Albuquerque, gave notice to my landlord, packed my things and moved up to the Lama Foundation. It felt right. I was trusting something that wasn't logical. I took a leap of faith.

Natalie Goldberg taught for many years before turning to writing. Her books include Writing Down the Bones, Wild Mind, *and* Long Quiet Highway: Waking Up in America, *from which this story was excerpted. She lives in New Mexico.*

✳

Every one of us is called upon, probably many times, to start a new life. A frightening diagnosis, a marriage, a move, loss of a job or a limb or a loved one, a graduation, bringing a new baby home: it's impossible to think at first how all this will be possible. Eventually, what moves it all forward is the subterranean ebb and flow of being alive among the living.

In my own worst seasons I've come back from the colorless world of despair by forcing myself to look hard, for a long time, at a single glorious thing: a flame of red geranium outside my bedroom window. And then another: my daughter in a yellow dress. And another: the perfect outline of a full, dark sphere behind the cresent moon. Until I learned to be in love with my life again. Like a stroke victim retraining new parts of the brain to grasp lost skills, I have taught myself joy, over and over again.

It's not such a wide gulf to cross, then, from survival to poetry. We hold fast to the old passions of endurance that buckle and creak beneath us, dovetailed, tight as a good wooden boat to carry us onward. And onward full tilt we go, pitched and wrecked and absurdly resolute, driven in spite of everything to make good on a new shore. To be hopeful, to embrace one possibility after another—that is surely the basic instinct. Baser even than hate, the thing with teeth, which can be stilled with a tone of voice or stunned by beauty. If the whole world of the living has to turn on the single point of remaining alive, that pointed endurance is the poetry of hope. The thing with feathers.

—Barbara Kingsolver, *High Tide in Tuscon: Essays from Now or Never*

LYALL WATSON

* * *

Out of the Depths

There's more here than meets the eye.

WE WERE THREE—TWO JAVANESE CREWMEN AND I—IN A TINY wooden *prau*.

She normally served the fishing rafts anchored in the shallow waters off Surabaja, but had been lured into the Banda Sea by my interest in the islands east of Bali, and by more rupiahs than the crew could normally earn in the course of an entire year.

I had had to resort to bribery because none of us had ever been into that part of the eastern archipelago, and, despite my eloquent appeals to their manhood, their national pride, and the souls of their seafaring ancestors, the other two were quite happy to leave things that way.

It was not a comfortable way to travel.

The little boat was just twenty feet long and shaped something like a Chinese junk. The deck sloped downwards to the bows, and in the center was a thatched hut where we cooked rice and fish and, when it rained, spread our rattan sleeping mats. The sails were patchwork oblongs of canvas and matting held together and aloft by a thicket of bamboo and string that I never had the courage to examine too closely. The steersman sat high on a box at the stern, using his bare feet to work an ironwood rudder hanging in a plaited sisal sling.

19

I needed a boat, but never even considered this unlikely craft until the day I saw her speeding close-hauled and bone-dry over a tidal race that left a visiting American yacht three times her size looking very wet and miserable.

And until I discovered that her name was *Kembang Chili*—the *Little Flower.*

Six weeks and many islands later, we lay becalmed and out of sight of land.

I enjoyed this brief respite from the tyranny of wind, but the crew kept looking up at the sky and saying nothing at all.

By midafternoon, streaks of high and icy cirrus had appeared overhead, all converging towards the east as though gathered in there by a giant hand.

It was the wrong month and too far north for cyclones, but in recent years the weather factories have shown scant respect for calendars, and sailors have learned that they can no longer afford to rely on seasons and predictions.

Nothing happened until sunset, when a long and unaccountable series of swells came rolling up out of the east.

Then we knew.

Revolving tropical storms are vast whirlwinds with a center of low pressure. Whether going under the local name of hurricane, cyclone, or typhoon, they all go clockwise in the Southern Hemisphere and travel along at about ten knots. This speed may increase later as they swing around the pivot at the western limit of their track before recurving to the east, but most of the time they churn along a fairly straight and totally invisible line.

The best way to find out where you are in relation to the storm is to locate its center. Stand, if you still can, and face the wind. In this position south of the Equator, the vortex will lie at right angles to your left. If you raise your left arm until it is parallel to the ground, and reach back as far as you can without twisting the body, your index finger will be pointing provocatively at the calm and evil eye of the beast. If the wind remains steady, then it is coming directly towards you.

It did, and it was. We turned due north and ran.

This way the wind would always be behind us or, at the worst as the storm swept by, hitting us on the aft quarter or the beam.

It did all those things in the next ten hours as we lay flat on the decks.

I was glad the dark made it impossible to see what was going on. What I could feel was bad enough.

Sometime during the night the deckhouse blew away, carrying with it all our food and clothing, but the first hard gray light revealed that we were all there and, incredibly, so was *Little Flower*—a little faded perhaps, but with every improbable petal of her hull and rigging still intact.

For a while the sea continued to stand over us with its fists clenched, but it was clearly running out of wind.

We had no idea where we were, but decided to set sail and swing south again, where we ought to run into one of a long chain of islands. And at sunset the following day, after another 40 hours afloat, we did catch sight of land. A distant volcanic peak that rose up out of the waters like green and welcome Ararat.

By then it was too late to attempt a landing on an unknown shore, so we drifted under bare bamboo beyond the reefs and waited for the light.

The night was dark. We were in between moons, and the sky was still curtained by the cyclone's trailing skirts of cloud.

It was also very calm.

I could see a white line in the distance where the sea surged over the reef, but the water beneath us was black and a little hard to believe in. I lay on the deck and let my fingers fall until the warm and gentle grasp of surface tension restored it to liquid reality.

I let the mood take me, living only as it allowed, thinking only what it permitted me to think, but breathing deeply, very glad to be alive.

I have no idea how long that meditation lasted, but eventually something intruded sufficiently to attract my conscious attention.

Cassiopeia?

There was a pattern of light in the dark, one so reminiscent of the lazy shape of the Lady in the Chair that for a moment I thought the sky had cleared and I was seeing a reflection of the familiar constellation.

I even looked up, but it was black as ever overhead.

Then I realized that the lights were underwater, and somehow, this was a terrible shock.

Light belongs to the sun. Even before we knew it destroyed four million tons of matter a second in an endless thermo-nuclear blaze, it was obvious that our star was afire. A great fire, worthy of considerable reverence. The only local events that could touch it for power and majesty were forests in flame and volcanoes in the process of eruption. For most animals these were dangers to be avoided at all costs; but somewhere in the chain of circumstance and selection that set man apart from his ancestors stood an individual who stopped to take a closer look.

But journeys to strange lands produce more than culture shock and this first challenge requires more than coping with cultural differences alone. Though often very important, culture represents just part of the new ecology usually encountered in those lands. In a given journey it may or may not be the most important part. Other ecological differences described earlier—in the people and places, in what we see, hear, feel, smell, and taste, in the technologies we use, and the power, structure, and support we have— can affect us significantly as well. That is why the general term ecoshock *is more appropriate for these journeys.*

—Gary Fontaine Ph.D.,
A Sense of Presence

We know that Peking Man and at least one of the African ape-men kept a fire burning in their caves from time to time, but there is absolutely no evidence to show that either of them used this hearth for cooking. They may have valued it for the warmth it gave, or because it kept competitors and predators at bay; but I believe the truth is simpler and much more exciting.

Almost every culture has a myth that recounts the capture and domestication of fire. And in all these, fire was sought not because it might prove to be useful, but because it was fascinating. It still is. Despite all our sophistication, the minds of our children glow with the simple magic of matches; and even moribund adult imaginations are ignited for hours on end by the flickering expressions in a log fire. We are inflamed. As they were when they first captured the spirit of the sun and danced around it, or simply sat and watched this new and fascinating fetish come to life on the floors of their caves. There they tended it and fed it, keeping it alive and well: the earth's first divinity, enshrined on the altar of its hearth.

In the beginning it was an adventure. Not *just* an adventure, because it was probably our first. The first time any species in our system had made a major change in its way of life purely for the hell of it. Simply because it was fascinating, and because it seemed like a good idea at the time. Later we got down to the serious business of controlling fire, of exploring the night country and burning our way free of the shackles of gravity. And yet even today, when we build fires that blaze more fiercely than those in the sun itself, a single candle flame can still hold us in thrall.

It is because we attach so much significance to fire that we tend unconsciously to attribute all illumination to enlightenment. Lights in the night mean fires kindled and controlled by other men, by beings whose purposes are comparable and comprehensible to the human mind. So it comes as a shock to find them doing it where neither men nor flames belong—to see the lights burning deep underwater.

When I recovered from my initial disquiet, I realized there must be a biological explanation.

Many organisms make light.

At times the whole surface of the night sea glows with a sheet of cold fire that blazes wherever it is disturbed.

Schools of fish become rivers of flame, and dolphins burst through the surface like rockets trailing showers of silver sparks.

Every moving vessel pushes ahead of it a billow of liquid phosphorus which is sometimes so bright that, standing on a tropical shore, I have been able to read the name illuminated on the bow.

All this glory can be attributed to tiny protozoans and crustaceans that harness chemical reactions, sparked by special enzymes, which produce a very efficient light with little heat.

To distinguish this kind of light from phosphorescence, which depends on previous illumination, biologists call it biolumines-cence and know a little of its chemistry, but nothing of its purpose.

This is distressing, but the lights I saw in the deep that night dis-turbed me for quite another reason.

They had none of the flare and glitter one sees on the surface, producing instead a number of discrete cool pools of light like fluorescent tubes glowing in the gardens of a village in the valley.

As I watched, they grouped and regrouped, running through a whole zodiac of patterns, and then suddenly they all went out as though they were under some sort of central control.

Many deep-sea species of fish carry their own torches which act as lures and can be turned on or off at will. I have seen some that have lines of flares down the whole length of their bodies in pat-terns that differ from species to species, perhaps even giving each individual the chance to have his name up in lights. But nowhere have I come across any mention of the possibility of coordination, although I must admit it happens on land.

In Malaysia I have seen synchronous fireflies, perhaps ten thou-sand to a tree, all turning themselves on and off in perfect unison, transforming a line of mangroves on the bank of a moonless creek into a sparkling fairyland that creates itself anew with every pulse-beat. They seem to be all males, gathered together in one of the world's most extravagant mating displays. Each species has its allotted frequency, and the right sequence on an ordinary pocket flashlight in that part of the world can soon make you the center of an appropri-ate swarm of admiring female fireflies. And then what do you do?

I thought about this and tried to equate the firefly system with what I had seen down there deep beneath the *Little Flower*.

I felt certain there was a crucial difference.

There had been nothing mechanical or automatic about the pat-tern and position of the lights; and something very deliberate about the way they had all turned off together and without warning.

Perhaps *as* a warning?

Something could have frightened them, maybe even my casual dabbling at the surface.

I did not know, and I saw very little chance of ever resolving the mystery. I was busy mulling it over in my mind one last time before putting the whole experience away in a hoard I keep against hard times—when all heaven broke loose.

The lights came on again all over the deep, and this time there were many more of them and much closer to the surface.

I did not move. I could not.

I simply lay and watched open-mouthed as the galaxy glowed there beneath me and came drifting slowly up, in perfect formation, towards the surface.

As they came closer, their resolution improved and I could see that each light was a sharp ovoid of cool blue glow with two lighter green flares within it near one end.

They came to a halt about ten feet below the boat and it was clear that each was itself about eighteen inches long.

All this time the *Flower* had been drifting in her usual quiet way, but then a larger swell flowed by and she leaned over on her side and grumbled a little about it.

Instantly the lights changed character.

Several went out altogether, a few turned from blue to green, and two very close to me flared up in a bright white burst of luminescence—and suddenly I knew who they were.

Squid!

The oceans abound in squid. They form the sole food of sperm and bottle-nosed whales and are eaten extensively by dolphins, seals, and oceanic birds. Huge concentrations of squid hovering just below the illuminated zone of surface waters may even be responsible for producing the phantom bottom reflections that haunt echo soundings of the deeper ocean basins.

We assume that squid occupy a wide variety of ecological niches in the sea, but most of our information about them is inferential, because they are so seldom seen. In the clear blue halls of a coral lagoon you may be lucky enough to find a chorus line of little ones swaying gently near the surface. On one wonderful occasion I saw a squadron jet right out of the water to man height and glide slowly back to the surface with their mantle flaps fully extended. Trawlers sometimes catch sick and slow-moving squid in their nets, but of the rest we know little except that some small ones leave the chitinous quills of their skeletons on the tidelines of our beaches, and some of the larger ones leave circular sucker scars the size of dinner plates on the skin of giant sperm whales.

In the thin skin of squid are small flexible bags of pigment connected to sets of radiating muscle fibers. Excited individuals blush in a variety of hues as these sacs change shape and send waves of color sweeping over their bodies. A dark squid floating over a light sandy bottom can blanch instantly and vanish without moving. It had not occurred to me before, but from what I could see that night from the deck of the *Little Flower,* it was obvious that the same sort of nervous control, and perhaps even the same pigments, were involved in displays after dark.

This was exciting enough, but there was more to come.

All the illuminated squid were now within three feet of the surface, forming a complete circle around the boat.

I counted sixty and then gave up. There must have been several hundred. Every single one hovered with its short trailing group of tentacles gathered into a point that faced me like a nose between the bright green auras of its eyes.

I believe that the eye glow was a reflection produced by an almost metallic shield of tissue around the eye, because the main source of radiance clearly was within the leaf-shaped mantle sac which blazed with a strong still light.

At first I could see little difference between individual squid; some glowed brighter than others and a few seemed more green than blue, but this variation was cancelled out as the emphasis shifted from one part of the circle to another.

Then one of the crewmen stirred from his sleep and sat up and coughed.

In a flash the circle of squid grew several feet in diameter and, from this new and safer distance, began to throb with light like the display board on a giant computer.

And yet it was never that mechanical. From the moment the

behavior began, I had absolutely no doubt it was purposive. As my Javanese companion stood up and walked round the deck to join me, the stress and frequency of the flashes followed him around the circle of agitated squid. It was not merely a luminous twittering of the sort one would expect from a flock of frightened starlings, but a controlled and excited exchange of emotion.

There is absolutely no way in which I can prove this assertion of intelligence, but I watched that group of animals very closely for a long time and there is no doubt in my mind that there was a conversation in progress—and that we were the subject under discussion.

We moved carefully up to the higher aft deck for a better view, and soon the entire squid community maneuvered itself into a glowing semicircle around us.

The illuminated conversation had now become desultory, confined to the occasional flash of casual comment, and I began to have the strange feeling that they were waiting for us to do something more interesting.

I tried waving my arms up and down and got a small neon response from the front row.

I would have loved to be able to respond in kind with a lamp or even a match. Several deep-sea sailors have told me of being bombarded by squid when they showed a light at night. But all our sources of illumination had been washed overboard in the storm.

I think a flashing torch might have evoked some fascinating reactions, but I am not sure it would have made a great deal of difference in the end.

The squid were indeed waiting, but not for us.

For a long time we simply watched each other.

At times it seemed their lights were suspended in air and we shared the same dark space. Then, gradually, the intensity of the squid luminescence began to fade.

When the change became apparent, I thought they were sinking back below the surface, but as I moved to look, they glowed again still in the same positions.

I grew a little impatient with the impasse and leaned over the side with the intention of splashing water at them, but my hand never touched the surface.

Directly below the boat I could see another light.

It was the same shape and color as those in front of me and seemed to be the same size until I realized, with a sinking sort of excitement, that it was still very deep down.

When I looked up to call my companion, I noticed that he had been joined by the other crewman and that all the surface squid had disappeared.

The three of us and our *Little Flower* were alone with a light in the chasm below us that kept on growing relentlessly larger.

On October 11, 1492, the night before his first landfill in the New World, Columbus found the *Santa Maria* floating on a sheet of luminous water. The strange, even glow disturbed his sailors, who were long familiar with the sparkle of phosphorescence. This phenomenon is now well known in the Bahamas and is thought to be produced by organic matter brought to the surface by convection currents that cause up-welling of cold bottom water. But the glow is still so bright that astronauts have been able to pick it out from space as the last light visible to them from the earth.

Many seafarers have reported sights of huge glowing wheels, hundreds of feet in diameter, turning slowly just below the surface of the Indian Ocean. The most likely explanation for these is that they are produced by bioluminescent plankton being excited, and lighting up in series, as a wave form—perhaps from a distant submarine earthquake—passes by.

But even when these luminous marine phenomena have been more or less explained away, there remain some that cannot be classified quite so easily. These are the ones that have a more compact form and seem to move in a way that demonstrates some kind of volition.

Thor Heyerdahl tells of one night in the Pacific when three immense luminous bodies followed *Kon-Tiki* for several hours. He estimated their size to be greater than that of the raft, which was fifteen meters long.

By the time our body had completed its ascent to a point perhaps fifty feet from the surface, it was already clearly twice the size of our craft. We could see it on every side—a soft, clear glow billowing at the edges like a fluorescent cloud. The shape was roughly ovoid, similar to that of the squid, but through a depth of water it was impossible to pick out any details.

The *Little Flower* was drifting slowly along with a current moving parallel to the distant line of reef, and the aurora was keeping perfect pace with us below.

The crewmen were terrified. One kept running from side to side looking for a way out, and the other refused to look at all, sitting resolutely in the ruins of the deckhouse repeating the ritual "Peace be on you, and the mercy of Allah" over and over again.

I didn't know what to do.

I tried desperately to see some detail in the illumination, some concrete feature that would allow me to identify and classify it, to give a biologically meaningful account of it to my colleagues; but there was none.

I remembered my own exasperation with the incomplete reports of others in similar situations and understood for the first time the difficulty of being an eyewitness to anything really unusual. Objectivity is all very well, but it is possible only when you can describe your experience in terms of standard weights and measures. I did not know the frequency of the intensity of the light I was seeing, I could not provide an accurate record of its size, shape, or weight, and I had no scientific way of assessing its intelligence or intent.

As a biologist in this situation, I was a total failure; but as a biological system, I continued to function very well. I can provide an account of my contact with the light that is totally subjective and of no practical value in any court of law or academy of science, but I believe it is nevertheless meaningful.

To begin with, I was both enthralled by the presence of the light and appalled by its size and my total lack of understanding. I do not remember feeling afraid; I was aware instead of a sense of privilege, the sort of synthesis of honor and awe that I usually associate with proximity to large whales. A feeling almost of exultation, of a kind of grateful elation that is very close to worship. A compound of

"Praise be!" and "Why me?"

We lack the instruments necessary for recording stimuli of this order, and we seem to have lost the capacity for providing an appropriate response. It would help to be born again, but perhaps all we need to do is redevelop a kind of organic innocence, recapture the receptiveness of childhood and show a willingness to take part in and be filled, or emptied, by whatever it is that happens. I am beginning to believe that there may be no other way to experience, or even begin to explain, certain kinds of reality.

When a man's nature is universalized, he feels himself within all the countless multitude of beings that breathe and also feels them all within himself. There is a breaking down of the barrier of exclusive particularity, and, in consequence, a direct and active contact with the currents of universal life.

—Haridas Chaudhuri,
Sri Aurobindo: The Prophet
of Life Divine

To make sense, you must have sensed. My sense of that light was overwhelming. I know it was alive and I believe it was conscious. During the time it was there beneath the boat, I felt a presence, the kind of certainty of life nearby that you have when you wake in a dark room and know beyond doubt that someone else is there with you. It was a presence that involved a certain amount of astonished recognition, like meeting for the first time in the flesh someone you already know well from film or photograph.

It did not last long.

As soon as I made that first fleeting contact, the light gathered itself together and shot off at tremendous speed back down into the deep and the dark.

We were alone again—and I felt like weeping.

It was a long night, and I spent most of it wondering what had happened. Until the moment the squid opened their illuminated conference, it had been only a field experience. A rare and magical episode of natural history of the kind that leaves you filled with wonder and delight. Then it had undergone a qualitative change and become significant in a totally different way. I couldn't put my finger on the moment that had first produced this shift in emphasis, until I remembered the light in the squid's eyes.

Squid are molluscs. Soft-bodied, unsegmented invertebrates belonging to a very old and diverse group of organisms. Most molluscs still have external shells and are restricted to fairly sedentary lives, attached to rocks or creeping along the ground, but despite this relative inactivity, some of them have excellent eyes. The common edible scallop lies on sandy undersea surfaces with the two halves of its corrugated shell held slightly apart to expose rows of vivid blue eyes, all focused and very much alert. In the tropics, there is a leaping conch that propels itself across exposed mud flats in foot-long bounds and will, if interrupted in this progress, extend a long fleshy tube and peer at you with an eloquent big brown eye. It is a very disconcerting experience to be scowled at by a snail. It is possible that the conch simply stares down all potential predators in this way, but it is very difficult on that ground alone to account for the presence of such an elaborate structure in a well-armored animal that does not need to be so sentient.

The development of this strange molluscan eye has gone even further in the highly mobile squid. All the oceanic squids have a complex eye with an iris, a variable-focus lens, and a retina with enough sensitive cells to make their color and pattern discrimination every bit as good as our own. Squid see as well as, if not better than, any other animals alive—or at least, their eyes have the capacity for doing so. This is uncanny, but what really worries me is what they do with so much information.

All molluscs have a nervous system consisting of just three small sets of knotted nerves, or ganglia. One lies around the mouth and seems to be involved only in feeding; another is positioned below the oesophagus and is responsible for the movement of fins, mantle, tentacles, and pigment cells; and a third rests on top of the gut. In the squid this third delicate tissue of nerve cells shows some differentiation, which suggests that it may be responsible for a variety of functions connected with complex behavior patterns that involve learning and association. It is in effect a brain, but a very simple and rudimentary brain. One too elementary to even begin to cope with the vast amount of information provided by the incredibly complex eye. It is a little like taking an expensive telephoto lens and sticking it on a shoe box.

The whole thing is absurd, but as a biologist I cannot just leave it at that. Nature does at times seem profligate and to produce some implausible schemes, but in the end they all tend to fit neatly together. There has to be a good reason for squid's eyes, but at that particular moment I could think of only one—and it still sounds so wildly improbable that I hesitate even to mention it. And yet, even now, it makes a mad kind of sense that is very persuasive.

Suppose, purely for the sake of argument, that the eye is exactly what it seems to be—a highly developed sense organ for the detection and collection of electromagnetic information in the range of frequencies occupied by visible light. And that the squid just happens to be attached to the back of this instrument to give it mobility.

Can you think of a better camera platform for oceanic observation? Squid are sleek, speedy, and ubiquitous. There are billions of them, by day or night, on every level, at every temperature, in every part of the world's ocean. Seeing without being seen.

Visitors are warned that this facility is under constant closed-circuit surveillance.

Lyall Watson, a self-proclaimed "scientific nomad," travels the world in the pursuit of the paranormal. Born in Africa, educated in Holland, Germany, and London, he now lives in Ireland. He is the author of Supernature *and* Gifts of Unknown Things, *from which this story was excerpted.*

⋆

In the Western world, we believe that scientific truth lies in the objective observation of events—or, as it is commonly put, that "seeing is believing." But it must be obvious that there is a great deal of confusion in this area. After all, almost everyone believes that the earth goes round the sun, and we are fairly well convinced that the solar system is on the outer edge of a spiral arm of a huge galaxy, despite the fact that most of us haven't seen these things. We accept them not because they have been demonstrated to us, but because we believe they could be. In other words, someone has been able to *convince* us of their existence. Most of us take this to mean that their existence has been "proven." We believe science advances by demonstrating the existence of previously unknown or unexplained phenomena, when in fact it reformulates our view of the world in a way that allows us to accept them.

—George Simon, *The Science of Non-Verbal Communication*

JANIS ROZE

* * *

Call of the Jungle

Dwarfed by unknown nature, the monkey
ego beats a chattering retreat.

THE AGE OF EXPLORATIONS AND DISCOVERIES OF THE GEOGRAPHY and natural history of our world is essentially over. Our communication and transportation technology has increasingly helped to link and to reach what few areas of "unknown worlds" have been left unexplored. In light of our shrinking world, it was particularly gratifying to be able to participate in an expedition that penetrated into what is one of the last major corners of the earth that has escaped human attention and remained until now practically untouched.

The author was coordinator of an expedition to Cerro de la Neblina, Venezuela in the 1980s. At the time, this was the most significant cooperative effort in 50 years to study the biology and ecology of one of the last major unexplored regions of the earth.

—SO'R, JO'R, and TO'R

Because hundreds of square kilometers of impenetrable jungle surround Neblina, our initial camp at the base of Neblina and several high-altitude camps were established and supplied by helicopters. During the rainy season, however, helicopters could not fly in because of poor visibility and the absence of any reliable maps. Our particular task was to gather a flotilla of several river boats: *falcas, bongos,* and *curiaras*—local names for larger and smaller, single-trunk boats with flat bottoms. From San Carlos de Rio Negro, we were to journey several hundred kilometers to the base camp through the swampy, almost impenetrable jungle world.

The nine-day-long journey to reach Neblina started on the wide, quietly flowing Rio Negro, continued on the Caño Casiquiare and Rio Pacimoni as a smooth, motor-propelled voyage. We stopped at the last village outposts of the Baré and Kuripaku Indians. Beyond that point, no humans penetrate the jungle except, perhaps, some Yanomani travelers.

Entering Rio Baría, the swamps engulfed the jungle around us. Except for a few solid sand mounds, for several days there was no firm land. The river grew narrower and narrower and became fragmented into many small "side-roads" among which we had to choose the right passage. Our Indians chose well, even though at times the river channel was reduced to a size barely wider than our boat. The narrow "river-path" was frequently closed with bushes and fallen trees. It had to be opened with machetes and axes; and the only way to continue was by pushing the boats with long poles, day in, day out.

The lusty, tropical rain soaked us nearly every day or night. Nights were spent on whatever little patch of land could be found. A simple tarp among trees under which we hung our *chinchorros* (hammocks) provided for our night refuge. At sunrise we were already moving on.

Breakfast was before sunrise. During the day we nibbled at whatever was available without interrupting the journey. Supper was at sunset because soon thereafter we disappeared into the *chinchorros* unless a night exploration was called for. Although we had food with us, especially dried food, the Indians preferred to hunt for fresh food. Many evenings a wood fire cooked curacao, egret, monkey, caiman's tail, or any of the several kinds of fish. The aroma enticed the tired, hungry scientists to eat these jungle delicacies.

On the fourth day, the forest became so dense above the narrow river that it formed a magnificent green tunnel enclosing us completely. It was so dense that large numbers of bats were flying around the river tunnel.

The jungle itself was a kingdom of all kinds of flying and biting arthropods. Ants, spiders, and wasps—mosquitoes surprisingly less so—delighted in falling upon us as we disturbed the green tunnel roof above us. The variety and abundance of spiders was most remarkable, a true paradise for arachnologists, students of spiders. We were bitten abundantly, incurring pain ranging from a slight tickle to that which elicits a pained "ouch"; four-letter words were not excluded in some particularly nasty encounters. Actually, spiders usually only bite when they are squashed by mistake, and so do ants and wasps as well. Unfortunately, there were plenty of "mistakes."

The narrow streams harbored an abundance of the most unusual aquatic life. Notorious were the electric eels that can discharge more that 1,000 volts of electric shock, painfully stinging freshwater rays, a rare species of black caiman, not to mention the abundant piranha for which we fished. Surprisingly, we had no difficulties though, as humans are neither their prey nor their natural predators—so they will attack only when felt threatened.

"Hípana, Hípana," shouted my Kuripaku friend when on the ninth day our small flotilla suddenly entered a lager river: Rio Mawarinuma. The magnificent Neblina Massif—Hípana, as the Kuripaku call it—was before us. Hípana blessed us with a beautiful sunny afternoon and a breathtaking sunset. After a few hours, we reached the Neblina base camp and, for the first time in nine days, we could dry out our clothing, shoes, and all our other possessions. The next morning the real work could start.

For a month, we took trips lasting from one to several days, moving in the jungle, up the different ravines, around small streams and rocky mountains. Provisional camps were established where needed, plants and animals collected, and many ecological and behavioral studies made. With the exception of the few larger peaks, neither hill nor river had names. Not even Indian names exist, because nobody lives within a radius of hundreds of kilometers—"It is too far away," says our guide. The journey of days and days by boat through swampy jungle without any land around discourages them. The Indians need firm land to live on.

Collections grew rapidly. Botanists estimated that about eighty percent of the plants, especially from the higher altitude are unknown to science. The high plateaus—mostly covered with blankets of fog and clouds—have a plant world of their own. Some unusual, previously unknown amphibians, reptiles, and fishes were also gathered, not to mention the extraordinary abundance of insects, spiders, and other arthropods. One of my prize specimens was a nearly-meter-long cecilian, a snakelike amphibian that is more closely related to frogs and salamanders than to snakes. Yet, some of the most intriguing specimens were tiny frogs with pointed noses and lizards only two centimeters long!

A month passes quickly. Nobody counts hours, not even dates. The day is measured by what is done and the night by the time required to rest the tired body.

Soon, very soon, some subtle changes in perception and behavior take place. The sense of our civilized world becomes reduced, and the immediate need to deal with unfamiliar and changing surroundings becomes the dominant mode. There is a natural caution not to make mistakes or ignorant moves that would endanger physical well-being, health, and survival. But reaching our goal—the Neblina Massif—is an ever present drive, which demands that some risk be taken. Fallen trees, narrow bends of the river, and hidden obstacles under the surface mix with surprised animals, richly diverse flowering trees, sun-bathed or rain-drenched thickets to offer an unpredictable, ever-changing and always new panorama. Yes, we are on a journey into an unknown world, guided by a vague, yet firmly held conviction that "out there" is a goal to be reached.

As the journey progresses, a whole new set of living conditions and behaviors begin to substitute for the ones we cherished in the world left behind. But while some old habits and expectations are easy to let go, others stick like dried burrs—hard to detach and eliminate. A challenge to their existence causes discomfort and irritation, producing an illusory threat to survival. Is this what psychologists—back in a fast-receding, little-remembered world—call defenses of the self?

Days and nights in Neblina create a whirlpool of activities with shorter and longer trips in the jungle and up and around the mountains. Travels to penetrate deeper and higher into Neblina have a pace of their own.

The wholehearted involvement in the explorations of the external environments and landscapes, with their varied flora and fauna reveal certain rhythmic flows in nature unperceived before. The Mountain of the Mists unveils its nature, showing itself sometimes shyly covered by clouds, sometimes as powerfully naked with sharp angles, forbidding walls, and protruding bulges reaching high up into the sky. It is an imposing mountain chain, totally pure, totally undisturbed, reaching so high and so far, radiating an unmistakably benign presence that pervades its world.

In their ancient richness the landscapes somehow begin to make sense. They invite one to explore one's inner world, the world within, and learn about its ways. At some moment, living and being with the natural rhythm of Neblina, the outer and inner landscapes begin to look similar. It is as if they converge in equivalent harmony. While each seems to tell and complement the story of the other, a much greater sense of wholeness emerges with the revelation of their similarities. Together they provide a glimpse of an integrated reality, life made whole. Nature has done its task of completing and revealing the external landscape. We have to complete ours. Neblina whispers an opportunity and responsibility to integrate and redeem nature and humanity.

A realization bursts into the mind: it is not only "as above, so below," as it is engraved on the ancient Emerald Tablets, but also "as without, so within," as re-

> *There is much hidden within us, covered by the kind of consciousness required to function in our driving and driven material world. But to experience the fullness of our humanness we need to turn again to nature and open ourselves to what it has to say to us.*
>
> —Margaret P. Stark,
> *How Deep the High Journey*

vealed by the magic of Hípana.

What makes this world so different? Why does the mind and intuition flow so freely, see new relationships, perceive new wholes, seize new opportunities in the midst of the basic sameness of nature, however different and strange to the individual experience? It isn't one particular thing or event but rather several interdependent peculiarities. Together they create a magic combination that bends one's perceptions and ponderings by revealing a world of essentiality and invites participation. In this kind of world, one cannot remain indifferent.

Quickly but silently my Indian friends taught me that in order to be successful in the jungle, one has to root one's own ways in the ways of the jungle. Entering the jungle, the eyes and ears are fully open. There is an intensified general readiness to meet any surprises that might occur at any moment that is sustained in walking for hours of uneventful distances. The machete is always ready: sharp and handy. My Indian friends saw to it that my machete was always sharp and singing as it should be. How close this natural concern is to what the Samurai warrior of another world felt for his sword— the soul of the Samurai.

Walking in the jungle, one constant task is to mark the *pica,* the path. With quick, economic swings of the machete, a path is marked by cutting down a small bush, making a sight dent in a large tree, or breaking a small branch. "Reading" the marked *pica* is the only way to find the way back in an area covered by hundreds of square kilometers of jungle, so varied and yet so uniform. The jungle floor is relatively open ground covered by a soft, thick layer of dry and rotting leaves and teeming with life. There are a few saplings, still fewer bushes judiciously spaced, and medium tree trunks. The big trees reach up and form the green ceiling above, preventing the growth of bushes and grass by shutting out the light. Vines crisscross the spaces in between, at times forming considerable obstacles.

But above all else, the jungle is in deep silence because we are in the area of the equatorial doldrum. Here no wind shakes the leaves or the branches. When on rare occasions a very soft breeze gently stirs a few leaves above, it is an almost unbelievable event. Because there is no errant wind, every noise, every movement has a reason. One learns to be aware of the many unknown sources. In the silent world, the sounds create a unique language, telling the story of the dance of nature.

Leaving the camp behind and walking in the jungle alone, one soon becomes submerged in the silent world. One's own "internal noise" becomes louder and louder against the silent background. God, is there ever plenty of emotional and mental garbage that, unnoticed, has been accumulated! The needs, wants, fears, denials, self-explanations, self-generated expectations, and plain mental and emotional business become so conspicuous. They affect and modify one's relationship to the surroundings. They stain and strain what is seen and what is done. It seems almost imperative that this internal dialogue (a colleague calls it the "infernal dialogue") and business go on, driven by the need to explain (oh, to be in control of everything!), to justify everything. What becomes more painful is the realization that every self-directed desire and self-centered thought restricts the ability to perceive and to be more fully in the environment. It is a reminder that there are two separate worlds: the jungle and the self.

And then in the jungle silence the mind cannot stand it any longer. The internal world with all the self-generated noise gradually dissolves. The external silence pervades everything. Consciousness gets reduced to a small point, an inner/outer focus without space, perhaps without time, that just is—that's all. The ways of the jungle enter freely because there is no clatter in the emptiness within. Alertness to and perception of the surroundings are so intense that everything is taken in, within and without. No detail in the jungle is irrelevant. Everything has its fullness, its complete message, because everything in nature is a complete part of the totality. The wholeness of the jungle lights up, complete, without additions and subtractions, without particularities. Suddenly, wherever my attention is directed, it discovers an incredibly beautiful, rich world. It does not have to be explained because it reveals itself through the togetherness—in complete silence, inner and outer. Everything is so absorbingly interesting and new, nothing is trivial or trite.

After a while, in the silence of my consciousness, the dance of nature fills everything, without beginning and without end. God, what an incredibly splendorous world! How can one not love it?

The walking ceases to be random and uncoordinated. Full alertness accompanies every step, strong and deliberate, because it is part of the dance of nature. Every animal and plant and dry leaf dances it. Every stream and rock and white patch of sky takes part in this magnificent choreography. And the "I," reduced to a silent point of intense alertness, takes part in it but in a previously unknown way. There is a kind of will, a directing force, not quite within and not quite without. It is rooted in an unknown "place" that moves not only me but somehow also that which is around. The power of the human spirit! It is so clean and effortless that it has no description, no characteristics. It radiates an incredible sureness and naturalness that flows through everything. No one can touch me or hurt me because my walk is one with the dance of nature. With the human spirit, no move-

After visiting the Muktinath temple high in the Himalayas, we were descending towards Jomsom on a narrow dusty trail high above the Gandaki River Valley. It was late afternoon and the dreaded wind of the world's deepest gorge lashed our faces. The trail sloped gently; the dust was an inch thick, cushioning our feet that had been trekking since early morning. And at one undefined moment, I became acutely aware that I had fallen into a certain rhythm which made walking effortless. I also felt an immediate connection with everything around me. The blue of the sky, the white of the Himalayan peaks, and the snaky, silvery slither of the river below took on a brilliance that, instead of blinding me, induced in me a state of pure ecstasy. I realized with great amazement-and, oddly, tremendous humility-that I was actually gliding above the Kali Gandaki gorge. If I had been a Zen monk, I'd have had my satori right then and there.

—Rajendra S. Khadka, "Gliding Above the Kali Gandaki"

ment, no step can be wrong, nothing can be partial. New and different levels of being are reached.

A blue bee on a leaf not only demonstrates the dance of nature
but also begins to tell me something that encompasses time: the bee
is also weaving on the loom of evolution. Hundreds and thousands
of movements in the dance of nature weave on the loom of evolution! The whole jungle is one busy world doing just that. I, all my
Indian teachers, my companions left in the camp and in Caracas
and in the United States and in the rest of the world unknowingly
weave on the loom of evolution! Everything that we do, strive for,
dream about, fight for, is part of the all encompassing superreproduction.

From somewhere an invitation issues forth: come, brother of
mine, and travel with me into the unknown. Come, sister of mine,
and share with me the discovery of a world whose natural beauty
and splendor is unrehearsed, generous, and free. Come, all my
fellow travelers; in our journey together the fullness of life shall be
revealed!

*Janis Roze, a specialist in tropical biology, reptiles, and amphibians, teaches
at the City University of New York and does research at the Museum of
Natural History.*

✳

We know very little about the nature of our minds. They are the basis of
all our experience, all our mental and social life, but we do not know what
they are. Nor do we know their extent. The traditional view, found all
over the world, is that conscious human life is part of a far larger animate
reality. The soul is not confined to the head but extends throughout and
around the body. It is linked to the ancestors; connected with the life of
animals, plants, the earth, and the heavens; it can travel out of the body in
dreams, in trance, and at death; and it can communicate with a vast realm
of spirits—of ancestors, animals, nature spirits, beings such as elves and
fairies, elementals, demons, gods and goddesses, angels and saints. Christian
versions of this traditional understanding were prevalent all over Europe
throughout the Middle Ages, and still survive in rural societies, for example in Ireland.

By contrast, for more than three hundred years the dominant theory in the West has been that minds are located inside heads. This theory was first propounded by Descartes in the 17th century. Descartes denied the old belief that the rational mind was part of a larger soul, mainly unconscious, pervading and animating the entire body. Instead, he supposed that the body was an inanimate machine. Animals and plants were machines too, and so was the entire universe. In his theory, the realm of soul shrank from nature into man alone, and then in the human body contracted yet further into a small region of the brain, which Descartes identified as the pineal gland. The conventional modern theory is essentially the same, except for the fact that the supposed seat of the soul has moved a couple of inches, into the cerebral cortex.

—Rupert Sheldrake, *Seven Experiments That Could Change the World: A Do-It-Yourself Guide to Revolutionary Science*

JOHN R. HOWE

✦ ✦ ✦

The Green Halo

Is there a ladder between
Heaven and Earth?

The Self is the sun shining in the sky,
The wind blowing in space; he is the fire
At the altar and in the home the guest;
He dwells in human beings, in gods, in truth,
And in the vast firmament; he is the fish
Born in water, the plant growing in the earth,
The river flowing down from the mountain.
—Katha Upanishad, II.2.2

I AWOKE SCARED, STRANGLING, TOOK THREE QUICK BREATHS AND remembered: the Himalayas, 15,000 feet, blizzard…trouble, big trouble. No wind. Snow whisked steadily against the tent fly. A muffled boom in the distance and the long, dull roar of an avalanche coming…still coming…silence. I took a deep breath and checked my watch: 11:10 p.m. Bob's voice came suddenly out of the darkness: "How you doing, John?"

"O.K.!" I said, startled by my cheeriness.

"Hey man, that's a lot of snow out there," said Bob.

"I know," I said. "We in *trouble*."

Strange…I did feel good. Was it the altitude, or was I avoiding the truth? Or maybe the truth hadn't sunk in yet; maybe it had and I was relieved it was so obvious: we had to stay put until the storm cleared and we could start back down.

Bob's voice broke in again: "Gotta get the snow off the tents!" He sat up and shouted in Nepali. "Pemba! Ram! Harka! Get up and dig out your tent!" No answer. We struggled out of our bags. Bob went out first. I heard him breathing heavily as he plowed over to the porters. "They're mightily freaked out," he said as he crawled back in. "Pemba was just sitting and staring at a candle. When I walked up I could see his silhouette and it was like I had x-ray vision and could see the mournful expression on his face. The other two were just lying there, looking blank. Maybe they're praying."

In the long hours before dawn, *National Geographic* images of gaunt, frost-rimmed mountain climbers nudged at me as I drifted in and out of sleep. The snow piled up and pressed in on us until we were curled against each other in fetal positions. We hadn't asked for this, I kept thinking; we hadn't come looking for trouble, we just wanted to go for a long walk, immerse ourselves in Nepali culture, and see as much wildlife as possible. Until now it had all been so easy. Arriving in Kathmandu in early September we had hired Pemba, a young Sherpa, as a cook and porter and left for Pohkara a week later by taxi. From there we set out on foot, north and west more than a hundred and fifty miles to Jumla, walking six or seven hours a day, confident we could beat the first winter snows. On October 14th, four days ago, we arrived in the village of Pheri, at 9,000 feet our last chance to re-supply before crossing an 18,000-foot pass into the Langu River valley.

Early the next day we started for the pass, led by Ram and Harka, two Pheri men, each of us carrying about fifty pounds. The first morning we followed a roaring river up through a mixed for-est of bamboo, spruce, and birch; all afternoon we bushwhacked along the steep sides of the valley, often inching along cliffs or haul-ing ourselves up muddy slopes, finally camping, exhausted, on a tiny sand beach. Yesterday evening, right on schedule, we reached the tree line at 12,000 feet, emerging from the forest into a broad valley where the river ran gently down between brown, grassy hills studded with rock outcrops.

A clear sky at dawn gave no hint of the approaching storm; it wasn't until just before dark today, as we hurriedly pitched our tents, that the first flakes began drifting down. At first we took little notice, expecting to find only a few inches on the ground by daybreak—perhaps enough to make our footing a bit more slippery going over the pass, but nothing to worry about. Snow this early in the year wouldn't last long, we told ourselves, and we were only a few thousand feet from the top; by tomorrow afternoon we would be safely down the other side. By seven o'clock, when Bob and I turned in, the snow was about five inches deep: I felt my first jolt of fear, the kind that hits when nature suddenly takes charge. We were so far from help. If anything happened, no one would miss us until Bob's wife arrived in Kathmandu three weeks from now.

My eyes opened to dark clouds of snow lying thick on the tent. Though it was still coming down lightly, the storm appeared to be breaking. Visibility was almost fifty feet. Better to start back down now, we decided, while we still had a chance. We ate a quick breakfast, packed up, and were on our way by 9:30, breaking trail through powder up to our knees. "I don't want this role," Bob said as he dropped back to encourage the porters. "Cast me for a Tennessee Williams play in the tropics, not this one."

I hadn't gone more than a hundred yards before the storm blew back in and I was pushing against blinding, swirling whiteness and fierce gusts of wind. I heard Ram say something and Bob answer him sharply.

"What did he say?" I asked as Bob heaved up next to me, gasping for breath.

"He says we're going to die."

I gave him a pained look—"Great attitude!"—and turned back into the storm, trying to remember the shape of the hill I had climbed only yesterday.

The land sloped gently down, then leveled off. Now the drifts were up to my waist. I swept the tip of my walking stick back and forth in front of me, mapping the ground as I advanced step by slow step, a blind astronaut lost in space. Suddenly a large, fluffy mouse was flying fast across the snow toward me. With my stick I arced a quick warning line in front of it. It swerved, then swerved back and came for me again. Space encounter! Alien ship! I jabbed at it and it turned and was swallowed by the storm. A vague dread flipped in my stomach and sank in deep: the mouse wasn't an alien, it was a desperate, lost animal looking for anything but whiteness—like me.

Three more steps. The ground sloped down more steeply. I stopped to look back at the others and could just make out their dark, blurred forms stalled in a tight line about thirty feet behind me. Bob was yelling something at Harka, who was standing on one leg, pointing at something in the snow. I saw Bob lean down and dig out a shoe and hold it up and then the ground fell out from under me and I was flying, tumbling, spinning, caught by a huge wave like the one that grabbed me off a beach in San Diego years ago, tracking the surface, waiting to be released, for my next breath, and then I wasn't in California any more, I was deep in a rushing, roaring white river and there was no up, no down, no air and I had to have air—now! This could be it, this really could be it, The Big Moment! Then the ocean wave took me back and I was swimming again, I wasn't sure where, and saw a green halo with light shining through it from above the mountains I knew were out there some-where and I reached for it with both arms, became a soaring angel, and the roaring stopped and I could breathe again. I was buried up to my neck, struggling, terrified, like an animal caught in a trap. What if another one came? A deep voice I didn't recognize boomed up from my gut: "Help!... Help!" Exclamation points burst loose from the cartoon bubble over my head and whirled away into the storm.

I calmed myself and shrugged my right arm free, pawed out my left arm, wriggled out of my pack and quickly dug out my legs. Then I was standing up and the others were pushing toward me down the hill. Bob shouted above the wind: "What happened?"

"I almost died," I shouted back, "I'll tell you about it later."

"We gotta get one of the tents up! The guys are almost gone!"
As he and Pemba began stomping down the snow around them
Ram and Harka stood hugging themselves, shivering desperately. In minutes the tent was up. I grabbed Harka and shoved him in, yelled at Ram, pointing at the door—"Get in!" Once inside I felt a clear, lonely energy struggling to escape. I told Ram to get into his blankets and quickly pulled out my sleeping bag and wrapped it around Harka, yanked off his shoes and began rubbing his feet. Bob was shivering so hard he had to ask Pemba to help him light the stove. Before long our clothes began steaming and we were drinking hot soup. A huge gust of wind roared up the valley and slammed hard against the tent. Bob and I looked each
other long in the eye. "This is bad, John," he said.

Najmoddin Kobra writes: "...the heart is a light in the depths of the thrown." Initially when the well is revealed it has a depth to which no depth perceived physically can be compared, but as the seeker ascends toward the light shining above, the whole well below is transformed into a well of light or of a green-colored light: "Dark at the beginning, because it was the dwelling-place of devils, it is now luminous with green light, because it has become the place to which descend the angels and the divine Compassion."

—Paul William Roberts, *In Search of the Birth of Jesus: The Real Journey of the Magi*

"You're right."

"Hey, think we'll make it?" he asked, cheerfully ironic.

"We have to make it," I said. "We have no choice."

I described the avalanche and he reached over and squeezed my shoulder. "I didn't see it take you. I was so preoccupied with Harka. He was almost hysterical. Ram saw you go down and was sure you were dead." He was silent for a while then said he'd been thinking about his wife and son. "My life is too sweet right now," he said, his eyes glistening. He turned to the others and began talking in Nepali: "Ram, you have a wife and three children. Harka, you've only been married six months but you need a chance to make some children. Pemba has a wife and a six-month-old baby, John has family in America too, and my wife and son are coming to meet me in Kathmandu in a few weeks and what will they think if I'm *just not there*? What will they do? So many people depend on us. We're going to get out of this. It may take a few days, it may take longer, but we're going to get out. We are *all* going to get out."

The porters quietly listened, though when Bob finished they looked just as scared as before. We checked our supplies: two pounds of flour, fifteen small packets of noodles, a pound of beans, a pound and a half of dried pumpkin, four ounces of sweet potato leaves, one bag of granola, a dozen packets of Lipton's "Cup-A-Soup," eight apples, a small box of tea, a pound of sugar, a handful of chili peppers and spices, a cup or two of cooking oil, two liters of kerosene for the stove and a half a liter of scotch. It was enough—not much, but enough—for three days. Even with no snow on the ground it had taken us that long to get up from Pheri; now we would have to break trail through deep snow at least as far as the tree line. We would be lucky to get out in three days. And what if the storm didn't break?

For the first time I let myself remember the roaring white river, the green halo, and the light shining through it and something melted inside me. Tears flooded my eyes. I turned aside to wipe them off before the others noticed. I'm a space cadet, I told myself—it hasn't really hit me yet. Still, there have been other times when I've looked at death and looked past it and kept on going. We'll get out. It'll be rough, but we'll make it. We have no choice. We were in our bags long before dark, five of us and most of our gear crammed into a seven-foot circle. I slept fitfully, waking often to listen to the wind howl, the Nepali word for wind, *hawaa,* becoming "horror" in my mind.

By morning the storm had passed. Outside all was brilliant whiteness and pure indigo sky. Soon we were making our way cautiously across a steep snow field that plunged several hundred feet down to the river. Ahead we could see the next section of mountain and beyond it, far below, a broad, gently sloping valley. Wending our way slowly across steep ravines, through deep snow to grassy knolls and rock outcrops blown bare by the wind, we often came to cliffs or cul-de-sacs and had to retrace our steps. The words of a Dylan song, "knock, knock, knockin' on Heaven's door," played and replayed in my mind. Where the river fell suddenly away into the lower valley we had to abandon our horizontal traverse and angle higher up the mountain. Scouting ahead, I was stopped by more cliffs and chest-deep snow and then, inches from my face, inches from each other on a rock, placed neatly together like a museum exhibit, the scat of a snow leopard and a pearly shell was on a ride that had taken it up 14,000 feet in thirty million years.

That may have been when I knew we would make it, for although the next few hours were grueling, I hardly noticed, enraptured as I was by the pure, still, immensity of the mountains, the perfect, clear light, the valley below us beckoning like the Promised Land. I have only hazy memories of the rest of our long, hungry retreat down to Pheri: struggling for two more days through snow up to our thighs…the first patch of bare earth just below tree line…the lush, nostalgic scent of the forest…idyllic pastoral scenes of families cutting grass in the fields outside the village…excited children escorting us back to a house where we gorged on sheep meat, apples, and milk.

That night, asleep on the roof of a house by the river, I heard a loud roaring, and as I swam, terrified, to the surface, the snow in my dream melted and all that had happened flooded away: it was only the river, the deep, soothing bass tones of the river. I got up and went out to look at the stars, aware how relieved I was just to be standing there naming constellations. I remembered a night on the way down when I looked up and saw, as if for the first time, an infinite expanse of sparkling light. I was back now, I told myself, back to attaching words to stars, though I knew it would be a while before I found the source of the light that shined through a green halo from somewhere higher, much higher than the mountains above me.

John R. Howe lives in Cambridge, Massachusetts with his wife Anne-Marie and Spencer, a small, fluffy dog. He owns Clearwater Communications, which provides writing and editorial services to environmental technology companies and government environmental agencies in New England. In the wee hours he works on a book about the wildlife of the Gobi Desert in Mongolia.

*

The world has signed a pact with the devil; it had to. It is a covenant to which every thing, even every hydrogen atom, is bound. The terms are clear: if you want to live, you have to die; you cannot have mountains and creeks without space, and space is a beauty married to a blind man. The blind man is Freedom, or Time, and he does not go anywhere without his great dog Death. The world came into being with the signing of the contract. A scientist calls it the Second Law of Thermodynamics. A poet says, "The force that through the green fuse drives the flower/Drives my green age." That is what we know. The rest is gravy.

—Annie Dillard, *Pilgrim at Tinker Creek*

MARIANNE DRESSER

_* * _*

Passing Through

You are more than you think.

IT'S ONLY A SHORT WALK THROUGH THE SMALL VILLAGE OF BODH
Gaya, a quarter-mile or so down the main dirt road to the *vihar*, the
Burmese monastery and pilgrims' lodge at the edge of town where
I am staying. But to reach the road I have to pass the gauntlet of
beggars lining the Mahabodhi's outer wall. They arrange themselves in an intricate hierarchy: first, the wild-eyed *sadhus*, renun-
ciants lost in an ecstasy of self-chosen self-abnegation, clothed in
little more than the sacred dirt of Mother India. Next to them, the
more conventional beggars whose abject poverty and homeless-
ness, not sanctioned by religious choice, is correspondingly less
auspicious.

Last in line, well after devotees' purses have already been opened
and closed again, are those whose credentials are simply their tortured and incomplete bodies, entire limbs missing or ending in
puzzling shapes. With cruel logic, the begging business deems that
contributions to the holy poor carry a greater karmic reward than
giving to those who are merely destitute for all the usual reasons—
caste and color, bad luck or bad timing on the cosmic Wheel of
Fortune. I dispense a few rupees at strategic intervals, hoping the
greatest number receive part of a contribution that will never be

enough. A dull ache accompanies this brief ritual; I have grown accustomed to its presence in my sternum.

Once past the patient gallery of beggars, I'm immediately assailed by the bright cries and alert glances of the rickshaw-*wallahs* who gather just outside the temple grounds. Eager to win my paltry patronage for a five-minute ride, they shout, *"Sister!" "Look, sister!" "Best ride here, sister!"* By now, after three months of this nightly ritual, we mostly recognize one another. Though I'm not a likely customer they give me their most eloquent entreaties anyway, eyes smiling. I smile back, nod gently, do not break my stride. I stroll out into the main road, past the closed-up box-carts that by day are one-man shops dispensing necessities: candles, date-expired antibiotics, warm, syrupy soft drinks. I can feel the pores of my sandaled feet soaking up warm dust. Woodsmoke, spices sizzling in oil, sweet sandalwood, dung—a rich brew of smells crowds for space in the air, clouding my nostrils and stinging my eyes.

The four most holy places for Buddhists are Lumbini in Nepal where the Buddha was born; the other three, all in India, are Bodhgaya where he became enlightened, Sarnath where he gave his first sermon, and Kushinagar where he died. Of the four, Buddhists consider Bodhgaya to be the most important pilgrimage site; and for the traveler, Bodhgaya too may the most interesting because it is much more a working Buddhist center than a spot for archaeological explorations.

—Rajendra S. Khadka, "Amongst the Buddha"

Down the road, past the souvenir hawkers, who all offer the same cheaply printed postcards, the same rough-hewn replicas of the sublime stone deities scattered throughout the temple. In my first few weeks in Bodh Gaya, I had spent many an evening perusing these offerings, choosing the little figure whose creator, with the luckiest slip of the chisel, had rendered the archaic smile intact. But I no longer thirsted for the perfect *bodhisattva*. The makeshift altar in my quiet, small room at the *vihar* already had a full complement of tiny images. And behind them rested a leaf from the sacred Bo tree that floated to the ground as I sat beneath its protective canopy. Dried by the Indian heat, the tear-shaped pipal leaf had become a crisp, slightly shrunken but perfect replica of itself.

On the other side of the road, groups of travelers and pilgrims congregate at the *chai* shops, dipping *gulab jamen* into cups of the strong milky brew and talking animatedly. The foreigners indulge in the queasy pleasure of comparing digestive-tract horror stories, another ritual I used to take part in. Lately, the brief exchanges, nods, and smiles I exchange with the familiar locals along the road are all the society I crave. I walk past the whitewashed statue of Gandhi, his slightly comical oversize eyeglasses rendered in thick black enamel. In Bodh Gaya, the architect of India's liberation is just one more saint, a latecomer to the vast Hindu pantheon that keeps growing like a benign B-movie monster. A reflex of the spiritual generosity that recognizes and accepts all exemplars of holiness—from the Buddha to Christ.

I walk past the snack vendor who always charges me an extra rupee or two for a packet of stale popcorn. He has liquid brown eyes and such a beatific smile that I pay the difference willingly. I pass the shop of the Muslim tailor, working under a single bare bulb suspended by a thin wire over his elderly machine. I know the shoemaker's shop by the brightly colored poster of Ambedkar, the modern-day founder of a religion for his kind, India's untouchables. I nod to the cloth merchant who sold me the khadi cloth for the loose, long shirts I wear, comfortable in the close heat and safely androgynous. He is lounging with his cronies on a thick woven rug, framed by colorful bolts of fabric. He sips his tea, laughs and gestures, looking all the world like a 13th-century pasha.

Quieter now, farther away from the temples and monasteries and the religious heart of town. Bodh Gaya is home to a host of major and minor deities, and a yearly round of festivals in their honor—raucous crowds celebrating the Goddess Durga; the whole town lit by thousands of flickering candles for Diwali, the Festival of Lights; the Mahabodhi ablaze with oil-lamp offerings to the Buddha; Surya Puja, when the village women bathe in the river at dawn and pass out *prasad,* divinely blessed food, like candy at Halloween. At *puja* time, the town is a booming spiritual marketplace serving the steady stream of wayfarers who buy the small terra cotta figures for worship, the candles and incense to burn, the flowers to scatter. The streets are clogged with ecstasy, and all those transient prayerful bodies need food to eat and a place to sleep. Now, between festivals, it's just a few itinerant pilgrims and me, on this dirt road dodging bicycle rickshaws and sacred cows.

Buzzing clouds of insects clot the meagerly interspersed street-lights. A soft luminous shudder, thousands of tiny shadows. I walk steadily through the circles of light, passing quickly through the fluttering wave of small frantic life forms brushing against the bare skin of my arms and neck. I know to keep my mouth closed and breathe out slowly. Off to the right is the Nilajan, its turgid, broad brown sweep dissected by a sliver of reflected moonlight. Flat cow-shaped silhouettes stand in matte-black relief on the near shore. The failing light mercifully obscures the river's slow cargo of animal carcasses, debris, and the occasional half-burned body, its soul long since released into the ocean of time from the *charnel* grounds upstream.

On the road, I'm nearly home now. Russet twilight stains the western sky long after the sun has slipped behind the fringe of trees at the edge of the world. The beauty of it commands my attention, the tenacity leaves me breathless. A subtle pressure in the air: the body of time. Countless births and deaths and rebirths, and in between the elastic span that we call life. This place is very old, and weary, and yet an invincible spirit permeates everything, animates even the tiny diamonds of light darting off the water.

I take refuge in these images: the molten river, a gnarled tree, a brackish pool in which a single white lotus, now closing gently against the evening coolness, will again miraculously bloom. Three women pass me, giggling at my cropped hair, my indeterminate features. Do they think I'm a boy? Do they know I'm a woman and wonder at my aloneness, here on this road? Each one wears the vermilion streak lining the part in her glossy black hair—the fur-row split by the plow—signifying her married status. A young tea vendor pours a cup of milky brew the color of his palms and flashes a radiant gap-toothed grin at me. "*Chai,* sister?" he beckons earnestly, forcing another refusal from me; the momentum of my stride carries me on. A thin old man drives his dusty gray and blue-black bullocks leisurely toward the patchy fields on the riverbank. Their massive haunches heave a lazy rhythm as they move past me, their tails halfheartedly flicking away flies. I run my hand over their broad backs, touch the pungent skin of the world.

Where am I in all this? A spectator, a ghost?

A guest.

Suddenly I become lighter, transparent. Things pass through. My senses are as permeable as a membrane. Someone is laughing.

Walking on a dusty road in the gauzy half-light of an evening passing into night, lost to the gracious anonymity afforded by the gathering darkness. For an instant that stretches to infinity, there is no "I," only seeing. A moment of freedom from the bounded entity, the name and story that shores up the fragile and tenuous sense of self on which a life—my life—has been built in great earnestness.

The earliest texts speak of the moment of the Buddha's realization as "burning down the house." The figure on the road is straw, dry kindling, just waiting for a spark.

Writer and editor Marianne Dresser is the editor of Buddhist Women on the Edge: Contemporary Perspectives from the Western Frontier *and is at work on a collection of stories from her years of travel. She lives in San Francisco and wanders off to Asia every few years for a different taste of life.*

★

The Hindu Vedas and yogic texts assert again and again that the universe is God's dream. In Christianity the sentiment is summed up in the oft repeated saying, we are all thoughts in the mind of God, or as the poet Keats put it, we are all part of God's "long immortal dream."

But are we being dreamed by a single divine intelligence, by God, or are we being dreamed by the collective consciousness of all things—by all the electrons, Z particles, butterflies, neutron stars, sea cucumbers, human and nonhuman intelligences in the universe? Here again we collide head-long into the bars of our own conceptual limitations, for in a holographic universe this question is meaningless. We cannot ask if the part is creating the whole, or the whole is creating the part because the part is the whole. So whether we call the collective consciousness of all things "God," or simply "the consciousness of all things," it doesn't change the situation. The universe is sustained by an act of such stupendous and ineffable creativity that it simply cannot be reduced to such terms. Again it is a self-referenced cosmology. Or as the Kalahari Bushmen so eloquently put it, "The dream is dreaming itself."

—Michael Talbot, *The Holographic Universe*

* * *

Hearts with Wings

Ain't no disco dancing here.

The land of Egypt is in a state of turmoil these days. The face of Cairo is that of a stranger, one that I hadn't encountered on my previous travels here. I know the language of the city and its dialects, but the people seem to be speaking a different language. I see the city as a sick man on the point of tears, a terrified woman afraid of being raped at the end of the night. Even the clear blue of the sky is thin, with clouds laden with an alien fog that has come from distant lands....

—The fictional Venetian traveler Visconti Gianti describing Cairo in 1516 from the novel *Zayni Barakat* by Gamal Al-Ghitani

"THERE ARE *BASSASSIN* EVERYWHERE," MOKHTAR TOLD ME, AS he wrapped a length of turban around my face and adjusted the old *gelabia* he'd brought over to the hotel. A *bassass* is a spy. Mokhtar had promised to take me to witness the gathering of a Sufi *tariqa*—the word means "way to attain union with God."

Sufism is a mystical sect of Islam that is all but outlawed in most strictly Muslim countries, although it has gained popularity in the West through the writings of Gurdjieff and others who adapted its rituals to suit their own needs. The word comes from *suf*, the crude woolen garment worn by itinerant holy men. One aspect of Sufism is a veneration for the Prophet that goes far beyond the tenets of orthodox Islam. Many Sufis came to regard Muhammad as the eternal manifestation of the force that created and sustains the universe, and the only channel by which God may be approached and known. Inevitably, supernatural qualities were thus conferred on Muhammad, something both the Prophet and mainstream belief had been careful to avoid. Like members of other mystical sects, the Sufi ascetics cultivated an ecstatic union with the divine through various disciplines, and an overwhelming love of God. Their philosophy of the faith was developed from the 8th century on by defining mystical experiences. Some even believe Sufism is in fact the ancient Egyptian priestly wisdom adapted to Islam. Quite late in its development came the designation of saints—an aspect that still appeals greatly to ordinary Muslims. Besides major poets like the Persian Rumi, the order produced numerous Sufi masters who were, and are, believed to possess spiritual powers and the ability to perform miracles. The tombs of these saints—there are several in Egypt—have become places of pilgrimage. This reverence has led to some abuses in Sufism, so modern Muslims seeking to purge Islam of superstition have effected a decline in the sect among the educated classes throughout the Islamic world. However, it retains a powerful hold on the masses, as do the *zaar* and other cults. Because of the *bassassin*, fear of whom, whoever they are, seems to affect the private lives of many Cairenes, it was necessary for us to take great precautions before visiting this Sufi *tariqa*.

We were accosted rudely in the hotel lobby by a security officer, who apologized to the point of groveling when I pulled aside the cloth covering my face. Both Mokhtar and I concluded that my disguise was convincing enough. He, too, had exchanged his business suit for the rough garb of the *fellahin;* he was something in "Research Planning," whatever that is.

We drove across Cairo through another hooting, squealing rush hour, heading up to the plateau of the original city fortress, or Citadel, where, low behind Muhammad Ali's gigantic, imposing mosque, a sunset of pale smoldering gold turned the smog into a sprawling wreath of gilded mist. Halfway up a steep hill leading past the City of the Dead into old Cairo, we parked on a patch of waste ground where a house seemed to have simply collapsed of its own accord. On what must once have been a section of wall, a young woman sat with a cabbage the size of a beach ball balanced on her black-veiled head and a miserable-looking chicken, its legs tied together, under one arm. Perhaps it had been her house?

"Ask her," I urged Mokhtar.

"You don't talk to *those* women," he told me. "Their husbands would cut your balls off and eat them. Anyway, houses are always falling down here. Mud brick is fine as long as it doesn't rain." Fortunately it doesn't often rain in Cairo—but it *does* rain.

The City of the Dead, Cairo's necropolis, covers many square miles and looks at first glance like a large walled village of vaguely prosperous houses. The buildings contain only tombs. On holidays, families can still go over to their deceased relatives' homes and include them in their festivities.

As we passed one of the necropolis gates, a stout woman in about an acre of black *abaya* staggered out carrying an army-style gasoline can (stamped War Department—1943) and two huge snot-nosed babies. Behind her, at least six more children were beating up a donkey.

"What do the dead want with gasoline?" I asked Mokhtar.

"Oh," he said, indicating the woman, "she probably lives there."

"What do you mean, *lives there*?"

"Housing shortage. People are renting out places there now. It's not cheap, either. You have to put about three thousand down just to get in, then it's around thirty pounds a month, which is steep for almost anyone."

Mokhtar, I learned, paid three pounds a month for his spacious three-bedroom apartment overlooking the Nile, although he was making at least a thousand a month. Rent control here means the rent stays at what it was when the place was built. Little wonder owners are not inclined to do much in the way of maintenance.

"So," I asked him, "you mean people live in mausoleums? What about the tombs?"

"I hear they make serviceable dining tables." He laughed. "Honestly."

We turned into a dark, twisting alley where the eaves of ancient houses nearly touched above us, blocking out what little light was left in the sky. No one was paying any attention to us, a real novelty for a foreigner in the Orient. Old men sat in their doorways smoking *sheesha* pipes and shooting the breeze. An occasional mule tottering beneath the weight of two big sacks of earth or vegetables or grain would make us flatten ourselves into the nearest recess while it passed. The smell of cooking wafted from windows and passageways. The place was such a labyrinth I'd need a thread to find my way out again....

A would-be seeker asked a Sufi:
How long will it take to arrive at the point of true understanding?
The Sufi answered:
As soon as you get to the stage where you do not ask how long it will take....

—Idries Shah, *A Perfumed Scorpion*

Looking all around in a manner so furtive anyone watching would have known we were up to no good, Mokhtar suddenly bundled me up a short stone staircase and through an open arch that led into a long and very dark passage. At the end we came to an ancient door studded with large metal knobs and thick enough to hold off an army with battering rams.

I said, "*Now* I die?" I wasn't really joking. No one knew where I was, and I hardly knew Mokhtar from Mephistopheles, *or* the people who'd introduced me to him, for that matter....

Silencing me with a gesture, my escort pulled a creaking metal ring until it appeared to come away in his hand and then recede back into the heavy wood. The sound of a distant bell ringing solved this enigma. Soon footsteps could be heard shuffling slowly toward us from within. A voice more like the bark of an old dog with laryngitis uttered two syllables through the wood. Mokhtar replied with a simple "*Aiwa.*" "Okay," or as close to an approximation of "yes" as Arabic seems to allow itself.

A recalcitrant bolt was drawn back, a key turned, and the mighty door was dragged open a couple of feet. Then the turbaned head of a man old enough to have known the Prophet personally appeared in the space. The umber skin on his face looked like desiccated mud flats, and he wore a Solzhenitsyn-style beard the size, shape, and color of a small cumulus cloud. Behind him I could make out an open courtyard and, on the far side, a house with heavy carved shutters. It was dark, apart from a dim yolky light framed by an open door. Squinting first at me, then at Mokhtar, the old man growled again, revealing three lonely teeth like thick, spent matchsticks. The door didn't appear to open any farther, so, following my companion, I squeezed through the gap, and the two of us helped the old man, who wore what resembled a black academic gown over a white satiny *gelabia*, heave the monstrous door shut again. We slid back a bolt as thick as my arm, and he turned a key as large as a squash raquet in the kind of lock you see in bad parts of New York City.

"Wow," I remarked. "*This* must have been made when a door still *meant* something…."

I followed Mokhtar and the old man across flagstones worn smooth by the feet of centuries and into the house. The place was huge, and palatial, if run-down. It certainly wasn't what I'd expected, given the area we'd been walking through. The ancient woodwork was exquisitely carved with Islamic patterns and, in places, inlaid with stained ivory and dusty mother-of-pearl. The curving masonry was similarly festooned with geometric and floral designs. I later discovered the place dated from the 14th century. That was probably also when it had last been cleaned. Down corridors we went, our pace as painfully slow as the old man's, and up an uneven staircase missing so many stones that some steps were virtually three feet high. Another corridor contained a huge mercury-backed mirror in a frame so ornately carved that it must have constituted someone's lifework. The mercury had worn so badly that when I looked, half my head was missing.

Finally, we were led into a tiny room containing two cheap metal folding chairs. The old man grunted, hawked, and shuffled noisily off.

"Not much room for a gathering here," I said.

Mokhtar just nodded toward what I'd taken to be a carved wooden panel at the end of the room. "Look," he told me, somewhat smugly. The panel was actually a kind of *mashrabiya* window, the kind used by women sequestered in *purdah* to look out while remaining unseen. Through the delicately fashioned peepholes I could see a large hall-like room lit by dozens of candles or oil lamps in turquoise glass shades hanging from the roof beams. Below, some thirty feet beneath where we sat, two dozen or so men in lavishly colored silk caftans and blood-red turbans sat in a circle around an old white-bearded man. This figure was dressed entirely in black robes, with a black turban so large it looked like a bag of laundry on his head. "That's the sheikh," Mokhtar whispered.

"Are you sure we're supposed to *be* here?" I had grave doubts.

The sheikh appeared to be talking in a low, even tone to the men around him. The hall was constructed from floor to ceiling in pale white marble and even contained, at one end, a small fountain, also of marble. Its waters, though soundless from our vantage point, sparkled in the bluish light.

The sheikh's voice suddenly rose several octaves, and he broke into what sounded like a song. This atonal wailing yodel was clearly a big hit. His audience started swaying to and fro, clapping their hands, and eventually even singing along. Mokhtar and I drew up our chairs and looked down on this ridiculous spectacle in silence.

Now I'm not sure if my eyes deceived me or not in the poor light, but I could have sworn that the old sheikh didn't stand normally; rather, he seemed to float up to his usual height and then lower his legs to the ground beneath him. The other men certainly stood in the conventional manner—some with the obvious effort of old age—and, once they were all standing, proceeded to walk in their circle around the sheikh, slowly at first, but gradually gaining momentum until they were virtually running, old and young alike.

This continued for some minutes, and then, as a loud chanting began, they started to weave in and out as they ran, still keeping their circle perfectly symmetrical. The effect, from above, was of an unbroken human braid. Their movements grew faster and more complex, as did the chanting, until I found it impossible to believe that anyone, let alone anyone as old as some of these characters had to be, could be capable of such faultlessly choreographed and sustained physical exertion. They couldn't have been better synchronized. As they spun and weaved, even their robes seemed to swirl and billow in unison. Faster and faster the circle turned until it was one continuous blur of color.

Then, with a loud clap of his hands, the sheikh stopped the men completely. No one teetered, no one appeared remotely winded, let alone tired or dizzy. The sheikh held up both hands, palms facing out. He next made a slight movement, as if pushing an invisible wall, and began to turn around very slowly, continuing the same movement with his upraised hands. The section of the circle he faced would rock noticeably, as if he were pushing the men themselves. This went on until the old man had turned several times and the whole circle swayed like flowers in a breeze.

He lowered his hands until they were parallel with the ground and started clenching and unclenching his fingers violently. I was wondering why when I saw what looked like liquid begin to shoot from his fingertips, as if he were flicking a basin of water. Turning again, he showered the circle of men with…what? Sweat was the best I could come up with. He must have incredibly sweaty old hands, I told myself. He then clapped his incredibly sweaty old hands twice, and the circle of men once more sat down. So did the sheikh, in the conventional manner.

Just then, following a spectacular demonstration of throat-clearing, the old creature who had let us in materialized near the doorway and barked something at Mokhtar.

Mokhtar looked visibly shaken. "We've been invited to go downstairs," he told me.

"What do you mean?" I said. "We've been asked to leave?"

"No. The sheikh has summoned us to join the *tariqa*."

"But how could he have…I mean, *he hasn't left the room….*" Meekly I rose and followed Mokhtar and the old man. I hoped the athletic segment of the gathering was over. I hoped I didn't have to speak to the sheikh (*So, what's it like being a Sufi then? Nice, is it?*). Was I expected to become the human sacrifice in stage two of their ritual?

Following the old man gave me much time for reflection and observation. I reflected on what I'd just seen. Pretty quickly I observed that we were heading back via a different route from the one we'd taken on our way in.

We passed a wall I'd never seen before, and it was certainly a wall I'd have remembered. On it was emblazoned a mural from floor to ceiling that, judging by the leprous condition of the paintwork alone, had to have been executed when Shakespeare was still a toddler. Pharaonic paint jobs are in better shape. As far as I could make out, the corrugated and peeling shapes depicted a fat heart with wings, hovering over a glade pullulating with wild animals who clearly wanted to take a bite out of it. There were certainly tigers, bears, jackals, crocodiles, and leopards. And there were bits of what could have been pterodactyls, carnivorous giraffes, and saber-toothed hippopotamuses. An odd spirit of unity prevailed among them. In fact, they all seemed oblivious to one another. It was that big, juicy winged heart they wanted. Yet the expressions on their faces conveyed a depressed resignation; they knew they'd never get near the heart. Even the tiger, who was nearer than his fellows, looked somewhat foolish, as if he knew he was wasting his time. Clearly, the mural was symbolic of something. But what?

"Hey, Mokhtar," I said. "What's a winged heart mean?"

"The soul in love with God" was the answer, delivered deadpan. At least it was better than those grotesque images of Jesus performing open-heart surgery on himself with his bare hands.

Descending a wooden staircase that creaked beneath our feet like choral music by dying cats, we passed a grandfather clock made, according to the faded lettering painted on its face, in Birmingham in 1823. Its hour hand and pendulum were missing.

Pulling aside a tapestry decorated with a large and complicated tree full of birds, the old man revealed a narrow archway leading into an area so dark it could well have been an entrance to the Underworld.

"If there's anything you feel I should know, Mokhtar," I said, "feel free to tell me. For example, why are we in this unlighted dungeon?"

"Do not be scared."

"Who's scared? I'm not scared—unless you think I *should* be scared?"

We walked like blind men, pausing when our guide did. A muffled fiddling with metal objects, punctuated by Olympic hawks that propelled pieces of the old man's lungs around the invisible space in worryingly numerous directions, resulted in the opening of a door about four feet from me. Light so dense it seemed almost liquid poured out in blinding waves.

> We are above the skies and *more* than angels...
> Although we have descended here, let us speed back:
>   what place is this?
>
> —Jalaluddin Rumi, 13th century

We had been led into the marble hall where the sheikh still sat with his devotees, a point within a circle, like the ancient symbol used by occultists to designate the sun. Immediately facing the door we'd just emerged from stood porcelain bowls raised five feet high on lacquered stands and holding clods of blazing magnesium ribbon. As a fine thread, magnesium is the flash in old-fashioned camera flashbulbs. I was about to tell Mokhtar I'd just about had it with this farce when I realized the sheikh, beneath his preposterous black turban, was standing by my side.

"The mind is a monkey," he said in faultless English. It struck me as an odd statement. Had he meant to say *"manqué"* or something else? I glanced at Mokhtar. He'd bowed his head reverently.

"A monkey?" I repeated, smiling inanely at the sheikh. His eyes, set in a wizened, noble old Semitic face, seemed much younger than the rest of him. They were clear, bright, full of humor, yet I had the curious sense that no one was looking through them. Eye contact is a profound form of communication, yet, as my eyes met his, there was no communication between us at all. The only analogy I can offer is with looking into the eyes of a mad person.

"The heart cannot fly with a monkey on its back," said the sheikh, his voice gentle, soft, and low.

The mural came to mind. But the human heart didn't have wings or a back upon which a monkey could sit; yet at that very instant I saw a ferociously clear mental picture of my mind as a restless and mischievous monkey engaged in countless unrelated, pointless activities, unable to stop itself, incapable of not responding to an unending stream of stimuli. A monkey, of course, has no set goals in life. It is not the least bit bothered by a lack of continuity, any absence of achievement. Morality and ethics are no problem, either.

This mind flash took maybe a second, but it thoroughly unnerved me. In the sheikh's eyes I next saw something that convinced me beyond all doubt my thoughts and his will were, at that moment, one and the same. I don't think I've ever felt such raw panic. *Tame the monkey*, I recall telling myself. But *was I the monkey?* Never again will I wonder what it's like to lose one's mind. No thought can be trusted—including *that* thought.

"The best way to tame monkey is to make him climb up and down a pole until he gets exhausted," the sheikh confided. His tone was that of a man who's learned everything the hard way.

This latest remark left me baffled and increasingly bad-tempered. What pole? It wasn't even *fair* to the monkey….

"Come," the sheikh told me, lightly tugging my elbow, "our ring of power is ready to receive you. There are voices in eternity that need to speak of many things to those who'll listen."

I felt about six years old as the sheikh took me by the hand and led me across the marble tiles to where the others still sat, their eyes half-closed, not registering me or Mokhtar or any other intrusion. I had a strong urge to say, *Can I sit next to Mokhtar, please, sir, we're friends.* I recalled experiencing the same feeling on my first day in school.

As it happened, the circle wriggled apart to make a space big enough for Mokhtar and me to sit together.

"You're so lucky, my friend," Mokhtar whispered.

"What's going on?" I hissed back. "This is weird stuff. *Too* weird."

Without warning, a man who could have been James Joyce's twin brother in Arab drag leapt up and started rocking back and forth on the balls of his feet, shouting, "Allah! Allah!" at the top of his lungs. He reminded me of a cheering sports fan. I half expected to hear rival supporters encourage their boys in the same fashion: "Siva! Siva!" After all, religion is a team sport.

The man shouting for, or at, God, far from being silenced for his disruptive behavior, was joined by others, until everyone apart from Mokhtar, me, and the sheikh was rocking and roaring out his God's name. It reminded me of a passionate woman in the throes of a ferocious orgasm.

Looking at Mokhtar, I realized he realized what I realized: we could hardly continue to sit down. Within a moment both of us were bobbing along with the rest of the circle, hollering for Allah. I hoped Allah wouldn't mind my doing this. These, and other bizarre anxieties, flew like mosquitoes through my mind as I swayed and chanted, an impostor among the faithful.

After ten minutes or so I found the name of Allah I'd repeated a hundred-odd times began to sound as if it were repeating itself

> *It seems awareness functions like a radio. There are millions of stations we can tune in to, but only one channel can be played at a time. The Buddha taught that the dial of this radio is in the grip of the monkey mind, which cranks it around and around, twiddling from frequency to frequency. The radio plays a jumble of disconnected noises, part of a word, then static, a note of a song. This is the normal state of human awareness. The listening consciousness screens out most of this jumble, selecting fragments here and there across the band. From these it fashions human thought, like an archaeologist reconstructing an ancient civilization from a few fragments of bone and pottery.*
>
> —Tim Ward, *What the Buddha Never Taught*

independently of me. My brain fizzled with inane streams of consciousness as my lips uttered God's name. *The mind is a monkey*, I remember telling myself. *But who am I? Who is I?* The vibration of the chant in my chest was beginning to kindle an extraordinary sensation of well-being, a warm glow like love, or finding a large check in the mailbox. I felt great, and I shouted out for Allah without even having to think about doing it. I dimly recalled a similar feeling of confusion and joy when taking acid. When I *could* think, my thoughts made no sense. Gradually this fuzzy warm feeling changed. My mind shifted to a state of abject panic. I tried at one point to stop the chant and found with bemused horror that I truly couldn't. *Was I chanting,* I wondered, *or being chanted?* I could hardly hear my own thoughts at times, and when I could, I found myself lost in long forgotten memories from the distant past, which wove seamlessly into entirely unrelated thoughts, vivid sexual fantasies, angry feelings connected with incidents and people I hadn't thought about in years or even decades, all of them as immediate as if they were really happening. Yet the whole boiling stew that was my mind simultaneously recalling everything it had ever retained seemed remoter and remoter from the "me" who perceived it. The sun glowing in my heart overpowered my life now, my sole reality. That and the name of Allah speaking itself through my lips. My awareness of the room and everyone in it dimmed.

At some point I noticed people were beating their breasts in frenzy, and the noise of chanting pounded like the deafening roar of jet turbines. But then I noticed I, too, was pounding my chest with my fists, tearing at my clothes, jerking like a person with Saint Vitus' dance.

Only when I found myself staring directly into his eyes did I see the sheikh, immobile, a black outcrop of rock at the center of a tempest-torn forest. This old man was more than I could comprehend. In some way he controlled everyone in that room. His power was tangible, emanating from him toward each of us like the spokes on a wheel. Or did it flow from us to him? You could almost see the energy. I could not decide whether the power was good or evil. It did not feel like either.

Whatever was happening kept shifting gears, too, changing its mood but always appearing to be heading somewhere. All the hysterical rigmarole we'd been participating in seemed to conjure up a force field of energy needed to get us to that obscure ultimate destination.

orcerers are experts at shifting levels of awareness. Some are so adept they can shift the level of awareness of others.

—Florinda Donner, *Being-in-Dreaming*

The controlled chaos now appeared to be getting out of control. Some of the men were beginning to salivate, frothing like epileptics. A man opposite me suddenly collapsed in a shuddering, untidy heap....

I must have done the same thing, for I next found myself sprawled on the bare marble with my nose buried in Mokhtar's hairy calf. The sheikh stood once more, walking slowly around the ring of tangled bodies. He looked bigger, younger, and altogether more potent than he had earlier. When he clapped his hands this time, the sound was almost deafening. Instantly everyone sat up and resumed his former calm, cross-legged posture. Some of our clothes were torn, and only the sheikh still wore his turban; the rest, mine included, lay scattered around us all like multicolored rocks.

"Allah Akbar," the sheikh said, his voice rich with power. He continued in Arabic, an odd-sounding Arabic, for some minutes, then switched to English: "The bridge across worlds has been built. The light is with us. The light has dispelled all darkness. The light that was before all things shines once more...."

In fact, the room was now in almost total darkness. Only one dim oil lamp still burned, and were it not for the abundance of white marble, you'd have had trouble seeing your own feet.

"The light is the bridge," the sheikh continued. "The blessed who walk in light are now ready to cross over. Who among you will summon them?"

"What *now?*" I whispered at Mokhtar. "What's he going on about?"

"Ssssh! He's invoked the *djinn*. You must keep quiet now."

"The gin?" I presumed there were easier ways of ordering cocktails, even in Islamic nations.

"*Djinn* are powerful spirits who rule the other worlds. Now *sssh*!"

Humor, of course, is a nervous reaction. I'd always pictured *djinn* as turbaned phantoms that lived in magic lamps. Something like an electric shock suddenly sparked deep inside my brain.

A moth made love to the oil lamp's dim, flickering flame. By its vague strobe light I saw the sheikh had closed his eyes and was sitting quite rigid. A couple of men were swaying slightly again and muttering under their breath. Then, for a moment, I had the distinct impression a figure on a large horse had galloped silently across the far side of the room.

"How can you expect God to be pleased with you when you are not pleased with Him?" a voice like the sheikh's appeared to ask me explicitly.

Emerging from the sheikh's body seemed to be another, larger body. When I looked closely, it appeared to be merely a trick of the light.

Was I supposed to answer? I didn't anyway, I didn't *have* an answer. I felt as if I'd been touched by some vast force, fierce yet gentle. It left me with an extraordinary sensation of calm. Dead calm.

The rest of the proceedings—a series of dialogues—was in Arabic and seemed not to concern me anyway. I sat in my cocoon, content with the peace that I didn't even try to understand.

"Well?" asked Mokhtar, when we stood once more in the darkened alley. I just shook my head. "That sheikh has great powers," he said, as if the thought had never occurred to him before. "He can bring the dead back to life."

He got no argument from me. We'd left the *tariqa* as furtively as we had entered it. I didn't have any more questions about Sufism. It was enough to know that the magic of ancient Egypt lived on....

That night I went to sleep feeling we live in many worlds at once, some an endless night, some still teeming with wonders, with the light of that innocence we knew as children, then lost, only to spend our lives striving to find it again.

Paul William Roberts has written for many magazines and newspapers, including The Toronto Star, Saturday Night, Toronto Life, *and* Harper's, *and is an award-winning writer-producer for Canadian television. Born in Britain and educated at Oxford, he currently lives in Toronto. He is the author of* In Search of the Birth of Jesus: The Real Journey of the Magi *and* River in the Desert: Modern Travels in Ancient Egypt, *from which this story was excerpted.*

★

Remember that moment in *Star Wars* where the spaceship shifts into over-drive, and suddenly we are hurtling through time, having broken through that final barrier, the speed of light? The dancing was like that. Into this space crowded with dancing figures, this little space in the middle of the jungle overwhelmed with moonlight, the black shadows of great trees, the frenzy of cheap, loud music—suddenly—there is a click, a meshing of psy-chic gears, a hurtling into another dimension. It is though we are all sud-denly drenched in a flood of tribal energy. The sound of the music fades away to a background noise, the night draws away and disappears, that area beneath the shed, now illuminated with an inner light, begins to pulse and glow. In an instant the souls of the dancers, deeply hidden within their egos, are drawn out of their bodies. Everyone is simultaneously aware of what has happened, this synchronization of individuals into a single, tremendous, and mysterious entity. The faces become intense, thoughtful, profound, the bodies become spiritual. (If I were to walk into this and take Ester or Ramón by the shoulders and shake them would they recognize me?) By surrendering himself each individual has become something much more powerful than himself; by giving himself to the group, to the tribal imperative, he takes on and shares the power of all. If death is the scattering and sharing of one's atoms, then this little death among the dancers would seem to prove that death is a joyful thing. Or could it prove even more? That the whole point of life is in dying? That God is not more than that rhythm that has dissolved and freed this yearning group of dancers?

—Moritz Thomsen, *The Saddest Pleasure: A Journey on Two Rivers*

ANNIE DILLARD

* * *

A Man of the World

Into the well of the human spirit.

WE ARE BEING FETED AT A BANQUET IN BEIJING, IN ONE OF A restaurant's many private banquet rooms. The room is drab and charmless; the food is wonderful.

Our hosts, members of the Beijing Writers Association, are mostly men and women in their fifties, sixties, seventies, and eighties. They are people who have witnessed, participated in, and in some cases sacrificed for, the liberation of China. In their early lives they saw civil war, and world war, and foreign occupation, and more civil war—all turning around in January 1949, when Mao's Communists, many of them veterans of the 1935 Long March, walked into Beijing. They deposed the local warlords and made it their capital. By the fall of that year they had taken the big port cities on the east coast. It was all over, essentially, but the shouting, which has continued on and off ever since. The Cultural Revolution, which lasted ten years until 1976, was only the most recent and ruinous of a series of internal purgative campaigns. Most of the Chinese people in this room, as intellectuals, were to various degrees among the Cultural Revolution's victims. Some of them, however, were bureaucrats who were canny enough to stay out of trouble.

My attention now is on one of our many hosts, seated beside me. Wu Fusan, I will call him, is a politically powerful man in his late sixties or seventies. I have watched him in action for days; he is the sharpest of sharpies, the smoothest of smoothies. The others at the table interest me more, I think, but here he is—beside me, speaking English.

Wu Fusan is a tall, soft-voiced old man with a ready, mirthless laugh. His arms are long; his fingers are light and knobbed, like bamboo. He wears a tailored gray jacket. He jokes a lot, modestly, about his powerful position. When he laughs, his face splits open at the jaw, revealing a lot of gum and teeth. His white hair is just long enough in front to hold the suggestion of a part; the hair shoots out diagonally in two directions from this part, giving him a wind-blown look, as if he were perpetually standing in the bow of a ship.

He is infinitely relaxed. He lounges in his chair; he tilts back his long head and brings out his words slowly, crooningly, from deep in his throat. He makes no effort to be heard; if you want to hear him, you must lean into him and lower your head, as if you were bowing. We chat.

His eyes do not seem to be involved in his words at all. Instead, from their tilted-back position, his eyes are studying you with a bored, distant, amused look—the way we would watch Saturday-morning cartoons on television for a minute or two, if we had to. He laughs his mirthless laugh at whatever you say, and at whatever he says, as if some greatly successful joke has been made, or some wonderful coincidence has been discovered, which makes the two of you accomplices. Usually this is the laugh of a nervous woman in society—but the woman uses her eyes, and Wu Fusan does not. He nods vigorously and tightens his legs; he is absolutely breathless with laughter; the lower half of his face is broken with laughter; he murmurs "Yes, Yes," in an educated British accent—and his eyes continue their bored appraisal. I have written him off as a hack, a politico, a man of the world without depth or interest. I am, as usual, wrong.

I learn later that Wu Fusan's class background is excellent: his father was a poor peasant. I learn still later—in a manner I will shortly relate—that his personal background is so impeccable that in the Cultural Revolution he lost only his books. Red Guards confiscated them because he spoke English and was known to have relatives overseas.

It is rude to drink alone in China. When someone at your table wants to drink his *mao-tai*, he raises his glass to you, and you are obliged to drink with him. Our host, Wu Fusan, has offered several formal toasts to us foreign guests seated at this table. Now, as the conversation splinters, and the beautiful, fragrant dishes pass before us one by one, he raises his tiny crystal glass to me, and we drink.

As we drink, Wu holds my eyes. As we lower our glasses and tilt them briefly towards each other, Wu holds my eyes. There is something extraordinary in his look. This occurs a dozen times over the course of the banquet; I have ample opportunity to see just how extraordinary this look is.

The man is taking my measure. He is measuring what I can only call my "spirit"—my "depths," such as they are. No one has ever looked at me this way. There is nothing personal or flirtatious about it. He is going into my soul with calipers. He is entering my eyes as if they were a mineshaft; he is testing my spirit with a plumb line.

His gaze is calm and interested. He is not looking at my face, nor my eyes, in any usual way; he is not particularly even looking at me. He is examining something inside me; he gauges my "strength" as if he were counting the coils of a loaded spring. All this takes less than a minute. We put our glasses down. The first time it happens, I think, What on earth was *that* all about? But there is no time to think about it; we resume small talk around the table. With us are other "literary workers"—Chinese and American publishers, scholars, and writers.

Every time we drink together, Wu Fusan and I, it happens again, and I learn more. I hate to think what *he* is learning—but I won't lower my eyes. I let him look; I hide nothing. What's to hide? I don't even know *how* to hide. You need to know, I think, that the ideas to which I have committed my life have required no more effort of me than occasional trips to the library. My life has set me at little risk, put me under no hardship. In this, I and many

Americans my age differ from most of the world's people. I am a light-hearted woman born at the end of World War II into American peace and plenty. He can see all this easily, I believe. I wonder why he bothers. I think it is a habit with him. The conversation is desultory.

My strongest impression is this: that Wu Fusan has been down this particular well—the well of the human spirit—many times, and he can go a hell of a lot farther. The deeper he goes, the more interested he gets, but, I stress, his is an analytical interest, and, I stress, he hits bottom. My depths are well within reach of his plumb line. He pays out his line slowly, drink by drink, double-checking, and gets his answer. I wish I were deeper, but there you are.

His look is neither sexual nor combative, although there was considerable sizing up involved. He was sizing up my spirit, my heart and strength, my capacity for commitment. This is what counts to a Maoist—in a friend and in an enemy—why shouldn't he be in the habit of looking for it?

Still, it was an odd, unverifiable impression for me to have, and I doubted it. It was too vague, internal, and groundless to count as anything but imagination.

Later I met a woman in China whose thinking I trusted. She was an Italian who had lived in China for years and had close Chinese friends. I tried to describe to her Wu Fusan's deep, measuring look.

"That's right," she said. "That's what they do. You weren't imagining it. This is their great area of expertise. Have you read much Chinese literature? Most of it, for thousands of years, is about this one thing: the human spirit in all its depth and complexity. Whole stories hinge on some small human variation, some quirk of the interior life. There is nothing they do not already understand. It makes them peaceful, at ease with all people. When I am alone with a Chinese man, I am as peaceful as if I were alone with only myself. Everything is known. Western men," she added unexpectedly, and not unsympathetically, "cannot see any of this."

Now the waitress brings the final soup to our banquet table. We are chatting politely. I am not thinking of our extraordinary toasting; I will sort all that out later. Not much is being said. Wu Fusan continues his paroxysms of social laughter, clapping his bony hands on his bony knees. Is this your first visit to China? We hope you will soon return.

I ask Wu where he's from. This is a standard polite question in China. He is not from Beijing, he says; he is from Sichuan Province—which is over 1,000 miles away. Paying very little attention, I continue.

"How long have you lived in Beijing?"

Unexpectedly he gives me a little amused glance and shrugs.

"Since we took it."

Annie Dillard has written a book of poems, a book on literary theory, a collection of essays, and a Pulitzer Prize-winning book of prose, entitled Pilgrim at Tinker Creek. *This selection is from her book,* Encounters with Chinese Writers. *She lives in Connecticut.*

＊

I must, before I die, find some way to say the essential thing that is in me, that I have never said yet—a thing that is not love or hate or pity or scorn, but the very breath of life, fierce and coming from far away, bringing into human life the vastness and fearful passionless force of non-human things...

—Bertrand Russell, *The Selected Letters of Bertrand Russell*
Vol. I (1884–1914), edited by Nicholas Griffin

RABBI DAVID A. COOPER

✦ ✦ ✦

The Old City

*In Jerusalem, the author encounters
ancient knowledge.*

DAWN APPROACHED THE HUSHED CITY OF JERUSALEM LIKE A parent entering a sleeping child's room—softly, gently, on tiptoes. It did not matter that the child had been naughty. Indeed, this child had been a problem for thousands of years. But she is special, endearing; she still draws the attention of the world.

I love walking the Old City's narrow, stone streets in the early morning hours. It is the time of transition, neither night nor day— a time when the spirits that live in shadows whirl and dance in one last frenzy before their murky playground recedes into oblivion. Pivotal points like this, the mysterious passage between moments, the blur where one thing is thought to end and another begin, are the gateways to other realms. In the hushed corridors of the slumbering Jewish Quarter, whispers of past eras can be heard— softly—like cats' paws on a dusty path.

For a while I went to the Old City *mikvah* every day to experience the ritual purification of immersion in "living water"—water gathered naturally from springs, streams, or even the rain, in an amount sufficient to submerge the entire body at once. Many *mikvahs* are close to freezing, but through procedures approved by rabbinical ordinance there are ways to heat the water. The Old City *mikvah* has two pools: one quite cold and one deliciously warm. I preferred the warm.

Some things are dulled through repetition, but for me the *mikvah* always had a profound effect. I also loved my daily routine in the Old City: getting up before dawn, practicing yoga with quiet concentration, walking the streets in contemplation of some mystical idea, submerging in the warm waters of the *mikvah*, and afterward going to the holy Western Wall to participate in the sunrise prayer service.

Jewish legend tells us that there were two stupendous beasts formed at the time of creation: the Leviathan and the Behemoth. They are magical creatures, but at the end of this era they must destroy each other in battle to make way for the world to come: messianic consciousness. It says further that the flesh of the Leviathan will be fed to those who are worthy of it, and after consuming this flesh the meritorious ones will live under tents made of the Leviathan's skin. The remaining skin, the part that is not needed for this ongoing feast, "will be spread by the Holy One, blessed be He, upon the walls of Jerusalem, and its splendor will shine from one end of the world to the other, as it is said: 'And nations shall walk at thy light, and kings at the brightness of thy rising' (Isaiah 60:3)."

The Leviathan has intrigued commentators for two thousand years, and Kabbalists suggest this is a great mystery that holds within it the secret wisdom of creation. It is said that the Leviathan could easily destroy the earth. In fact, a Talmudic text describes that the archangel Gabriel was given the task of dragging the Leviathan out of the sea. He succeeded in hooking the monster, but was unable to budge it. It turned out that only God could overcome this beast.

Another tale reveals a different, but similar aspect of the Leviathan's power. When Jonah was swallowed by a great fish, he was taken to the Leviathan, the master of all sea life; but when the monster saw that Jonah was one of the righteous people who in the days to come would devour him, he immediately fled.

Kabbalists believe that the Leviathan represents evil incarnate, which is more powerful than everything but the source of life itself. Messianic consciousness will come when evil is somehow conquered, when we transcend mundane existence and enter a purely spiritual life. All these tales conceal weighty secrets about the nature of evil. What does it mean, for example, that the light of Jerusalem, the holy city, will stream through the canopy of evil, resulting in messianic consciousness illuminating the world? It teaches us that our task is not to eliminate evil, but to search at its core for a spark that is a necessary element in the transition to higher consciousness.

This is a dangerous thought, and it is why the rabbis have been persistent in keeping Kabbalistic teachings hidden and inaccessible. Like all mystical wisdom, if misused or misunderstood, it is the gateway to hell; but if our vessels are properly prepared to receive this light, it will illuminate a path to realms beyond our conception.

The Old City *mikvah* is on a side street that few tourists use; it is not easy to find. In the dressing room, an old man sat in a corner, bent over like a sunflower in autumn, his narrow, rounded shoulders formed a valley to cradle his chin where a chest had once been. His skin hung in little bags, like pushups of old memories, younger years in Poland when the *mikvah* was a mud hole in the summer, and an opening through ice in the winter. His *peyot,* the long sideburns that identify a pious Jew, hung below his chin; his beard would reach to his waist if he could stand up straight, but now it touched his knees. I wondered if he was past a hundred years in age—good chance.

On another bench a man and his son were getting dressed in Hasidic garb. Both had shaven heads, but long, luxuriant *peyot* hung dripping down their cheeks: the floor was wet, and the man had to hop on one leg, doing the jig I had seen often, trying to get the second pant leg on without dragging its cuff through the muddy swirl on the floor. He slipped for only a moment, and a gray smear blotted his cuff. He shrugged briefly and then helped his son stand on the bench to get dressed.

I was dressed in yoga pants and a sweatshirt. A few of the regulars knew me; but many eyes stared across the room. I had tried to conform for a while by wearing the regulation slacks and white shirt of a yeshiva student, but people stared anyway. It did not matter what I wore, I did not fit in. So I decided to be comfortable, wear my normal clothes, and try not to be self-conscious. Nonetheless, I made it a point to come early, when there were fewer people.

Women are given privacy when they go to the *mikvah*. They are alone most of the time, except for the few moments when they are actually in the water; then a female observer is usually present to be certain that all body parts and hair are submerged at once. The *mikvah* is an absolute necessity for Jewish women at least once a month, as they are the vessels in which conception takes place—spiritual purity in this instance is essential.

Males also use the *mikvah* for spiritual purification, but more as a preparation for the fulfillment of daily practice and religious obligation, particularly prayer, study, handling or reading the Torah, or writing or saying the Holy Name of God. Male Orthodox practitioners regularly go to the *mikvah* just prior to the Sabbath or Holy Days, and many of those who are stringent in observance attend the *mikvah* every day before the morning prayers. Thus the male side of the *mikvah* is often crowded.

Aside from the implicit act of sanctifying this holy vessel we call our body, a good deal of the male ritual in *mikvahs* is similar to behavior we all learned in locker rooms. Like little boys who battle with their golden fluid swords streaming into a toilet bowl, men size up each other through the great equalizer of nudity. At the *mikvah*, we solemnly soap in the showers, rarely able to expunge the pervasive scent of maleness, and then immerse ourselves side by side in deep tubs of water; just as the Torah describes that the high priest had done in days of old. Some traditions beat drums, dance, hunt, and conquer for male bonding; Judaism uses the *mikvah*, prayers, and the constant process of learning Torah with a male partner.

The pool was all mine. I had waited a long time in the shower, peeking around the corner, hoping for a few moments of solitude. This was my reward: I was alone. As I hastened into the steaming tub, I pulled out the large rubber stopper in the wall that connected this water with an unseen source. The inflowing stream was cool. As the waters mixed, my tub was spiritually impregnated and validated as an authentic mikvah. Somewhere within my being, I felt a charge when this coupling occurred. I was secure, encased in a womb, warm, supported, caressed, gently rocked in the spiritual amniotic fluid, lulled by whispering steam leaking through exposed pipes near the ceiling.

They say that every person has many souls, each of which resides on a different level; the highest aspects of the soul are connected with the angelic realms. Each time we sleep at night, one of our soul levels—called the neshamah—flies away to the heavens, learning things of mystical delight. This soul force must return to us before we awaken, and the first blessing we make, as consciousness informs us that sleep has ended, is a thanksgiving for the reinstatement of our soul—we could not live without it. The truth is, the soul would rather be somewhere else.

Today, when I immersed under the mikvah's waters, I felt my neshamah communing on ethenic planes. Bubbles streamed past my face as I slowly sank to the bottom in a fetal position. I felt myself melting into a unity, suspended in equilibrium—no gravity to remind me of my substantiality—and I lost all sense of body and form.

Echoes reverberated; a low, murmuring buzz that arose and fell from no particular direction was everywhere. The four Hebrew letters of the Holy Name etched themselves in my inner vision, and like a blast furnace pouring molten steel, flames streaked out from each letter. The fire intensified like mammoth sun flares traveling enormous distances, approaching me in slow motion as if through a gigantic telephoto lens, constantly coming nearer. I spread myself open, welcoming: "Come here, come to me; please."

There was a tug, an awareness, then another. My chest was straining. Something slowly realized that this body was under water—not breathing. The "I" consciousness began to return; there was a burning and ache deep in my lungs, far away. How long had I been here, and how long could I remain? I knew in that moment why the neshamah does not want to return. Quite simply, the womb of eternity is incomprehensibly serene, gentle, and loving.

I was curled near the bottom of the pool. The tugging became insistent. Slowly, I found the tiled bottom and pushed myself upward. As I broke through the surface into the world of mundane reality, I gently allowed my lungs to fill with the pervasive damp, warm air, and I knew something had

been revitalized within me. In this daily experience of Jewish baptism was
an affirmation and direct realization of a kabbalistic secret: We are reborn
each day—indeed each moment—and we begin afresh with the possibility
of new perfection in every breath we draw.

My favorite time at the Western Wall was three o'clock in the morning. I had always enjoyed this time of deep reflection in the stillness of predawn hours, but my recent Vispassana meditation experience added a fresh perspective to my readings and prayers. In truth, up until this time, I had found the prayer service too long, too fast, and too repetitive. My goal had been to learn the pronunciation and to try to stay up with the prayer group. It was often a frustrating, numbing experience.

But now I began to prepare myself for the prayers by sitting quietly and emptying my mind. When I was ready, I would begin slowly, absorbing the meaning, dwelling in the rhythms, not concerned about how far I would get. Some days I spent hours on one phrase—and that was my prayer for the day; other days I felt the flow of the words pouring forth, and I would dance through dozens of pages, skimming the waves of emotion like a sleek canoe as I paddled from one poetic cove to another.

Not only did my prayers become more alive and more meaningful, the texts I studied assumed completely new voices. I had had glimmers of this earlier in the year, after my mother's death, but now the experience became robust, and I realized that these texts cannot be fully appreciated in everyday consciousness because their authors were themselves operating in an altered state.

Thus, strangely, my appreciation for Judaism was profoundly inspired by Buddhist practice. Indeed, if it had not been for the contemplative refinement of strenuous meditation, I would have missed a vast world of Jewish insight and wisdom that is hidden just below the surface—but few of the teachers or institutions I had yet experienced offered guidance along these lines. This was such an enormous void for me—and the fruits so readily available— I decided to pursue and gain some level of mastery with the meditative technique, all the while deepening my relationship with

Judaism. Thus, I spent months going to the Western Wall long before the crowds appeared, and sat alongside the huge blocks of granite for many hours—in stillness—absorbing the aura and history of the Jewish people.

There were always a few devotees at the Western Wall who spent entire nights as self-appointed guardians of the sacred space, but normally wide sections of the ancient stone blocks were unattended, and I could sit and meditate without being disturbed. When dawn approached, large numbers of men began to fill the square, and my meditations had to cease. Many *minyanim* (prayer groups with a minimum of ten men) formed, each with its own style and pace. The cumulative effect was chaos. This was diametrically opposite to the atmosphere of my silent meditations. Visitors to the Wall who are not acquainted with Jewish prayer are often shocked or amused that every prayer group, and every individual within each group, seems to be going off in a separate direction.

Religious law requires the morning prayer to take place within a certain period after sunrise. It also emphasizes praying in a *minyan*—Judaism is a communal tradition—and so pressure is brought to bear on all individuals to join in group prayer. My experience had been that few groups had a rhythm or orientation to

> *L*ate afternoon. I am standing above the Western Wall, also known as the Wailing Wall, in the old section of Jerusalem. All the cracks [in the Wall] are filled with paper. Some are brittle and yellow, some are mere fragments, and some are on air mail envelopes and hotel stationary. I could see a few with words exposed: there was one in French, others in German and Hebrew and Russian and English. I wondered what these prayers were all about. Were they praying for someone who was ill, for friends, for family, for peace or prosperity? What were their hopes and their dreams? Did they really believe they could get a message to God through this wall? Every single crack in the wall to my right and left, above my head and beside my feet was filled with paper. I kept looking. Three meters above my head was a hole the size of a tennis ball. I crumpled my note up into a tight wad, looked around, hoping that no one was watching. I leaned back and tossed my message up.
>
> —Lynne Cox, "To Aqaba"

prayer that was compatible with mine, but I found a way to meet these group obligations at key moments during the prayer sequence while still cloaking myself in a kind of invisibility—a psychic separation—so that I could continue the quality of my meditative prayer. I longed, however, for a like-minded group who could meditate and pray together because the power of a group working harmoniously in spiritual efforts far exceeds the sum of its parts.

My spiritual solitude was never a deterrent for dozens of *shnorrers,* people who ask for money, who always appear at the Western Wall on weekday mornings during the hours of prayer. Although I could manage to gain some distance from the other people praying, it was hopeless to try to avoid the *shnorrers.* Nothing stops them.

Americans have a difficult time with collections of charity because most of us view begging with disdain. *Shnorring,* however, is a highly honorable profession. Many of these people are collecting money for others as well as themselves, and their self-image is that they are vehicles through which other people can do good deeds—because it is a great *mitzvah* (good deed) to give money to the poor. Thus a *shnorrer* "expects" people to give, and is not particularly grateful when they do—which is misinterpreted by many uninitiated contributors as arrogance.

It should be noted that this attitude is not unique to Jewish beggars. A well-known Zen story tells of a man named Umezu who brings five hundred gold pieces (called ryo) to his teacher, Seisetsu, for the expansion of his school building.

"Seisetsu said: 'All right, I will take it.'

"Umezu gave Seisetsu the sack of gold, but he was dissatisfied with the attitude of the teacher. One might live a whole year on three ryo, and he had not even been thanked for five hundred.

"'In that sack are five hundred ryo,' hinted Umezu.

"'You told me that before,' replied Seisetsu.

"'Even if I am a wealthy merchant, five hundred ryo is a lot of money,' said Umezu.

"'Do you want me to thank you for it?' asked Seisetsu.

"'You ought to,' replied Umezu.

"'Why should I,' inquired Seisetsu. 'The giver should be thankful.'"

I made it a rule when in Israel to try to give something to every person on the street who begged openly. It did not matter what the individual looked like or how aggressively he or she approached passersby. The less I felt inclined to give, the more I made an effort to increase the amount. Almost every time I tried to pray at the Wall, a *shnorrer* would approach me from the side, peek into my prayer book to be certain I was at a point where acknowledging him was permitted, and then lean close to my face, mumbling something. I always tried to have pocket change handy, so when this occurred I would transfer coins to him without removing my eyes from my book as if this were simply another component of the morning prayers.

Many people resent this kind of intrusion and will avoid going to the Western Wall for this reason alone. I had little difficulty with this, however; my distraction came from the crowded conditions— the loud voices of many prayer leaders, the shoving and elbowing of people jockeying for space, and the general mood of socialization, all of which contributed to the disruption of my concentration. The *shnorrers* were simply color added to the grand swirl of events that fill the canvas of the epic work known as Daily Life at the Western Wall.

The mind tenaciously grabs for something each moment, like a frog unrolling its sticky tongue to capture an insect, and instantaneously a mosquito is buzzing in my thoughts. Sometimes I track it through an aimless series of associations; other times it is joined by a swarm of images flooding into repetitious patterns—and I forget where, and what, and who I am.

Indeed, there is more forgetting than remembering. Only in moments like this do I realize that I live almost entirely in a state of forgetfulness. When I am able to cut off the drone of these thought-mosquitoes, I have a twinkling of remembrance. It never fails to shock me, this remembering; it dwells in a radiance that instantly soothes my aching psyche. It brings me back into the garden filled with delight that has often been my home—a place of serenity and perfect peace.

Around the garden's perimeter a fruit tree grows. The scent of it offers irresistible promise: divine wisdom. But the instant the fruit is tasted—in the repetition of the mythic cycle—the veil of forgetfulness descends and we are condemned to an endless motif of remembering and forgetting.

This is our mind. Constantly seduced by the aspiration for divine wisdom, only to discover it is not something to be attained but is inherent in our own stillness. Yet the paradox remains that in the stillness "we" no longer exist, and the fear of absorption into this nothingness fuels the endless chain of forgetfulness. Our ambition is self-defeating; letting go is our only hope.

The seven-day holiday of Sukkot was nearing its end. The morning prayers during this seasonal celebration are the most festive of the year. Each person carries four distinctive plants: an unopened palm branch, called a *lulav;* three branches of myrtle, called *hadasim;* two branches of a willow, called *aravos;* and the fruit of a species of citron, called an *etrog.* Each person has his own set of the four plants, and at a specific time during the prayers he waves them in six directions. According to one of the major Jewish mystics, Isaac Luria, the directions must proceed in the following order: south, north, east, upward, downward, and, finally, west.

This ritual is not only a thanksgiving for the harvest, it is a rain dance. A circle is formed around the Torah, and the men chant songs of praise as they circumambulate the holy scroll. At the end of the week, the willow branches are beat against the ground, and the prayers for rain begin in earnest.

When I first learned about and participated in this ritual, I was rudely awakened to the fact that Judaism has a fair share of primitive ceremony, and I was embarrassed to be involved in what appeared to be superstition and magic. But the more I became involved in these activities, the more I appreciated the power of our primal nature—its mystery transcends the farthest reaches of the intellect. Modern man continues to admire the amazing abilities of Aborigines who commune with nature, but most of us have surrendered this link in the name of being civilized. Religious traditions, however, have often retained rites that actually open passageways to a wondrous primeval energy within us.

Thus, over the years, the Sukkot ritual has become one of my favorites, particularly the requirement to dwell for a week in the *sukkah,* with its roof open to the skies, completely dependent upon the vicissitudes of nature. Sukkot has become for me the Jewish paradigm of an annual spiritual retreat—I love its raw, primitive flavor and the profound mysticism that is associated with it. The days of Sukkot each autumn provide a marvelous combination of spiritual insight that never fails to inspire new and penetrating self-realization.…

I have noted that the Jewish calendar is filled with days of ritual celebration. When I first encountered this ongoing procession of Holy Days, I was impressed by the experience of reflecting on the past, reliving ancestral events thousands of years old. Having repeated these rituals for many years, however, I have found that while the cycle invites contemplation upon the past, each experience—although repetitive—seems to sharpen my awareness of the present moment.

Long ago, I read about the famous Dr. David Livingstone, who was found in the African jungles by Mr. Henry Morton Stanley, the news reporter. One day Livingstone was attacked by a lion, and was virtually in its claws before the lion was killed by a gun bearer. When asked later how he felt, Livingstone replied that when he realized there was nothing he could do, his terror transformed into an oceanic calm, a peacefulness he had never before experienced. When I first heard this story, I thought Livingstone's euphoria was the result of an ultimate release in the clutch of death, the final realization of: "So this is how it is going to end!" In later years I discovered an important nuance in this supreme level of resignation: simply that the utter release of our survival impulse leads to breaking the bonds of all sense of past and future. When we are not clinging to life, we enter the continuous experience of the present moment. And so it turns out, paradoxically, that our grasping for life is self-defeating; it is only when we let go completely that we can be fully alive.

Similarly, whereas the ritual of traditions at first draws us into the past, its repetition, year after year, begins to generate a feeling of an endless cycle. Eventually, this leads to the realization that although we have a degree of choice, we are also encapsulated in our bodies, limited by our minds, products of creation bound by the laws of this universe. While we might conclude that the reality of being constrained by the nature of existence would result in a sense of fatalism, the actual experience in quite the opposite. Just like Dr. Livingstone, once we clearly recognize that we are securely in the jaws of fate, we release into the sublime state of transcendence that is commonly known as being fully present in the everlasting NOW.

Rabbi David A. Cooper has been a student of mysticism for over thirty years, traveling and studying extensively the mystical elements of a variety of traditions. He spent almost ten years living and studying in Jerusalem before moving to the Colorado Rockies. This story was excerpted from his book, Entering the Sacred Mountain: Exploring the Mystical Practices of Judaism, Buddhism, and Sufism.

＊

"Let's face it, when you meet people, you find out in two or three minutes whether or not you're comfortable with them. You say, 'I'm not comfortable with this guy, but he's going to do something for me,' so you pursue that course…and somehow you're off the road and you're in the mud." Dan Pearson [San Diego businessman] is certain that's bad business.

"If there's a word in the common vernacular," he says, "it's *go with the flow.* I raise a lot of money, but I never force it to a close. I'm always asking myself, Is this the thing I'm supposed to be doing? The ancient writings talk about *dharma*, doing your own thing. It is better to be moderately successful at what you're supposed to do than wildly successful at what you're not."

But how can a person know what his or her truest instincts are? "Well," he says, "I meditate twice a day, and the phrase I use is *checking in with the boss,* the cosmic computer." When he has doubts about a business deal—about anything—he looks for some sign. "And then invariably the next day or two someone calls me or walks in," and the solution presents itself. "It's why I always return every phone call. If I've learned one thing, it's that there are people out there you're supposed to relate with."

The Hindu sage Patanjali believed a person runs into the same few significant people again and again during the course of his life, without recognizing them, until the time comes to make a connection dictated all along by fate. The woman who ends up as your wife might have passed you on the sidewalk ten years ago—"these people are walking through the movie set all the time. And, depending on how quickly you go *Aha!*, you interact." That's why Pearson returns every call: a man never knows how the mystery will unfold.

He leans forward at his desk, a by-gosh-if-it-don't-ring-true Indiana grin on his face. "You've done it yourself, sleeping on a problem instead of trying to 'solve' it. It boils down to having the courage to trust your instincts. You have to realize"—still grinning, shrugging as if he's baffled himself, almost whispering—"that life...was not...designed...to be as hard...as you want to make it!"

—Tom Huth, "The Man Who Levitates Hotels," *California*

* * *

Beyond the Sky

*Creativity and love come
from the same source.*

I WAS DRAWN AS IF BY MAGNET TO A LIFE WHICH ALMOST immediately led me to explore immense, uncharted wildernesses in the heart of my native continent, the greatest of which was the Kalahari Desert, and for some years I devoted myself to exploring these "known unknowns." I did all that—in so far as I was conscious of what I was doing—because instinct and opportunity and a love and gift for making do in bush and jungle and desert matched the opportunities put in my way, and seemed to be the most honest and worthwhile kind of employment for a person like me who had to start rediscovering himself and resuming a way of his own.

I was soon to find that, in exploring vast tracts of country where no Europeans had been before, the impact on me went far beyond what my senses conveyed, significant and vivid as their transmission turned out to be. The simple, overwhelming fact was that exploring the physical unknown became, from the beginning, more and more an exploration of an immense unknown in myself, so that although the journeys themselves and what appeared to be of interest to a larger world have been recorded in several books of mine, there were special moments almost like phases on a kind of pilgrimage of providence, and some six years of my immediate

post-war life-stand out now like the lighthouses I have seen in the
many oceans over which I have travelled.

The first of these moments came one day when I was lying in
the grass on a mountain top in central Africa with the earth underneath me warm and alive. Through all my body I seemed to
feel it like a kind of electric blanket holding me warm and secure
as if a gift direct from the caring and loving heart of our great
mother, the African earth. Between the tassels of grass high above
me the sky, as so often in Africa, was a sort of midnight blue, and a
great feeling of exhilaration broke through me and the thought
presented itself, bright and quick to my slow tongue, and I could
only catch it in retrospect on my return to Europe in words which
found a place in my book *Venture to the Interior*. It was a form of
certain faith, of even more than the Pauline conviction so beautifully
expressed by perhaps the greatest writer in the Bible. It was for me:

> ...*the not-yet in the now,*
> *The taste of fruit that does not yet exist,*
> *Hanging the blossom on the bough.*

These words expressed a thought that remains constant, and I
am amazed how many letters I still get and how often I am asked
from which Chinese text that quotation came, or from which
poem of Eliot the lines are taken. The answer, of course, is that I
merely wrote them down; they came to me out of Africa and the
kind of journeying I was doing then.

And its importance has continued to grow and its light in the
dark of myself increase because it came out of a bitter experience
in prison where, taken out to what we thought could be our own
execution, we were made by the Japanese to watch the most brutal execution of others; and, during the watching, an officer, standing between me and a great friend and great prison commander
whom we all called Nick, fainted on trembling, thin and weak legs.
Nick and I had to support him as he stood there, and in the process
we all touched hands and I was startled, because throughout my
physical being there was an inrush of what I can only describe as
electricity, which was not just a thing of energy but was also

charged with a sense of hope, certainty, belonging and life forever.

I knew then, and the knowledge has grown and not dimmed, that this is what flesh and blood is about and is meant to be, and but for this I do not know how I could have steered my course in the years that have followed up to today, because the external scene of the post-war human world appears to be stubbornly determined to deny and destroy that one-ness of life we are meant to share.

Sir Laurens van der Post was born in Africa in 1906 and was the author of over twenty books including A Far-Off Place, The Lost World of the Kalahari, The Dark Eye in Africa, *and* About Blady: A Pattern Out of Time, *from which this story was excerpted. Made a Knight of the British Empire in 1981, van der Post lived in London until his death in 1997.*

✳

Around Vega there is a brim of dust, half a light-year wide and as warm as toast. Comet dust. The dust of meteors. Grains of nickel and iron. Silicates. Ices. Dust that entrains volatile gases and water vapor. Enough dust to make a dozen planets, planets with seas and atmospheres. But not planets yet. The dust is still dispersed into a flat disk, but slowly it is yielding to the clumping tendency of gravity—the halo is condensing into grains, the grains into nuggets, the nuggets into asteroids, the asteroids into worlds—worlds as numerous as flakes of snow condensing out of a storm, as same and as different.

A grainy stuttering of heat on a simulated photograph—knowledge condensing from a sea of mystery, extending the shore along which we might encounter God. (Can that ancient, much-abused word still have currency in an age of science? Perhaps not. But let it stand, like a distant horizon, like a foreign shore.) *Este saber no sabiendo,* "this knowing that un-knows," is what John of the Cross called it, the knowing that takes place *just here* on the surface of the eye where Vega and the thought of Vega are one. Photons of radiant energy stream across the light-years, wind-whipped whitecaps of visible light and the longer swells of the infrared, to fall upon the Earth out of the dark night—denying, revealing, hiding, making plain. I am soaked by starlight; I am blown by a stellar wind. I am bent low in that downpour of revelation.

—Chet Raymo, *Honey from Stone: A Naturalist's Search for God*

PAUL MCHUGH

✦ ✦ ✦

The Pure Jones of It

Or, the tai chi *of the critical moment.*

EVER SEEN A DOG WITH A PURE JONES FOR RUNNING AS HE FINALLY gets taken out, his leash is unsnapped, then he sprints free and wild down a beach?

Recall the shining eyes, the lolling tongue, the tiny sand cascades from paws digging deep for traction on a high-torque turn, the deliriously joyful barks, the breeze that ripples the red-bronze fur, the wet black nose rooting with eager frenzy through heaps of seaweed, flotsam, and wrack…but the dog abandons it on a whim to wheel directly into splashing runs out through wave spray, followed by teasing escapes from a tug of undertow and backwash of surf?

Riding a motorcycle is like that.

You see, this joyous sense of play, this pure delight in motion is part of the fuel of the physical animal, and part of our birthright as well. Motorcycles so amp our senses that we are reached in deeper places, and inspired to thrust our minds into more captivating sensual levels than those strata which we ordinarily so fussily and fretfully manage.

In such shining instants, our inner animal is seduced to leap forth and dance through our skins. But much more than the rapture of a playing animal makes itself manifest when grave and proximate danger is added to the summons.

As a dog rides in the bed of a pick-up, his experience is amped by the power of the machinery, and each major sense is stimulated to the maximum. His nose is jammed with a stream of odors both subtle and strong, his eyes filled with a blur of passing landscape, his ears tune into a symphony borne to him through undulating white noise of the slipstream wind.

By contrast, most human drivers of automobiles remain well-insulated from the world through which they pass. Manufacturers may hype a certain hot model's handling, but primarily, a modern car is created to isolate you from the landscape. There's cushy suspension to homogenize the surface of the terrain, stereophonic music to mask its sounds, plus an air-conditioner capable of wiping out any ambient climate.

On a motorcycle, you're more like the dog in the pick-up. The warmth of each ridge, the cool of every dell wrap about you immediately as you wend through them. The fragrance of each earthen bank, dank willow-clad creek, or field of wildflowers washes around and up under your helmet only to be instantly replaced by the new bouquet of odors awaiting you around the curve…which may just happen to include a freshly squished skunk—PHee-YEW!!

And visuals sharp and crystal clear rush toward you from straight-on, blur to abstract streaks in your peripheral vision, then take real shape again briefly in the rear view mirrors shortly before they vanish forever. This is the 360-degree movie through which you fly….

A thin shriek of wind whistles past your helmet, the bass thrum of the big engine vibrates right up through the seat into your spine, as do a hum and mumble of the tires on the pavement. Part and parcel of this sensory stream is a gamut of logistical meaning that's speedily weighed by the brain, then fed flowing back through the body in the opposite direction, rushing back out through the nerves of your feet and fingers as a continuous stream of operating commands to the big mechanical beast humming between your legs.

You grab just the right amount of rpm's with a throttle twist from your right fist so the beast drops onto a power surge at just the precise spot, so you can snap open your left fingers just as if your clutch lever was a bowstring, and you yourself become the arrow that darts straight out from the nadir of the curve in the swale.

In such a fashion, you not only grow to appreciate undulations of the terrain in a manner known mostly to low-flying goshawks, you also feel a telepathic communion with a road engineer, that very one who designed this sinuous sequence of banked curves which permits you to swoop and recoup your carefully invested momentum instead of having to jerk it around or chop it roughly back with your brakes. And you wonder if somewhere back in that engineer's mind way back then there wasn't the germ of this thought, "Ah, this road of mine is one smooth and beautiful sumbitch, it'll be pure delight for someone to charge out and snake it up on a big roaring chopper some crisp fall day."

It is an ultimate sensation to shape all that information rushing into and out of you, so that your mind, the terrain, and the beast all unite in the experience, and the motorcycle is raised like Frankenstein's monster into near sentience and obvious animation by the kiss of your pleasure in its movement.

But all of that experience, and all that conditioning and pleasure pale in comparison beside the forces that emerge when one is forced to put all one knows, and more than all one knows, to a test, a test in which matters of life and death must be decided in an instant.

Here's the scene: a crisp autumn night in Tallahassee, Florida.

It's about 1 a.m., and I'm riding a black Triumph Bonneville motorcycle back from an evening of wine, cheese, and literary blather at a college professor's home.

Now this "Trumpet"—our slang term for Triumph bikes back then—was one hot putt. It had been a track racer, reconverted for street use, and its 650cc vertical twin engine packed a potent 210 pounds of compression in both cylinders. So I'm cruising down Monroe Street to the major intersection in town and yeah, I'm ballin' that jack at maybe twice the speed limit. Hey, I'm young, and there's few cops around at that early a.m. hour, and those shortie exhaust pipes I had on emitted a burbling roar that I loved to hear reverberate back off those big storefront windows as they rattled in their frames.

Those big bikes had a bass toot that stimulated every major gland in a teenager's body. Could be, that's why we called 'em Trumpets.

As I rumble blithely up the low hill where Tallahassee's two major highways cross under a traffic light, suddenly my mildly ecstatic, high-speed cruise turns into an invitation to die.

This turkey coming the other way in a red sportscar just cranks a left turn right in front of me.

That's bad.

Next, he sees me coming, freaks out, hits his brakes and stops. Sideways, and blocking the road. Dead in front of me.

That's real bad. "Oh Fuck," are two words that spring to mind.

Amazing how your mind just shoots right into hyperspace when something like that occurs. Time itself seems to slow down. An astounding number of perceptions and choices and moves seems to fill the silences between heartbeats.

OK. No room to swerve. Gotta bring the speed down as much as possible before impact. Crank down hard on those mushy Triumph brakes! Oops. Rear wheel's locking up and the back end of the bike is sliding around past the freewheeling front end. Balance is fragile and dicey. Don't want to lay the motorcycle down because then I'll go under that low sportscar and probably get his transmission embedded in my cerebrum.

If I'm absolutely gonna hit it, I'd rather be riding high and have the chance to launch my body up and over the car.

But sliding the Trumpet in this crazy sideways screeching posture ain't something I can handle for more than a microsecond! But wait—my mind goes plunging like a wildman through a haystack of solutions in a crazed search for that one straw that might possibly be turned into a magic wand—I suddenly and luridly recalled a scene from a movie I'd just seen, a documentary of motorcycle riding called *On Any Sunday,* with some cameo scenes in it by actor Steve McQueen. There had also been some scenes of flat-track racing that showed guys going into broadslides on dirt curves, then slowing down without brakes as they steered by goosing the throttle.

Seemed like a real good idea to pull off a broadslide now.

I'd never done anything even remotely like it before.

But necessity can be a mother.

So, let's just assume I can do it.

Keep the rear tire sliding now, bozo, keep the front tire rolling so you can steer, use rear brake pressure to keep the rear tire where you want it, keep your balance on the foot pegs, and Hey! ain't this something?

Now you're broadsliding!

My tires and front brake drum are screeching, doom is still rapidly approaching, and my emotional state can be summarized as terrified. But somewhere in my brain I am also smiling: God bless those limey bike builders. They may have made Trumpets with the crummiest electrics since Benjamin Franklin's kite string, and scumbag carburetors that are impossible to tune, but man, the sweet-handling of this frame geometry on this here motorcycle is an ergonomic marvel.

As disastrous as the overall situation is, something about my barely balanced, skittering slide across pavement towards that sportscar feels just absolutely perfect.

However, goddammit, although this broadslide lets me slow without putting the bike right smack down into a medley of grinding metal on the pavement, my situation is only marginally improved. Now it looks like I'll just crash into that sportscar with the right side of my body, instead of head-on.

It does not seem as though this shift in my circumstances really constitutes a significant improvement.

But that distracting thought is immediately swatted out of my mind by a much larger concern. How can I possibly get out of THIS part of the fix?

Well, why not shoot the moon!

I WAS able to assume that I could broadslide.

Now, let's assume I'm psychic.

Thus, I can broadcast a special, mental message to the driver of the sportscar, with the force of a billion candlepower lighthouse lamp lens that beams into his grey and swirling foggy mental fog with a dense and swiftly transmitted ditty that goes something like this:

HEY THERE STUPID, THE BEST WAY FOR THREE HUNDRED POUNDS OF BRITISH STEEL TO NOT WIND UP IN YOUR LAP BY WAY OF CAR-OMING OFF YOUR GIRLFRIEND'S FACE WHO SITS NOW BESIDE YOU IN THE FRONT SEAT WITH HER JAW HANGING DOWN TO HER BELLY-BUTTON IS IF YOU TAKE YOUR GOLDDANG FOOT OFF THE BRAKE PEDAL, PUT IT ON THE ACCELERATOR, AND CHUG ON OUT OF MY WAY!!!

And I'll be darned if he didn't respond.

He did just as I'd instructed him.

But he did it with agonizing, heart-wrenching slowness. Or was my sense of his forward motion only relative to the awesome speed of neurons firing and synapses snapping in my brain as my body's internal tachometer soared past redline? Had I entered into some surreal state of overdrive, where thoughts and impressions and choices whirled through my consciousness with a speed that would make a tornado look like a zephyr?

Perhaps even the second sweep of a wall clock would look

> "*Qi is a kind of force that resides in the lower abdomen and circulates through the body. A soft-boxing master can direct it to any part of his body, or even out of his body to another person's body.... In the old days, masters were so good they could hurt or heal you without even touching you.*"
>
> —Mark Salzman, *Iron and Silk*

to me now as if it was groaning, staggering, taking an eternity to swing from one second hatch mark on the clock face to the next.

In any case, even though he was now moving, I foresaw I'd still mightily crash into his rear bumper unless I could somehow turn this broadsliding sled back into a rolling motorcycle and swiftly swerve around him.

So. Right now. How do I get out of this friggin' broadslide?

Again, the mind leaped.

I take no personal credit for this, by the way. Whatever was happening within me was as outlandish as stumbling onto the dance floor behind your new girlfriend in dread of your very first major junior high school social embarrassment and suddenly discovering you'd been demonically—but magically—possessed by the ghost of Fred Astaire.

This time, the mind leaped into a dark sea of unconscious intuition gradually accumulated from the past six years of riding motorcycles on everything from sand and gravel to wet pavement. How do you get out of a broadslide? The answer seemed to resonate right up out of my nerves. Take your foot off the brake, unlock the rear wheel, and goose the throttle. The envisioned sweetness of the move just seemed right. It harmonized with the situation.

> *Mystical—or poetic— experience is somehow very simple, like drawing aside a curtain, or turning on a light switch. But if you blunder into a completely dark room, you may feel the walls for hours before you find the switch. Turning on the light is simple when you know where the switch is.*
>
> —Colin Wilson,
> *Poetry and Mysticism*

And there were no more milliseconds left for a second guess.

I twisted that throttle grip like I was turning the doorknob on the portal to my personal future, and the Trumpet swerved back into a straight line of travel as the squeal of the rear tire was supplanted by the motor's roar. And so my body and that motorcycle whipped around the rear bumper of that still slowly moving sports-car with nary a centimeter of space to spare.

Then I pulled to the curb, switched off the bike, took a breath that seemed like the first deep breath I'd had in weeks, and sat there shaking. My pulse hammered so furiously, it felt as if it was about to blow my forehead off. Shadows and streetlights seemed to shift and waver in color as my perception of time wound gradually back down to normal level, and it was like I could feel the hum of a dynamo fading down to its ordinary rpm.

Very, very carefully, I restarted the bike and drove home. But lying awake that night—and for years since then—I pondered the remarkable, magical transformation that had occurred. That spontaneous and wondrous shift in my time sense, perceptions and reactions during those few heartbeats when my life had seemed at risk. It had seemed that at every fast-paced critical juncture there had been a path laid out in my mind with the absolute lucidity of a neon arrow glittering in the void. All that had been required to survive was the boldness to choose and commit instantly to that path.

To mint some words and coin a phrase; let's call this transformation The *Tai Chi* of the Critical Moment.

To experience this high-speed transmogrification is our birthright.

Man—and Woman—the animals—come equipped with the biochemical gear to take on a sabertooth. To experience that transformation in all its hair-raising glory is to discover something important about our identity. It is to plunge our bucket into a well-spring of innate power.

One blessing and curse of human affairs in the very late 20th century is that we barely allow ourselves to experience just an overture to that powerful and ancient reflex. But involving

ere is the world from a subatomic physicist: "Everything that has already happened is particles, everything in the future is waves." Let me twist his meaning. Here it comes. The particles are broken; the waves are translucent, laving, roiling with beauty like sharks. The present is the wave that explodes over my head, flinging the air with particles at the height of its breathless un-roll; it is the live water and light that bears from undisclosed sources the freshest news, renewed and renewing, world without end.

—Annie Dillard,
Pilgrim at Tinker Creek

our bodies in "risk sports" not only permits a reconnect to the vibrancy of our animal nature, it also allows a complete, physical follow-through to a conclusion.

One makes tremendous discoveries in that process.

My friend, mountaineering writer Eric Perlman, has said: "High-risk sports are mentally and physically addictive. Forget cocaine and LSD—those are just synthetic triggers that send the real drugs into action. When an avalanche rakes the climbing route, or the kayak flips in a gnarly hole, every eye-opening, pain-killing drug in your body rips through the nervous system like a Chinese fire drill.

"Muscle fibers fire faster. Emotions hit warp speed. Thoughts kick into hyperdrive. The higher the risk, the hotter the dose. Adrenaline, epinephrine, endorphins, dynorphins and dozens of others—those are the pure stuff that money can't buy."

Perlman is right about the delicious intensity of this hormonal cocktail. When the hormone-amped body presents its possible moves to the crisis-focused mind, life becomes absolutely dazzling in its clarity and vigor; and awareness becomes simultaneously sweeping and sharp.

Tai Chi refers to an old Chinese martial art, and the *Chi* that is summoned and nourished is the essential life force. To feel it erupt and dominate decisively a critical moment is not only to be exhilarated, but to be informed in no uncertain terms who we are at our core. It gives us a hint of the sort of talents we might unlock if we could only pay more attention to them.

I quit riding motorcycles. I grew entirely too sensitive to their dangers to continue. Besides, I had taken up white-water kayaking, and I told myself. "A man doesn't need TWO things like this. Only so much luck to go around!"

Then in 1989, after nine years of doing without, I bought a BMW R100GS, and began again. I had come to realize that it wasn't only moments of high crisis that had energized my nerves. A steady growth of awareness had once come to me from just riding around on bikes. What had made me such a conscious and defensive driver nowadays was the motorcycle experience in toto. Constant exposure to risk had rubbed the nerves ripe and ready, whenever I was on the road. Constant work on processing rogue variables had made me program in a response to always look for escape routes far in advance of need.

When riding a motorcycle, your own skills and abilities are also among the things that should never be taken for granted. Even apparent constants—the adhesion of your tires to the road surface—will not remain the same. A patch of oil, a streak of mud, or an unanticipated need to hit the brakes can suddenly turn your magic carpet into a tumbling bucket of bolts.

Of course, that unpredictability permeates all the rest of life. But riding a motorcycle makes it obvious.

I guess the key argument that swung me back into the doggone beautiful world of big putts was something I heard from a biker who had never taken a break from the sport. For a newspaper story on motorcycling, I was interviewing Dennis Casey, who rode on weekends, and worked the rest of the time as a carpenter in the East Bay. When I learned he'd ridden steadily for the past twenty years, I wondered why the inherent dangers hadn't slowed him down or stopped him, in the name of all the presumed responsibilities of adult life.

"Sure," Casey said on the phone. "Bikes are dangerous. But, you know, another school of thought goes, you could step out your door tomorrow, stroll down the sidewalk and still get hit by a truck.

"So, my idea is when death comes to you, you might as well be doing what the hell turns you on. Don't want to wind up at the age of ninety saying, well, I may have watched a lot of TV, but I sure was safe."

Born during Hurricane King at the edge of the Florida Everglades, Paul McHugh lived there until leaving home at sixteen to study for the Roman Catholic priesthood. After completing his education at Florida State University, he jumped on his motorcycle and traveled the U.S. He ended up in Northern California, where he worked as a fair hawker, custom carpenter, candle carver, masseur, commercial fisherman, logger, and rancher. McHugh made environmental movies for PBS during the early '80s, serving as a producer and writer, and in 1985 was hired as chief outdoor writer for the San Francisco Chronicle—*a position he has held ever since.*

✳

The laws of nature become simpler and more elegant when expressed in higher dimensions.

To understand how adding higher dimensions can simplify physical problems, consider the following example: To the ancient Egyptians, the weather was a complete mystery. What caused the seasons? Why did it get warmer as they traveled south? Why did the winds generally blow in one direction? The weather was impossible to explain from the limited vantage point of the ancient Egyptians, to whom the earth appeared flat, like a two dimensional plane. But now imagine sending the Egyptians in a rocket into outer space, where they can see the earth as simple and whole in its orbit around the sun. Suddenly, the answers to these questions become obvious.

From outer space, it is clear that the earth's axis is tilted about 23 degrees from the vertical (the "vertical" being the perpendicular to the plane of the earth's orbit around the sun). Because of this tilt, the northern hemisphere receives much less sunlight during one part of its orbit than during another part. Hence we have winter and summer. And since the equator receives more sunlight than the northern or southern polar regions, it becomes warmer as we approach the equator. Similarly, since the earth spins counterclockwise to someone sitting on the north pole, the cold, polar air swerves as it moves south towards the equator. The motion of hot and cold masses of air, set in motion by the earth's spin, thus helps to explain why the winds generally blow in one direction, depending on where you are on the earth.

In summary, the rather obscure laws of the weather are easy to understand once we view the earth from space. Thus the solution to the problem is to go *up* into space, into the *third dimension*. Facts that were impossible to understand in a flat world suddenly become obvious when viewing a three-dimensional earth.

Similarly, the laws of gravity and light seem totally dissimilar. They obey different physical assumptions and different mathematics. Attempts to splice these two forces have always failed. However, if we add one more dimension, a *fifth* dimension, to the previous four dimensions of space and time, then the equations governing light and gravity appear to merge together like two pieces of a jigsaw puzzle. Light, in fact, can be explained as vibrations in the fifth dimension. In this way, we see that the laws of light and gravity become simpler in five dimensions.

—Michio Kaku, *Hyperspace: A Scientific Odyssey Through Parallel Universes, Time Warps, and the Tenth Dimension*

Fire Beneath the Skin

Born of stars, how can we not burn?

SMOKE HUNG OVER THE CITY AS WE RODE TOWARDS THE *GHATS*. IN the distance over the river, we saw fireworks flash, bringing the jagged outlines of temples into dark relief, followed by thudding like artillery shells. Our rickshaw driver tried to avoid the crowds by following side roads. Off the main avenues, instead of electric lights, dozens of small oil lamps and candles had been planted in rows along the ledges of the homes. Strings of firecrackers burst like machine-gun fire from the city centre. The explosions came with greater and greater frequency as we neared the river. A young boy stepped out from between two buildings and hurled a banger into the middle of the road. It detonated in the path of our rickshaw, frightening the driver. He swerved, rocked on two wheels, and narrowly avoided a head-to-horn collision with a wandering cow. Roman candles flared across the sky, fizzling gold above us. The sacred city could well have been at war.

"I *am* a *Dis*-co *Dan*-cer," the current hit song from a popular Hindi movie, blared out from loudspeakers set up along the main market streets. Young men gyrated to the beat in front of garishly painted plaster idols of the God-king Rama and Queen Sita, spotlit and strung round with coloured lights. A mass of dancing worshippers, all clapping hands above their heads, jammed the next intersection, making further rickshaw travel impossible. I paid the driver and we dismounted into the crowd. Clutching each other's hands, Sabina and I pressed our way through the frenzy into the back streets at the centre of the city, trying to find a way to the river.

Wet, dung-filled paths, too narrow for cars or even ox carts, covered the heart of Varanasi like a skein of dogged veins. They twisted and turned, dead-ended and looped back upon themselves. Through one doorway, I spotted a flash of red and the glitter of candles; a rear window into a shrine room was filled with praying, white-robed devotees. In the next alleyway, a water buffalo munched softly on a pile of dried grass. All the shops were still open, their wares spilling out onto the street: silver bangles, pewter pots and water jars, row upon row of small golden idols. Candles and coloured lights covered every ledge. Young boys huddled in small groups, daring each other to hold the tips of red bangers in their hands. The explosions made Sabina jump, and her skittishness attracted the boys' attention. They threw their tiny bombs directly at her sandalled feet, laughing as she shrieked, and giving chase as we tried to escape through the winding alleyways.

The boys fell back when we joined a train of well-to-do women in white saris. The procession led through the inner-city maze to the shore of the holy river, just upstream from the burning *ghats*. We had inadvertently joined the final steps of a funeral march. The cremation fires seemed muted under a hundred bright electric lamps, each hanging on the end of a long bamboo pole. Lamps for the dead, Sabina explained.

A second power failure struck, dousing the city once more in darkness. But the momentary blackness soon gave way to the yellow glow of cremation fires. Orange embers flickered upwards to the sky. Looking over the Ganges, we saw hundreds of small oil lamps set afloat as offerings to Rama. Moisture rose up from the river and drifted inland, swirling warm and fishy around us. A dog barked near the water's edge, then growled. We stepped down the dark stairs of the *ghats* and heard a voice call to us from the river.

"Hello, Mister, you want go boat ride?"

We heard the gentle slap of oars. We could not see the hull against the black water, just the boatman's glowing white turban as he slid towards shore. He held out a near-invisible hand to steady us as we boarded. We sat close together on the wooden planks in the bow, and the boat surged slowly upstream away from shore, into the current of tiny river lamps. Sabina urged the oarsman to be careful not to overturn any of the fragile offerings. He allowed the current to take us farther out until a thousand dancing lights bobbed between us and the shore. Beyond the banks, the city's darkened profile was shot through with dots of candlelight.

"Oh, so beautiful," said Sabina. "It's as if the stars have settled on the city."

Where was the rational Indologist now? I thought with a grin. But it vanished the next moment as I felt her fingers touch my cheek, slide down my neck, press lightly against my chest and rest there. The sudden intimacy of her touch inflamed me. I placed my hand on her thigh, felt her muscles tighten and relax. After a minute she placed a hand over mine, holding it still.

"I have an idea," she whispered. "Another secret. I'll show you, back on shore."

When we reached the *ghats* she took me by the hand and led the way once more through the city's inner maze until we arrived at the gates of an ancient observatory. She quickly coaxed the watchman into opening the iron door for us, then drew me in after her through a confusing network of walkways and walls to a spiral staircase. It had charted the course of the sky. As we looked down on the city spread out beneath us, the power failure ended. Varanasi flashed out of the darkness with a million multicoloured lights. A spontaneous cry from thousands of voices rose up from the streets. "Disco Dancer" surged through the loudspeakers. A sudden volley of Roman candles filled the sky with luminous pinks and greens. The smoke that followed covered the city with a misty glow. Sabina leaned against my side and put her arms around my waist. She pressed against my chest, her breasts warm beneath her *kurta*. "I give you Varanasi for Diwali, Tim," she said, holding me close.

It was past one by the time we made our way back through the combat zones of the old city and the still-crowded market streets

Diwali, also known as Deepavali, is perhaps the most joyous festival in the Hindu religion. It is a celebration of good over evil (typified by the Hindu epics Mahabharata and Ramayana). During this five-day festival (known as Tihar in Nepal), oil lamps or candles are lit at night by doorways, windows, and rooftops. The houses are thoroughly cleaned and tiny "footsteps," made of rice flour, lead from entranceways into the main room of worship. These "footsteps" are supposed to lead Lakshmi, the goddess of wealth, into the house and thus bring prosperity and wealth during the coming fiscal year. Besides worshipping Lakshmi (symbolized by the cow), the crow and dog (again, symbols and icons in the Hindu cosmology) are also worshipped. On the fifth day, sisters invite their brothers to their homes and food and gifts are exchanged. Children especially love Diwali because firecrackers are part of the celebration, and in Nepal, gambling is open and "legal" and every street corner or alleyway is crowded with young boys and men who temporarily possess that crazed frenzy one associates with casino addicts.

—Rajendra S. Khadka, "Diwali, Deepvali, Tihar"

to the Maharajah Hotel. The moon-faced manager sat outside on the steps, keys in hand. When we entered, he drew an iron gate shut behind us and locked it with a chain. "Ah, Diwali!" he said dreamily as he climbed the stairs behind us.

"Good night!"

Sabina's eyes slowly surveyed the room. She smiled at the sight of the pomegranate, guava and red bananas I had piled in a bowl in the centre of the wide blue bed. On one of the night tables the small white elephant she had given me raised its trunk playfully. I lit four candles around the bed, then turned off the light. Bicycle bells rang in the street below. A burst of firecrackers popped dully in the distance, and the occasional Roman candle sent bars of light in through the cracks in the shutters.

"This is our room," I said, glad for how she lingered over the small details I had prepared.

I left her briefly for the sink, quickly sprinkling droplets of water to scare away the ants. They scurried in panic all across the porcelain bowl and back into the cracked ridges in the plaster. I returned to the room and sat on the bed, legs crossed, eyes closed in a final moment of meditation, listening to her brushing her teeth, peeing, flushing the toilet. Even such earthy sounds filled me with bliss. I felt exhausted and exhilarated, drugged by Diwali, one corner of my mind still wondering if she was going to come back out and announce she had to leave for an important meeting with some Buddhist monks.

She returned and lay on the bed beside me, her head propped on one arm, looking straight into my face. I sank into her gaze. I couldn't speak. We didn't move. After a few minutes, she reached out and touched my cheek.

We caressed, easing each other out of our long Indian shirts. She touched me like an accomplished ballroom dancer leading a novice through his steps, sweeping me along in her grace. She guided my hands, my lips, to where she wanted me, pulled my head to her breast, drew my fingers between her thighs. I felt her muscles tense with pleasure. Her hands stroked my back, my neck, nails scratching lightly across my shoulder blades, her eyes watching me closely in the candlelight, as if learning how my body moved and taking delight in mastering it. Her touch felt cool and I trembled. I clutched at her shoulder, panting. She smiled, inscrutable, shifted her hips and pulled me from my side to lie on top of her.

I rolled between her legs, felt her wet heat and pressed into her, gasping for air, blood roaring in my ears. It was too intense, too fast. I wanted to thrust wildly, claw her flesh, but instead dug my fingers into the bedclothes. I froze, afraid to move in case I burst, and an old spectre of shame rose up. Her eyes tried to catch mine, but I averted them. She too was breathing heavily, but stilled her hips. We hung together motionless for a while. Then slowly she began to rock, sliding me in a little deeper with each gentle movement, and the intensity held, did not spill over prematurely as it had done all too often in the past. She wrapped her ankles around the insides of my calves and strained to pull me tighter into her, increasing her rhythm. I opened my eyes and this time met her gaze, the blue sparking dark, honey hair tumbled all about. She threw back her head and I kissed her neck, breathless with the quickening roll of our hips. Our breathing came together now, shorter, faster, her body quivering beneath me. She groaned, and I felt it through to my belly, triggering a shudder, a brief second of bliss, spasms of pleasure coursing outward as I rocked hard against her, and then lay still.

We made love once more in the late Diwali night, and again at dawn as the ringing of bicycle bells filled the alleyway below our room. After we made the great bed rattle one final time, she kissed my belly and slid off towards the bathroom.

"Where are you going?" I asked dreamily.

"Oh, I have a breakfast meeting with Strauss. He has—"

"I know, a Buddhist monk or scholar he wants you to meet for your research."

She grinned at me and closed the bathroom door.

"Ack—Ants!"

This existence of ours is as transient as autumn clouds.
To watch the birth and death of beings is like looking at the movements of a dance.
A lifetime is like a flash of lightning in the sky.
Rushing by, like a torrent down a steep mountain.

—Diamond Sutra

I hated to let her go, marvelled that she could separate herself so easily. I pitied Strauss, so infatuated with her, but denied the pleasure of her touch. Yet I felt no pride. Rather, a sense of awe that someone so beautiful, so sexually accomplished had chosen to be with me. It was almost religious. After she left, I lay in the blue bed, thoughtfully munched a guava and picked up my journal. My skin still tingled from her touch. A lazy, drugged warmth ran through my muscles, as if I was drunk on mulled wine.

"Technically," I wrote, "this has been the most intense, longest, most exhilarating night I have ever spent with a woman. I think I have a blister."

Technically.

I stared at the word in my notebook and pondered how it had flowed from my pen. Sabina was certainly a master in the arts of love, but I wondered if I and all men were for her just canvases on which she expressed her art. We had made love passionately and energetically, and I felt an acceptance of my sexuality—even desire for it—that I had never felt with previous lovers. Yet we hardly knew each other. This acceptance was exactly what I had longed for all my life; better, in fact, than I had ever imagined it to be. But somehow dissatisfaction was creeping in already. I picked up my pen again.

"Somehow it feels 'surface,'" I wrote. "Passion, but not real intimacy. I suppose that's not surprising on a first night. It just feels as if somewhere underneath there ought to be a lot more."

"If Strauss insists on coming to the station, can you just meet me on the platform?" she said after our second night in the blue bed. She was on her way out for a final goodbye breakfast, and I had agreed to meet her at the ticket office for our trip to Patna later in the day.

"No, I'll jump up and kiss you."

She laughed nervously and bit her lower lip.

At the station, she was late. Ten minutes before departure, I decided to leave our meeting place for a minute to confirm that our train was on time. As I passed through the gate leading to the inquiry desk, a heavyset white man with a goatee came through the other way. He didn't recognize me, but the blonde woman at his side in the dark blue Punjabi-style pantsuit certainly did. She blanched, eyes pleading for silence. I brushed past her, not saying a word.

I inquired about the train, found that it was on time, and turned to see Sabina behind me.

"Meet me at the platform, please," she asked, out of breath from running.

I nodded. She turned and ran back through the gate.

"He wanted me to stay another day," she told me when we at last pulled out from the station, leaving the luckless professor behind. "But I told him I sacrifice myself for scholarship."

"Did he try to seduce you?" I asked.

The jealous tone of my own question annoyed me. I wasn't so much as uncomfortable at the apparently lighthearted way she had used his desire to accomplish her own ends. Of course, Strauss seemed a willing enough volunteer. Still, I could all too easily picture myself in his shoes, and was glad I could not be used to further her career.

"No, he didn't try," she replied, "except in a very academic way. We were discussing Mara's daughters and he told me he didn't think their temptation of the Buddha was really about sex. He said he thought it symbolized the attraction of the world in general, and that it would be a misinterpretation to infer from the story that the Buddha was anti-sex."

"Quite a come-on. But it is a good question. What do you think about it? It seems pretty central to your work."

"I told you," she said, irritated, "my research is to catalogue and describe. It's science. You Western Buddhists, so concerned about whether or not Buddha thought sex was dirty! But I don't care."

"I'm not a Buddhist," I grumbled uneasily.

"Then tell me, what were you doing meditating in the mountains?"

"It's difficult to explain," I said awkwardly. "But let me try. When I became a Christian at eighteen, my perspective on the world changed radically. Suddenly God was everywhere. The devil, too. There were new spiritual meanings for things that I previously didn't think of questioning. Everything from events in the State of Israel to my sex life, or rather, sudden lack of one, had a place in God's plan. My non-religious friends thought I had lost my mind. Don't smile. Evangelical Christianity was just a different world, with its own quite consistent internal logic. After I started studying philosophy and travelling in Europe, it hit me there were lots of different worlds, each valid from its own particular point of view. By becoming Christian, I had changed viewpoints, but not necessarily come any closer to the truth. And the Western cultural background in which I grew up was still determining how I saw things. I wanted to experience something radically different in order to really shake up my perspective. I went to a monastery not to become Buddhist, not to get enlightened, but to see how the world looks to a Buddhist, and in doing so, loosen the grip my own culture has on my mind. Ideally, just to get more free."

"You would have liked my father," she replied, surprisingly softly, for I suppose I had expected her to dismiss my philosophizing with an impatient wave of the hand. "He was an atheist, but very drawn to Zen. I remember he used to tell a story about being captured by the Russians during the war. He was a doctor in the German army. They sent him to a prisoner-of-war camp. He thought he would never see anyone he knew again. When he arrived, they stripped him of everything, down to his skin. They left him with absolutely nothing. 'This was the happiest moment of my life,' my father used to say. But he said as soon as they put him in prison, he started searching for a pencil to write a letter to his family to tell them he was still alive."

Suzuki Roshi once said about questioning our life, our purpose, "It's like putting a horse on top of a horse and then climbing on and trying to ride. Riding a horse by itself is hard enough. Why add another horse? Then it's impossible." We add that extra horse when we constantly question ourselves rather than just live out our lives, and be who we are at every moment.

—Natalie Goldberg, *Long Quiet Highway: Waking Up in America*

We stayed in Patna for five days, wandering through its museums and ruins, sketching and photographing Buddha statues of Mara and his seductive daughters. In the 3rd century B.C., Patna was the site of the imperial city of the Buddhist king Ashoka, and it remains the capital of modern Bihar State. Bihar comes from *vihar*, the word for a Buddhist temple. For some fifteen hundred years the region was the heartland of a thriving Buddhist culture, rich in monasteries, temples, and universities, all of them wiped out by successive waves of invading Muslims who dispatched those unwilling to convert. It was now predominantly Hindu once again. For Sabina, Bihar was a treasure-house of research material, although by any economic standard, the state ranked among India's poorest.

One unique feature of the city made its most dismal streetside slums seem festive. Slum dwellers spray-painted their wandering goats and cows with bright Day-Glo patterns: hot pink, electric blue, lime green. Some streets looked like living, mooing, art exhibits. Presumably the markings identified the animals and kept them from being stolen; and in a land where the cow is sacred, paint struck me as a lot more humane than branding. The animals excited Sabina. Sometimes as we rode she would call to our rickshaw driver to stop just so she could take a picture of a passing neon cow.

"You should be doing your thesis on cow art," I teased her.

"Oh, wouldn't that be wonderful!" she replied in earnest. "I love the cows of India. They are so beautiful, so gentle. No wonder they are sacred to the people. They give only good things: milk, dung for cooking fuel, and urine, which used to be taken as a medicine for certain sicknesses. I have often thought about doing a photo book, you know, a coffee-table book, *The Cows of India.*"

We stayed at the Patna Tourist Guest House through the hot and humid nights. Our bed was covered with a white cotton mosquito net, which looked to me like a silken desert tent, closing out India and the world, or so we hoped. The wooden bed frame squeaked. I told Sabina I imagined the janitor sweeping one spot outside our door for fifteen minutes every morning, gradually being joined by other workers until the entire hotel staff congregated at our doorstep, hand brooms whisking in time to the rhythm of the bed, straining to hear the sounds coming from underneath the foreigners' door. We could shut India out, but could not prevent it listening in.

In Varanasi I had been forced to play the stranger for the sake of her reputation. In Patna, that same concession to Hindu morality demanded that we pretend to be husband and wife. Eyebrows were raised at front desk over our respective Austrian and Canadian passports, but provoked no objections. One elderly Brahmin, a visiting Congress party politician who spent his days chewing betel nut in a plush chair in the lobby, quizzed us thoroughly on our international marriage. For his sake we quickly created three young daughters and a family home near Vienna.

Sabina's public persona changed as radically as her marital status. She kept her hair pulled straight back, the blonde ponytail usually knotted into a bun, and carried not a single sari in her heavy duffle bag, just pantaloons and long-sleeved pullover *kurtas*. In Delhi and Varanasi she had always seemed soft and feminine, relying on her charms to get what she wanted. In Patna she displayed a hard edge I had never seen before in public. She was blunt, imperious, almost sneering towards rickshaw drivers, porters, even peons at the museums. She bestowed not a single smile, except to museum curators, and her instructions in Hindi to those required to serve her sounded harsh, even to my uncomprehending ears.

"You sound so sharp," I told her once after she had snapped out our destination to a rickshaw driver.

"Yes, I have become a real *memsahib* in India, like the wife of some British general," she said as the three-wheeler jerked us out into traffic. "If I show any softness at all, then they are cheating me and grabbing at me. Men here are not used to taking orders from a woman. Especially a blonde European. They see me, and all they think of is American movie sex scenes. But they understand a *memsahib's* voice, a *memsahib's* scorn. If I keep my head high, never look at them, and yell orders, then they don't bother me."

Until that moment I had not fully appreciated what it took for her to negotiate India. Her yellow hair was a candle for over two hundred million sexually repressed male moths. Beating them off would be an exhausting task for anybody, yet she managed not only to deflect them but to conduct research at the same time. I respected her for her daily battle, and had a new understanding of my role as her assistant. Having a "husband" along helped with much of the deflecting, and that, far more than lugging her bag or searching with her for statues, sped up her work. It felt good to be useful to her, after all, and quite wonderful to be the one man in all Bihar with whom, in the privacy of our room, she dropped her defences and smiled upon.

At dinner our fourth night in Patna we sat side by side at a table for four so that we could hold hands beneath the white tablecloth without attracting too much attention, although the waiters grinned widely with every visit to our table. Sabina asked if I had ever been in love. I told her about my years of celibacy, about trying to love Tina, my sense of inadequacy, both emotionally and sexually, and then leaving her to go to India. Sabina gazed at me.

"Is it such a long way to you?" she said.

"Yes. For you, maybe not so long. What you would find there, I don't know. Some of it scares me."

"I love you," she whispered to me as a waiter approached, then turned to him, "And now I would like the milk sweets for dessert."

I wanted to speak the words back to her, surprised at how quickly they were forming on my lips, but ordered a bowl of mango ice cream instead.

That night as we slid out of our clothing and under our gossamer netting, I caught something fragile in her mood, a sense of something slipping away. The way she held me when we embraced seemed almost mechanical, as if after several days of warming intimacy she had reverted once more to plain technique. It felt to me as if she was marking out a safe distance in the field of our loveplay. I wondered for the first time if she paid a price for her sexual freedom with men. I wondered if another kind of protective shield, far different from the *memsahib* act, had formed inside of her. Somehow it seemed her sexual expertise permitted her to embrace without being vulnerable enough to get hurt, as if she kept a divider between sex and love—almost like a man. Almost like me. Now the divider was sliding down once more, right in the midst of her caresses.

I thought I knew all too clearly what caused it. I had held back from her at the table. But not out of lack of loving, for now that the field was clear of rivals, I had abandoned my futile attempts at Buddhist detachment. Indeed, our sex was the best I had ever experienced, and she was a confident, informative and intriguing travelling companion. As far as watchful India was concerned, we were a happily married couple, and I found it rather to my liking. But to say the words was difficult, more so because if I was going to really love her, I felt first I had to confess something that I was afraid to say. She might conclude I was crazy and just leave. But if she was going to love me, it was only right that she should know.

I held her firmly in my arms, stopped her stroking fingers, and put a stilling hand on her shoulder.

"There's something I have to tell you," I said, cursing the tremor in my voice. "It's going to sound strange, and I don't know what you are going to make of it."

"All right," she said, uncertainly propping herself up on her elbow, eyes intent.

"It's not like I'm about to confess a murder or anything. You can relax. It's something that happened to me during my meditation in Ladakh, perhaps the most revolting and disturbing experience of my life. It takes a little time to explain. Do you mind?"

She shook her head, encouraging me to go on.

"You see, the text I was working with started out with a section on freeing yourself from desire by meditating on the composite nature of all being. Basically, the instructions were to visualize a beautiful woman—or a man for a woman student—someone who fills you with desire, and then focus the meditation to find out where the desire is located. So, for example, say I feel desire for my lover's beautiful long hair. Then I examine the hair through each of the

You thought you could do without [matter] because the power of thought has been kindled in you? You hoped that the more thoroughly you rejected the tangible, the closer you would be to spirit; that you would be more divine if you lived in the world of pure thought, or at least more angelic if you fled the corporeal? Well, you were like to have perished of hunger.

—Perrre Teilhard de Chardin

five senses: do I desire the sight of it, smell, touch, taste, or sound it makes maybe when she swishes it back and forth? Wherever you find desire, you look more closely, as if through a microscope with a zoom lens. If I desire the sight of my lover's head of hair, do I desire a lock of it? A strand? Well, perhaps a strand? A four-inch piece? Two inches? There comes a point where there's no more desire for the speck that remains. Then you build it back up, strand by strand, back to the lock, to the full head. If desire returns, you go back to where it disappears once more, until you realize no feature of a woman is desirable in itself. Desirableness is something the observer superimposes on the object of his desire. This may seem like a fancy way of saying beauty is in the eye of the beholder, but discovering it for myself, it no longer seemed a cliché."

"And you wonder why I have no time for this spiritual foolishness?" she said angrily. "So, you're telling me you have mastered desire?"

"Oh, God, you, better than anyone else, know that isn't so." I gripped her arm for a second to make sure she wouldn't leave. "In fact, it took me a few days just to get started on the exercise, because I didn't really want desire rooted out so viciously. The text said to look on the body as a 'dirty machine, a frothing scum or heap of sticks, stones and pus.' And I couldn't do it. It seemed to me intent on fostering aversion. I didn't want to do that, but I did want to get into the rest of the text. It was my whole purpose for being in Ladakh. So I decided to do the meditation without bias. If disgust arose, I would just accept it. And if desire stayed, I would just accept that, too. At least in the end, if desire persisted, I would have a much clearer idea of what turned me on.

"Slowly I worked my way down from hair, forehead, ears, eyes, nose, mouth, through chin, neck, shoulder blades, armpits, nipples, elbows, wrists, each finger and the navel. It was exhausting work. Each single part took at least an hour's meditation. Some parts much more than others. But feeling all this desire every time I sat down to meditate proved good incentive for the work. It was amazing how clear the image grew, as if I could really see a woman in front of me, and could then get close-ups almost to the cellular level. It was working, too. In most cases, I could observe how I was adding the component of desire to the image, and then watch it disappear, but with some exceptions. For example, no matter how much I analysed my imaginary lover's eyes, I couldn't shake the feeling that this was more than looking into little black holes. Even in certain photographs or paintings, it's just ingrained in me that there's someone in there, someone I desire.

"After about two weeks of meditating four or so hours per day, I made it to the waist. From there on down, it was really slow going. Cutting through desire was as much work as clearing a rain forest with a pocketknife. Fortunately, by this point the process was moving almost automatically. Focus. Zoom. Analyse for desire. Repeat. Finally I got past the mons veneris. The genitalia were hell. They took forever to get through, and kept me in a pretty constant state of horniness that just wouldn't go away. In the next session I turned my attention to the buttocks.

"When I zoomed in close on the buttocks, I felt desire take on a new quality, something dark. I tried to focus on it and suddenly it ballooned in intensity. It was as if a carefully controlled experiment was going into meltdown. From inside my chest a creature sprang out with a yell, leapt into my meditation and grabbed violently at the imaginary buttocks with long, bushy arms. It thrust itself fiercely, sexually, into the image—a dirty, hairy, ape-like little creature, hunched over, furtive. It reminded me of Gollum, you know, the obsessed, repulsive cave creature from *The Lord of the Rings*.

"It realized it had been lured into the light, and the beast froze. It cowered like a thing long used to caves and subterranean passages. It appeared as distant and real as if it was physically standing in front of me. I knew perfectly well it was a hallucination. But it was a real hallucination. It had come out of me. Luckily, I kept calm. I didn't break from my focused, meditative state, just noted the extreme aversion the vision aroused. It revolted me, this stinking, filthy animal. It chilled my flesh.

"'Stop,' I said, forbidding the beast from slinking back into my chest. It trembled, rooted to the spot by my voice, and obeyed. 'If you are my lust, my dark nature, whatever, all right,' I said out loud. 'I don't want to kill you. I won't deny you exist. Not any more. You are a part of me I—I never knew—did I do this to you? Did you have to be this way? Now I know what you are, and I will accept you. You do not lunge in real life. You are under my control. I just want to look at you, see if those sick emotions can be lost without denying or repressing you.'

"The creature glared at me, frightened and malevolent, while I looked it over.

"'Now go,' I said.

"In a flicker, the beast leapt back inside my chest. I felt it lurking there, prowling, angry at being tricked into the light. I fell back on my cot, completely exhausted. I never dreamed this part of me existed, so twisted and ashamed. I almost quit the meditation, Sabina, because I wasn't sure how to guard against the beast returning. But I had come to Ladakh to study Buddhism. To break free of my culture, get another perspective—you remember what I told you? I had to laugh. What I had wanted was so abstract, so analytical; instead I hallucinated a personal demon that feels more real than any philosophical truth I've known. I couldn't deny it. So I continued with the meditation, staying on my guard, without incident, right down to the toes.

"What I need to tell you, Sabina, is that it's still in here, this creature. It's a part of me. But I think I feel him changing since I've met you. Maybe it's possible for it to grow into something healthy? I don't really know."

I looked at her, eyes barely visible in the darkness. She said nothing. I knew how she scorned metaphysics, and this one was right over the top. But I continued.

"You said to me at dinner that you loved me, and I didn't say anything back, and you must wonder: Did he hear it? Is it making him afraid? Does he love me too? Yes, yes, yes. I do love you, without even knowing what the words mean. Here and now, I do. Does any of this make sense to you at all?"

"No, it sounds pretty confused," she said gently, stretching her arms around my neck, and pressing her breasts against my side. "But it doesn't matter. The last part is sounding better. Keep talking."

She crouched over me and kissed my shoulders, my nipples, ran her fingers through the hair of my chest, then bit my stomach. Her hands ran down my legs, and she slid down to take me in her mouth. I stopped talking. The feeling of impending orgasm grew in the centre of my belly. But instead of driving outward towards her body, the energy began to burn within. Heat seared up and down my limbs from inside. My nerves tingled like pins and needles, as in a leg that has gone to sleep and when the feeling returns it's so painful at first you can't walk. I began breathing fast and deep, hyperventilating, trying to absorb the strange sensation so that it would pass quickly, but its intensity kept growing. Bursts of white light flashed behind my eyes. It scared me. I felt I was losing control of my body. I pulled Sabina up, then rolled over to lay on top of her, anxious to have an orgasm and get rid of the sensations. My head, hands, feet and belly felt on fire, the nerves incredibly sensitive to touch. The rush was weirdly ecstatic, electrifying, almost unbearable in its intensity. My body shuddered like paper before it ignites. The image of a curling corpse aflame in the burning *ghats* flickered through my mind. My hips thrust down at her, desperate for release. Suddenly I realized my erection was gone. My penis lay limply against her while the sensations inside my skin seared white hot. I felt I was losing consciousness. Beneath me, Sabina moaned and clutched. I could barely feel her, but held on, frightened and amazed as everything began to whirl around, and she was all that there was I could cling to.

I don't know how long it lasted, but gradually the burning ecstasy faded from my twitching nerves. It took perhaps another half-hour for me to slow my breathing. Exhausted, slick with sweat, I turned to her and stroked her hair. Her eyes met mine uncertainly.

"This has never happened to me before," she said, her voice quavering, "that I have orgasm without penetration, without you...touching me." She felt my belly and the shaft of my penis. "You're still hot, but no sperm. It's very strange."

I nodded. For a while I could not speak. My mind searched for some frame of reference to connect this to, and an image surfaced from a visit to a remote mountain monastery in Ladakh. A lama friend had taken me to the special red chamber where the guardian deities dwelled. He permitted me to draw back the curtain to gaze on the wrathful aspect of the deity drawn on the temple wall. The ancient being radiated rings of flame. Its blue head was that of a snarling, fanged bull. Four of his arms bore tantric objects of power: a sword, a bell, a sceptre, a human skull filled with blood. The other two pair of hands caressed a green-skinned female goddess pressed against him in sexual embrace. She gripped him, standing, one leg wrapped around his waist. Their red tongues met, and in graphic detail the icon showed the thick blue shaft of the bull-god's penis entering her.

Such graphic sexual depictions of celestial and demonic beings were metaphors, so my Western commentaries on Tibetan Buddhism had said, for the spiritual union of the female and male poles of existence: yin and yang, darkness and light, potency and fertility. Yet I had also read that some tantric Buddhists and Hindus lived out their metaphor in their own secret practices, transforming sex into a spiritual force so blinding, so powerful, it consumes all pleasure, all lust, all personality in its purifying fire.

I shook my head and sat up in bed, wondering if we had inadvertently touched that power together. It scared the hell out of me. What if we had been sexually united, had carried it through to orgasm? It felt as if I would have exploded, unable to contain the energy. My body would have broken open and shattered like a shell. But from that shell what would have emerged? I wondered with a brief laugh if Sabina did this to all her lovers, like some goddess in disguise. God, she'd laugh at me for that, I thought. I'm enthralled enough with her as it is.

"You give me so much," Sabina murmured, placing a hand on my back.

The remark caught me totally by surprise, for in all honesty, I had hardly been aware of her. Her gaze, her stroking, her subtle movements and sounds of passion that usually delighted me in our

> *If our universe is only a pale shadow of a deeper order, what else lies hidden, enfolded in the warp and weft of our reality? [Physicist] Bohm has a suggestion. According to our current understanding of physics, every region of space is awash with different kinds of fields composed of waves of varying lengths. Each wave always has at least some energy. When physicists calculate the minimum amount of energy a wave can possess, they find that every cubic centimeter of empty space contains more energy than the total energy of all the matter in the known universe!*
>
> —Michael Talbot,
> *The Holographic Universe*

lovemaking, they were all lost in the storm. All I remembered was gripping her and once hearing her groan. She reached up and clasped my waist from behind, drawing me back down into her embrace. I realized it must have been late into the night.

"Sabina, I think we may have touched something here," I said, reluctant to lie down, but unable to resist her arms, "some kind of tantric energy. What was it like for you?"

"You were wonderful."

"That's not what I mean!"

"Hush, let's sleep a bit."

She put her fingers over my mouth and curled against me, one leg sliding up on top of my stomach. Metaphysics loses another argument, I sighed, and, suddenly feeling very weary, went to sleep.

Tim Ward is a Canadian journalist who spent six years in the Orient. He is the author of What the Buddha Never Taught, The Great Dragon's Fleas, *and* Arousing the Goddess, *from which this story was excerpted. He lives in Maryland.*

✳

Do you know the story of the Buddha and the prostitute? It is the story that moves me most, I think, of any that I know. When he was young, the Buddha was considered very handsome. Some of his enemies wanted to discredit him, and so they sent to see him the most famous courtesan of his time. The Buddha liked her and they spoke of many things. She was very beautiful and witty. She offered herself to him. The Buddha smiled at her and said, "I will love you when no one else loves you; I will love you when every other love has abandoned you." At this, she grew very angry and left him. Almost forty years later, the Buddha was dying and being carried to his final resting-place on a wooden bier. He saw a figure huddled in rags in the shadow of a wall. It was a leper, a woman, an old hunchback with half her face eaten away. The Buddha dismounted from his bier, and walked across the waste between him and the woman and folded her quietly in his arms.

—Andrew Harvey, *A Journey in Ladakh*

PART TWO

Changing Your Life

Monk without a Robe

In fine old mendicant tradition, the author
hits the road without a dime.

I'M SITTING IN MY CAR, PARKED IN A CONDO COMPLEX DOWN THE road from my office near San Francisco. It's lunchtime, but the turkey sandwich rests untouched on the passenger seat. I barely notice a doe and her fawn step by the window. It is a golden California day, and I am crying.

I turned 37 this week. I've been a newspaper reporter for a decade. The pay and perks are good. I've traveled all over the world. I live in a nice apartment with a beautiful girlfriend. There are people who love me.

But all of that is little consolation when you know you're a coward.

If I were told I was going to die today, I'd have to say I never took a gamble. I played life too close to the vest. I was never up and I was never down—the perfect shill.

Wiping tears from my eyes, I know it's time to bet or fold. Just this once I want to know what it feels like to shove all my chips in the pot and go for broke.

When I get back to the office, I corner my boss before I lose my nerve.

"I'm a long yo-yo on a short string," I say. "I'm ready to snap."

"Do you need some time?" he says.

"Yeah, all I got left."

I drive up to Lake Tahoe to say good-bye to my family and tell them the logic behind chucking a perfectly good job in the middle of a recession.

It's a spiritual sojourn, I say. I'm making a leap of faith a continent wide. I'll go from the Pacific to the Atlantic without a penny. A cashless journey through the land of the almighty dollar. If I'm offered money, I'll refuse it. If I see a coin in the road, I'll step over it. I'll accept only rides, food, and a place to rest my head. Wait and see, it'll work.

My relatives line up to attack the plan like children going after a piñata.

"I hate being broke and having to scrounge," says my younger brother, Pat, who has struggled financially most of his adult life. "Why would you want to deliberately put yourself in that position?"

"You'll get rousted by the cops," says my dad.

"We'll see how far he gets," says my stepmother.

And this encouraging note from my grandma: "You're going to get *raped* out there."

My final destination is Cape Fear, North Carolina, chosen as a symbol for all the fears I know I'll have to conquer if I'm to go the distance. If I make it to Cape Fear, it will be as a different man from the one who starts the journey.

I'm afraid.

I've been afraid my whole life.

I was born scared.

I grew up afraid of the baby-sitter, the mailman, the birds in the trees, the next-door neighbors' cat.

I'm afraid of the dark. I'm afraid of the ocean. I'm afraid of flying.

I'm afraid of the city and I'm afraid of the wilderness. I'm afraid of crowds and I'm afraid to be alone. I'm afraid of failure and I'm afraid of success.

I'm afraid of fire, lightning, earthquakes.

I'm afraid of snakes. I'm afraid of bats. I'm afraid of bears.

I'm afraid of losing an arm. I'm afraid of losing a leg. I'm afraid of losing my mind.

Yes, and I'm afraid of dying, too. But what really scares the hell out of me is living.

I'm afraid.

A Toyota pickup with a camper shell pulls over, and I have to squint to make sure it's not a mirage. I hoist my pack onto one shoulder and will my legs to carry me swiftly to the truck before the driver changes his mind. The cab is littered with McDonald's bags, burger wrappers, coffee cups, stir sticks, and hash brown containers. The guy, Randy is his name, was down near Los Angeles, checking on some property in the desert. He's heading home to Humboldt County.

> *What gives value to travel is fear. It is the fact that, at a certain moment, when we are so far from our own country we are seized by a vague fear, and an instinctive desire to go back to the protection of old habits. This is the most obvious benefit of travel. At that moment we are feverish but also porous, so that the slightest touch makes us quiver to the depths of our being. We come across a cascade of light, and there is eternity. This is why we should not say that we travel for pleasure.*
>
> —Albert Camus

"I've got a small nursery up there," says Randy, who has red hair and a wispy mustache. "I make seventy-five dollars a week off it at the farmers' market. My wife's got a good job. I used to grow pot, but I got busted, so I can't do that anymore."

Humboldt County is famous for two things: giant redwood trees and some of the finest marijuana to have ever graced a bong. The growers were mostly hippies, content to make a quiet living. Then pot hit $6,000 a pound, and everybody got in on the act, even redneck ranchers and grandmothers. A cult of greed descended on a region long known for its counter-culture values. Volkswagen buses were traded in for Jeep Cherokees. Grocers openly sold the number one cash crop at checkout stands. The government answered with Operation Green Sweep, a crackdown with whirlybirds, paramilitary troops, and German shepherds. A neighbor snitched on Randy. He got 90 days, plus probation. But the feds never found the fifty grand buried on his land....

He pulls off at the McDonald's in a small lumber town, and my stomach growls with anticipation. But at the drive-thru intercom, Randy barks, "Gimme a large vanilla milkshake," and reaches for his wallet. There's a long, sad moment before he turns to me and says, "Do you want something? Do you want a hamburger?" I say, great, and sit a little higher in the seat. Randy leans over to the squawk box and says, "And gimme two cheeseburgers and a glass of water."

Randy sets the bag of burgers on the seat between us and pulls back onto the highway. The bag just sits there, like a third passenger. I know one of those burgers is mine, but I don't want to be rude. Finally, Randy reaches in and tosses a burger on my lap. "There you go," he says. "It isn't much."

Oh, but it is. At long last, meat! I take small bites and chew long after the food has been broken down into mush. Randy harps more on the government. I nod a lot, and say "yeah" and "hmm" and "it's insane." But I'm not hearing much. I'm transfixed by the burger wrapper in my hands. I study the yellow and red sheet of paper, carefully reading every word of it, as if it were literature.

We reach Garberville, in southern Humboldt, late in the afternoon. Randy has to go west, so he stops to let me out. Dark clouds roll over the ridge. I know what's coming.

"Does your nursery have a roof on it?"

"Yeah," Randy says cautiously.

"Do you think I could crash there tonight?"

"It's way out in the woods."

"How far?"

"Twenty-six, twenty-seven miles."

I take that as a "no" and thank Randy for the burger and the ride. I get out of the truck and almost step in a cardboard box sitting in the dirt. It's funny how quickly perceptions can change. Three days ago, I would have said the box at my feet contained spoiled produce. Now, all I see is food. Sure, that rotten tomato and shriveled celery aren't fit for pigs. But the head of cauliflower looks like it might be edible—after some salvage work. I carry the vegetable to a gas station and hose off an army of ants. The black fungus won't wash away, though, so I crack open the head and eat it inside out. All in all, a tasty snack.

Things are looking up.

I ask a local merchant if there's a safe place I can lay out my sleeping bag tonight. He tells me the nearby Humboldt Redwood State Park has 155,000 acres. "It's probably illegal, though," he adds.

"Yeah, but is it safe? I mean, are there wild animals out there?"

"We have some bears, and there are some mountain lions." Enough said.

I walk down the main drag. A woman with hairy legs appears from behind my pack and says, "Hi, do you need any help finding anything?"

I ask if she knows a spot to camp.

She says, "The best thing is to make friends with somebody." I'm about to say, "Do you want to be my friend?" but she skips ahead. "I'm in a hurry now," she calls back. "I've got to coach a soccer game, but I'll look for you later." I know that's the last I'll see of her.

It hasn't rained since spring, but the sky doesn't look like it has forgotten how. I spot an outdoor restaurant with covered picnic tables and figure I can sit out there tonight after it closes. At least I'd stay dry. I walk on, hoping for something better.

I hit the edge of town and turn back. A man stops me. He's in his 50s, wearing jeans and a baseball cap that reads, "Beef."

"You look like you need some directions."

"No, not really. I'm just kind of wandering."

"How far you wandering?"

"All the way to the Atlantic Ocean," I say. Then I add, "Without a penny."

A smile fills his face. "Say no more. Follow me."

Next thing I know, I'm standing in the studio of the local radio station, KMUD. The man, Roger, is a rancher who hosts a talk show twice a month called "Life in the Country." He's in a bind. One of tonight's guests has canceled. Could I pinch hit?

I tell Roger I'm always happy to do my part for public radio.

"I'm gonna have you on the air with a local fire fighter who's just back from fighting two fires in the Tahoe National Forest," he says. "We'll have sort of an over-the-back-fence talk."

I'm still reeling from the sudden turn of events when I see what appears to be a man dressed as a woman stroll across the parking lot and enter the studio. His long blond hair is held in place by a white bow, and he's wearing a pink tank top and red lipstick. Beard stubble pokes through caked makeup. What really gives him away are his arms. They're the size of howitzers. I'm six-foot-four, and we stand eye to eye. He grips my hand and pumps it hard. He says his name is Diana. He's tonight's other guest.

"Roger, I'd like to keep the conversation more on fire fighting," Diana says, "rather than the cowboy logger turned cowgirl logger."

"Okey-dokey."

In the few minutes before we go on the air, I learn that Diana used to be called Dennis, and he's not what he seems. He really is a she. The sex change—"gender reassignment," in the parlance of transsexuals—was done years ago. All that remains is some electrolysis. Diana tells me that's the worst part, but I can't imagine anything more painful than losing the family jewels.

The three of us squeeze into the tiny sound booth. As Roger greets his listeners, I steal glances at Diana. I've never met a transsexual, not that I know of, anyway. Fatigue, anxiety, and hunger combine with the surrealism of the moment to leave me giddy. I fear I may laugh like a hyena. I consider gagging myself with a handful of foam from the soundproof wall. But Roger asks the first question, and I settle down. Though penniless, I am, after all, a professional.

Roger proves an able interviewer. He pulls my whole story from me, and then some. Callers ask about my travels to 35 countries, most of them as a journalist. I tell them how I went skiing in Bosnia during the war. How I witnessed the return of the condor to the Colombian Andes. How I found Romanian orphans living in the sewers of Bucharest. I hear myself talking and think, *How could you quit such a fascinating job?* But one thing I've always found frustrating about being a reporter: you're never able to fully enter the world of your subjects. When your notepad fills up, they go back to their lives, and you return to your hotel to order room service and watch TV. On this trek, there won't be an expense account standing between me and a fuller version of the truth.

By the end of the show, KMUD listeners have concluded that my trip is nothing short of a pilgrimage, a spiritual journey. I'm heartened by their enthusiasm, as I sometimes think of this adventure in similar terms. Then

The whole object of travel is not to set foot on foreign land; it is at last to set foot on one's own country as foreign land.
—G. K. Chesteron

again, it's an easy audience. This is Humboldt County, where welfare recipients are called gurus. I'll have to wait to see how my enlightened poverty trip plays in Peoria.

Diana hasn't said boo. With Roger's encouragement, I've hogged the whole hour. It's too bad. There's a lot I'd like to have learned about her.

So it's a pleasant surprise when Garberville's only transsexual fire fighter leans over and says, "Mike, if you don't have any other plans, I'd like to take you to dinner."

We go to an Italian-Mexican restaurant where a football game plays on a giant video screen. Roger and the producer, Mitch, join us at the table. There's also Linda, from nearby Redway, and her eight-year-old daughter, Iona. Linda heard me on the radio and rushed to town to buy me dinner. Now that Diana's springing, Linda insists I spend the night at her house. I happily accept, with one regret: I'll never know how Diana intended our evening to end.

I'm glad to see I still know how to read a menu. I order lasagna, garlic bread, and the salad bar. The ache camped out in my head the last three days will soon be folding its tent.

In her previous life as a man, Diana was known as a fearless fire fighter and one of the region's top loggers. As a woman, not much has changed.

"I dropped a tree the other day that was seven-foot-four at the butt," she says. "I'm still a redneck, I'm just a little different now."

Diana's taco salad arrives, and she takes a bite, smearing her red lipstick. "I've always been maternal. My crew called me Mom, even before I was a woman."

Linda asks how her family reacted to her sex change. Diana's relatives have raised cattle in the area for several generations.

"My dad said it'd be easier if I was dead," she says softly. "With ranchers, you always want to breed up. You want your next calf to be better than the last. He looked at me and figured that I was a throwback."

The table falls silent.

"People come up to me now and say, 'Hey, I like to wear dresses sometimes.' And I say, '*Eeoo*, how weird.' They think I'm gay. I'm not. I've known I was this way since I was four. The thing is, when you go through your inner change, I can't see it. When I go through my change, it's there for everybody to see."

Diana spent last winter in the San Francisco area, in group counseling with other recent transsexuals. She worked a construction job to pay the bills. One day, she was remodeling the kitchen of a wealthy family's house. The couple saw how well she got along with their kids and invited her to move in as the nanny. She became the auntie for the whole upper-crust block, a real-life Mrs. Doubtfire, and no one was ever the wiser, not even her employers. On nights off, she went out with her six-foot-eight boyfriend.

"I could wear heels everywhere," she says.

We all erupt with laughter.

The check arrives, and Diana snaps it up with her sausage fingers. I've planned this journey in my mind for a year, but I never came close to imagining who would be buying my first dinner.

I look at Diana and think, *Kindness is strange, but never long a stranger.*

I load my pack into Linda's minivan, and we head for her house. She stops at the supermarket in Redway and asks if I want anything. I'm too shy to say, so she fills a plastic bag with trail mix. Perfect. At the checkout, we see Diana come in and grab a cart. She waves. The whole scene now seems normal.

Linda is forty-two and twice divorced. Besides Iona, she has two other daughters: Fauna, aged ten, and Sequoia, sixteen. Iona and Fauna split time between Linda and their father, who lives in the same neighborhood. They attend one of Humboldt's many self-styled alternative schools. Sequoia, who studies dance, lives with Linda's first husband, in Santa Cruz. Linda and her second ex founded two hugely successful mail-order record companies, specializing in children's and world music. They've just been bought out by a Hollywood entertainment conglomerate. Linda is a rich hippie.

She grew up poor in San Francisco, the only child of an Irish merchant seaman and a Swedish maid. Her mother was an alcoholic who died in an insane asylum. When Linda last saw her, she was strapped in a straitjacket, her head shaved for electroshock therapy. She swore at Linda in Swedish, blaming her daughter for her wretched life.

Ashamed of her background, Linda compensated by entering the glamorous world of high fashion. She became the buyer for an upscale San Francisco department store. A blond woman with stunning Scandinavian features, she was squired about town by wealthy men. When that lifestyle rang hollow, Linda dropped out to study herbal medicine. She arrived in Redway in the '70s, part of the second back-to-earth wave of hippies to invade Humboldt County. She delved into yoga, astrology, Eastern religions, quantum physics, and Indian mysticism. She set about repairing her soul.

Linda owns one of the area's original hippie mansions, a two-story octagonal structure built with scraps of redwood left behind by logging companies. A skylight in the shape of a pyramid crowns the roof. The house is circled by wooden decks. The trees are so close you can reach out and touch them. It is a most unconventional home. Forty African drums fill a corner of the living room. There is no TV, no curtains in the windows, and the girls call their mother Linda.

After the girls have gone to bed, I sit with Linda on a wicker sofa, gazing out the picture window into the dark forest. The house is still. Linda says she is inspired by my journey. After a decade as a cynical journalist, I've developed a pretty accurate bullshit meter.

Nothing registers on it now. Linda seems to possess an inner calm, an unshakable sense of her place in the universe. I feel like a sham in comparison. I want what she has. I confess to her that I am not brave and wise. I'm a frightened boy in the body of a man. I'm afraid of the dark, the wind in the trees, the animals in the forest.

Linda smiles kindly. "When I first came here, I lived in a cabin I found out I shared with raccoons and skunks and bats. They'd all nestled away in there. I snipped pot for a living, ten dollars an hour. I did it at night by lantern. The bats swooped all around me, and I worried. But I learned that they weren't going to hurt me. They'd fly past and swirl around in these same patterns. After a while, I saw that they recognized me. They knew who I was.

"An Indian taught me something I'll never forget. He said, 'We don't have a word for loneliness in my language.' I said, 'Why, because you're always surrounded by uncles and aunts and grandparents?' He said, 'No. It's because we think of nature as our kin, so we are never alone.'

"I thought, How great. When you realize that the bears and the bats and the trees are all your relatives, you can never be lonely."

Linda looks at me and says in a solemn tone, "Reverence. You can't repair your soul until you have reverence. Don't be afraid of the dark, Mike. Don't be afraid of nature."

We talk late into the night, then Linda shows me to the guest room. A bed! With flannel sheets, no less. I drift toward sleep, feeling safe and warm and profoundly grateful. Diana bought me

> *Buckminster Fuller was absolutely convinced that mistakes are how we learn: "Mistake-making is the cosmic wisdom's way of teaching each of us how to carry on."*
>
> *In his standing-room-only speeches, sometimes pacing the floor with eyes shining through his thick black-rimmed glasses, he implored people to think for themselves: "Please get yourself educated as quickly as you can. Don't get mixed up by the crossfire of information. The only way you'll get there is by doing your own thinking. So simply begin to dare, dare, dare. Listen to your own mind."*
>
> —Otto and Stephen Silha,
> "Remembering a Man
> Bubbling Over with Ideas,"
> *The Christian Science Monitor*

dinner, but Linda gave me food for thought. And sometimes that's the best meal of all.

In the morning I shave and shower, washing my hair with Linda's Irish moss shampoo. The shower is made of stone and stands in a corner of the greenhouse, butting up against a wall of glass. I bathe, naked to the world, or at least to my cousins, the redwoods.

Linda fixes French toast, with honey in the batter, as I eat sliced cantaloupe and sip grapefruit juice. Fauna and Iona turn cartwheels across the hardwood floor. I've never been a comfortable guest, even in good friends' houses. But I feel totally at ease in this stranger's home. My stomach churns, but not from hunger. I must soon leave, and I know the uncertainty of the road is about to resume.

Linda hands me the bag of trail mix, along with a mutzu apple and two lemon zucchinis from her organic garden. The load adds a good seven pounds to my pack, but it's weight I'll gladly carry. She and the girls drive me back down to the highway in Garberville. I thank Linda and tell her that if the rest of my trip goes a tenth as well as it has here, it will be a great journey.

"Well, if you settle for ten percent, that's what you'll get," she says. "On your journey, don't compromise your vision. You're on a vision quest. You're an archetype. You represent middle America, who just got fed up and wants to discover the real America. Maybe America is now spelled with a small *a,* and you're out trying to find the capital-A America."

Linda leans over and hugs me, and gives my cheek a kiss. I say good-bye to the girls and step out of the van. I'm standing in the same spot where I found the cauliflower yesterday.

"Remember," Linda says through the open window, "don't compromise your vision."

Stuck in a job he no longer found fulfilling, journalist Mike McIntyre felt his life was passing him by. So one day he hit the road to trek from one end of the country to the other with little more than the clothes on his back and without a single penny in his pocket. He wrote about his journey in The Kindness of Strangers: Penniless Across America, *from which this story was excerpted.*

*

Each soul takes upon itself a particular task. It may be the task of raising a family, or communicating ideas through writing, or transforming the consciousness of a community, such as the business community. It may be the task of awakening the awareness of the power of love at the level of nations, or even contributing directly to the evolution of consciousness on a global level. Whatever the task that your soul has agreed to, whatever its contract with the Universe, all of the experiences of your life serve to awaken within you the memory of that contract, and to prepare you to fulfill it.

An unempowered personality cannot complete the task of its soul. It languishes in an inner sense of emptiness. It seeks to fill itself with external power, but that will not satisfy it. This sense of emptiness, or something missing, or of something wrong, cannot be healed by satisfying the wants of the personality. Gratifying needs that are based upon fear will not bring you to the touchstone of purpose. No matter how successful the personality becomes in accomplishing its goals, those goals will not be enough. Eventually it will hunger for the energy of its soul. Only when the personality begins to walk the path that its soul has chosen will it satisfy its hunger.

—Gary Zukav, *The Seat of the Soul*

✦ ✦ ✦

If You Meet the Buddha on the Road

Why do you want things?

As the empty pedestals and barren niches of a thousand temples attest, people have been taking away Asia's treasures for centuries. Perhaps, along with their Buddhas and Bodhisattvas, they hope to possess something that cannot be possessed—the intangible mystique of cultures that hold these images sacred. I was as willing as any materialist that came before me. Yet, one acquisition eluded me until the end of my expatriate days.

Every Westerner I knew in Asia, it seemed, not only owned a Buddha, but a big, impressive Buddha at that. I spent a great many of my days in Asia wanting one too.

Early in my expatriate life, I met the Buddha of my dreams, sitting cross-legged on a lotus blossom in a Bangkok antique shop. Its crown was a spire, its ancient patina a dull, brownish green, flecked with particles of gold leaf. It was a Buddha that few practicing Buddhists would want: its arm from shoulder to wrist had broken off leaving a jagged hole in its side. Despite this, I noted, the perfect peace of its smile remained unaltered. I could not afford to buy that Buddha, but took its photograph and left.

And traveled. In Bangkok, where the immense reclining Buddha shimmers with gold leaf pressed there by the hands of the faithful.

139

To Indonesia's Borobodur, huge as a gothic Cathedral, where a constellation of larger-than-life Buddhas sit meditating on lotus blossoms under fretwork bells. To Burma, where the Buddha on Mandalay Hill gazes benignly upon the shaven heads of saffron-robed monks, the sweet smell of incense heavy in the air, and where, in the dark caves of Pagan, white stone statues glow in the brave light of hundreds of candles. To Kyoto, Japan, where the wasp-waisted Buddha Nyorai, said to have been hijacked from Korea during the fifteenth century, inclines its head in reflection, and Kamakura, where the huge Buddha that has survived tsunami tidal waves sits placidly on a hill above the sea.

I visited the stylish motherlode of expatriate collections in Bangkok, in the museum that was the home of Jim Thompson, the American who parachuted into Thailand in the last days of World War II and remained to turn Thai silk into an international business. There, I glided barefoot across hand-planed teak floors, marveling at mah jong tables used for dining. Ming plates, carved cabinets and a variety of Buddhas, an astonishing array of Asian artifacts in an urban Eden. Thompson's house, itself a collection of traditional Thai structures poised overlooking a canal, seemed to epitomize the expatriate experience, and his Buddhas—some valuable antiques, some not—seemed a necessary part of that experience.

To inform myself as a buyer, I tramped through temples and historic sites, poured over art books, attended lectures, ignored the boredom of friends while I lingered in museums to read exhibition captions. I learned the 36 characteristics that denote the true Buddha image, such as the elongated ears, the rings of flesh around the neck, the mound of curls atop the head, the circle in the center of the forehead.

Caught up in Expatriate Buddhalust, I scoured antique shops large and small, from Bangkok, to Seoul, to Kyoto, to Hong Kong. I bypassed the souvenir shops with their fat-bellied jocular Buddhas for tourists. In the dim corners of dusty lofts, I wiped the grime from a hundred cheeks, examined faces, assessed smiles. There were Khmer Buddhas, stone heads with taut smiling lips and wide, flat noses, decorative elements lopped off temples in the jungle. Thai Buddhas, their topknots curving upward like the flames of chalices. Burmese Buddhas in the Mandalay style, their swirling robes trimmed with vari-colored glass. Meditating, standing, teaching, sitting cross-legged, in the posture Southeast Asians seemed always to have liked best, with the downstretched fingers of one hand "calling the earth to witness." Their expressions—serene, all-knowing, eternally smiling inscrutable smiles the Mona Lisa might have envied.

As a changing parade of shopkeepers poured tea and told stories about the hundreds of Buddhas before us, I found no other that matched the first I had loved, no other that spoke to me like that one had.

The more I saw and learned, the more remote the perfect Buddha seemed.

In Tokyo, I tried to satisfy myself with a new, inexpensive wooden Buddha from Okinawa. Its hands were folded in its lap, index fingers and thumbs circled and touching. I took it home, and, as I put it on a shelf, I saw sawdust inside one hand. Picking out the dust with a knife. I discovered a small worm—by Western standards an imperfect creature—had hewn that hand smooth and perfect, while the other retained rough edges. Apparently, I mused, imperfection can be a path to perfection.

The first component [to the Law of Dharma] says that each of us is here to discover our true Self, to find out on our own that our true Self is spiritual, that essentially we are spiritual beings that have taken manifestation in physical form. We're not human beings that have occasional spiritual experiences— it's the other way around: we're spiritual beings that have occasional human experiences.

—Deepak Chopra, *The Seven Spiritual Laws of Success: A Practical Guide to the Fulfillment of Your Dreams*

Though the telling of the worm story increased the charm of that humble Buddha, Expatriate Buddhalust demanded I acquire a more "important" one.

Finally, after eight years in Asia, I found the object of my desire in a Chiang Mai antique shop. It was a Burmese bronzed, seated, its fingertips touching the earth, its pointed face and quirky smile typical of the Shan style. My expatriate days were at an end; the price was a fraction of the first statue I had loved in that antique store long ago. Plunking down my American Express card, I bought the Buddha, and we drove away in a hired car, the statue in a box beside me on the backseat.

As the driver steered my purchase and me down dusty lanes, past rice fields, beneath overhanging palms and between walls dripping with yellow trumpet vine and pink bougainvillea, uneasiness overcame me. Not, oddly enough, about the considerable amount of money I had just spent. The thing is—I am not a Buddhist. I grew up as many Christians do without even an image of Jesus in my home. For me a statue of the Buddha was a trophy. I thought about the Buddhist teaching that desire and attachment block spiritual understanding. And the parallel lesson in Christianity that life's true treasures are spiritual, not material. Returning to the shop, I returned the Buddha, who—without having been taken from his box—had reminded me of one of the most important lessons of all. Here *was* an irony—through a material obsession, I had acquired some spiritual understanding too.

If you meet the Buddha on the road, kill him, says a famous Buddhist aphorism. Unencumbered by either Buddha or Buddhalust, I stood outside that antique shop in Chiang Mai, amid the swirling dust of passing cars, in the scalding and searing brightness of the mid-day sun and grinned, I'd like to think inscrutably. And, unburdened, if yet unenlightened, I set forth on the road unfolding before me.

Gladys Montgomery Jones is an ex-expatriate writer having lived and traveled in Asia for eight years. In addition to authoring articles for Discovery *and* Far East Traveler, *she has co-authored several books on the Philippines. An Okinawa Buddha meditates on her desk in Reading, Massachusetts.*

★

We have no idea what his fantastic head
was like, where the eyeballs were slowly swelling. But
his body now is glowing like a gas lamp,
whose inner eyes, only turned down a little,

hold their flame, shine. If there weren't light, the curve
of the breast wouldn't blind you, and in the swerve
of the thighs a smile wouldn't keep on going
toward the place where the seeds are.

If there weren't light, this stone would look cut off
where it drops clearly from the shoulders,
its skin wouldn't gleam like the fur of a wild animal,

and the body wouldn't send out light from every edge
as a star does...for there is no place at all
that isn't looking at you. You must change your life.

—Rainer Maria Rilke, "Archaic Torso of Apollo," *Selected Poems
of Rainer Maria Rilke*, translated by Robert Bly

HOLLY MORRIS

✦ ✦ ✦

Homewaters of the Mind

Reeling in a big one.

IT IS FIVE O'CLOCK ON A DARK AND DAMP NORTHWEST MORNING.
What I thought was a brilliant idea only six hours ago now seems
lunatic. As I will the coffee maker to brew more quickly, I remind
myself that the invigoration of a predawn angling adventure out-
weighs the unpleasant exhaustion of the moment. Last night when
I was going through my dusty, stiff gear, choosing a collection of
nymphs, caddis and stone flies, and reframing my mind, I realized
that being an armchair angler had become far too comfortable.
This morning it felt just comfortable enough as I huddled under
my blankets. But my father is coming to town next week, and I
need to prepare.

Fishing has long been an escape for me, and of course, escape is
complicated. Escape is good when it means freeing oneself from
the weight of an obscure and explosive father or the constant grat-
ing of a mind embattled by memory. Escape is bad when it means
ignoring the kinds of memories powerful enough to turn a life into
a fortress, a man into stone. Few images of lessons fondly passed
from father to daughter linger in my memory. I never fly fished
with my father. We spun no stories together. No line connected us
in silence. No metronome. He never knew the meter of his own

life, or mine. But he inhabits my fishing life. His image rises like a rainbow to disappear elusively or be hooked and tangled with.

The day after my eighth birthday marked the first of many flights. I was in the back room playing with my new Zebco fishing rod and reel that my grandparents had given me. From the living room came a thunderous "Gaaahd Dammit!" Not the usual I've-added-this-column-sixteen-times or where's-my-other-shoe-god-dammit, but the clinched jaw profanity that was just a prelude to the real rage to come. I stiffened. I knew the glint in his eyes. Although my father governed through intimidation, the threat of violence was always lurking, ready to ignite. I began to tick through the things I'd done wrong, but before I got very far he was in the doorway and starting toward me. My mother appeared, shaking, and tried to put herself between us and hold him back. Her interference signaled that a line had been crossed. She sensed violence. I grabbed her cue, my pole, and ran like hell.

After a quarter-mile barefoot sprint, I walked on the hot, cracked pavement steadying my emotions, testing the pain on my feet and concentrating on the fish that I would catch. The pond was about a mile from our house, and I doubted he knew it even existed. I made my way down a winding trail and nestled in among the swaying grasses at the water's edge. In many ways the place was unremarkable: a midwestern pond filled with blue-gill and bass, surrounded by tall grasses and few trees. On other days, I would discover the pond rough and alive, gun-metal gray like a pre-tornado sky. But on that day the water was blue and still and heavy as the humid summer air. I threaded a freshly dug worm on my hook, cast my line and rested my mind on the tip of the pole, waiting for a nibble from the darkness to tell me what to do next. The thick air wrapped around my refuge. It was my world, one that I was determined my father would know nothing about.

Twenty years later, I am driving the hour to North Bend, the launching point for a simple day of fishing the Snoqualmie River. Six-thirty in the morning and the reason for this day comes back to me. I feel lighter, happy with anticipation. Caffeine helps. A wet fog blankets the evergreens that spread up hillsides from the shoulder of the four-lane highway. The spaces between the mountains invite my eyes: rich valleys multiply and offer something beautiful and new with each one I look into, and beyond.

A dirt road leads from the highway down to where I leave my car next to the river. I know this stretch of water, but it can still surprise me. I slide into my brown neoprenes and the place that fly fishing takes me. The comfort of ritual and the draw of another world: cold and shadow, wonder and fear, currents that offer both danger and movement. Fishing offers me new ways to look at a sunrise, a small feather or a fork in the river. The rhythm of the casts and the power of place untangle the knots of my emotions. Problems get loose and wet, slide apart, become just a part of the landscape of my life, no longer the line that binds it.

I check my tippet and leader and fumble a clinch knot twice before successfully tying on a #12 nymph. Then I choose my line, that is, the line I'll travel when I enter the river. The holes and currents will frame my movement. I feel exhilarated by the strength of the river and by the cold that I think will never reach me.

My first casts are about as gracious as the Tin Man's movements upon Dorothy's arrival. Cast number five wraps around me. (Must be the breeze that has picked up.) Sometime around cast number twenty-two things start to go right. I begin to relax, forget about mechanics, and start to think about placement, and place.

Gray moss-covered boulders scatter the water's edge. Brown and green bushes mask the trunks of the tall evergreens that secure the banks. The fog lifts from the Cascades revealing crisp, snow-covered peaks and soppy-looking brown and green foothills. The beauty makes me realize I've noticed little beyond the confines of my mind for a very long time, and I feel arrogant and small. Rivers and mountain trails have always led me to places where truth means less and there exists a simple clarity. I come here to know my own life and transform it. To revive my senses, to smell, to see, to hear. To turn everyday politics and responsibility into distant phantoms and to put the dissonance of pain into its proper place. The pull of the land, the texture of its body, the slow rhythms of growth and death—these things teach me grace.

In Montana, strip farming dehydrates the soil and intensifies its saline content. Toxic concentrations of salt enter the ground water only to resurface elsewhere in the form of salt deposits. Saline seep. When I fish, decades-old secrets and feelings bubble to the surface, and my foundation of carefully constructed logic washes away in a current of uncertainty. Emotional seep. Much of the time I choose to avoid these feelings, but, in truth they carry the ability to erode pain and leave me resensitized, feeling, able to see possibility beyond this bend, that boulder.

The last time I saw my father he seemed slight, not the towering man from my youth, not the powerful figure that occupies my memory. Was it his age or my own growth that reduced him to mortal? For the first time there emerged a vulnerable person whose navigation of life left a trail of both blunder and accomplishment, and portions of love that were by turns cloaked and confused. I saw myself as a little girl trailing behind him pausing at these strewn obstacles; hoisting them on my back to be carried along or deeming them too heavy and foreign, leaving them behind. His parting grip was gentle and his eyes seemed soaked with decades of unspoken emotion. The scar tissue that embalmed his own wounds of youth parted and he whispered "I love you." When we said goodbye that day, I packed away that new, incongruous image of my father. But that image comes to me now.

My father's world is silent and dark and has been as much a wonder to me as the primeval world of forests and fish. The latter anchors my soul and offers mysteries with depths to be plumbed; but I've let the former become a counterweight that, in some ways, still guides my movement, or prevents it.

Rousing myself from the haze of emotional sleep, I move to

There is an idea based on the central tantric notion, found from Sufism to Buddhism, that if you enter a lower state or even a defiled state with clear awareness, then that state will transform into its corresponding wisdom. So if you enter passion with awareness, you will find compassion. If you enter anger with awareness, you will find clarity. And so on.

—Ken Wilber, *A Brief History of Everything*

catch a fish. I change to a Royal Wulff #10 and cast in earnest. My pulse picks up as I anticipate the unique elation that comes with take. In spite of the preparation and forethought fishing requires, in a strange way, I never expect to catch a fish and am always surprised, and slightly panicked, when it happens. The moment of the take is a mix of chaos and elation and a connection that never ceases to catch me off-guard. Like Spalding Gray's sought-after "perfect moment." You never see them coming and they are best had alone. They give closure and tell you when it's time to go home. A sixteen-inch rainbow bearing down on a #14 Zug Bug. That's a perfect moment.

Eight-thirty and still no action. I crouch and cast and feel that the morning's slight breeze has calmed. A good sign. Behind a boulder a roiling hole beckons. Was that a rise? For at least the fifth time, I wish I'd remembered to bring my polarized sunglasses. Two false casts and the first lay falls short. My second cast is close, but the fly immediately hooks a passing twig. On the third try, it lands right on the sweet spot. At the same instant of my tiny celebration about the perfect lay, the water explodes; I see the flash right before I feel the strike. The line sings. I play the fish and try to imagine her size in between the cracks of my panic that I'll lose her. Twice she takes line and heads into deep, midriver current. Twice I bring her back slowly, cautiously. After ten minutes she's next to me, twelve inches long, exhausted and beautiful. A rainbow of color courses down each side melting into her sleek belly. I hold on to the moment, the meeting of our worlds for as long as possible, but know it must be fleeting. I gently remove the hook from her lip and revive her. She fins for a few seconds, then darts back to another side.

After the rainbow is gone, I glide through the water easily, my casts are satisfying, no longer stilted by tension. My brother's words come back to me. "He's changed. He's really trying. Come on, always making him the bad guy is the easy way out." My brother's opinions, which have lingered in the recesses of my mind for the past year, seem almost plausible. I dare, tentatively, to imagine what it would be like to have a dad.

As I take off up-river to fish and think for a few more hours, I wonder...perhaps I'll ask my father if he'd like me to teach him to fly fish.

Holly Morris is the editorial director of Seal Press and the editor of its imprint, Adventura Books. She has edited two anthologies about women and fishing, Uncommon Waters *and* A Different Angle, *and is the creator and host of the television docu-biography series, "Adventure Divas." She lives in Seattle.*

❋

Since the only real geography is consciousness, it is not where we are but what we have become that makes the difference.

    —P. M. H. Atwater, Lh.D., *Future Memory: How Those Who "See the Future" Shed New Light on the Workings of the Human Mind*

GERARD WOZEK

⋆ ⁎ ⋆

Paris Angels

Download this.

ANGEL OF THE VEIL. ANGEL OF WHIRLWIND AND SMOKE. ANGEL OF
the unknowable rune. What angel did I invoke, that sends me
jetting 4000 miles from Chicago to Paris, to board a Métro that
clatters now through an early April drizzle, as it careens through a
landscape of blinking green pharmacy crosses, twisted rain spigots,
vacant market pens, Plexiglas towers and countless billboards ad-
vertising Sade's *Love Deluxe CD*. Sultry, pop singer Sade is trapped
in a pose of carnal rapture. Our goddess-elect of the underground
tunnels is whispering, "this is no ordinary love, no ordinary love."
Sade, with her smooth golden skin glossed over in amber honey
tones, is folding the quaking city to her breast.

I think of the letters that have brought me here. Your postcards
of the city, delicately scented with ambergris. The promises of
walks through the Tuilleries at dusk, the *bateau-mouche* ride at
midnight, *riz au lait* and biscuits at your favorite café near the
Opera, then our nights, sequestered together at the Hôtel
Vendome. You write to tell me that this is where Fred Astaire
stayed in 1936 after making *Swing Time* and my mind begins to fill
with images of dancers in a plush ballroom, a Gershwin tune playing on the piano, and the intoxicating tug of love. I pass over the

lines of your last letter which indicate the directions to our meeting point. Though we have never actually seen each other, we have held each other through our phone calls, our correspondence, our thoughts. I write in my journal: *Paris angels, protect me. Protect this new love that needs to fly.*

Wedged between my knapsack luggage and a train window that's held open with an old copy of *Le Figaro*, I'm suddenly thrown back to a Saturday afternoon when I'm eight or nine years old. I am sunk into an old Charlie Chan movie from the '30s. Warner Oland is suited in taupe linen and Keye Luke hovers nearby as his dutiful number one son. From the terrace of some swank deco apartment terrace, this detective duo surveys a hazy view of the Eiffel Tower—

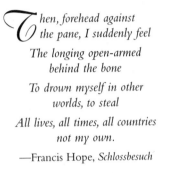

*hen, forehead against
the pane, I suddenly feel
The longing open-armed
behind the bone

To drown myself in other
worlds, to steal

All lives, all times, all countries
not my own.*

—Francis Hope, *Schlossbesuch*

and I'm completely swept into the lushly painted backdrops of this pot boiler mystery: wisps of gray smoke curling around lampposts, mustached crepe venders in striped t-shirts, cafés with netted candle globes on tables, strollers in their tilted berets—Paris dressed as a Hollywood myth.

In my memory, it seems as though it is always twilight when Chan is out sleuthing in Paris. Leaning my fey belief structure on the hokey plot line laced through *Chan Goes to Paris,* I deduce that Parisians are nocturnal creatures who speak English with an exaggerated French accent, breathe through their Gitanes, and subsist on *croque monsieurs* and *café noisettes.* At ten I decide that I want to be just like Charlie Chan, looking for clues and solving mysteries on the Left Bank, as a gray clouded moon peers over the sullen gargoyles of Notre Dame. I want to wear soft beige suits with a light cast strategically on my face. I want to lean over the railing of a *bateau-mouche* with a fair amount of urbane nonchalance as I observe the ancient bridges and spires.

For years I ate up all those Hollywood archetypes of Paris where

the city is more a cutout facsimile of its true essence: Irma La
Douce and her tame desolation in the Red Light District, Gene
Kelly twirling in a red bandanna over an effigy of the Arc de
Triomphe, and Maurice Chevalier eyeing pubescent girls in the
Tuilleries. These and so many cliché travelogue film clips fed my
dreaming: the image of cobblestones nudged against the banks of
the Seine, the whirligig jag of Montmarte's sidewalks, Edith Piaf
singing *La Vie En Rose* over a café crowd, the rust of fountain water
over mute and solemn statuary in the Luxembourg Gardens.

In my journal I write: *What angel presides over the hour when a
pilgrim finally arrives at the entrance to his or her destination? Angel of
doorways. Angel who holds the key to all locks. Have I done all that was
necessary before passing through the gates of this city? Paris, can I walk your
labyrinthine streets and become your own fleshy angel—solid and faithful
to your stones? Will you welcome me the way you have always welcomed
lovers, poets, and dreamers? Will I reinvent you in my diary, in my recollections of you? Can I fall in love with your skies, your arches, your
revenants, the way so many others have before me? Paris, have I wished
hard enough for you?*

The drizzle seems to be turning into more of a fervent pulse as
I emerge from the dank Métro tunnel near Sainte-Chapelle. It is
within the confines of this sacred spot that you and I will finally
meet. I will recognize you by
your self-description and the
photograph I downloaded last
summer on the Internet. I still
remember that afternoon I was
browsing the international chat
rooms and stumbled onto your
poetry. I e-mailed you instantly
and knew I had found a soul mate through your words. You spoke
of twirling spheres of light, of celestial realms that were waiting to
be explored. You spoke of angels as though you were part of their
hierarchy. When you entreated me to come to Paris I was cautious.
I had always wanted to lose myself in this mythological world.
Now, I'm half-dazed thinking that I will embrace this magic with

> *And which of us,
> seeing that nothing
> is outside the vast wide-meshed
> net of heaven, knows just
> how it is cast?*
>
> —Lao Tzu, *The Way of Life*

another soul kindred to my own.

I walk the bridge that leads over the Seine and find it hard to catch my breath as I scan the spires of Notre Dame. I feel like Fred Astaire as he raced to meet Audrey Hepburn in the musical *Funny Face*. From the open window of a passing car I can hear Sade's honey voice singing out, "Did somebody say that, a love like that won't last?" I make my way towards the chapel entrance, pay my fee and enter the area where light is falling through the tall stained glass window panes that depict various scenes from the Bible. The tourist brochure explains that Sainte-Chapelle, erected in 1248, is the city's most significant medieval monument and the place where Louis IX and his family worshipped.

I whisper a prayer under my breath. Angel of Translucent Hope. Angel of Winged Love. Whatever Angel brought me here, let me find the love that I have craved my whole life. I smell smoking beeswax and burning cedar as I wait for the arrival of my French companion. There is something like the beating of wings as you approach. Something like a halo of light around your face as you lean towards me and say, "You've found your way to Paris, you've found your way to me…welcome home."

Gerard Wozek is a teacher at Robert Morris College. His poetry has been widely anthologized and he is at work on his third play.

✳

Helping clients recognize people who were destined to have an impact on their lives is a fascinating aspect of my practice. I believe those who come to see me about relationships are not in my office at a certain point in their lives by chance. Am I spoiling the purpose of their spiritual recognition class by assisting these subjects in recalling clues? I don't think so, for two basic reasons. What they are not supposed to know yet probably won't be revealed in hypnosis, while on the other hand, quite a few of my clients only want confirmation of what they already suspect is true.

I can speak about recognition signs from personal experience, since I was blessed by three specific clues to help me find my wife. Thumbing through *Look* magazine as a teenager, I once saw a Christmas advertisement for Hamilton watches modeled by a beautiful dark-haired woman dressed in white. The caption in the ad said, "To Peggy," because she was holding a wristwatch as a gift from an imaginary husband. An odd sensation came over me, and I never forgot the name or face. On my twenty-first birthday I received a watch of the same make from a favorite aunt.

A few years later, while attending a graduate school in Phoenix, I was washing a load of white laundry one Saturday. Suddenly, the first trigger was activated in my mind with the message, "It's time to meet the woman in white." I tried to shake it off, but the face in the ad pushed all other thoughts away. I stopped, looked at my Hamilton watch and heard the command, "Go now." I thought about who wears white. Acting as if I was obsessed, I went to the largest hospital in the city and asked at the desk for a nurse matching the name and description.

I was told there was such a person who was coming off her shift. When I saw her, I was stunned by the resemblance to the picture in my mind. Our meeting was awkward and embarrassing, but later we sat in the lobby and talked non-stop for four hours as old friends who hadn't seen each other for a while—which, of course, was true. I waited until after we were married to tell my wife the reason I came to her hospital and the clues given to me to find her. I didn't want her to think I was crazy. It was then I learned that on the day of our first meeting she had told her astonished friends, "I just met the man I'm going to marry."

My advice to people about meaningful encounters is not to intellectualize coming events too much. Some of our best decisions come from what we call instinct. Go with your gut feelings at the time. When a special moment is meant to happen in life, it usually does.

—Michael Newton, Ph.D., *Journey of Souls:
Case Studies of Life Between Lives*

SCOTT ERICKSON

Wake Up Call

What totem awaits you?

I WAS SITTING AT MY DESK, AT A CORPORATE JOB I'D HELD FOR five years, when the idea came to me: a backpack trip around Lake Superior, largest freshwater lake on earth. I knew that moment that I would do it, no doubts, no questions. It didn't matter that my longest backpack trip had been for only six days. All I can say is that I *knew*. There was a feeling of utter certainty which is very difficult to explain to others, and which I cannot fully recall myself. I have yet to experience anything like it quite so intensely. Its power was not by force, not by high volume, nor by deep tremors shaking the foundations of the soul. It was not a breakthrough of mystical oneness or a blazing epiphany of bright light and inner awakening. It was very subtle: a deep and wordless feeling, a quiet yet firm "yes" which seemed to come from within me but also from beyond me—a silent yet overwhelming voice anchored through time to some firm bedrock of absolute *knowing* whose existence I had never even suspected. That "yes" was utterly beyond question—beyond the need to question, beyond the desire to question.

I was 25 years old at the time and had been living in Minnesota since escaping from Los Angeles at the age of 19. I ended up in Minneapolis, where the well-paying corporate careers were located.

155

I was not tremendously satisfied with my job, nor with my life in general. Yet my dissatisfaction was vague—I could not name it or locate it. But one aspect of my life was unquestionably satisfying: my frequent journeys into the natural world. It is not too much to say that I lived for them—or maybe that I only truly lived *during* them. In a life in which the years merged into an amorphous regularity, my time was marked and measured by my major backpacking trips: the Canadian Rockies, Yosemite, Grand Teton, the Bighorns, the Wind Rivers.

I had also discovered the rugged beauty of northern Minnesota. During extended weekends I traveled to the Boundary Waters Canoe Area, canoeing in the spring and backpacking in the fall. In the winter I went cross-country skiing and even tried a little snow camping. On all these trips I dragged along a camera plus three lenses and a tripod, and gradually developed the ability to capture images worthy of being published in several magazines. Through the camera I had discovered a magical process which focused my attention in a search for something I knew was vitally important but could not fathom. If my journeys into nature were my life, then my photography was something like the distilled essence of that life—an objective record of a deeply subjective experience.

> *The basic psychological problem of human beings is the tendency of consciousness to "congeal." When Wordsworth looked at the Thames from Westminster Bridge or the daffodils beside Grasmere, his consciousness was somehow free and fluid like running water in the sunlight. When we are in the same situation for any length of time, consciousness thickens, becomes a jelly, then eventually turns into a kind of thick mud.*
>
> —Colin Wilson,
> *Poetry and Mysticism*

I vividly remember my first trip to Lake Superior. It was the first weekend of October, close to my twentieth birthday. The fall color was at its peak, and this was an especially colorful year. The advice to visit the north shore came from co-workers at my new job in Minneapolis, who knew of my enthusiasm for the outdoors and told me, "You *have* to see Lake Superior!"

My first view of the lake was from a high overlook called Thompson Hill, a ridgeline at the head of a series of steep hills whose crest was once the shoreline of an ancient and much larger body of water called Glacial Lake Duluth. Interstate Highway 35 climbs gradually from the south until it crests Thompson Hill and suddenly the view drops below and opens out into vast distance—to an immense body of water expanding to shoreless horizon, to strips of land stretching out in two directions—to the left the high ridges of the Minnesota north shore, and to the right the gentle expanse of Wisconsin. Nestled far below at the confluence of north and south is the city of Duluth, sprawled in a thin line and hugging the least-steep strip of land directly on the shore—land that was once 500 feet under water.

Each time I come upon this view it is still breathtaking, but nothing like that first time. It was one of those instances where I literally stopped breathing—time compressed to an extended moment as my sense of scale was suddenly pulled and stretched toward the infinite. Some part of me kept my truck on the road and steered it into a roadside viewpoint just over the crest, where I sat for a long time absorbing the view without the distraction of the highway and the barrier of a windshield. The impact of that first view led me to immediately choose Thompson Hill as the starting and ending point when I planned my hike around the lake.

That first weekend was packed full of activity yet didn't feel rushed. I remember a childlike sense of discovery—exploring each area with incredible curiosity until fully satisfied, then moving on. There was so *much* to see, and I knew I was seeing only a fraction of it. But there would be other visits. I knew this as an unspoken assumption, with no need to think it out or go through the trouble of forming words into concepts. I saw many of the well-known attractions: Gooseberry Falls, Cascade River, Split Rock Lighthouse—plus many non-famous places such as small creeks and brief stretches of rugged shoreline where I was fascinated by tiny beaches of brown pebbles among cliffs and boulders. I brought my camera along, which at the time was a small fixed-lens 35mm rangefinder—very compact and lightweight. Photography was an extremely intuitive process then, innocent of style and without any purpose or justification beyond recording what caught my interest.

I got as far as the town of Grand Marais, not far from the Canadian border, and made camp at dusk in the municipal campground. The next morning I spent exploring the harbor and rocky breakwater at Artist Point, and a beautiful stretch of shore just south of town which has become one of my favorite spots on Lake Superior. That first visit gave Grand Marais a magical quality for all future visits—a guarantee of something interesting happening every time, although I could never predict what it would be.

Over the next four years I made many trips to the Minnesota north shore, finding new places to explore and re-visiting old favorites in different seasons: Baptism River High Falls in winter when they became an 80-foot-high mass of ice, or the nearby shoreline by Shovel Point where frozen spray from crashing waves had created a glassy coat of smooth ice over branches and boulders. During spring thaw the rapids and falls ran high with the deafening rush of water stained root-beer brown with tannin leached from decaying leaves.

Over the years I knew that someday I would have to see the entire lake. And during this same time I had been reading books by long-distance hikers: Peter Jenkins who walked across America; Colin Fletcher who walked the length of California and completely through the Grand Canyon. The idea of doing something similar interested me, and remained an ongoing thread in the back of my mind—as did the idea of someday seeing all of Lake Superior. Yet I was not making a conscious effort toward doing either—they were merely two interesting spaces I held within me, two very compelling possibilities. These two threads ran parallel for a long time until one day at work they touched—two ideas coalesced, two spaces merged. That moment was an opening: a depth was reached and something entered. I was pulled away from myself and the task I was doing, pulled away from all conceptual roles to which I was identified.

I had a focus now—a direction to move, plans to make. I did not understand it, and felt absolutely no need to understand it.

✷

Why does someone do something like walk around Lake Superior? Why give up a secure career and stable lifestyle to spend nearly half a year living out of a backpack? Why was I so instantly sure that it was the right thing to do and that I could do it—from where did that profound certainty come? Is it crazy to do such a thing, or is it crazy to *not* do such a thing?

I sensed early that something special was going on by the enthusiastic response of people

> *Every man has two journeys to make through life. There is the outer journey, with its various incidents and the milestones.... There is also an inner journey, a spiritual Odyssey, with a secret history of its own.*
>
> —Dean William R. Inge, "More Lay Thoughts of a Dean"

to what I was doing. My large backpack was a sort of advertisement which drew attention and curiosity. A typical interaction went something like this:

"Where ya headed?"

"I'm walking around the lake."

"What, *that* lake? Walking? The whole way?"

Then whoever I was talking to would light up and ask me a string of questions: "When did you start? How much does your pack weigh? Aren't your legs sore?" I never tired of answering questions. It was fun to see people get so excited about my trip. Such interactions were an unexpected bonus, and through them I received validation and boosts of confidence. They also made me realize that what I was doing was special to others besides myself.

My journey brought out qualities in people that I seldom see. I was invited into the homes of strangers I had just met to share meals and spend the night. I was given tours of a few towns, treated to a sailboat ride, and on more than one occasion was invited to share in the consumption of large amounts of alcoholic beverages. People couldn't seem to do enough for me. Many times after giving me a gift of food or a cold beer there were apologies for not having more. For the entire trip the reactions from other people remained a surprise and mystery. Exactly why did people react so strongly to what I was doing?

Simply to have done a trip like this draws widespread interest—not only my own trip, but many others. Books by people such as Peter Jenkins and Colin Fletcher are widely read, and stories which can be loosely classified as "Travel and Adventure" arouse perennial interest—seeming to call to something deep within us. I sold a major magazine article about my trip before it was written, despite having no writing experience, on the basis of a few photographs and the simple fact of having done the trip. Last year I was interviewed for a book about people who left a "regular" life for extended travel, and I got so excited that afterwards it took me several hours to calm down. The interviewer felt it too, and said she felt a similar stirring within herself which she received from everyone she interviewed. People still light up just by mentioning the trip, and whenever I find others considering doing some sort of extended journey I feel an upswell of that familiar stirring within which rises together with theirs to become a mutual voice of "Yes! Do it!"

Only with time have I begun to realize what was happening. My hints during the trip itself were like the thoughts and feelings we have as children that we cannot understand or communicate until we have the language and conceptual framework of an adult. I understand now that the process of "growing up" is never complete, and that our growing awareness makes some things easier and some things more difficult.

How is all of this related to Lake Superior? For certainly I was not aware of any of it before, and it was only because of a process that Lake Superior began in me that I am aware of it now. In my previous life I had a naiveté that spared me deep despair but also profound joy—a false bliss coming from ignorance. Until Lake Superior I had lived to a great extent within a gray nether world, not really in touch with myself inside or the world outside. I am certain that many others live to various degrees in this same place, and like I was once, are unable to realize they are living there.

I now understand that the feeling of *certainty* I experienced came from the soul—the life-force inside searching for ways to realize itself. Lake Superior was a "gateway"—a creative message by which something universal could be heard in a way that would entice a particular person to respond. The message was a spark through the gray of my life that I was fortunate enough to act on, despite having no idea what it was or where it was leading. Such understanding was not possible then, since the impulse was from a self which I could not have known about and did not suspect even existed. The journey is not over—and can never be over. Belonging to the cultural mainstream, to the surface of life, was easy yet empty. Belonging to a more genuine movement is a life-long journey of continuous challenge.

Lake Superior gave me my first sense of what it is to be truly alive. In ways I am still in the process of understanding, the walking trip was a metaphor for how life should be lived. There was a childlike simplicity which was deeply satisfying: for nearly half a year I met every morning with enthusiasm, and each day was an adventure which sustained a wide-eyed curiosity. If the human journey is to recreate Eden as a conscious Heaven, then the goal of my life is to somehow contain the essence of my Lake Superior walk in every aspect of my life. And I am continually discovering how difficult it can be to be simple. But new understandings await discovery, understandings extending toward a mystery I can barely fathom.

I will always be thankful to Lake Superior. Whenever I think of that incredible body of water there comes from within me a deep silence, a humbleness, a reverence. These feelings are both for the beauty of the lake itself, and for the greater reality it represents—for me, and for all of us.

Over a period of five and half months, Scott Erickson walked over 1,620 miles through three states and one Canadian province. He has since moved to Oregon and developed a career in nature photography and travel writing. His photographs and articles have appeared in Sierra, Wisconsin Trails, Skipping Stones, Earth and Spirit Journal, *and many other publications. This story was excerpted from his manuscript* Reflections Upon the Water.

For eleven years I thought up possible journeys, drawing faint pencil marks on imaginary maps, planning vague timetables that came to nothing. I was in no hurry. The gaudy days of youth looked as if they had no end. I had no desire to cut short my endless strolling through early manhood. Then, after three years as a journalist in and out of Northern Ireland, I learnt that the present was only a flicker, and the future no more than a possibility. One night on a ferry to Liverpool, looking over the Irish Sea for the last time and feeling cynical and disillusioned at the physical and moral deaths of people who were close to me, I realized that I could no longer shelve my journey. I was in my mid-twenties. The regions of early youth were slipping behind me and I saw ahead that "shadow line," as Conrad called it, beyond which the future becomes no more than a series of dull repetitions. I became haunted by the vision of myself as a middle-aged young man tortured by envy of the things I might have been.

—Richard Trench, *Forbidden Sands*

SEAN O'REILLY

⋆ * ⋆

St. Peter's Black Box

An apostate is humbled.

THE PLAZA IN FRONT OF ST. PETER'S BASILICA IN ROME IMPOSES itself on the imagination. It is humbling to stand at the religious center of 2,000 years of creative and passionate spiritual endeavor. Here in the presence of the unthinkable successor to the mighty Roman Empire, the mind tends to implode, to shift into reverie and things besides mere thoughts enter the heart. So much history in one place creates a kind of soul warp where the collective consciousness of untold generations creates images in the mind and leaves the vision slightly blurred to accommodate the intrusion. One staggers through this psychic doorway to discover that nothing is as it seems....

I was a second year student in the University of Dallas Rome program. We were to spend three days a week in class and the rest of the time roaming Europe. We went just about everywhere— Paris, the coast of Spain, Germany, Austria, Switzerland and even North Africa but it was in Rome that I experienced the unusual.

The first thing that I noticed after entering the Basilica of St. Peter's and gaping about were the confessional lights bright against dark wood, then the signs in many languages above the confessional boxes. They seemed forbidding and ritual-encrusted, archaic technology left over from a vanished yet still vital world.

Confessions were being heard in Spanish, English, Chinese, Malay, Polish, Czech, Russian, and God knows how many other tongues. I thought to myself, "How convenient, anyone could go."

A black box is anything for which the reader has to suspend disbelief.
—Dennis L. McKiernan, "Science Fiction, Fantasy, Black Boxes, Energy, and Substance"

Immediately, I mentally countered with the thought that it would be convenient for those who wanted to go—myself of course not being included. I could not tear myself away, however, and for some reason I kept looking at the lights. I then forcibly walked the other way, thinking that there would be many other interesting things to look at. I wandered over to the Pieta and marveled at the flow of the marble. Only the real masters can make marble look like human flesh close up. The work of Praxiteles comes to mind and the stunning statue of Antinous at Delphi—small wonder that Hadrian had been so captivated by him.

After a few minutes with Michelangelo, I found myself back in the same place. I started to become annoyed. What bullshit! Who could need confession? I was surprised that this was even an issue for me, as I had left the Catholic Church at fourteen and at twenty-one had no intention of returning. I was suddenly caught in the gravitation of the struggle that was going on and recognized that I was in fact having an argument with my self. What occurred was one of those rare moments when you catch yourself looking at yourself and wondering what the problem is. From this illumined perspective, desires whether for good or ill are transparently clear. You either want something or you do not. I experienced what in retrospect might be called a paradigm shift. I caught myself denying what appeared to be a bizarre desire (from my perspective at the time) and simultaneously realized from an entirely different and larger perspective that what I wanted was tantalizing and possibly beneficial in a way I could not understand.

I knew at that point that I had to go into the confessional—there was no honest way out. I simply wanted to go and there was no denying it. I felt a subtle shuddering as if I was standing at the edge of a cliff and there was no turning back. At the same time there was an immense clarity to what I was about to do. The fulfillment of my own history, a venture into the unknown, a vast quantum leap into the future seemed to be at hand. I hesitated; what sins would I confess? The answer bore down on me with awful certainty. "Confess all of them." I realized that if I was going to do this, there was no point in doing it halfway.

So I went in and confessed all my misdeeds from age fourteen to twenty-one—a seven year accumulation of sexual misconduct and a host of other failings. I do not remember all that I confessed or even what the priest was like but I do remember stumbling out of the confessional like a person facing a new dawn after a reprieve from some long incarceration. I felt lighter and also re-oriented—as if something had been out of focus and was now suddenly much clearer. I immediately wrote it off to psychological relief but could not quite escape the sense that something extraordinary had happened.

> *You succeed by harmonizing yourself with forces that are more powerful than you are, rather than by trying to force them to your will.*
>
> —Tim O'Reilly, "Knowing When to Let Go"

My life was never the same after that. I had many moral lapses from that day on but always went back to confession, and astoundingly, the relief from spiritual oppression and darkness always seemed to occur. If I had to describe it another way, I would say that before I go to confession, I feel fragmented, vaguely depressed, somewhat inverted and upon receiving the forgiveness of Christ, set aright or made joyfully whole in a mysterious manner. What is certain is that in Rome, St. Peter's black box opened a window onto a different reality for me.

Sean O'Reilly is editor-at-large for Travelers' Tales.

★

Last summer, in church in Italy
        I prayed for all of you: asked not for forgiveness
                and strength, but that all the sadness of our days,

all the grief of our lives,
        all the loneliness given us be taken away
                without judgment—asked for life and light.

That was the first time in twenty-three years something
        like that happened to me. Not knowing the modern prayers,
                I fell back on the old way of ending prayer, recited:

Glory be to the Father and to the Son
        and to the Holy Spirit, as it was in the beginning,
                is now, and ever shall be, world without end

then dropped some lire coins in the metal offering box,
        walked through the heavily curtained doorway into the
                Mediterranean heat, into the hard traffic of the village,
                        into the harsh light of the afternoon
                                into this world without end.

                —Thom Tammaro, "A Church in Italy," *When the Italians*
                                        Came to My Home Town

* * *

Luzviminda

Strangeness in the night.

SHE HAD ONE OF THOSE NAMES THAT ARE SO COMMON IN THE Philippines, like Lucy or Linda. Maybe it was Dinah. I can't remember. I met her on the Manila waterfront. True to what I had been told, she did look a bit of a tramp, and an older one at that. You might even have called her mannish for her shape. But she was a she to the core, as all good ships are, and which I found when I boarded her. I'll speak no ill of her. Under the maritime subdivision of the Masculine Code, it is a bad thing to defame virtuous females, whether terrestrial or marine.

I was going to ride this cargo liner to the southern islands where I could relax in a place where nothing ever happens, and feel nostalgic. This was one of my many return journeys to the countries of the South China Sea since the end of the Vietnam war. It was in this region I came of age, and lived many years.

I was almost too young when I was sent out to this end of the world in the final years of the war. I was that guy everyone called "the kid" in so many old war movies about better wars. A navy man, I did duty sometimes on the "gun line" along the coast, and sometimes up the river. This is not a war story, so I'll just say that in the battles without and the battles within there was plenty to

167

make a man crazy, I mean really truly bad crazy, unless he had something with which to ground himself. Some men got religion. Some took drugs. Others wrote songs or poetry. Still others just went crazy.

Me, I was lucky. I was able to get away frequently to the Philippines, Thailand, Indonesia, all over the South China Sea, where I took my comfort with women. It was the Tribe of Women who kept my mind and spirit whole. I found I could sail to the antipodes, fight all the hordes of Ho Chi Minh, live in fire, go without beer, if I could but lie in the arms of a woman. I drank deeply from their cup, and their female powers sustained me. And there didn't always necessarily have to be any sex involved, although that was certainly a plus. Indeed, I remember times when the woman whose arms I would have most preferred were my mother's. Maybe you'll find it questionable that a grown man wants to nestle in his mother's arms, but any man who has been in war knows whence I speak. We all know stories of men dying in battle with the word "Mama" on their lips. You may be sure the stories are true.

So there I was in the islands again, roving southerly in a tramp steamer with no particular destination, and ready to put ashore on any island where a lady might find me good company. My cabin was located port side amidships and contained a bunk, wardrobe, sink and toilet, a little desk and chair, and a port hole. We had been at sea several hours when I decided to tour the vessel. I started at the bottom and began working my way up the decks, having the bridge as my ultimate goal. When I reached the level of the crew's quarters and the chart house I noticed a closet-sized space that held a swivel chair. A cigar box full of scissors, combs and other supplies sat on a makeshift shelf. A hand lettered sign above the door read, "Barber and Beauty Shop."

Oh as I was young and easy in the mercy of his means,

Time held me green and dying

Though I sang in my chains like the sea.

—Dylan Thomas

I kept climbing upward intending to reach the bridge. One level below my goal, I found a small bar. "Hot damn!" I thought, and walked in; the bridge be damned. The place had a port hole on each side, but otherwise no access to outdoor light. No electric lights were burning so the room was pretty dim. It was seedy looking, kind of like the ship itself, a tramp bar. Only a few passengers were in there. I figured it was mainly for the comfort of the crew. It looked like a waterfront dive. But I had drunk in many a waterfront dive, so that was okay with me.

I took a seat at the counter and ordered a San Miguel beer. The sleepy looking barman served it up with no glass but it was icy cold, and I downed it quickly then ordered another. I was taking my time with the second beer, gazing out a port hole when I heard someone sit down near me. I didn't turn around, but I heard a woman with a husky, Lauren Bacall voice order coffee in a Philippine accent. I heard the cup set down on the bar, the spoon tinkling in the cup as it stirred in sugar and milk, then short little sipping sounds. I realized that she was sitting right next to me. And all the other barstools were empty. I made a quick, silent prayer to Aphrodite that this woman be attractive, then turned, as casually as possible.

She was dressed in a kind of jumpsuit, but the sleeves and legs were short. It looked clean, but rather old. She was very slim and lithe looking, in the manner of one of Balanchine's dancers with their characteristic small breasts and hips. Her skin was the same color as her coffee with milk. Her hair was shoulder length and fine. She had big brown puppy dog eyes. She was not beautiful, but in no way was she undesirable. To my eye, her most remarkable features were her hands. They were very graceful and expressive, and looked like they belonged to a sculptor. In one hand she held her cup and saucer, in the other, her spoon, with which she drank her coffee, just as a child might do with a cup of hot chocolate. She held the cup close to her mouth and looked at me over its rim. Her name was Luz.

A lot of women in the Philippines are named Luz. In Spanish Luz means light, as all Filipinos know from their time as a Spanish possession. In the islands Luz is short for Luzviminda, a contraction of the names of the three island groups that comprise the Philippines. Luz, then, is a female patriotic name with a lovely double meaning.

Luz: Luzon
Vi: Visayas
Minda: Mindanao
—SO'R, JO'R, and TO'R

"Are you going to Cebu?" she asked in her Lauren Bacall voice, and took a little sip from her spoon.

"Yes," I answered. "Are you?"

She nodded a yes and said, "But I'm not going to be stopping there. I work here in the ship. I have my beauty shop."

"Oh, yes. I noticed that."

"Do you want a haircut?"

"No. Thanks."

She put the spoon into her mouth, upside-down, like a lollypop, and drew it out slowly between pursed lips. We made small talk. I offered her a beer but she declined, preferring more coffee. "Do you have a girlfriend in Cebu?" she wanted to know.

"No. No I don't. I'm just on a pleasure tour. Do you have a boyfriend? In Cebu?"

She looked into her coffee for a moment, stirring thoughtfully. "No," she said. "I don't got no boyfriend no more. I leave him because he's always hitting me."

What do you say to something like that? I tell you, it always upsets me to hear about men who beat women. I come from a long line of cowboys and lumberjacks and frontier sheriffs and other Neanderthals who have the quaint and outdated notion that men are to protect women and guard them against abuse. I have brawlers aplenty among my kinfolk in the Tribe of Men, but from earliest times I can remember their admonition: "Never hit girls, even if they hit first. It's a bad thing to do." I take it near personally when I hear of men who violate the code. You can call me old-fashioned, patronizing, patriarchal or sexist, but there it is. And I don't care.

I mumbled something I hoped sounded sympathetic, because I was, and because what else could I say, and she said, "Don't worry. That's okay. He's not going to hurt me anymore because I leave him forever."

"Good for you," I said.

She sipped another spoonful of coffee and then slowly licked the spoon, her puppy dog eyes on mine. We made some more small talk. I drank more beer. She even bought me one. Now and then, with the back of her spoon, she painted her lips with coffee and then licked the sweet creamy brew from them. She did none of these spoon maneuvers blatantly. Rather, each action was very subtle, as though she had learned to do it in some kind of finishing school where young ladies of position study social comportment and how to snare a man.

At length she said, "Can I come visit you in your cabin?"

"When?"

"After they serve the dinner."

"Why not have dinner with me?"

Nearly all the best things that came to me in life have been unexpected, unplanned by me.

—Carl Sandburg

She shook her head. "We're not allowed to do that. But I will come to visit you after the lights are out. After ten o'clock."

After dinner I killed some time in the bar and by walking on deck. At 10:00 p.m. all the ship's white lights were extinguished and only her running lights shone on the exterior. The moon still made plenty of light, and it reflected brightly off a mirror-calm sea. In the enclosed passageways the claret red night lights were on. I smiled as I remembered from navy days about red lights. They preserve your night vision, in case you have to go quickly between exterior and interior, where such a sudden change in light could temporarily blind you.

I returned to my cabin and waited. I opened the port hole and the moist scent of the warm sea filled the room. Only the dim reading lamp above the little desk was burning. Not long after, Luz tapped on my door. I opened it, and her silhouette stood in the dim passageway. She wore a sleeveless pullover and a full length cotton skirt, sandals on her feet. In the night vision claret light I could faintly see the gleam of her lip gloss. I stood back as she entered the region of languid light in the cabin. She reached across the desk and turned off the reading lamp. "I'm shy," she explained in a curiously small voice. I closed the door. The moon-light streaming through the port hole would be enough.

We sat on the bunk, not touching, leaning against the wall. "Did you enjoy your dinner?" she asked.

"Yes. It was very good. And there were a lot of interesting people to talk to." My eyes were adjusting to the moonlight and her features were becoming clear.

"Yes, I meet many people in the ship. Sometimes they send postcards to me. I like to see a view of other places." She slipped off her sandals and curled her legs up on the bunk. I know my breathing was coming deeper, and I could see her bosom rising higher. Her features, although muted in the shadowy cabin, as though in sepia, were clear now. Her head was inclined toward me, and she twirled a lock of hair in her fingers. She looked up at me in a sidelong glance.

"Maybe you think I'm bad," she said.

"Maybe you think I'm bad," I countered.

"No. You're not the bad kind of guy. You don't hurt nobody."

"No. I don't. I try not to, anyway."

She shifted the weight of her body in my direction. A few inches of space lay between us, yet I could feel her body. That tactile zone that surrounds the human body, lying normally close to the skin, was expanding outward, as it does in times of passion or tenderness. That special sensory reaching-out was in play. A shiver ran down both our bodies and our tactile zones swelled out to engulf each other. I became aware of our mouths, sealed together, breathing in humid kisses. Lips pressed urgently. Breath came short. I thought to break away for a moment to recover my composure, but neither my body nor hers would obey anything but desire.

Our mouths inseparable, I reached behind her and caressed her buttocks, then up under her pullover to caress her back. I realized she wore no bra, so I reached around the front where I cupped a willing breast in my hand. It was unusually firm and the skin quivered at my touch. I held the nipple between thumb and forefinger and began to squeeze, ever so gently at first, but with increasing pressure. She moaned and almost sobbed into my mouth.

Suddenly her mouth broke away from mine with a gasping sound and she desperately began kissing my neck and chest. I tore at my shirt buttons while she, shaking, wrestled with my belt and zipper. My groin was throbbing so intensely, pressing so hard against my trousers that I was in near pain. Luz pulled the trousers down to my knees. She grasped through the cotton underwear with her sculptor's hands and I cried out with excitement.

She tugged my underwear down to my knees. She knelt over me for a moment, looking, panting, collecting herself. She brought her head slowly down to my breastbone and kissed. She followed the line of hairs that grow from breastbone to navel, kissing, biting, kissing, biting. I could feel her hot breath at my crotch. Her mouth poised over me and she waited, waited, waited until her desire was so strong that her will gave in and she fell upon me. Using one of her hands she forced me into her mouth as deeply as I could go, pressing me to the back of her throat. She trembled, and little desire sounds emanated from her. The universe contracted upon itself and all that there was were Luz's sculptor's hands, her mouth, me and the little sounds she was making. It all spun dizzily.

I felt that I was going to come at any moment, and that was too soon, too soon. Shakily I sat up, reaching for her skirt. Luz's mouth uncoupled with a wet sound as I pulled her skirt up and reached for her panties. She gave a little cry of protest, as though she were menstruating and didn't want me to see. But it was too late. I had the panties down below her crotch and was kissing upward when I plainly saw the little shriveled, flaccid cock and balls made lifeless by long use of estrogen.

I told myself I was seeing shadows, that it was the dizzy effect of passion. I touched to make sure. My hand recoiled of its own accord, snake-bit. Nausea billowed in my gut. My own tool went quickly as limp as Luz's. Luz's? Hers? His? I stood up in a haste and pulled up my pants, zipping and buckling them securely. Luz sat on the bunk, adjusted his underwear and covered his legs with his skirt, demurely. He sat there, hands on his lap, face down but eyes looking up at me, mortified, ashes of sepia. He trembled. His lip gloss was smeared and I knew that it was also smeared on my cock at that moment. I could feel it shriveling and withdrawing into my body.

With the back of his hand Luz wiped the saliva that had flowed out of his mouth and across his cheek and chin. "Spit that gushed out of his mouth while he sucked my cock!" my thoughts roared. "The pukey little lying, perverted faggot!"

I hit him, open handed. I slapped him full across the face as he sat there, and the blow jerked his head to one side. The smacking sound was satisfying and the stinging in my hand told me I had hurt him. But it wasn't enough.

I asked George to do something about my nightmares & he said "what's the matter? you want em in the daytime?"

—Geoffrey Brown, from "Ringing the Changes," *Road of the Heart Cave*

Luz had made no sound, but sat there quietly, his head slightly awobble. I hit him again, this time on the other cheek. It was the one that had the passion spit on it and the residue came off on my hand. It felt like poison and I wiped it off on Luz's hair saying, "There! Let it poison you, you little queer!" Luz's head bobbed with the force of the wipings.

He stared straight ahead as I punished him, making no sound, no protest, no defense. A fat tear welled out of one of his eyes and ran in a stream down the hot cheek I had just slapped. "How dare you sit there and cry after what you just did to me," I spat. Then I slapped him again, as hard as I could. I grabbed him tightly by the hair, drew back my arm and spun my body towards Luz so as to put all my weight behind the blow. It landed perfectly on the cheek I had first hit and I felt the impression of the jaw and cheek bones on my palm. It landed with enough force that it made Luz finally cry out. It knocked him over, too, and he would have landed on his face had he not thrown out his hands to break the fall.

I took a step back, and watched as Luz slowly, effortfully sat back up. He put his hands on his lap and stared straight ahead, eyes not seeing. He took a deep, shaky breath. And so did I. Both his eyes were streaming tears now, silent ones. They were pain tears, yes, from the punishment I had meted out to him. But even in that dim light, nothing but the moon through the port hole, I saw the pain that went much deeper than his cheeks. These tears were the distillate of suffering, rejection and abuse. Luz's mouth quivered, but then set firmly. He swallowed hard. "At least he's taking it like a man," I thought. "At least in this he's honest."

But he had lied to me to get me into bed. I recalled something I had read by Gloria Steinem. She wrote that seduction was rape by other means. I had given it no thought at the time, perhaps even scorned the idea. Now I knew what she meant. Luz had seduced me, willingly misrepresented himself. He had violated me, stolen from me. He had taken a chance, doubtless not for the first time, and it had turned out badly for him, equally doubtless not for the first time. But at least he had the guts to take his medicine without complaint. And it was bitter.

"Why did you do it?" I asked sullenly.

In a misty voice he said, "Because…I want to. Because when I see you…I like you."

"You shouldn't have done it!" I insisted.

Luz just nodded his head and turned his gaze to the deck. He looked very small. Regarding him now, I noticed the tell-tale signs of the pre-op transsexual whores I had seen and resolutely ignored as they prowled the waterfronts of a dozen ports of call: larger hands, broader shoulders, narrower hips than most women; an Adam's Apple. None of them

> *Travel offers a whole new frame of reference for our identity: none. We are blank slates to anyone we meet, and that allows many of us to do some shape-shifting. "It's a sense of trying on a new persona," explains Margaret Backman, a psychologist who teaches travel clinics in New York. "Sometimes you're being something you always wanted to be but wouldn't show at home for fear of being criticized, not accepted, laughed at, so you try it out, and nobody's going to comment on it. And it doesn't matter if they do. You feel invisible. Nobody who counts sees you— nobody back home. There's an intensity to these encounters based on the fact that you're never going to see that person again."*
>
> —Joe Robinson, "Altered States," *Escape*

in themselves meaningful, but taken together with exaggerated gestures and a low voice they're pretty suggestive. I looked at Luz's breasts. One was larger than the other; they pointed in different directions. "Must have had a back-alley surgeon," I thought. "Couldn't afford anything better. Probably saving what money he can to get chopped and channeled by the same guy or one like him. I wonder how often he gets beat up?"

"What's your real name?" I demanded.

"Luz," he squeaked. "Luzviminda."

"Isn't that a girl's name?"

"Luzviminda," he quietly insisted. "Luzviminda."

I went to the tap and filled a cup with water. I gave it to him and he said, *"Selamat."* Thanks.

I watched as he drained the cup. A realization came to me that made me shudder: I felt sorry for Luz. Some part of me even wanted to reach out and kiss and caress this crazy confusion of genders and make it better, for his were crazy-maker pains, pains he had to bear alone, with no one to comfort him, neither men nor women. A deep and unknown part of me even wanted to let him have his pleasure with me, let him have his way if it meant so much to him. After all, the damage was already done, he had already deflowered me, as it were. It wouldn't hurt me, and it seemed a world of satisfaction to him. But how could such a thing be? I quickly banished such thoughts.

He gave me back the empty cup. I took it, looked into it dumbly. I turned away and rested my hand on the little desk. And I stared at the wall, inches from my face. There in the half light I stood mutely facing aft while he, or maybe she, sat facing midships, drying his, or her, tears.

"Look," I said in the direction of the steel wall. "Look...uh...why don't you go back to your cabin now. It's late."

The clock stopped somehow. We shared a long long silence that didn't seem to register in time. The moment just hung there and stayed current.

"Before I go," Luz finally said in a small voice that yet filled the room, "will you embrace me? One time?"

I know I did not quite hear those words at first. But they echoed in my mind until they finally registered on my ear.

"Embrace?" I thought. "Embrace him? Embrace her? Embrace whom?" Luz looked awfully pitiful, and in need of some comfort. Like a wet puppy. I would have known what to do in the case of a wet puppy.

I would have known what to do if Luz were a man. I could have put one arm around his shoulders, given him a brotherly punch somewhere and said, "It's okay now. Your buddy is here." But Luz sat there in a dress, and woman's underwear.

A sound man's heart is not shut within itself
But is open to other
people's hearts:
I find good people good,
And I find bad people good
If I am good enough;
I trust men of their word,
And I trust liars
If I am true enough;
I feel the heart-beats of others
Above my own
If I am enough of a father,
Enough of a son.

—Lao Tzu, *The Way of Life*

I would have known what to do if Luz were a woman. I'd have gathered her to me gently, stroked her hair, and held her closely until the pain subsided. I'd have kissed away her tears. But Luz had a cock and balls, and no breasts of Mother Nature's making.

On the other hand, I could just throw Luz out. I knew how to do that. I'd just open the door, grab the nearest body part and walk the intruder out. After all, I had had enough trouble. Hadn't I? Hadn't I? The code gave me no guidance, but this seemed the nearest possible solution.

I do not know what moved me. Certainly it wasn't thought or knowledge. But I do know that my mother, whose principal motive is to nurture, would be disappointed if her son caused or allowed the needless suffering of a fellow creature, however crazed or confused. And while I am a man, my father's son and a warrior, so am I my mother's son.

And so my arms reached out. My hands found their way to either side of Luz's face, to those same hot cheeks that those same hands had so recently assailed. I lifted up his tear-wet face, and drew him to his feet. I gently pressed his head to mine, temple to temple, and stroked his hair. Luz trembled delicately. Then, as though it were the most natural thing in the world, I inclined his head forward, pushed back his bangs, and kissed his forehead. And then kissed him again. It did not seem a bad thing.

I lowered my arms and allowed them to encircle his waist. Whatever bosom Luz professed, I drew to mine. He lay his head upon my shoulder, and sighed many sighs. And I watched through the port hole as miles and miles of moonlit sea slipped gently by; the good old ship, the Lucy or the Linda or maybe the Dinah, sailing smoothly on, bound I knew not where.

Richard Sterling is a graduate of the University of California, Berkeley, and a veteran of seven years in the U.S. Navy. It was while serving in Southeast Asia that he was first able to indulge in his lasting passions for culinary discovery, adventurous travel, and great literature. He is the author of Dining with Headhunters: Jungle Feasts and Other Culinary Adventures, The Eclectic Gourmet Guide to San Francisco, Travelers' Tales Food: A Taste of the Road, *which won a Lowell Thomas award (silver medal) for best travel book. He is currently at work on* The Fearless Diner. *He lives in Berkeley, California.*

✳

My last night in Cairo. From the A-l Stables in Giza I rented a white Arab stallion an hour before sunset, galloping far out into the desert until the pyramids were on my horizon, the only sign of human existence visible. I was in better shape than Flaubert. The horse was a magnificent creature, rippling with power and eager to run with me forever into the night, beyond the bounds of earth and time, back to the gods of ancient Egypt. We paused in a silent wilderness of jagged stones and sprouting shadows to watch the body of Re touch the earth somewhere over Qattara, near the Sand Dune Sea. I recalled a translation I'd read of one of the Old Kingdom Pyramid Texts:

> I know his name, Eternity is his name,
> "Eternity, the master of years" is his name,
> exalted over the vault of the sky,
> bringing the sun to life every day.

And then another fragment came unbidden, a comment made by the supreme Lord of Creation in a magical text called *The Book of the Two Ways* written over four thousand years ago: "the gods I created from my sweat, but mankind is from the tears of mine eye."

Re's blood now streaming in the firmament, staining even the sleek white coat of my restless stallion a raw, fleshy pink. I felt myself outside creation, a lone speck of consciousness in an empty void. What secret did those pyramid builders know? Why *did* God create man? I tied my *kaffiyeh* back to stop the crazy wind troubling it, and as I did, the answer arrived, so obvious: because man is more moral than God.

—Paul William Roberts, *River in the Desert:*
Modern Travels in Ancient Egypt

CLAUDIA CAREY-ASTRAKHAN

★ ★ ★

Gidget Would Go

She rides the electron pipeline.

I STARTED SURFING A FEW MONTHS AGO AT MALIBU. I HAD BEEN dating a surfer for about a month. After one afternoon sitting on the beach at County Line watching him and his friends surf, I decided I wasn't cut out to be a surf widow. Touching up my lipstick and adjusting my underwire bikini top for maximum eye thrust on shore while the boys were out having fun didn't quite make my top ten list of adrenaline rushes.

I told my surfer babe that I wanted him to teach me to surf, half hoping he wouldn't think I was trying to create new ways for us to spend too much time together, half wondering if that wasn't the real reason for my interest in the sport. Bottom line, I thought, at least I will have tried it. When I'm 90, I'll be able to say, "Yeah, I surfed once." Who knows, it might even be fun.

On our first day out, we sat on the beach at Zuma and I received instruction. The Surfer drew a surfboard on the sand and had me lie down on it. "Back a little. You want to keep your nose out of the water about four inches. Otherwise, you pearl." He accompanied himself with sound effects and pantomime, to be sure I understood.

"When you think you're on it, when you think you've got the wave, paddle hard four last times: wshhh! wshhh! wshhh! wshhh!

Then pop to your feet. One motion: Pop! Let's see you try it."
And I was paddling and popping on the sand. "Bend your knees
more, keep your butt in, lower! Lower!"

After a while, the lesson ended and we both sat there watching
the surfers in the water and the waves. I don't think my Surfer ever
expected me to get into the water. But I have always maintained
(and sometimes even manage to approach my own life with) the
philosophy: Do it NOW or you'll NEVER do it. So I postponed
my plans to change the world that afternoon and we decided to hit
the evening glass-off at Malibu.

I was outfitted in a spare men's wetsuit with a distinctive nub
stitched into the crotch and stretched out to house a set. I thought
this a dangerous thing, since the resultant air pocket might very
well hold me bobbing upside down, breathing in saltwater, should
I get knocked unconscious by the board. Hell I was new to it all.
It might have been a legitimate cause for concern.

Paddling out to the Point, I thought the muscles in my upper
arms were hemorrhaging. It had been a while since I had used
them in any major way. But the pain passed quickly, soothed by
the idea of being offshore, wrapped in rubber and paddling on an
actual surfboard.

The Surfer swam by my side, paddled when I got tired, and
looked like even more of a babe out there than I'd found him on
dry land: his skin glowing, his eyelashes dripping saltwater kisses,
his eyes mirroring the ocean and the sky at once. Did I mention
the way the muscles on his shoulders and back throbbed and pul-
sated through the black rubber when he paddled? No doubt, the
surf widows on shore had never feasted on a sight like this!

We paddled out through a three-wave set and I got my first
practical lesson in duck-diving. "I can't push the board down! I'm
too light! It won't go!" I choked out after each foaming whitewa-
ter disaster.

"Use your knee. Push down hard! You'll get it," the Surfer
assured me.

Out at the Point, he lined me up with the boys and I got my
first chance at diving over the falls nose-first. I don't know how

many surfers I took with me. I had been taught about etiquette and rights of way and all that, but I had no understanding of the waves, where they came from, when they were building, or where they were going. I just couldn't see it. So when I pearled, it was complete chaos.

Still, there was something in this, something in the salt of the ocean and the force of the waves that bit into me, compelled me to roll back onto the board and keep trying. Later, lined up again, I was paddling my guts out to the shrieks of my Surfer.

"Paddle. PADDLE! No…WAIT!!"

But it was too late. The saltwater wall snapped me backward and up to teeter at the top, and then snapped again like a kitchen towel, twirled up and knotted. I was on the monster. I dropped down the face on my belly: forward, down and out. I had no idea where I was going. The wave had whipped my hair into my eyes, and I was too busy hanging on to the board to risk wiping it out of my face so that I might see. For fat seconds, I whooshed along, as blind as Cousin It, not knowing if a surfer might be bearing down on me at full trim, about to cut me in half.

For the first time, I felt the rush: of my independence as a human, of my interdependence with Nature. I was riding the power of an ocean wave, ripping across the surface of the ocean like Jesus walking on the water, heading toward shore, the sun throwing colors off the Malibu landscape only for me.

Hmm. This was cool.

I've had more moments of pure joy in the ocean than almost anywhere else. Giddy happiness and connection to everything including the snot pouring out of my nose and the roar of the waves. This to me is a form of religion as exultation is always followed by gratitude to my Creator.

—James O'Reilly,
"I Was a Teenage Yogi"

Again and again, I paddled out toward the Point, cursing God with every obscure vulgarity I could come up with as I was held inside in the piss-warmed kiddie pool when all I wanted was to get back out to where the boys were. Finally, exhausted, I laid my head on the board, bit the insides of my cheeks, arms still windmilling in an agonizing but feeble paddle, and whined to no god in particular, "Please. Oh please, I only want to go from here to there." I envisioned being back outside at the Point. "Only from here to there. Just let me through these next few waves." And somehow, eventually, after lots more cursing and crying nobody but the ocean could see, I was out in the lineup again.

I stood once that first day. I did. Stood too high and flipped backward off the side of the board like a cartoon character who'd stepped on a banana peel. But I stood.

My second day out, I rode on my knees. I think I stood; I had to stand to prove that the first day wasn't just a fluke. I rode on my knees, kicking off a bad habit, but getting my first sense of controlling the movement of the board all the same. The paddling was still hell, but I knew I would have to develop the muscles somehow. Paddling in the water seemed a more logical method than using some strange apparatus in a gym.

There was no glory that second day, but the excitement hadn't diminished in the least. After, on shore, in line at the movie theatre or parking the car, I would be overcome with the desire to feel saltwater burning up my nose and dripping down the back of my throat. I wanted to sail across the surface of the water on my knees or any damned way I could manage it. Even being torn apart and spinning in the funnel of a collapsed wave, not knowing up from down, began to hold a strange appeal for me.

My third day out was on my own board: a six-foot orange and green goddess named Lucy I'd picked up at Manhattan Beach and christened in the orange-foamy water in the shadow of the waste-treatment plant at El Porto. That day, I stood and rode for real. Yes, it was straight toward shore, and yes, I was in the foam, but at least I was up and going. Now I know how *homo erectus* felt that first time up.

It's been several months now and I've been out as often as possible. I haven't been chain-smoking or swilling six packs. I've been surfing. It has given me another part of myself, a part I never expected to find. Surfing has given me the Me that paddles out through overhead closed-out waves at Zuma, thinking, "Well, maybe I can drop in and ride a little foam." Yes, the Surfer is history, but my passion for the surf remains.

And when it gets too big and too hard and I've been hammered enough, I crawl onto shore and watch the sets pound. And when one comes in that has some shape, I curse myself: "Damn, there's a nice one left for me. I should be out there!"

Claudia Carey-Astrakhan is a native Cape Codder who spent her formative years singing in a punk rock band in Berlin. After two years spent sneaking into classes at the American Film Institute in Los Angeles, she started up the nonprofit Aurora Project, which is dedicated to creating job training and production opportunities for women and minorities in filmmaking. She reports with great sadness that the Malibu beach where she learned to surf is currently closed due to pollution. She is directing her first film, The Red Wave, proceeds from which will be donated to Big Sisters of Los Angeles and a homeless teen shelter called Options House.

★

Deep in his or her heart, every surfer believes that the act of riding a wave is somehow different than anything else a person can do. Not better, necessarily, just different. Something you can't understand until you've tried it.

Now, this may seem like an obvious point at first glance. Of course you can't know what surfing is like unless you try it. The same could be said of skiing, or skydiving, or jamming a screwdriver up your nose. But I am convinced, as are most surfers, that there is something truly special about our sport. Something that goes beyond the sun and the water and babes on the beach. It has to do with the waves themselves.

What most people don't realize and many surfers often forget is that surfers do not ride moving water. They ride bands of energy moving *through* water, and that is what separates the sport from every other human experience.

When you catch a wave, you are being propelled by a phenomenon that plays a fundamental role (perhaps *the* fundamental role) in the way the universe works. Waves sit at the heart of the 90-year-old debate that defines quantum mechanics: Should the subatomic world be regarded as matter or energy? Albert Einstein realized at the turn of this century that light waves sometimes behave like particles. Thirty years later, another physicist, Louis de Broglie, alternately reasoned that electrons, always thought to be particles, sometimes behaved like waves. But it was Erwin Schrodinger, an Austrian, who eventually won the hearts of surfers everywhere when he worked out the equation that accurately predicted the motion of de Broglie's electron waves.

"The electron is not a particle, [Schrodinger] argued, it is a matter wave as an ocean is a water wave." Heinz R. Pagels, the theoretical physicist, wrote in 1982, "According to this interpretation...all quantum objects, not just electrons, are little waves—and all of nature is a great wave phenomenon."

All of nature is a great wave phenomenon. If you surf, you have to like the sound of that.

In theory, the swells we surf are no different than the light waves that travel from Alpha Centauri to your eyeball. Once the wind kicks up a swell, ocean waves move with the predictability of billiard balls, abiding by the same mathematical principals that govern all waves. Like their high-speed counterparts, our waves come in a variety of frequencies and amplitudes. They can be focused, diffracted, refracted. They decay.

Of course, measured against other waves with which humans are familiar, surfable swells move like lumbering beasts. They are the Schrodinger equation writ large—abstract mechanical principles magnified from the subatomic to a scale even Brian Wilson could grasp. Where sound waves travel at about 760 miles per hour and light waves at 186,000 miles per second, we detect only a byproduct of their oscillations: a barrage of sound waves beats against your eardrum; your eardrum activates your auditory nerve, your auditory nerve sends a signal to your brain; your brain tells you to dance. Out in the surf, no such translation is needed. You can feel each undulation, each pulse of energy, as it moves through the universe.

With a little practice, you can ride it.

—Steve Hawk, "Einstein, Moondoggie and Me," *Surfer*

✦ ✶ ✦

Psalm Journey

The ancient concept of sanctuary
acquires new meaning.

"ARE YOU CATOLICA?" ASKED SISTER MARCELLINA.

Oh God, what was I *this* week? Unitarian, Hindu, Jewish, Born-again, something New Age? My religion usually depends on what holiday I do or do not want to celebrate, or the biases and proclivities of the country or people I happen to be visiting. (Recently I became an instant convert to the Pentecostal sect of the mechanic who was performing a tricky smog inspection on my emissions-tampered race car.)

This was an easy call—I was living in a convent in Assisi, Christmas was a *long* way off—and the demonic speedster back in California was legal for another two years. Yeah, sure, I was Catholic.

"It doesn't matter," she said, "but I wonder because you're following in the footsteps of St. Francis."

St. Francis? The bird-and-animal lover, right? Wonderful! I adore animals—even the ones I eat. On the other hand, those vows to poverty, obedience, and chastity were my three most hated virtues.

The sisters had me wrong (or so I thought). I hadn't come to their convent to contemplate the life of St. Francis—my presence was purely an accident. A few weeks earlier I'd been brutally attacked by a drug-crazy teenager (also a bird-and-animal lover)— a puny surfer who had punched me in the jaw, banged me against my own wooden walls and well-worn antiques, and then nearly strangled me to death. It was a pathetic scene. I had cowered defenseless, hysterical, shaking, sobbing—like a beaten animal, a bird without flight, like the battered woman I had been in what had seemed like a thousand incarnations ago. What was it he'd said before he left (appeased by $200 cash and his newly discovered "power")? "You've been beaten before." Yes, yes, I remember nodding, like some cheap bobbing-head souvenir. His arrogant shrug cocked me a line: "If you've been beaten 2000 times, what's 2001?"

It was the one that sent me to the convent.

I'd only come for two days—a brief respite from visiting friends in France where I'd been headed to an ashram about 30 miles from Assisi. My plan had been a dive into meditation (and ever deeper into my bare-handed-castration and hired-hit-man fantasies) while cooking my nightmares away inside cauldrons of vegetarian stew. It didn't work out. By the time I'd found the ashram—a three train, one bus, and thumb out ride from Florence—the place had been shut down by the Italian government. I'd been pointed to the convent where, for some inexplicable reason, every two days I requested to stay two days longer. I'd been there for weeks.

The convent was home to the Swedish Sisters of something-or-other, though none of the sisters were Swedish but Italian, Ethiopian, Pakistani, and such. They wore gray habits with a peculiar type of headpiece, fastened by a clamp-like device which made them all look as though they'd had frontal lobotomies. Two of the older sisters were suitably severe and unsmiling.

My room was on the second floor with views of the rose garden, the Umbrian hills, the lowlands beyond. It was long and narrow—blissfully austere—with a long, narrow single bed made up with stiff unsoiled white sheets and a weightless virgin wool blanket. A cheap imitation of the magical cross that spoke to St. Francis hung over my head, and a mass-produced print of our

Swedish patron saint stared from the desk. Cappuccino was served each morning and Chianti was poured at night. Everyone was celibate, everyone was sane. I was locked in. Safe.

The rooms were polished, perfectly kept. No one dared touch the classic volumes in the library, nor the ebony piano in the drawing room. The dining tables were always set with linen, heavy silver, hand-painted china, and spotless water glasses. Two younger sisters would arrive at my room each morning with cleaning supplies, only to find I had already made my bed (with hospital corners), wiped out the sink and bidet, and hung the thin woven towels out to dry.

The sisters thought I was very strange. And, of course, they were right.

I was a fairly well-to-do homeless person. An escapee, a woman on the run. All of my belongings were contained within one cheap, made-in-China roll-aboard—a long black wool (nun's?) dress, two pair of blue jeans, a couple of t-shirts, my most unsexy underwear, a practical nightgown, sensible shoes, no makeup, and a blue cashmere turtleneck pullover. I wore the pullover every day, carefully folding the neck to hide the deep scarlet gashes left by my near-strangulation—even though they'd become invisible to every eye except my own after about 48 hours. Without that covering I could see my burnished scars reflected in every piece of ancient stained glass, in the mirror of a cupboard used to store old habits, in the dark reaches of my crystalline memories.

I had no idea what my mission was, nor the meaning of my longer and longer stay. Each day—like some gumshoe detective in search of an unfaithful spouse—I tailed St. Francis to one of his haunts: the huge very *un*-Francis-like basilica where his tomb posed for tourists' cameras; the monastery where he began the Franciscan order; the room where he baptized Sister Moon Clare; the garden where he plunged his flesh into the thorny roses; the chapel where the cross spoke to him; to the very spots where he was born, punished, revered, had preached and died. I mused Giotto's colorful scenes and Raphael's seductive angles, made sketches on a stupid souvenir notepad with St. Francis's image embedded on every tissue-y leaf. I sucked oranges with a dread-locked teenage girl in the middle of an olive grove, resisted the advances of that Pietro-guy over at the parking garage with his easy access to an isolated toilet. I pressed my hands against the glass that housed St. Francis's tunic—it's fabric so thick, so textured, beautifully patched with a painstaking overlock stitch in some places—pocked with gaping holes and tattered edges in other spots.

Eventually the Swedish sisters told me, "Be out by Friday!" A feast was approaching and they needed my room. It was time to leave anyway—I was out of money, my Visa card kept getting rejected, and my clothes were filthy and falling apart (I'd already had to darn the pullover several times). I needed to get back to work. I needed to go home.

Home. I suddenly realized that most of my anger and despair had dissipated during my stay in Assisi and my murky following in the pink-marbled footsteps of St. Francis. And though I was hardly at the point where I *loved* my enemies, at least

> *To let understanding stop at what cannot be understood, is a high attainment. Those who cannot do it will be destroyed on the lathe of heaven.*
>
> —Chuang Tzu

I didn't *hate* them. What had changed? I'd been living much like Francis and his followers—cloistered, adhering to poverty, obedience, and chastity. There was a time I'd viewed those vows as the most dire of punishments (just a few weeks earlier, in fact). Now they had metamorphosed into valuable survival tools—more useful than a top-of-the-line Swiss Army knife and a flask full of cognac. I had followed Francis into and out of his world, brazening some sort of internal mercenary training camp for beaten, flightless, and battered beasts.

Come Friday morning, I left my Swedish sisters and Assisi to catch a pre-dawn train—the first leg of my long journey home. Looking back at the walled city through the tricky morning mist, it was easy to imagine a solid figure clad in a raggedy, loosely belted tunic. I tugged at the neck of my darned pullover, feeling the stitching give way, and a gape of fresh air.

Marael Johnson, with roots in Russia and Motown, is a bonafide alumnus of Hollywood High and one of the few students in her graduating class who is still alive and has never been incarcerated. As a freelance writer and poet, she works and travels throughout the world. Among her published words are Outback Australia Handbook, *winner of a Lowell Thomas journalism award, and a collection of poetry,* Mad Woman on the Loose. *A sun-hating, non-swimming avid reader, she makes her home in a Southern California beach town filled with deeply tanned shallow thinkers.*

★

"I was lucky to catch a glimpse of Mother Teresa herself before she left for Ethiopia. She was leaving her convent, Mother House, on her way to the airport. She looked old, more bent over than I had imagined. There was a car in the lane waiting for her. Three ragged beggars pushed their way in through the side gate. They threw themselves down in her path and raised their empty hands to her. They pleaded for her to give them something. I don't think it mattered what. One of them, a man with a matted beard and torn grey undershirt, was in tears. Mother Teresa patted him gently on the arm. She met his eyes and shook her head. Then she calmly walked around them into the waiting car. She left me stunned. She wasn't sucked in at all by the beggars. Even if they really did need money, she knew they had just come for a handout. She didn't try to be responsible for them. She wasn't distracted from her task at hand. If they had a need, there was probably some way her organization could help. But she was not affected by emotional pleading. The lady gives her life to the poor. If she turned them down, it wasn't because she was too busy. She knows what is and isn't her work. Still, she didn't treat them like dirt, like everybody else does. I can't describe how gentle was her touch on the man's arm. She saw them as people, not beggars. To me that's how a saint lives in a crazy world. Do the task at hand without delusions that you can cure all suffering."

—Tim Ward, *What the Buddha Never Taught*

Treading Water

Change can be glacial, but glaciers
are made of water.

I'D NEVER SEEN ANYTHING LIKE IT. THE SURFACE OF PUGET SOUND boiled with turbulence, then was calm as a pond. One minute waves rocked the kayak and I had to brace with the paddle, the next minute the surface seemed pocked with rain. Ahead, the waves ripping the sea looked like a river dropping into rapids, to the left and right, upwellings belched like the breath of serpents.

I'd never been so low to the water on a body so large and animated, but at that moment on the Sound I understood for the first time that the sea is alive. Its personalities were popping up all around me. I watched the surface with every paddle-stroke, reading the currents, anticipating the waves, riding up one side of a swell and down the other, concentrating, always concentrating. The black clouds overhead threatened rain or worse, but the sea was still friendly and I was cautious but not afraid. We had just another mile to the safe harbor of Turn Island, and I was optimistic we'd get there in time.

My mind shifted to a small lake in Minnesota, in the warm sun of summertime. Blue dragonflies glinted like jewels as they alighted on the edge of the boat. Lily pads sparkled. The lake shimmered. Everything was glassy and brilliant and fresh. I loved the dragonflies but was anxious that they'd bite, and my five-year-old mind couldn't formulate the questions or understand the anxiety as my father silently fished. There were air bubbles in the paint on the rowboat's planks, and when I poked one with my finger my father warned, "Be careful, if you break that the boat will leak." How numerous the air bubbles seemed, how fragile the boat, how far away the shore. I hardly dared to move.

When I was growing up it seemed every winter we'd hear on the radio or read in the paper a story about another accident on a frozen lake. The ice should have been thick enough to support a car, but one went down anyway taking a family to their deaths. My child's mind couldn't express the fear I felt when we went ice-fishing and my parents drove the car out onto the frozen surface. They were always cautious, and I knew they'd never do anything to put us at risk. But every winter I heard the stories.

I never really thought about my fear of water. It was something that existed, had mass and weight and reality like a mountain or a meadow. Others somehow weren't afraid, and it just seemed to me that their reality and mine were different and unchangeable in the way that you couldn't change your height, your freckles, or the color of your eyes.

I wasn't eager to take my first swimming lesson, but I think it had as much to do with my older brothers' lack of enthusiasm as my own. Mornings in Minnesota in early June can be cool, and the few lessons I did take were awful. We spent so much time shivering on the pool deck in the morning breeze that when we were told to get into the water it was something I could hardly bear. I learned only that swimming lessons were painful and my parents mercifully allowed us to stop after two or three. As it turned out this might have been a mistake, but it's impossible to say because without better conditions we may never have learned the value and joy of swimming anyway.

Like me, my brothers Bruce and Gene couldn't swim. We never talked about it as we grew older, but I think they felt more or less the same as I. We were filling our lives with other things, dreaming other dreams. Water played little role in our plans.

When I was 16, I was the youngest player on a baseball team. We were playing our way toward the state championship but facing a strong team in a divisional championship game, and I was called on to pitch. I pitched well on that hot August day, but not well enough and we lost a close game. The loss ended our season and I was soaking in the bathtub at home, feeling despondent, when I heard my father on the phone in the kitchen and from the tone of his voice I knew there had been a far greater loss that day.

I never got the whole story. I always imagined Gene reaching too far out with the paddle, maybe pointing at something, maybe reaching for a stronger stroke. I don't know why I always saw it this way, but I also always wondered if he'd ever been in a canoe before. I don't think he had been, don't think he understood how unstable they can be. I also never completely understood how it affected me, but in my sleep I could feel his fear, his panic, the terror of knowing he couldn't escape; I could feel his suddenly slow slide into unconsciousness and death. It terrified me, and I don't remember when I first got in the water again after Gene drowned.

To graduate from Dartmouth I had to pass a swim test or take a year of swim classes. That requirement is probably long gone now but it was good for me. It got me into a class that wasn't completely awful, the first such experience I'd had. I learned that I could do an elementary backstroke and continue to breathe, and I could jump into just about

"Let me tell you a story about a woman who came to us," Levine continued. *"Her ten-year-old daughter had disappeared while she was swimming. A few days later, the mother was called to identify what was left of her daughter's body at the morgue. She went completely out of her mind with grief, but when her heart broke open, she was transformed. Her own agony left her exposed to the agony of the world. She realized that it wasn't just her pain—it was the pain, the communal pain—and this opened her to other people. When she told me her story, I said that horrible as this accident was, grace had, in fact, come to her in the form of a shark."*

Savage grace, I thought.

"Whatever it takes to break your heart and wake you up is grace."

—Mark Matousek, *Sex, Death, Enlightenment*

any depth of water if I planned my escape and knew how to get there. But I didn't come out of the class comfortable with water.

Some years later I was planning an extended trip around the world and something told me that I would face death before I returned. Somehow I knew that death would come to me in the form of water. Was it a warning from Gene? A vision of another destiny I shared with the brother who shared my childhood? I didn't know, but I hired a private instructor in San Francisco to teach me to swim. She worked with me for several sessions, helped me a little, but, like others before her, couldn't get at the root of my fear. Nor could I. My only model for overcoming problems was to push through them. I'd been a successful athlete since I was a boy and all the coaching I'd received stressed fighting through obstacles. I didn't understand the subtleties of finesse. So I left for Southeast Asia with death by water lurking in the back of my mind.

> *Remember Heisenberg's rule: one who engages in foresight alters the future by the choices he makes.*
>
> —Robert D. Kaplan, "Last Redoubt of the Nation-State," *The Atlantic Monthly*

I tested it in many places: body surfing at Kuta Beach in Bali, swimming in Lake Toba in Sumatra, snorkeling at Koh Samui in Thailand. Never was I quite comfortable, and my next attempt at snorkeling in Trincomalee, Sri Lanka, was different.

I was traveling with a Canadian and a New Zealander, new friends discovered on the world travelers' circuit who were heading my direction for a time. Together we made our way to Trincomalee on the eastern side of the island, and in time we found snorkeling gear to rent and a place to wade into the sea. We scouted it from the rocks above and I didn't like what I saw. Waves rolled in and broke over successive reefs of coral, creating rows of shallows and depths and lots of froth. I couldn't see any easy way in or out, and my anxieties began to build.

Nick and Tracey were ready to go but I couldn't do it. I couldn't see my way out once in, and the tightness in my chest made breathing difficult.

"I'll wait and watch from here. Go ahead without me." It was the best I could do.

They made their way down to the beach, entered the surf, and gradually swam farther out, timing the waves and moving gingerly over the rocks and coral. The waves pushed them around, but in time they got to calm water and explored the depths, diving, coming up to the surface, blowing streams of water out their snorkels, enjoying themselves. I watched and waited, but the tightness in my chest remained. Sometime later they came out, again moving cautiously over the rocks and coral as the surf shoved them around, then walked up the beach toward me.

We decided to try another spot, some distance away, and when we got there it was more to my liking. The sea was calm, settled blue and deep and tranquil in a wide, protected bay. The rocks dropped down to the water and I could see an easy way in and out, at the backside of a rocky arm that protruded into the sea and acted as a natural breakwater. It would take little to climb down, ease my way in, and pull myself out when ready.

Tracey and Nick went first, swam out from the rocks, and soon all I could see were the humps of their backs, snorkels bobbing on the surface.

The first plunge is always the most difficult, and my chest constricted as I got in and felt the cool water against my skin. A short breath, then another, and another: the snorkel was working; I could breathe. I pushed myself away from the rocks, breathed nervously, paddled my feet to keep myself afloat and the snorkel above the surface. The sound echoed in my head, and the sound of air coursing through that plastic pipe was the sound of life, the sound of my survival.

I saw many things, but only with a fragment of my awareness. Most of my attention was on my snorkel, on the sound of my breathing, on the need to keep the snorkel above the surface.

My mask had a poor seal and began to fill with water. Many times I'd seen friends empty their masks while treading water, blow out their snorkels, and continue. I couldn't do this. My life depended on being able to breathe, and I didn't have the courage to tilt my head back willfully, empty my mask, and risk dropping my snorkel below the surface and losing my lifeline while I tried to tread water. I simply could not do it. But I was prepared, having planned my exit from the sea. I moved to the rocks, grabbed hold with one hand, emptied my mask with the other, then pushed away again and resumed breathing through the snorkel.

Sunlight shimmered through the sea, lighting up neon-colored fish. I paddled around on the surface, careful to remain near the rocks because my mask began to fill again. The salt water burned my eyes, and I had to repeat the procedure for emptying my mask: grab the rocks, empty the mask, replace it, head down, push away, breathe.

The third time I did this I noticed that Tracey and Nick were far away, out in the middle of the bay. I felt a momentary embarrassment that I wasn't out there with them, but that wasn't where my reality lay. Near the rocks I could fix my equipment, and I could continue to breathe.

When I went back out that time I noticed a new motion in the water. I sensed a gradual rising and falling, and I began to get splashes of water in my snorkel, surprising drafts of seawater inhaled with my precious air that sent jolts of adrenaline through my body. The next time I went to the rocks to empty my mask, a swell carried me up a couple of feet along the rocks and settled me back down again. This was new.

The sea continued to move, gradually up, then down. My mask continued to fill, faster than before. Now when I went to the rocks the swells carried me higher, then dropped me lower. I had to push myself firmly away from the rocks to avoid being scraped down them like soft cheese on a grater. Back in the water I sensed I had to get out, but I had drifted a short distance from my exit point. My mask was filling fast and I needed to empty it. This time the swell took me high up the rocks and dropped me hard along their sharp surface, scraping off bits of flesh, sending dull pains through my hip. My breathing was quick now. Coming in frantic bursts. My mask was still full of water. My eyes were burning, my vision blurred. I had to empty my mask, find my way to the safe exit point.

Back to the rocks again, rising with the swells, being scraped down the rocks like driftwood. At the trough of the wave I was able to clear the mask, then pushed away from the rocks. Breathing again, swimming now, toward the exit. But suddenly a force threw me backward and water rushed into my lungs. Gone. No air now, no breath, no lifeline, only one way out. The snorkel had come apart at the seams, leaving the mouthpiece wedged between my teeth in a bite forged by fear. But it was useless with the pipe disconnected, tangled now in the straps of my mask. I tried not to breathe, to keep the water out, but the panic forced me to inhale. Water, no air, just water burning my lungs, my eyes, my consciousness.

Suddenly I had a gasp of air. I'd surfaced. I kicked with all my strength toward the exit, toward the rocks where I'd entered, riding the rising swell toward land, toward air, toward the breath of life. I reached out with both hands and grabbed hold to pull myself out. But I was blasted head-on by a force almost too strong to resist. Water ripped my head back, poured into my mouth, tore one hand off the rocks and tugged at my body like a demon trying to drag me into darkness. All my strength, every electron of my awareness went into that one hand holding that rock, one finger now, just the fingertip clawing onto the rock against the force of that torrent. My whole being knew that I would be lost if that fingertip lost its grip, that I'd be swept into a vortex with no hope of escape.

It went on for an eternity, but finally the pressure abated, the water withdrew, the fingertip held. I scrambled out onto the rocks on rubber legs, gasping hysterically, stumbling this way and that, my motor functions stripped by the hormones of panic. Higher. I had to get higher. Away from the water. Higher, still higher. I could hardly walk, could hardly breathe. I fell, and fell again, scraping myself on sharp stones, climbing blindly away from the sea and certain death, knowing that I had to get far away from the water where it couldn't follow.

Finally I collapsed, exhausted, frightened beyond description, only raising my head once to see my two friends still paddling around in the sea, marveling at the sights beneath the surface. My breath came in gasps and all the images of Gene's death flooded back, images now hopelessly mixed with my own. But I was still here. I was still alive.

It's impossible to describe such panic to anyone who hasn't experienced it. Every synapse, every cell in the body gets infected by it, and I don't know how long it takes to work it out.

I have experienced nothing so debilitating as this raw terror. And whenever it happened after that afternoon I would descend into the depths of despair. Every ounce of confidence would drain from my body and my sense of self-worth would evaporate. My usual optimism would sometimes take only a few hours to return, but sometimes days, or weeks.

I didn't know how to change my reality. Much of my life was ruled by this tension between my grounded, confident self, and the paralyzed, helpless being I became when confronted with water. I refused to be daunted, refused to miss out on experiences I wanted to have, but equally was incapable of building my own skills to make having these experiences a safe and pleasant pursuit. I tried to fight through it, again and again.

Before I went off to raft the Zambezi River I visited a psychic healer hoping to find a key to unlock the fear I carried with me every day. She spoke to me and read the responses in my body as I lay on her table, going back over some of the key experiences in my history. She said she saw me with a close friend, on a river in Africa, two 19th-century missionaries crossing in a small boat. The friend was my brother in this life, and he'd come back to help me out. I died on that river, not by drowning, but by crocodiles when the boat capsized. My friend lived. And became my brother, Gene, who died a hundred years later.

You are what your deep, driving desire is. As your desire is, so is your will. As your will is, so is your deed. As your deed is, so is your destiny.

—*Brihadaranyaka Upanishad* IV.4.5

The Zambezi River is crawling with crocodiles, and the guides gave us a talk before we set out that chilled me to the bone. They were sober, clear and direct about the dangers. The river was huge and completely wild. Many of the rapids were Class V; some were unrunnable. Rafts would flip. We'd have only ourselves to rely on. "This is not about being macho," one said. "We'll be out of contact with the outside world for three days. We're not trying to freak you out. But if you have any doubts about this trip, back out now. This is your last chance, and no one will think you're a coward."

I had grave doubts. Could I last a week on one of the world's wildest rivers, running rapid after rapid in crocodile-infested waters? My gut told me no, but my rational mind said yes. When I saw the river up close I had to sit down and compose myself. The power of that water plunging from Victoria Falls, then racing down the narrow channel and ripping through a canyon of basalt was greater than anything I'd ever seen. When the first raft set out and snapped an oar at the first rapid, I should have left. But I didn't, and for once, my way of dealing with things head-on worked. We made our way downriver for a week, riding wild rapids but never capsizing or losing anyone overboard.

Two years later I wasn't so lucky. On a tributary of the Tembeling River in the heart of the Malaysian jungle, we were swimming beneath a small waterfall. There were numerous deep pools out of the current where I could leap in and get out without worry. But many of the group were swimming across the narrow river to a pool on the other side, and friends convinced me it would take only two or three good strokes to get there. I had my doubts, knowing that if I didn't make it before the current took me downstream I'd lose my safe exit and then I'd enter unknown territory. But three of them said they'd swim alongside me and help if I had trouble.

My strokes weren't strong enough, probably because of my fear. I got only halfway across before the current took me past the landing point and panic struck. I was immobilized, helpless, with three friends shoving me up to keep my head above water. Somewhere downstream they pushed me toward shore and I was able to grab the branches of an overhanging tree and get my footing, but I was devastated again. Confidence shattered, I sat in the sand trying to get my breath, and to understand the fear that steals my strength. My friends, too, were quiet, startled by this transformation. We were equally lost in this mystery of my psyche.

Later, when I had the opportunity to learn to scuba dive I faced the same old fears. I'd done a one-day walk-in scuba course in the Virgin Islands and had no fear of being submerged as long as I could breathe, and scuba gear didn't frighten me, but to go through the training, to sink beneath the surface, this was another matter.

The intensive scuba certification course we took on Bohol gave me a whole new level of confidence in the water, and in fact, the only part that scared me was when I had to take off my tank and pass it up to the boat at the end of the dive. Again, my guarantee of air, was essential to my comfort, and without it fear crept into every crevice. I managed to get through that and soon found myself enthralled by the depths.

But certified or not, I still couldn't leap into water that was over my head unless I had a sure way out. I couldn't tread water, and couldn't keep myself afloat except in the most benign of circumstances.

It was almost by chance that I saw an ad for a seminar at an outdoors fair in San Francisco: Swimming for Adults Afraid in Water. Was I afraid in water? Could I say no and look myself in the eye? It took me a while to take the step, but eventually I decided to drop in and see what the woman teaching the seminar had to say.

I was surprised at the number of people who came to hear Melon Dash speak. There were at least twenty. Were all of these people afraid in water? Melon spoke with calm, reassuring tones, and asked us to do a few exercises with her, to go back into our pasts and try to recall the very first time we were afraid in water, back to an experience when someone or something brought fear or anxiety into our lives, or when we brought it into ourselves unknowingly. I've never been very good at this sort of memory mining, and I never really got to any first experience, but after a while she asked people to talk about what they remembered. The stories were fascinating.

Few were similar except for the final result, that something in the experience had been connected to a paralyzing fear of being in water. The longer I sat there and the more stories I listened to the more I was convinced that she was on to something. I signed up.

Melon's teaching is simple at its core. She works with small groups, provides exercises to explore the source of our fears in water, encourages us to share these experiences with others, and emphasizes having fun. Never, at any time, should you do anything in the water that isn't fun. As soon as it's no longer fun, you stop, and go back to whatever you were doing that was fun.

Sitting beneath the surface in shallow water holding our breath until we want to come up. Lying on the pool bottom. Playing with each other. Through fun we begin to understand the dynamics of water and the human body, not through an intellectual or logical approach, but through fun. It was amazing how quickly fun translated into comfort, how quickly comfort translated into confidence, and confidence into learning.

Through incremental challenges accompanied by the mantra of "fun," I learned that the water would support me, that breathing was not difficult, that the water and I were of the same elements, that I could be comfortable and unafraid in water.

In six short weeks under Melon's tutelage I undid forty years of battles. There's no secret to it, no overwhelming challenge, no great epiphany—well, there were several small epiphanies, to be sure—I just needed to be guided by someone who knew how to help.

Near the end of my course I was at a convention in Puerto Vallarta, and a friend and I

From the Ramayana: Listen my friend, there is another kind of chariot, which brings certain victory. Its wheels are made of strength of mind and patience. Truth and dignity are its firm flagstaff and its flag. Strength and discretion are its two horses. Forgiveness and benevolence are its two reins. Faith in God is its wise charioteer. Absolute contentment is its dagger. Charity is its axe. Knowledge is its bow. Steadfastness is the quiver and self-discipline its arrows. Respect for the learned is its impregnable armor.... Listen patiently, O friend, the brave man who has this chariot shall be victorious over the greatest invincible enemy— which is life in this world.

—Ved Parkash Mehta, *Mahatma Gandhi and his Apostles*

needed to escape the stifling conference rooms so we ran out to the sea. We swam out past the breakers and talked about our lives and careers, friends and families, plans for the short and long term, all the while treading water in the swells. It was almost an afterthought for me, the realization that I was doing this, having a conversation in the sea in water over my head without a moment's worry. My passage had been so effortless, so gentle and so complete, that I hardly even noticed it. Melon would have understood entirely: I was just having fun. And it was only then that I realized how truly bound to my brother I was. I had resolved my fear of water as a way to resolve his death. I had learned to swim for me, but also for him.

On Puget Sound that day the sea's moods changed by the second. We paddled our kayaks through rough waters, across calm seas, over boils and swells and whirlpools. The rain came down but felt warm as it slid off us. And soon we broke into the lee of the island, and I thought of my long-lost brother, of my brushes with death and the deep-rooted fears that took so long to exorcise, that couldn't be exorcised by fighting through them, by attacking them head-on, by any technique I knew, but simply with the help of an extraordinary woman and by finding joy in the water.

The beach was only a few strokes away. We'd camp here for the night. I stopped paddling and let the kayak glide toward the sand.

I couldn't have done it without Gene's help, without Melon's help, and wherever I go they're with me, and I know we'll be paddling in together safely to harbor.

Larry Habegger is co-editor of the Travelers' Tales *series. He is also co-author of "World Travel Watch," a column that appears in newspapers throughout the United States.*

✷

Intuition can be thought of as a type of wiring that can be used by various sources. One of these sources is the soul. Intuition is a walkie-talkie, so to speak, between the personality and the soul. This happens through the higher self.

The higher self is the connecting link when the soul speaks to its personality. It is the dialogue between the personality and its immortal self. The personality-soul communication is the higher self experience, but the personality does not communicate with the fullness of its soul.

All of the energy of the soul does not incarnate. To incarnate, the soul creates a personality from those parts of itself that it wants to heal in the physical environment and from those parts of itself that it lends to the process of healing in that lifetime.

So powerful is the energy of the soul that it could not advance into a physical form without, literally, exploding that form. In the creation of a personality, the soul calibrates parts of itself, reduces parts of itself, to take on the human experience. Your higher self is that aspect of your soul that is in you, but it is not the fullness of your soul. It is a smaller soul self. Therefore, "higher self" is another term for "soul," yet the soul is more than the higher self.

—Gary Zukav, *The Seat of the Soul*

J O N A H   B L A N K

✦ ✦ ✦

The Labyrinth

You must discover the way out.

THERE IS A WAY THROUGH THE LABYRINTH. YOU MIGHT FIND IT
hard to believe, since every path you take seems to lead nowhere,
but you go on searching because you know a way must exist. If it
did not, the whole maze would be nothing but a cruel joke. And
that is something you can never accept.

The labyrinth is on the roof of the Great Imambara in
Lucknow. In the late eighteenth century an outrageously extravagant ruler of the princely state of Awadh built it on the upper three
stories of his palace as an entertainment for the women of his
harem. Somebody had decided that the pleasure dome of a de-
bauched *nawab-wazir* is hallowed ground, so you still must walk the
dirt-strewn passageways barefoot.

Down twisty tunnels, up steep staircases, through portal after
portal and round another bend, you walk and walk and wind up
back where you started. Promising hallways lead only to dead ends.
When the ceilings get lower and lower you have to duck to go on,
and you feel you must be nearing your goal. You run into a blind
wall and must retrace your steps in the dark. You're not even sure
just what it is you're looking for, but you know you haven't found
it. Perhaps there is not even anything for you to find.

Two young men were lost in the maze along with me. After we'd passed each other half a dozen times I stopped and pulled out a pack of cigarettes.

"Thanks, *bhai*," said the first man, leaning his head forward to the offered match. "Too much walking for one afternoon."

"Yes," said his friend, "and all in circles."

"Have you two been here before?"

"Oh, yes," said the first man. A large gap in his upper front teeth made most of his *s*'s whistle. "Many times. Sometimes we find our way to the balcony over the Grand Throne Room, sometimes we do not."

"But fun to try," said his friend.

Two cigarettes later, the whistler revealed that they were university students majoring in philosophy. Emboldened, I ran an idea by them.

"Perhaps," I ventured, "fate is a Borgesian labyrinth. We are perfectly free to wander through it at will, but the paths we tread are wholly determined by the walls of the maze. We can select any route we please, even change routes from time to time, but we still must follow the corridors wherever they may lead."

"Yes, indeed," said the whistler. He may have felt the analogy faintly absurd but was willing to play along. "If every road went where we desired, each of us would be a big movie star."

"But *bhai*," his friend addressed me earnestly, "we do not all have the same destiny."

"Quite true," I said, "the maze is different for every person."

"Why not just break through the walls?" said the whistler.

"Cannot be done," said his friend. "No way to alter fate, you know that. The walls of this maze," he said, turning back to me, "must be made of cast iron."

"Invisible iron," I said, spinning the trope out for all it was worth. "We can see the goals before us—"

"—the throne room," interjected the whistler, "the balcony, perhaps a pretty garden—"

"—more concretely," said his friend, "a good job, a beautiful wife, plenty of money, what have you—"

"—we can see the goals," I continued, "but we can't just step forward and reach them. We can't get there by a straight course— if we try we hit our nose on the thin air. We become angry and frustrated, because we do not realize we are in the maze at all. Instead, we should *feel* our way along the invisible borders, as we wind roundabout along our proper path."

Light was fading, I had no more cigarettes, and the student-philosophers had indulged me long enough. We went our separate ways back through the dusk-blackened maze of the Great Imambara.

As I edged forward with my hands outstretched to keep from walking face first into a brick barrier, I heard muffled echoes of other people trying to find the exit before nightfall. We all stumbled along, each in his own personal labyrinth, both blocked and guided by walls we could not see.

Fatalism is no call to inaction, no license for passivity. Even if your maze had a clear path to the finish, you will never find it by merely sitting still. You cannot change the world, but you can—and must—change yourself. The Hindu faith places greater emphasis on an individual's action than any other religion in the world. Christians, Muslims, and even some Buddhists see salvation as the free gift of God, bestowed on sinful humans as a reward for faith. For a Hindu, even a *bhakta,* salvation can never come from outside. It is something you must build for yourself. Something you earn.

> *What is the future?
> What is the past?
> What are we? What magic liquid
> is it that shuts us in, and hides
> from us the things that we ought
> most to know? We move and live
> and die in the midst of miracles.*
>
> —Napoleon Bonaparte

All of a person's future incarnations are determined by his or her karma, the eternal tally of good and bad deeds. By stoically accepting your destiny and following a strict code of ethics you can win rebirth as a millionaire, or perhaps as a Brahmin. If you accumulate enough good karma over the course of ages, you may even be able to escape the cycle of living altogether and reach blessed Nirvana. Fate governs your life, but ultimately you govern fate.

"It's no excuse for laziness," said a woman driving water buffaloes through the street of a town outside Lucknow. "You cannot simply say, 'If God intends me to eat I will be fed'—do you think the food will just jump off the plate into your mouth? No, you must take it yourself, and first you must earn the money to buy it. You will never eat unless God so wills it, but do not expect Him to ladle you out a portion from the pot."

The shaggy yoke-horned buffaloes stomped about in the muddy road, their ludicrously long, floppy ears idly whisking away fat flies, their cylindrical chests rolling like hairy casks of wine. I asked if it bothered her to have to suffer for sins committed in a long-forgotten existence.

"Bothered, why?" she asked. "Who should I be angry at?"

"You see," said a *pandit,* who had been silently squatting on his heels in a doorway nearby, "it is her own karma that controls her life."

Belief in absolute destiny would be depressing only if it came from outside. If Hindus saw some external force dominating all their actions, perhaps they would wallow in despondency, but in their view destiny is a power inside our very souls. Faith is the search for the power each of us carries within.

The *pandit* pointed at a buffalo with wildly spiraling horns. "You see that animal over there?" he said, jabbing his finger at the beast. "You see how his horns are curved all the way back to his ears? It is not an uncommon condition among water buffaloes. In a year or two, if the brute is unlucky, the horns will slowly start to grow into his skull. They will gradually break through the bone and enter the brain.

"Each day the poor animal will experience more and more pain. He will bellow and roll about, and he will never understand why his head is splitting open. He has no mirror, he cannot see that the cause is his own twisted horn, his own body. Even if he did know, what could he do about it? He is the cause of his own torment, but he is powerless to end it."

The woman tickled the buffalo on its bristly forehead, and the *pandit* continued.

"But we humans can saw off the horn," he said, "cut it short before it causes injury. As you can see by looking at the herd, this woman has sawed off several horns here already. To the animal, it must seem like a miracle—in a little instant the ceaseless agony ceases.

"Likewise, we humans are often afflicted with woes and torments we cannot cure and cannot even understand. Every day this is so, and many good people suffer. But we believe that the torments come from within, whether the fruit of past misdeeds or the perfectly logical result of some other chain of events we could never even imagine. We pray to various devas, to dozens of divinities, beg them to ease our pains, and often they answer our prayers. That does not diminish the power of destiny, nor the power of God."

The ability to cut off a buffalo's horn does not make man a deity, does not make him the master of fate. It merely makes him stronger than a buffalo.

Jonah Blank has worked as a newspaper editor and foreign correspondent in Japan, Sri Lanka, Sudan, the Philippines, Burma, Thailand, and India. He was educated at Yale and Harvard and lives in Cambridge, Massachusetts. This selection was excerpted from his book, Arrow of the Blue-Skinned God: Retracing the Ramayana Through India.

★

I have to know: Do human beings have a center of gravity? Could they lose it without noticing? Can they be toppled over, cast down just when they think they're most steady, upstanding and confidently striding forward? There is deceptive activity here, in the morning markets, steeplechase jockeying between taxis and oxen-drivers. Plenty of rickshawers, runners, cobblers, bobblers, chattel and rattle. Is this commerce or just the proliferation of cancer cells? Witnessing it makes the corners of the retina singe and curl up like burnt paper. And rooftops likewise shrivel in. At least, a town turning shanty makes for a fix-it-man's heaven. Plenty of trickling leaks needing new washers, lots of opportunity for unsupervised tinkering. In Calcutta, big changes would be wrought by a dozen nails. In Calcutta, no one can find a hammer.

—John Krich, *Music in Every Room: Around the World in a Bad Mood*

PART THREE

TRADITIONS
AND TEACHERS

MARK SALZMAN

* * *

The Master

Like the song said, "everybody
was kung fu fighting…"

I WAS TO MEET PAN AT THE TRAINING HALL FOUR NIGHTS A WEEK,
to receive private instruction after the athletes finished their evening
workout. Waving and wishing me good night, they politely filed
out and closed the wooden doors, leaving Pan and me alone in the
room. First he explained that I must start from scratch. He meant
it, too, for beginning that night, and for many nights thereafter, I
learned how to stand at attention. He stood inches away from me
and screamed, "Stand straight!" then bored into me with his terrifying gaze. He insisted that I maintain eye contact for as long as he
stood in front of me, and that I meet his gaze with one of equal intensity. After as long as a minute of this silent torture, he would
shout "At ease!" and I could relax a bit, but not smile or take my
eyes away from his. We repeated this exercise countless times, and I
was expected to practice it four to six hours a day. At the time, I
wondered what those staring contests had to do with *wushu*, but I
came to realize that everything he was to teach me later was really
contained in those first few weeks when we stared at each other.
His art drew strength from his eyes; this was his way of passing it on.

After several weeks I came to enjoy staring at him. I would
break into a sweat and feel a kind of heat rushing up through the

floor into my legs and up into my brain. He told me that when standing like that, I must at all times be prepared to duel, that at any moment he might attack, and I should be ready to defend myself. It exhilarated me to face off with him, to feel his power and taste the fear and anticipation of the blow. Days and weeks passed, but the blow did not come.

One night he broke the lesson off early, telling me that tonight was special. I followed him out of the training hall, and we bicycled a short distance to his apartment. He lived with his wife and two sons on the fifth floor of a large, anonymous cement building. Like all the urban housing going up in China today, the building was indistinguishable from its neighbors, mercilessly practical and depressing in appearance. Pan's apartment had three rooms and a small kitchen. A private bathroom and painted, as opposed to raw, cement walls in all the rooms identified it as the home of an important family. The only decoration in the apartment consisted of some silk banners, awards and photographs from the set of *Shaolin Temple*. Pan's wife, a doctor, greeted me with all sorts of homemade snacks and sat me down at a table set for two. Pan sat across from me and poured two glasses of *baijiu*. He called to his sons, both in their teens, and they appeared from the bedroom instantly. They stood in complete silence until Pan asked them to greet me, which they did, very politely, but so softly I could barely hear them. They were handsome boys, and the elder, at about fourteen, was taller than me and had a moustache. I tried asking them questions to put them at ease, but they answered only by nodding. They apparently had no idea how to behave toward something like me and did not want to make any mistakes in front

> *It is difficult to understand that a training which compels a man to remain motionless…in strict seclusion in complete darkness, which lasts three years and three months…can result in acquisition of peculiar swiftness. Moreover, it must be understood that the* lun-gom *method does not aim at training the disciple by strengthening his muscles, but by developing psychic states that make these extraordinary marches possible.*
>
> —Alexandra David-Neel,
> *Magic and Mystery in Tibet*

of their father. Pan told them to say good night, and they, along with his wife, disappeared into the bedroom. Pan raised his glass and proposed that the evening begin.

He told me stories that made my hair stand on end, with such gusto that I thought the building would shake apart. When he came to the parts where he vanquished his enemies, he brought his terrible hand down on the table or against the wall with a crash, sending our snacks jumping out of their serving bowls. His imitations of cowards and bullies were so funny I could hardly breathe for laughing. He had me spellbound for three solid hours; then his wife came in to see if we needed any more food or *baijiu*. I took the opportunity to ask her if she had ever been afraid for her husband's safety when, for example, he went off alone to bust up a gang of hoodlums in Shenyang. She laughed and touched his right hand. "Sometimes I figured he'd be late for dinner." A look of tremendous satisfaction came over Pan's face, and he got up to use the bathroom. She sat down in his chair and looked at me. "Every day he receives tons of letters from all over China, all from people asking to become his student. Since he made the movie, its been almost impossible for him to go out during the day." She refilled our cups, then looked at me again. "He has trained professionals for more than twenty-five years now, but in all that time he has accepted only one private student." After a long pause, she gestured at me with her chin. "You." Just then Pan came back into the room, returned to his seat and started a new story. This one was about a spear:

While still a young man training for the national *wushu* competition, Pan overheard a debate among some of his fellow athletes about the credibility of an old story. The story described a famous warrior as being able to execute a thousand spear-thrusts without stopping to rest. Some of the athletes felt this to be impossible: after fifty, one's shoulders ache, and by one hundred the skin on the left hand, which guides the spear as the right hand thrusts, twists and returns it, begins to blister. Pan had argued that surely this particular warrior would not have been intimidated by aching shoulders and blisters, and soon a challenge was raised. The next day Pan went out into a field with a spear, and as the other athletes watched, executed one thousand and seven thrusts without stopping to rest. Certain details of the story as Pan told it—that the bones of his left hand were exposed, and so forth—might be called into question, but the number of thrusts I am sure is accurate, and the scar tissue on his left palm indicates that it was not easy for him.

One evening later in the year, when I felt discouraged with my progress in a form of Northern Shaolin boxing called "Changquan," or "Long Fist," I asked Pan if he thought I should discontinue the training. He frowned, the only time he ever seemed genuinely angry with me, and said quietly, "When I say I will do something, I do it, exactly as I said I would. In my whole life, I have never started something without finishing it. I said that in the time we have I would make your *wushu* better than you could imagine, and I will. Your only responsibility to me is to practice and to learn. My responsibility to you is much greater! Every time you think your task is great, think how much greater mine is. Just keep this in mind: if you fail"—here he paused to make sure I understood—"I will lose face."

Though my responsibility to him was merely to practice and to learn, he had one request that he vigorously encouraged me to fulfill—to teach him English. I felt relieved to have something to offer him, so I quickly prepared some beginning materials and rode over to his house for the first lesson. When I got there, he had a tape recorder set up on a small table, along with a pile of oversized paper and a few felt-tip pens from a coloring set. He showed no interest

> *Grandfather also taught us the "wolverine" fighting techniques of the scouts, combined with the use of fighting weapons such as the short lance, fighting sticks, and knives. We learned to release the "animal within," which is the primal mind and body. The "animal," unlike the normal human consciousness, knows no limitations or restrictions, just action and reaction, where the primal self directs the body. Where thought is concerned, there is always restriction and slow reaction.*
>
> —Tom Brown Jr.,
> *The Way of the Scout*

at all in my books, but sat me down next to the recorder and pointed at the pile of paper. On each sheet he had written out in Chinese dozens of phrases, such as "We'll need a spotlight over there," "These mats aren't springy enough," and "Don't worry—it's just a shoulder dislocation." He asked me to write down the English translation next to each phrase, which took a little over two and a half hours. When I was finished, I asked him if he could read my handwriting, and he smiled, saying that he was sure my handwriting was fine. After a series of delicate questions, I determined that he was as yet unfamiliar with the alphabet, so I encouraged him to have a look at my beginning materials. "That's too slow for me," he said. He asked me to repeat each of the phrases I'd written down five times into the recorder, leaving enough time after each repetition for him to say it aloud after me. "The first time should be very slow—one word at a time, with a pause after each word so I can repeat it. The second time should be the same. The third time you should pause after every other word. The fourth time read it through slowly. The fifth time you can read it fast." I looked at the pile of phrase sheets, calculated how much time this would take, and asked if we could do half today and half tomorrow, as dinner was only three hours away. "Don't worry!" he said, beaming. "I've prepared some food for you here. Just tell me when you get hungry." He sat next to me, turned on the machine, then turned it off again. "How do you say, 'And now, Mark will teach me English?'" I told him how and he repeated it, at first slowly, then more quickly, twenty or twenty-one times. He turned the machine on. "And now, Mark will teach me English." I read the first phrase, five times as he had requested, and he pushed a little note across the table. "Better read it six times," it read, "and a little slower."

After several weeks during which we nearly exhausted the phrasal possibilities of our two languages, Pan announced that the time had come to do something new. "Now I want to learn routines." I didn't understand. "Routines?" "Yes. Everything, including language, is like *wushu*. First you learn the basic moves, or words, then you string them together into routines." He produced from his bedroom a huge sheet of paper made up of smaller pieces taped together. He wanted me to write a story on it. The story he had in mind was a famous Chinese folk tale, "How Yu Gong Moved the Mountain." The story tells of an old man who realized that, if he only had fields where a mountain stood instead, he would have enough arable land to support his family comfortably. So he went out to the mountain with a shovel and a bucket and started to take the mountain down. All his neighbors made fun of him, calling it an impossible task, but Yu Gong disagreed: it would just take a long time, and after several tens of generations had passed, the mountain would at last become a field and his family would live comfortably. Pan had me write this story in big letters, so that he could paste it up on his bedroom wall, listen to the tape I was to make and read along as he lay in bed.

Not only did I repeat this story into the tape recorder several dozen times—at first one word at a time, and so on—but Pan invited Bill, Bob and Marcy over for dinner one night and had them read it a few times for variety. After they had finished, Pan said that he would like to recite a few phrases for them to evaluate and correct. He chose some of his favorite sentences and repeated each seven or eight times without a pause. He belted them out with such fierce concentration we were all afraid to move lest it disturb him. At last he finished and looked at me, asking quietly if it was all right. I nodded and he seemed overcome with relief. He smiled, pointed at me and said to my friends, "I was very nervous just then. I didn't want him to lose face."

While Pan struggled to recite English routines from memory, he began teaching me how to use traditional weapons. He would teach me a single move, then have me practice it in front of him until I could do it ten times in a row without a mistake. He always stood about five feet away from me, with his arms folded, grinding his teeth, and the only time he took his eyes off me was to blink. One night in the late spring I was having a particularly hard time learning a move with the staff. I was sweating heavily and my right hand was bleeding, so the staff had become slippery and hard to control. Several of the athletes stayed on after their workout to watch and to enjoy the breeze that sometimes passed through the training hall. Pan stopped me and indicated that I wasn't working hard enough. "Imagine," he said, "that you are participating in the national competition, and those athletes are your competitors. Look as if you know what you are doing! Frighten them with your strength and confidence." I mustered all the confidence I could, under the circumstances, and flung myself into the move. I lost control of the staff, and it whirled straight into my forehead. As if in a dream, the floor raised up several feet to support my behind, and I sat staring up at Pan while blood ran down across my nose and a fleshy knob grew between my eyebrows. The athletes sprang forward to help me up. They seemed nervous, never having had a foreigner knock himself out in their training hall before, but Pan, after asking if I felt all right, seemed positively inspired. "Sweating and bleeding. Good."

Every once in a while, Pan felt it necessary to give his students something to think about, to spur them on to greater efforts. During one morning workout two women practiced a combat routine, one armed with a spear, the other with a *dadao*, or halberd. The *dadao* stands about six feet high and consists of a broadsword attached to a thick wooden pole, with an angry-looking spike at the far end. It is heavy and difficult to wield even for a strong man, so it surprised me to see this young woman,

> *You should strive to fulfill your own potential. You should try to put out all your energies in pursuit of your ends so that you go to the junkyard with no gas left in your tank.*
>
> —Stimson Bullitt,
> *River Dark and Bright*

who could not weigh more than one hundred pounds, using it so effectively. At one point in their battle the woman with the *dadao* swept it toward the other woman's feet, as if to cut them off, but the other woman jumped up in time to avoid the blow. The first woman, without letting the blade of the *dadao* stop, brought it around in another sweep, as if to cut the other woman in half at the waist. The other woman, without an instant to spare, bent straight from the hips so that the *dadao* slashed over her back and head, barely an inch away. This combination was to be repeated three times in rapid succession before moving on to the next exchange. The women practiced this move several times, none of which satisfied Pan. "Too slow, and the weapon is too far away from her. It should graze her back as it goes by." They tried again, but still Pan growled angrily. Suddenly he got up and took the *dadao* from the first woman. The entire training hall went silent and still. Without warming up at all, Pan ordered the woman with the spear to get ready, and to move fast when the time came. His body looked as though electricity had suddenly passed through it, and the huge blade flashed toward her. Once, twice the *dadao* flew beneath her feet, then swung around in a terrible arc and rode her back with flawless precision. The third time he added a little twist at the end, so that the blade grazed up her neck and sent a little decoration stuck in her pigtails flying across the room.

I had to sit down for a moment to ponder the difficulty of sending an object roughly the shape of an oversized shovel, only heavier, across a girl's back and through her pigtails, without guide ropes or even a safety helmet. Not long before, I had spoken with a former troupe member who, when practicing with this instrument, had suddenly found himself on his knees. The blade, unsharpened, had twirled a bit too close to him and passed through his Achilles' tendon without a sound. Pan handed the *dadao* back to the woman and walked over to me. "What if you had made a mistake?" I asked. "I never make mistakes," he said, without looking at me.

Mark Salzman is the author of Iron and Silk, *an account of the time he spent in China studying martial arts and teaching English. He has also written two novels,* The Laughing Sutra *and* The Soloist, *which was a finalist for the* Los Angeles Times Book Prize *for fiction. An amateur cellist, he lives in Los Angeles with his wife.*

＊

When we win it's with small things,
and the triumph itself makes us small.
What is extraordinary and eternal
does not want to be bent by us.
I mean the Angel who appeared
to the wrestlers of the Old Testament:
when the wrestler's sinews
grew long like metal strings,
he felt them under his fingers
like chords of deep music.

Whoever was beaten by this Angel
(who often simply declined the fight)
went away proud and strengthened
and great from that harsh hand,
that kneaded him as if to change his shape.
Winning does not tempt that man.
This is how he grows: by being defeated, decisively,
by constantly greater beings.

> —Rainer Maria Rilke, from "The Man Watching,"
> *Selected Poems of Rainer Maria Rilke,*
> translated by Robert Bly

JAMES HALL

* * *

The Vomiting Game

What goes down must come up.

THE FIRST TEST WOULD BE A VOMITING RITE, DONE IN PUBLIC LIKE all the tests, and using some of the most powerful spiritual medicines ever to enter my body, medicines fortified with the warm blood of a freshly slaughtered goat. Five goats were tethered outside the *Indumba* [spirit house], one for each of us. Vomiting herbal medicines on an empty stomach was one of several methods I had learned to administer our herbs, but on this day it would be done as a special ritual, a test of purification. Like a priest, a *sangoma* must exist in a state of inner grace bestowed by the *lidlotis* [ancestral spirits]. The speed with which the five of us were able to expel the undesirable element we had swallowed (the goat's blood) would show our state of grace. Retention of the blood or slowness to vomit were considered proof of spiritual disfavor and a public punishment by the *lidlotis* for some failing during the *kutfwasa* [initiation ceremony]. Such a humiliation had happened to MaZu the previous year when she found the simple act of vomiting a lengthy ordeal.

The author is a former screenwriter who went to Swaziland to become a traditional African healer or sangoma.

—SO'R, JO'R, and TO'R

Mahlalela entered the *Indumba* to give us the "line up": Makhanejose, the eldest, would be the first to drink the blood of her slaughtered goat, then Longdweshuga, then me followed by the two others. I wrapped a calf-length cloth around my waist, but other than underwear I had nothing else on; even our necklaces and amulets had been removed. We'd be cheating if we wore them. The medicines inside the beaded sacks attracted *lidlotis,* and we had to do this test ourselves, without spiritual assistance, to display our own states of grace.

We knelt in a line behind Makhanejose at the entrance. Beyond the *Indumba's* dark interior, the courtyard glared in the harsh sunlight. I could make out a hundred spectators and about two dozen *sangomas* with raddled hair and draped with beads, who were appearing for the first time in their most flamboyant ceremonial finery. They moved about and danced spontaneously to the beating drums. Those drums were like a second heartbeat to me, and sent my blood racing. Willie held Makhanejose's goat with arms so corded with muscle they looked like ropes, and Mahlalela, holding a knife, gave the signal.

Makhanejose leapt out quickly on her hands and knees. But she was confused, perhaps by the shouting of the spectators and *sangomas,* the drums, and her fatigue from the all-night dancing. She didn't know what to do, and as Mahlalela cut the goat's throat the first crucial flow of blood was wasted because she turned her back on the goat, expecting to be washing in the conventional way. Mahlalela shouted at her to turn around and drink. She did, and then was directed to go behind and drink some herbal medicine to vomit with.

Longdweshuga went next. I did not watch but murmured with eyes closed a petition to my *lidlotis* for their support. I wished I was in a trance, I wished they could possess me. I knew what was coming.

I opened my eyes and saw my black goat ahead, ten feet away; Willie held it up by its forelegs. Its ugly brass eyes with their slit-shaped pupils stared out above an opened, panting mouth. The moment Mahlalela severed its carotid artery, the animal would be effectively anesthetized and feel no pain. I steeled myself. Mahlalela held the knife to the goat's throat dramatically, like a Shakespearean actor. He gestured to me with his other hand, and I sprang rapidly out on my hands and knees into the blinding light, as drums pounded and voices shouted, covering the distance to the goat simultaneously with the plunging of the knife into its throat. The blade emerged when I arrived. My lips touched hot, pungent goat hair. A jet of blood shot out, pumped by the animal's frantic heart into my mouth and onto my shoulder. I closed my eyes and tasted hot, salty liquid. I swallowed as much as I could in the few seconds allowed. I felt light-headed and nauseous, and I knew there would be no difficulty vomiting when Mahlalela told me to move on.

On hands and knees I swiftly leapt past the roaring crowd to a ditch, six inches wide, that had been dug in the courtyard. Lined up side by side before it were five large, shallow bowls, each two feet in diameter, one for each of us. They were filled with an herbal medicine of a golden hue that I found lovely even in my febrile frame of mind. Makhanejose and Longdweshuga knelt at their bowls, drinking their fill in order to vomit. I quickly started to work on mine, not drinking so much as taking large, mouth-filling bites of the liquid. Soon Mzwane and Mkhwzeni were at their bowls on my left. People surrounded us, shouting, singing, shaking rattles, kicking up dust that settled on our faces. The drums boomed. I calmed myself with a sturdy Midwesternism, *"I'm cool as a cucumber."*

I felt no hurry. When my stomach was full, I leaned forward over the ditch and let go. Little at first, then a good gush, followed by lesser ones. But no blood. I stuck my head back into the bowl and drank. My stomach felt bloated. The bowl held five liters. I was nearly at the bottom. Someone poured more golden medicine by my ear; it rushed about, up my nostrils. I was swimming in it and suddenly felt full. The sensation propelled me forward, over the ditch. A rush came, then another huge one. Goat's blood poured out of me. Above the women ululated in celebration. The pitch of the people's shouting rose sharply in reaction. I let go again. Blood and medicine. More cheers.

An attendant told me to wash myself with the medicine, but I reacted slowly, feeling dim-witted. Then I saw my forearms, clotted with blood. I washed them in my medicine bowl. Hands took hold of me and pulled me up. I was finished. Two female *sangomas* on either side ran me to the *Indumba.*

Inside, I wondered why I was pulled away first. The others were still going at it. Several minutes passed before I heard more ululations greeting the successful vomiting of blood. Then I knew: I was the first to accomplish the task. My mind really was muddled, but this was the reason for the all-night dance: our bodies were purposefully exhausted and our minds dulled so there would be no doubt that it was the *lidlotis* who would perform the divination tests later that day. The attendants led Makhanejose in, and then the others came when they were done. They had had a more difficult time of it and looked worn out. I was glad I had been fortified by the medicine treatment the night before.

We sat together side by side along the curving wall catching our breaths. Mahlalela came in to give us a pep talk. "Hey, *thogoza,* don't sip, gulp!" Then he smiled and gave me the thumbs-up. "Hey Sibolomhlope! Number one!"

I was vague about what was to happen next. Although I had witnessed the previous year's *kuphotfulwa,* my mind was now a blank. The drums still sounded. *Sangomas* were trading off behind them, each new group of beaters announcing themselves with a thump, thumpa-thump so loud it was a wonder the drum skins didn't break. Mahlalela lined us up on our knees one behind the other, myself in third position, at the *Indumba* entrance. He waved at us to go, and we rushed out, propelling ourselves forward with leaping movements on hands and knees. Ahead was an attendant, pulling the top of a wicker basket along the ground at the end of a rope. "*Dlanini!*" ("Eat"), she shouted.

The five of us chewed the shallow basket top and pushed our faces down into it. Bits of cooked meat floated in a brown, peppery herbal marinade. Nuzzling in, I captured a piece in my mouth, then another. It was like bobbing for apples. We continued to scramble and follow the basket as the attendant dragged it around the courtyard. When I had four chunks of meat in my mouth, I didn't know what to do. I chewed but did not swallow. In the rush and confusion, people shouted at me. I thought they were telling me to spit out the pieces. I did. The attendant yelled, "Eat it! Don't be afraid!" If the meat was evil, as I suspected, I saw we were supposed to eat it anyway, and perhaps purge ourselves later. I plunged into the basket lid again. There were the chewed pieces I had discarded. I gobbled them up. By now, the attendant had led us back to the ditch, where our medicine dishes awaited. I saw now: we were to vomit again.

I knelt wearily at my dish, my weight on my forearms on either side. I drank. It was exhausting. I filled myself, leaned forward, and vomited. No meat. An attendant told me to continue. It was slow going. I drank and drank. On my second refill I felt the irresistible pressure. I let go. Medicine poured into the ditch and flowed away. My throat opened wide, and another gush came out. Ululations! The women were joyous, the men shouted. I looked down. Clinging to the bottom of the ditch were white chunks of meat, twice chewed by me, once spit out, now vomited out, I hoped for good. The attendants told me to wash, and then led me back to the *Indumba*.

I again found myself alone. The others straggled in one at a time. Longdweshuga was last; she looked like she was about to pass out. When we were reassembled, Mahlalela entered. "Sibolomhlope, you were number one again! Number one!" The buzz was all around the homestead, confounding the skeptics: not only did the white man vomit successfully, which clearly could not be faked, but he was the first to finish, twice! In my obsession with the afternoon's crucial divination tests, I had underestimated the importance of the vomiting ritual. Now it was over, but the biggest test awaited.

The five of us went down to the river by ourselves while objects for the divination ritual were hidden back at the homestead. It felt good to be away from the noise at the peaceful riverbank, just our group. Vusi brought down some bread and fruit from the hut, which I passed around. Makhanejose and the others were so relaxed—Mzwane and Mkhwzeni even washed some clothes in the river's placid flow—they seemed unaware of the make-or-break test that awaited us.

But I was very aware that all of *kutfwasa* had been reduced to the few moments to come. We changed into our new ceremonial garments, which felt stiff, fresh, and strange to me. The tall figure of Pashamqomo, made taller by his feathered headdress, appeared on the bluff above, dramatic against the sky. He raised his drum head and beat out our call. A nervous tremor ran through me.

We lined up and squatted on the ground, myself in the third position. Pashamqomo beat his drum head to march rhythm, and we stood and moved up the path to the road. Our *lidlotis* emerged, and announced themselves with cries tearing from our throats. My body yielded to their will, my consciousness again shrunk, and my senses dimmed until I observed what was happening around me imperfectly through veiled eyes. When we arrived at the road, I sensed a strange absence of people. The area was usually crowded on a sunny Saturday afternoon. But no one waited for a bus now. The food vendors were gone. The long span of the footbridge was still. Everyone was at Gogo Simelane's homestead, waiting for us.

We proceeded up the road. Pashamqomo's drum head was suddenly answered by the booming drums at the *Indumba* courtyard. Every drum in the area and others that had been brought in by the visiting *sangomas* were being beaten by the best. Their vibrations rolled over the field. At this moment, I knew, the person who had hidden the objects I now had to divine was blending into the multitude of onlookers. I had no idea who he or she was, but when we arrived I would be required to go directly to the person. There could be no delay, no going from person to person. That would be guessing. And even if I eventually located the person and successfully drew out the objects from their hiding places, I still would have failed because I would have shown that my insight was neither strong nor reliable. Who would trust their health and fortune to such a *sangoma?* I would have lost the confidence of the people, and without their confidence a *sangoma* could not work.

The drums increased in volume as, shouting in reply, we drew near the homestead. I was vaguely aware of entering the grounds, but it seemed as if we suddenly materialized before the *Indumba,* where we danced in place in a line. I was not aware of anything to my left, but to my right people were seated, packed tightly along the fence that extended forward from the spirit house. Others stood behind the fence and beneath a tree, and children sat in the branches. Any moment now, my *inhloko* insight would inform me of the person who was hiding my objects. I'd stop dancing and go to him or her.

But who? And where? I was still in a trance but felt much more in control than I ever had before while in that state. I could not think because the drums were too loud. The people were a blur. They were vague figures in my limited field of vision, as if I had blinkers on with gauze draped in front. Everyone was faceless.

> *T*he French call the relationship between doctor and patient "un couple de malade," *meaning paired-up, yoked together by illness, like a marriage. It is so. There is chemistry between the healer and the one being healed, and those who minister to the heart evoke a profound and tender connection. To be "yoked" like a pair of oxen is an image I liked, because it implies the dual effort it takes to get well or else die properly.*
>
> —Gretel Ehrlich,
> *A Match to the Heart*

Except for one person.

Twenty feet away, but seated directly in front of me as if placed there by providence and now spotlit by the *lidlotis,* was Tablamanzi. She didn't look at me. She was looking at something to her left. But I knew: she was the one.

Just as Makhanejose and Longdweshuga, responding to similar impulses, broke off to my right, I went directly to Tablamanzi. Only when I drew near did she look up. She seemed surprised. Was it a test of my resolve? My *inhloko* held firm: it was her, all right. I dropped down before her. The harsh, insistent voice that came when I was in a *lidloti* trance shouted *"Uyangifihlela, mngan wam!"* ("You are hiding something from me, my friend!")

At once, a second *sangoma,* a pretty and vivacious young woman who had come for the festivities, knelt beside Tablamanzi. They were partners in this, and together they snapped their fingers and replied, "*Sevuma! Sevuma!*" ("We agree; yes, indeed!")

I had caught Tablamanzi and the other one off guard, arriving as quickly as I did. The harsh *lidloti* voice that came from me shouted, "*Yebo! Asambe!*" ("Yeah! Let's go!")

"*Sevuma! Sevuma!*" my team replied with snapping fingers. "We agree! We agree!"

But *what* was hidden? I seemed to know. How? I was told: in visions too quick to glimpse and whispers too fleeting to hear, by impulses I somehow comprehended. Everything was happening fast. It had to, to show the power of my *lidloti*-inspired insight.

The ritual required that I cast my net over a wide area, then draw it in using ritualized phrases in SiSwati "You are hiding something from me. Something from the province of God!"

"*Sevuma! Sevuma!*" Tablamanzi and her partner agreed with enthusiasm.

"…Something from an animal!"

"*Sevuma! Sevuma!*" the women shouted.

"…Something from a goat!"

"*Sevuma! Sevuma!*" After each new declaration my team shouted back their replies—"We agree! We agree!"—as I tightened the net.

It seemed obvious to me which part of the goat they were hiding; a part used in these ceremonies. But then everything I had said so far seemed obvious, as if it was *a priori* knowledge within me. "*Yinyongo!*" ("It's the gall bladder!")

"*Sevuma! Sevuma!*"

But where was it? I knew this too: "*Isekhatsi kwendlu!*" ("It's inside a building!")

"*Sevuma! Sevuma!*" The women trembled with excitement as they snapped their fingers. I hadn't missed, yet. Words tumbled out of me.

"…In the *Indumba!*"

"*Sevuma! Sevuma!*"

"...On the floor...at the *umsamo* [the sacred spot furthest from the door]."

"*Sevuma! Sevuma!*"

Tablamanzi shouted with urgency, "*Hamba! Khokha!*" ("Go! Draw it out!") She and her partner were in competition with the other teams to see which of their graduates would be the first to draw out the hidden object. It was me. I leapt up, sprinted the brief distance back to the *Indumba,* passed the pounding drums and dancing *sangomas,* ducked, and darted inside. There, on the floor, just where I had "seen" it, was a robin's egg blue metal dish. Within it was a goat's gall bladder, inflated like a yellow, pear-shaped balloon atop a soggy hunk of black goat fur. I grabbed it. I spent only four seconds inside the *Indumba* before I emerged again.

> *Some Eskimos say that compared to shamans, ordinary people are like houses with extinguished lamps: they are dark inside and do not attract the attention of the spirits. Their word* qamaneq *means both "lightning" and "illumination"—because in their culture physical and metaphysical phenomena are considered to be the same.*
>
> —Gretel Ehrlich,
> *A Match to the Heart*

Into pandemonium.

For the first time I was aware of the courtyard to the left of the *Indumba.* At least five hundred people lined its sides, packed before the houses all the way back to the cooking hut. They were running toward me. I could not hear the drums, so loud was the shouting, the whistling.

"*SANGOMA! SANGOMA!*"

The *sangomas* reached me first. They grabbed the dish from my hand. Everyone tried to touch me. I thought, "But I'm not done yet!"

I broke away and ran back to Tablamanzi. I threw myself on my knees before her and her companion. "But you are still hiding something from me, my friends!"

"*Sevuma! Sevuma!*"

"...Something from the white man [a manufactured item]!"

"*Sevuma! Sevuma!*"

"...A thing of metal!"

"*Sevuma! Sevuma!*"

Everything thus far had come to me easily, but now I wondered what this new thing could be? It came to me "...It's a dish!"

"*Sevuma! Sevuma!*"

Another dish? Then it occurred to me the dish for vomiting!

"*Sevuma! Sevuma!*"

The dishes were still lined up along the ditch, filled with golden brown liquid. I sprinted to mine. The ring lay inside. I pulled it out, held it up. The roar of voices was like a physical force. A rush of people surged toward me and engulfed me. I was pulled up. There was no going back to Tablamanzi now! Someone snatched the ring. I was in a dream again as colors swirled around me. Two men lifted me into the air, Mahlalela and Sifundza, the hunter. When I was put down Mahlalela held on to my hand and broke into a frantic dance. Poor Mahlalela, I thought fondly, the tension he must have felt. He took a risk when he accepted a white man to study at his homestead, and could have been criticized if I failed. Now he was vindicated. Not only had I done it, I had done it first.

It was all I could do to break through the people dancing around me, the women ululating, the men whistling and yelling. I made it back to Tablamanzi, knelt before her, and clapped my hands in the *sangoma* greeting. This ritual formally ended with a litany of shouted thanks.

I began, "*Abe sengibonga inhloko yemadloti!*" ("I thank the insight of the *lidlotis!*")

The two women replied, "*Thogoza!*" ("You of the *Indumba!*")

"*Abe sengibonga luvela lwemadloti!*" ("And I thank the prescience of the spirits!")

"*Thogoza!*"

"*Abe sengibonga nesikhutsato sebangani bami!*" ("And I thank the encouragement of my friends!")

"*Thogoza!*"

I glimpsed Tablamanzi's round, generous face like a moon above. Her eyes were glistening with tears.

I backed away and returned to the *Indumba*. In a little while all five graduates returned. We had all found the objects hidden for us. Now it was time for informal divinations as we scattered to find whatever might be hidden for us by the people in the crowd. We were presenting ourselves and our skills to the community we would serve. I spotted Sifundza and knelt before him, sensing he was hiding something. He was: a coin in his pocket. A warrior was hiding a coin under the mat he sat on. A woman hid a pin in her hair. Another woman hid a seashell in her bag. I took each find to the drums before the *Indumba,* tossed it down amid cheering, then danced a few spirited steps to the *kukhokha* divination song. Then, following custom, I returned to the person who had hidden the object and gave ritualized thanks.

Our shared *inhloko* insights informed all five graduates that it was time for us to reassemble before the *Indumba*. We were joined by the *sangomas.* The drums changed their rhythm. A somber, stately beat was sounded. The *sangomas* formed a line with us at the end that proceeded around the perimeter of the courtyard. I was still half in a trance, but I was aware of women rushing up to me and placing gifts on my shoulder. A coin. A pecan. A vial of perfume. As they fell to the ground, a child picked them up to save for me.

It was late afternoon. Another night of ritual, another day of arduous rites lay ahead. But I felt fine; weary, but clear-headed as I took full possession of myself inside the *Indumba*. Vusi came in and sat beside me. Rubbing the sweat from my face with the towel he brought, I smiled and asked him how he thought it was going. He admitted he was scared when I drank the goat's blood and vomited—it must have looked wicked, I thought. But he was looking forward to eating the goat at the big feast tomorrow; everybody was.

Vusi grinned at me, "You found the *inyongo* (gall bladder)." And then, tentatively, he touched my head as if trying to feel the *sangoma's* insight lodged within.

James Hall is co-author of the critically acclaimed Makeba: My Story. *A magna cum laude graduate of the University of Southern California, he practices as a traditional healer in Manzini, Swaziland, where he lives with his wife and two children.*

✳

"Sorcerers," he went on, "make one see that the whole nature of reality is different from what we believe it to be; that is, from what we have been taught it to be. Intellectually, we are willing to tease ourselves with the idea that culture predetermines who we are, how we behave, what we are willing to know, what we are able to feel. But we are not willing to embody this idea, to accept it as a concrete, practical proposition. And the reason for that is that we are not willing to accept that culture also predetermines what we are able to perceive.

"Sorcery makes us aware of different realities, different possibilities, not only about the world but also about ourselves, to the extent that we no longer are able to believe in even the most solid assumptions about ourselves and our surroundings."

I was surprised that I could absorb his words so easily, when I didn't really understand them.

"A sorcerer is not only aware of different realities," he went on, "but he uses that knowledge in practicalities. Sorcerers know—not only intellectually but also practically—that reality, or the world as we know it, consists only of an agreement extracted out of every one of us. That agreement could be made to collapse, since it's only a social phenomenon. And when it collapses, the whole world collapses with it."

Seeing that I couldn't follow his argument, he tried to present it from another angle. He said that the social world defines perception to us in proportion to its usefulness in guiding us through the complexity of experience in everyday life. The social world sets limits to what we perceive, sets limits to what we are capable of perceiving. "To a sorcerer, perception can go beyond these agreed-upon parameters," he stressed. "These parameters are constructed and buttressed by words, by language, by thoughts. That is, by agreement."

—Florinda Donner, Being-in-Dreaming

✴ ✴ ✴

A Taste of *Satori*

*The author recounts his experience with
a Zen master in Kyoto.*

I WAS DRAWN TO BUDDHISM THROUGH D. T. SUZUKI, WHOSE
writings held out the prospect of at least a taste of *satori,* the enlightenment experience, if one practiced Zen. At that stage—my
mid-thirties—I wanted that experience more than anything else in
the world, so I entered Zen training, which led eventually to a
monastery in Kyoto and *koan* training under a Zen master.

"Rinzai Zen" (the branch that I was in) uses *koans* in its training. *Koans* are of different kinds, but the beginning ones are rather
like shaggy dog stories in that they involve questions—riddles
really—that make no rational sense. The one I was given was
longer than most, so I won't repeat it in full, but it came down to:
how could one of the greatest Zen masters have said that dogs
don't have Buddha-natures when the Buddha has said that even
grass possesses it? For two months, I banged my head against that
contradiction for eight hours a day. I was sitting in the cramped
lotus position and reporting to my *roshi,* or Zen Master, one-on-
one at five o'clock each morning, what I had come up with.
Precious little! It was the most frustrating assignment I had ever
been given. I seemed to be getting absolutely nowhere, though I
did discover as the weeks slipped by that the final word in the *koan*

"*mu*" (which translates into no), seemed to function more and more like the "om" mantra that I had worked with in Hinduism.

The climax came during the final eight days in the Myoshinji monastery—a kind of final exam period—where everything else gets tabled so the monks can meditate almost around the clock. As a novice, I was permitted to sleep three and a half hours each night, but I found that grossly insufficient and the sleep deprivation was the hardest ordeal I had ever faced. After the first night I was sleepy, after the second I was bushed, and it kept going from there.

I still don't understand how Zen training works, but it seems clear that the initial *koans* force the rational mind to the end of its tether, and that sleep deprivation figures in somewhere along the line. If you can't get your mind into an altered state any other way, sleep deprivation will eventually do it for you, for deprived of dreams, the mind becomes psychotic.

So you can have certain breakthrough Enlightenment experiences—satori, for example—but these are just the beginning of an endless process of riding the new waves of Form as they ceaselessly arise. So in this sense…you are never "fully Enlightened," any more than you could say that you are "fully educated." It has no meaning.

—Ken Wilber, A Brief History of Everything

Something like that happened to my mind two days before the monastic term ended. That afternoon I went storming into the *roshi* in a frenzy. Self-pity had long since become boring; that day I was in a rage. I was furious. What a way to treat human beings, I kept telling myself, and charged in to my *roshi* prepared, not just to throw in the towel but to throw it straight at his face.

I entered his audience room with the required ritual, palms clasped together. Turning only straight corners—no diagonal short cuts in Zen—I made my way to where he was sitting in his priestly robes with his short, heavy stick (for clobbering if need be) lying in his lap. Sinking to my knees on the cushion before him, I touched my head to the floor and flexed my outstretched fingers upward, an Indian gesture that symbolizes lifting the dust from the Buddha's feet. Then I sat back on my heels and our eyes met in a mutual glare. For some moments he said nothing, then, "How's it going?" He was one of the two *roshis* in the world then who could speak English. It sounded like a calculated taunt. "Terrible!" I shouted.

"You think you are going to get sick, don't you?" More taunting sarcasm, so I let him have it.

"Yes, I think I'm going to get sick!" I yelled. For several days my throat had been contracting to the point where I was having to labor to breathe.

Then something extraordinary happened. His face suddenly relaxed, its taunting, goading expression gone, and with total matter-of-factness he said, "What is sickness? What is health? Both are distractions. Put both aside and go forward."

What I despair of conveying to you is the impact those fifteen words had on me. Without reflecting for a moment, I found myself saying to myself "By God, he's right!" How he was able to spin me around, defuse my rage, and return me to lucidity in a twinkling, I will never comprehend. Never had I felt so instantly reborn and energized. It was as if there was a pipe connecting his *hara*—abdomen, where the Japanese locate the self's center—to mine. I exited in the prescribed manner, not only determined to stick out the two remaining days, but knowing that I could do so.

It didn't occur to me at the time that in that climactic moment I might have passed my *koan,* and I returned to the States assuming that I had not. But when I related my story to a *dharma* brother who had trained for twelve years under my *roshi,* he said he wasn't at all sure that I had not passed it. He reminded me that the answer to the early *koans* is not a rational proposition but an experience. That, at the climactic moment in my training, I was able not just to acknowledge the identity of life's opposites theoretically, but to *experience* their identity—in my case the identity of sickness and health— struck him as a strong foretaste of the enlightenment experience.

Apparently so. It still seems to me like genius. He knew exactly where I was, and administered exactly the light tapping that changed everything.

Huston Smith is the Thomas J. Watson Professor of Religion and Distinguished Adjunct Professor of Philosophy Emeritus at Syracuse University. He is currently living in Berkeley and is a Visiting Professor of Religious Studies at the University of California, Berkeley.

*

"There is one thing you must understand if you are going to take Buddhism seriously. You must not use it as an anaesthetic. I did, for years. I travelled, studied, went into retreats, gave up my job to go to Dharamsala, did all the proper things, had the most amazing experiences, insights…yes, indeed. I was very proud of myself, really thought I had got there, arrived, done and understood everything by the age of thirty. I was learned; I had met many of the great Rinpoches and had close friendships with them. I had become fluent in Tibetan. And I was happy, calm, suspiciously happy, in fact, suspiciously calm. I see that now. What I was doing was what many searchers do—I was building a great wall of experiences and meditative ecstasies and learning between me and the world."

—Andrew Harvey, *A Journey in Ladakh*

DAVID YEADON

⋆ ⋆ ⋆

Dreamtime Odyssey

The Aboriginals have something big to say.

I WAS COLD. VERY COLD. DESPITE THE DAYTIME FURNACE HEAT OF Australia's outback, a numbing nighttime chill invariably settles across the vast shrub-dotted plains of the interior, sending most living things—myself included—into a somnolent stupor. The silence was tangible—a Zen-like void—slowly filling with a delicious anticipation of dawn. The star-filled blackness of the night sky gradually eased into a purple-gray half-light and then…slowly—ever so slowly—the sun rose in a great golden yolk of light and heat and Ayers Rock emerged, red and wraithlike from the vast flatness. Colors spread in a slow tide across the desert. I was here—I was really here! After a long flight and a switch of planes in Alice Springs, I had arrived at last in the heart of Australia's Red Center, at its very navel, and was about to experience the daily rebirthing of the world's largest (1142 feet) sandstone monolith, set in the middle of over two million square miles of flat outback on the earth's most ancient landmass, eroded to a virtual peneplain over a billion years.

Years ago, Bruce Chatwin's unusual book, *The Songlines,* touched something deep within me. He was describing the Australian Aboriginal's "Dreamtime" creation-stories in which an unformed world had been shaped by ancestral beings—a myriad of giant-sized kangaroos, lizards, birds, snakes, caterpillars, witchetty grubs, even sea creatures, plants and cloud-beings—that emerged from the void and journeyed widely creating all living things and all the features of the landscape—waterholes, mountain ranges, scarps, rivers—everything. Ayers Rock and the nearby Olgas Cluster of 36 smooth-domed hills (now known jointly as the Uluru-Kata Tjuta National Park) remain today as physical evidence of the ancestors' feats enacted in the creation or "Dreamtime" period. The Anangu—or Aboriginals—who today number around 250,000 throughout Australia, are the direct descendants of these beings and have the eternal responsibility of perpetuating and caring for the land through "singing" the ancient rituals of stories, songs, dances and *"corroboree"* ceremonies along the Iwara (the dreaming tracks or "songlines" reflecting the ancestors' journeys). The secrets of these tracks are passed on by complex initiations from generation to generation in the form of the Tjukurpa or Aboriginal laws that rigidly define the relationships between people, plants, animals and all the physical features of the land. Chatwin wrote of the ancient ancestors that: "They wrapped the whole world in a web of song," which I found a wonderfully evocative description of Creation, and he emphasized the heavy duty placed upon today's Aboriginal ancestors to maintain the songlines through constant rituals, as "an unsung land is a dead land."

As I read deeper into Chatwin's book I knew that one day I would come to the Australian outback and learn more of its mysteries. And *voila!*—here I was—watching the sun turn Ayers Rock into a towering crimson reality and walking with a few others around its five and a half mile base as a guide told us the intricate Dreamtime tales of its creation, showed us hidden waterholes and led us under rock overhangs to peer at ochre-painted rock art created by Aboriginal ancestors over 20,000 (some experts claim over 50,000) years ago.

Despite all the charms of Ayers Rock and its modern Yulara hotel complex, I found the place far too overcrowded for my tastes and felt a need to pull away and seek out something less tied to

time and schedules and tourist pick up/drop off points. Something
that would allow me to explore the underlying realities of this
wild region, those tantalizing flickers of perception that came to
me when I looked into the eyes
of Aboriginal guides and sensed
whole timeless realms of knowledge and understanding that
seem so alien to our contemporary rush-rush, what's-next,
affluenza-plagued lifeways. So I
left the rock and "went bush"
with a guide, Lynne, on a long,
bone-jarring drive south along
red dust tracks. The scrub-dotted
desert, flat land seemingly fea-
tureless, makes you constantly
aware of the vast enormity of the
sky. Below is an infinite rust-red
nothingness, a place where distances are measured by the
earth's curvature and defined by shimmering heat hazes; above is
that arching sky dome so pure-blue it makes your eyes ache. When
the occasional cloud appears it is a singular event. I watched as a
huge thunderhead evolved out of the nothing in the west and ballooned ominously into an imposing object thousands of feet high
which gave the sky even greater vertical dimension and seemed,
by its very enormity, to compress the already-flattened earth into
even greater insignificance. A thought came: how small, alone and
utterly frail seems man against all this enormity. To survive here, to
find purpose and nourishment here, you *need* the company of
Dreamtime creatures, and the security of dreaming tracks or songlines for navigation, water and bushfood. You also need utter faith
in your one-ness with everything around you, bound unerringly by
Tjukurpa law, laid down and maintained in perpetuity, celebrated,
sung and resung to provide finite edges and realities in this otherwise unreal, edgeless infinity. Even if there wasn't a God, a greater

*When you live with
the bushmen you find
they are rich in a way in which we
have become poor. They pass on
something tremendous. They talk,
and they say the human being has
two hungers. There is the hunger
for food, but there is also the great
hunger, and that is to be part of
the creation. I found that this is
what wilderness did for me, and
this is what wilderness has done in
Africa, in Australia, in America,
and all over the world.*

—Laurens van der Post,
"Wilderness," *Lapis*

creative mind, you'd certainly have to invent one and learn to understand his ways, otherwise your ability to survive here and find daily nourishment would be destroyed and your rapid extinction guaranteed.

The next few days presented me with an experience I'll never forget. With Lynne as my guide and interpreter I lived bush-style in a small campground set against high red cliffs at the edge of a vast mulga bush plain studded with thousands of red-mud termite mounds. At night I slept under dazzling stars in the traditional bushman's swag (a hefty roll complete with pillow, mattress and sleeping bag all wrapped in sturdy waterproof canvas) and during the days spent most of my time in the company of two elderly Pitjantjatjara women, Nganyinytja and Tjulkiwa, their husbands Ilyatjari and Mutju, and members of their extended families. Nganyinytja was the spokesperson and explained how she welcomed visitors to her remote homeland: "I want to teach all people, black and *Gadia*—whitefellas—about the land and our way of living with it. If people will listen to our way then they will understand why we, the Anangu, still live in this country—our country—and keep the old ways, the Tjukurpa laws, and sing the spirit of our land. We want to increase understanding and acceptance of each other. The wind that blows across our country talks to everyone and they begin to realize that we all share the same spirit. We are all of one same earth."

Nganyinytja spoke softly and gently. "I do not talk badly of those people who do not understand," she told me, even though the terrible stories of her husband, Ilyatjari, about the mistreatment of Aboriginals by early white settlers and pastoralists, made me squirm with outrage. "There is a revival—people will come here from all over the earth and see how we live and they will learn that it is good—they will learn to care for the land again; they will take something valuable back with them."

My initiation into the "old ways" came slowly, but it did come. The apparent void of the land began to give of its secrets. I learned where to find witchetty grubs (deliciously crisp peanut-flavored snacks when roasted—honestly!) under the ground among the witchetty bush roots; I began to spot bushtucker in the sparse desert fruits—small bush plums, tomatoes, peaches and figs; I could tell the difference between old and new trails left by rabbits, kangaroos, lizards and snakes, and distinguish the liquid pre-sunrise calls of the black-and-white pied butcherbird and the chiming wedgebill from the rich dawn chorus of mulga parrots, cockatoos, willie wagtails, bowerbirds and cooing crested pigeons. I even learned the crafty ways of honey ants whose false trails and chambers eventually lead to a deep, subterranean cavern of delights where they hang in hundreds, their abdomens bloated like little grapes, ready to be sucked clean of their delicious life-giving nectar.

Family members showed me how to use simple but effective hunter-gatherer implements—the digging stick, the spear and spear-thrower, the boomerang, the *piti* and *wira* dishes carved from mulga tree bark, and the grinding stones for making breadcakes from grass seeds. They explained how ancient Dreamtime laws create a cohesive framework for mutual support and order; they told me how the constant singing and walking of traditional Dreamtime tracks (each initiated member of the family "mob" has his or her specific totemic ancestor that defines tracks and sacred places to safeguard) combined spiritual duty with pragmatic land-maintenance through scrub-burning and waterhole-cleansing. I learned of their bush medicines, the importance of secret male and female "business" rituals, the crucial initiation of young family members to perpetuate the Tjukurpa laws, and their delight in ancient ritual dances and in creating elaborate sand paintings. These exquisite dot-filled Dreamtime artworks are now produced on bark and canvas by scores of Aboriginal artists in outback communities and can be found in galleries and stores throughout Australia.

Despite all my experiences and insights, I still felt I was floating on the edge of Aboriginal Dreamtime, sensing vast timeless mysteries. At first my pragmatic Western mind dismissed the idea of supernatural powers possessed by Aboriginals as merely the ramblings of overactive minds entranced by the enticements of half-understood myths and superstitions. But the families' openness and unhyped honesty began to make me wonder about such abilities as bodily transcendence of enormous pain and near-starvation, the life-and-death power of "bone-pointing" rituals, the transmutation of form (from human to animal and vice versa), the possibilities of rapid-healing using ageless bush remedies, the existence of widespread mental telepathy between clan members, the ability to "go invisible" or appear in multiple form, even claims of levitation and instant bodily transference from one place to another.

My slow acceptance of these possibilities came, not in any hocus-pocus, drug-induced or magical sleight-of-mind manner but only after listening to the families and observing their quiet certainty, their matter-of-fact-acceptance of such actualities as a natural outcome of their ability to instinctively tap deeper energies and powers—powers that we have long since forgotten and replaced with more tangible and pragmatic realities.

I remember one small incident in particular. At night when the families decided it was time to sleep they moved away from the camp fire to different locations in the mulga scrub. Following the first coloring of dawn, when the birds began their liquid chattering, they would ease up out of their swags and sit in silence for a long time. I could see all the families doing the same thing—just sitting in silence, no one moving.

After maybe twenty minutes of the strange stillness, Mutju rose to stoke up the fire. I followed him.

She said that millennia ago, men and women were the possessors of a knowledge that allowed them to slip in and out of our normal world. And thus they divided their lives into two areas: the day and the night. During the day they conducted their activities like everyone else: they engaged in normal, expected, everyday behavior. During the night, however, they became dreamers. They systematically dreamed dreams that broke the boundaries of what we consider to be reality.

Again she paused, as though giving me time to let her words sink in.

"Using the darkness as a cloak," she went on, "they accomplished an inconceivable thing; they were able to dream while they were awake."

—Florinda Donner, *Being-in-Dreaming*

"Why all that long silence?" I asked him. He smiled—a little benevolently—on this uninitiated outsider.

"We were talking," he said.

"I didn't hear any talking."

He sighed—a kind of how-dumb-can-you be kind of sigh. "Not word-talking. That kind of talking is not necessary. We know each other. We understand each other…"

He could see I was still a little perplexed. "I am me," he explained slowly, "but I am also each one of them. They are they but they are also me. We hear one another quite clearly because we are all part of the same thing—the same person. The silence you heard was full of conversation…" Then he laughed. "Help me with the fire. You're hungry." And he was right. I was very hungry. Hungry for knowledge and sad that my time in the wild bush was drawing to a close.

On my last evening Nganyinytya suddenly announced it was "time for dancing" and supervised the elaborate body dot-painting of herself, Tjulkiwa, and young children of the family. She used her own white dyes and twigs whose ends had been pounded to fibrous paint brushes to create ornate whorls and spirals of dots on their chests, shoulders and arms. Within the patterns were ancient symbols of Dreamtime creatures reflecting the different songs that each member of the group is obliged to "sing" throughout their lives to keep the land and the law intact for future generations. The children were silent and serious as their bodies were slowly and meticulously painted. Nganyinyta smiled at their stern little faces. "They know this is not a game," she told me quietly. "They will do the same with their own children one day."

Then she and Tjulkiwa stood and, humming rhythmic, drone-like songs together, they led long shuffling dances with children as dust rose from the dry earth and turned the sunset into a mystical golden-tinged haze. They continued for a long time as dusk crept across the mulga. The monotone sounds of their voices and their stately movements were mesmerizing and for a while I felt I was living in pre-history times watching dances that had been danced by family ancestors for thousands of years. Willingly—I became a passive participant, sinking deeper and deeper into the old ways...into the Dreamtime...

Much later, when the dancing had ceased and we were all sitting together roasting just-caught rabbits on the campfire, Nganyinytja leaned over and touched my arm gently. "You are a little part of us now," she murmured quietly. I nodded and held her hand. My eyes were watering and it wasn't just from the campfire smoke.

Twenty years ago, David Yeadon took a two-month sabbatical from his job as a city planner to roam around the country with his wife Anne. Instead of returning to his job he turned to writing and has completed more than 300 magazine and newspaper articles and over twenty books, including Backroad Journeys of Southern Europe, Lost Worlds: Exploring the World's Remote Places, *and* The Back of Beyond: Travels to the Wild Places of the Earth. *He lives with his wife and cat on an idyllic lake north of New York City.*

✳

On the other hand, in a seeming paradox—at least to outsiders—the Dreamtime isn't a past epoch at all. Rather, it exists as a kind of metaphysical now, a mystical time outside of time, a spiritual yet nonetheless real dimension of time and space somehow interpenetrating and concurrent with our own. To Aboriginals, it lies just around the corner of the mind and perceptions, and, in a sense, can be physically entered by initiates—and only by initiates—during ceremonies and dreams. There, in that otherworldly realm, the Ancestor Beings still exist as always, continually renewing and maintaining the land and the cycle of seasons—indeed, the whole Universe—through a mystical communion with their loving Aboriginal descendants.

To this day Aboriginal groups and individuals trace their particular ancestry, or Dreaming, to one or more of these Dreamtime demigods. When an Aboriginal says, "I have a Crocodile Dreaming" or "I'm a Dingo Dreaming man," he refers to the Dreamtime Crocodile or the ancestral creator Dingo, who helped shape the landscape in that long-ago time and to whom he bears a special affinity and spiritual relationship.

—Harvey Arden, *Dreamkeepers: A Spirit-Journey into Aboriginal Australia*

JEANINE BARONE

* * *

Stone by Stone

Zen and the art of masonry.

"IF YOU'RE STARING AT A ROCK FOR MORE THAN A FEW SECONDS, it's the wrong rock," Ginou declared. I had just spent twenty frustrating minutes sorting through the pile, discarding each one as either too big, too round, too small, too flat, too irregular. With his weathered face, shaggy beard, and long curly gray hair topped by a shocking pink cap, Ginou surveyed the mound from over my shoulder. His brow wrinkled a moment with intense concentration, as he seized a rock with just the right dimensions and surface. He continued, "You'll find the right rock once you're in harmony with it." So began my first day restoring a medieval castle in southern France and my introduction to Henri Gignoux (Ginou), the chief mason of the project.

The evening before, I and 34 other volunteers from all over the world had settled into our accommodations at St. Victor la Coste, a medieval village that was dominated by a castle. There was a bit of a college feel, with the twin beds, spartan furnishings, and an old curmudgeon professor-type, namely Ginou. But instead of an alarm clock, we woke to the dependable, early-morning braying of a donkey; plump red grapes or a ripe plum picked from outside the window replaced the typical bags of chips.

Our main project was Chateau de Gicon, a 13th-century castle set on a hill half an hour from St. Victor. I had expected Gicon to be one massive structure reminiscent of King Arthur's days, complete with a moat and drawbridge. Gicon is actually a series of buildings, almost like a village, that had fallen three times in its history and was left in ruin for centuries. There was neither moat nor drawbridge, but the climb through the forest to get there certainly slowed our progress. This plus the stone fortification and sheer cliffs probably dissuaded many uninvited guests.

Some years ago, Ginou and his group of volunteer masons formed their organization, Le Sabrenenque, and began putting in stairs and windows, tiling floors, reconstructing archways and reinforcing roofs. The goal was not to bring Gicon back to its original form but to make it safe for the local wine cooperative to host tasting events—which would clearly be spoiled if chardonnay-toasting guests were to stumble off the nearby precipice or get knocked out by a section of crumbling ceiling.

From the start, it was clear this wouldn't be your average two-week stint in the French countryside. My hopes of a leisurely brick-laying class or two—complete with an instruction book for mixing mortar, aligning stones and the like—were promptly dashed.

Each day began with the bucket brigade: twenty of us lined up two flights of stairs, rapidly passing 30-pound buckets of sand from one individual to the next. Next came pails brimming with water. My first time was spent in fear that what felt like a lead-filled pail might slip at any moment. I quickly understood why the "old timers" came dressed in heavy hiking boots while I naively wore beach sandals. But after several mornings of this weight training, I progressed from a two-handed death grip to an almost casual one-handed swing. With 30 minutes of this daily, no wonder Ginou maintained his vital muscle tone. But, as I soon found out, there was no obvious explanation for his Zen-like aura.

We were divided in pairs, given a full bucket of mortar and a trowel, and led to the edge of the cliff top to begin wall construction. Atop a thick layer of fresh mortar, I laid one rock after another in no particular pattern, and was satisfied with my efforts. But I was quickly deflated by the sound of Ginou's deep baritone: "It makes me sad to see this." With a long sweep of his hand, he cast my rocks off the wall, and accused *me* of man-handling them. I looked up at him expectantly waiting for a demonstration of proper technique. What I got was unexpected, to say the least. Humming softly to himself, Ginou became a conductor, moving in time to the music while gently but firmly placing rocks on their long flat surface, one next to the other. "Be gentle in placing the rocks into the mortar. The strength comes from the rocks, not the mortar." For the next layer, he placed rocks crosswise with a good strip of mortar between. "Placing rocks in the mortar is like music," he said, "very fluid and rhythmic." Although amazed by his ease, grace, and artistry, I still had no solid understanding of how I was to duplicate his technique.

Alan Watts: What kind of yoga do you do, Joe?
Joseph Campbell: I underline passages.

Feeling deeply inadequate, I trudged to the stone pile to gather an armful of likely-looking prospects. Glancing to my right and left at the wall, I saw the others, for the most part, having no problem with Ginou's esoteric non-instructions. All seemed immersed in concentration, placing stones and laying mortar in an apparently acceptable manner.

After chatting with some of the more seasoned volunteers, however, I realized Ginou was trying to get us to know by doing and feeling, not by simple mimicry or rote learning. Kind of like an Outward Bound course where self-reliance is key. "Think of rocks like jewels," he said as he walked over to my side. It was time to discard logic and learn by intuition, not an easy task, as it turned out. I could neither get a feel for the right rocks ("meditating" made me feel silly) nor visualize how a finished wall would look. Either I was jinxed or genetically impaired.

Each night, I returned to my twin bed and, as the cold light of the moon streamed through the window, I'd mull over the day's lessons. I realized I needed to spend less time thinking and more time doing. So I decided I would try to feel what it's like to be a rock in order to fit each one on the wall properly—like method acting.

Following Ginou's lead, I began to relax and block out distractions, banishing all unrelated thoughts (whether they'd serve shepherd's pie for lunch, what kind of wines would be at the tasting this afternoon) from my head. I started watching the others with less envy. Carol had a knack for simply stepping up to a stone pile and finding the right rock, and Carrie always mixed the mortar correctly. I observed Genevieve who'd done this for five summers: First, spread a thick layer of mortar right to the edge; select big rocks that don't teeter but instead lay flat; place them on either side of the wall, making sure they're flush on the outside; and fill in the middle with smaller stones. Like many skills, masonry is best conveyed not by words but by experience. I soon became so wrapped up in my tasks, I no longer obsessed over what I needed to do; I just did it.

And with that, my masonry began, my confidence growing with each passing day. I found rocks that were big, but not too big; mixed mortar that was thick, but not too thick; and, like with a jigsaw puzzle, fit each rock almost perfectly next to its neighbor. Layer after layer, the wall rose to four feet high. Nearing the top, we used a plumb line to ensure that the rocks were flush on the top sides. Then, the plumb line was removed and we used a leveler. Finally, an approving smile and a hug from Ginou. I no longer felt like the unenlightened mason.

In the end, I stood back, hands on hips, trowel in hand, after topping my creation with watery mortar and large, flat stones—the final stage of a completed wall. Like a sculptor critically surveying the delicate curves of a shoulder or neck in a bust he's labored over, Ginou stood silently over our work. We'd all been transformed into proud artists.

With this, Audrey, one of many old-hands, sighed with the satisfaction of completing another successful renovation. For her, this was like a pilgrimage home after a long absence to see changes made while she was gone and relive memories of past projects, like the stone floor and archway she worked on a few years ago.

I relished the warm breeze and the burning sun on my arms, still feeling the smoothness of the mortar running between my fingers and the cool firmness of the rocks. Every day had been this perfect. Aloud, I wondered what we would have done if it had rained. Reflecting on the sense of magic here, Audrey replied softly, "It never rains in Camelot."

Jeanine Barone is a travel, fitness, and food writer who has trekked all over the world, from glaciers in New Zealand and castles in Scotland to the deserts of North Africa. Her writing has appeared in dozens of magazines, including Outside, Adventure West, *and* Walking. *She lives in New York.*

★

If you ask people in, or returning from, strange lands what their experiences are like they report that *everything to them is real and vivid and they feel very "alive."* They report an *experience of immediacy;* a *broad awareness* of everything around them; and a *feeling of being one with and responsive to the world.* Together they constitute a state of consciousness called a *sense of presence.* It's the signature experience of strange lands.

—Gary Fontaine, Ph.D., *A Sense of Presence*

* ✦ ⋆

The Great Holy Mystery

Visions come when least expected.

WHO ARE WE? WHERE ARE WE GOING? WHY ARE WE HERE? Imagine if more people searched the mystery of their lives for the answers to these questions. Imagine if more people understood the passion of the Lakota war cry: "It's a good day to die!" or the feelings of a man like Henry David Thoreau when he said that he would hate to face his death knowing that he had not lived. Imagine if the hearts of more people became like theirs…and the land became mother…and that which they share all things with became the Great Holy Mystery. Imagine…

I was a young man alone on my first vision quest.

It was dawn. A strong salty breeze swept across the turquoise sea. It caused Gulf waters to ripple and the waves to swell and break into cool white crystals of foam that carried in the tide. I sat on the shore on my turquoise mat within a circle I had drawn in the bone-white sand. Golden sea oats and tall sea grass swayed near me.

They cast shadows around a round stone I had placed on the ground. The small stone was about the size of a marble. It had been painted with a sacred red ochre by an Arapaho medicine man. Only he and one other Arapaho man knew where this sacred paint could be found. I knew only that it was a journey which took him deep into the Wind River Mountains of Wyoming.

I can remember the night he returned with the paint and held the small stone with the fingers of one hand while he placed the fingers of his other into a small deerskin pouch, how he moved them around inside until they emerged glistening in dark crimson, how he rolled the small round stone between his fingers, mixing it with the paint until the stone turned red too.

A few days before my first vision quest I had fallen into my old uncle's arms and cried, for I'd just been fired from my first teaching position at an Indian high school. My marriage was falling apart. I had lost any sense of purpose and direction. These things conspired to make the long trip from Wyoming to my home in Florida even longer. Crossing such a distance seemed only to give my emotions more time to well up inside of me, so when I finally arrived at Uncle Nip's I was a storm ready to release itself. And I did. It was as if all I had worked for in college and whatever semblance of identity I had struggled for was suddenly

> *Crucial for man is his attitude towards failure: whether it remains hidden from him and overwhelms him only objectively at the end, or whether he perceives it unobscured as the constant limit of his existence; whether he snatches at fantastic solutions and consolations or faces it honestly, in silence before the unfathomable. The way in which man approaches his failure determines what he will become.*
>
> —Karl Jaspers, *Way to Wisdom,* translated by Ralph Manheim

torn asunder. I was a broken man whose ideals were as scattered as a flock of frightened gulls. I seemed lost and afraid. I felt alone. And I cried in my old uncle's arms.

"Go for a vision," Nippawanock said, his wrinkled hands on my shoulders, his starry eyes penetrating my darkness. "It's time. If you are to walk the path of heart, then it is time…

"Take your red stone with you to a place where you can be close to nature…a place where people won't disturb you. Use your medicine stone as your intercessor. Speak through it to the Mystery. Go from sunrise as long as you can but no more than four days. Don't eat, and don't drink. Concentrate on that part of you that is all things. Concentrate on the Mystery. Meditate."

I did what uncle Nip advised and headed for the Island-Where-The-Great-Turtles-Nest. For days and nights I sat on my turquoise mat within the circle I had drawn in the sand as I called out into the Mystery for some understanding to my life. I wept for all the things I'd lost and for all those I had loved. Sometimes I shivered in terror at night, at having to face my own fears. Sometimes I lay silent, staring up at the stars. I remember how the sun rose each morning regardless of my state of mind and how the sudden emergence of dolphins made me feel light-headed and happy. I remember how the sun rose hot and lingered long and lasting…how it burned as I faced my own anger.

And although I received great insight that time years ago when I was a young man seeking a vision, no vision came to me. "The vision will come when you are ready," said Uncle Nip. "It will come at that special moment when time transcends reality and the Mystery of life reveals itself to you."

Unexpectedly, that would happen a year or so later on a cold wintry night in Minnesota. I had been teaching Indian children all day in the housing projects where the American Indian Movement school, Heart of the Earth, was located. And at night I had taught Indian adults in the basement of the Minneapolis Public Library. I had done this for days at a time, and living alone, I had no one to insist that I take time enough to eat or even to sleep.

I can remember the circle of elms and snowy, sloping hills across the street from Powderhorn Park, where I lived. I can still recall standing outside under one of the great elms and gazing up at the glistening stars…how many more there seemed to be that night…how some of them seemed so big and close I could touch them if I reached out my hand.

Instead, the stars reached out to me, and a Being robed in red appeared before me. His eyes were large and shaped like almonds and as black as the stone of Apache tears. He motioned for me to look, and I saw the spirit-breath of my people fading. Then he motioned again, and I saw a woman as old as the Earth. She spoke about lies and half-truths, about ambiguities and manipulations of words. When I turned away, the Being robed in red held in his hands a book of stars. He pointed to a certain place among them, and then the book of stars became the pipe that I would one day keep and protect with my life.

The vision I was given that night under the stars at Powderhorn, a thousand miles from the island where I first cried for one, became the guiding force and anchor of my life. Whenever I need to know whether or not I am doing the right thing for the People and the land, I recall my vision. If whatever I contemplate doing is connected to that moment of Vision, then I know it's the right thing to do. And though time and experience and living in the Wheel has provided me dreams and ceremony, nothing has ever been like the Vision. It has kept me on the path of heart. It is the one thing that I know can never be taken away from me.

White Deer of Autumn (Gabriel Horn) has taught in reservation schools, American Indian Movement survival schools, public schools, and junior colleges. He is currently a teacher in Florida as well as a member of the National Committee on American Indian History.

★

My backpack went heavily over my shoulders, and I closed five fingers around the handle of my water jug. It, too, was heavy—enough fresh water for two days of travel. It was 3 a.m., and we were getting a dark start on a long, rough journey to beat the day's heat. I was headed from Palenque in southern Mexico to the Usumacinta River on the Guatemalan border.

As I stepped out into the dark, I was suddenly confronted by a night sky that startled me. *This sky,* unlike the one in eastern Pennsylvania that I'm accustomed to, resembled a flat sheet of velvet, lusterless and black, and it loomed so close that it seemed I could touch it. A half-moon was rocking itself toward the horizon. Venus blazed, a stern eye. The southern constellations made hard, clear knuckles of brightness.

I shuddered. This was a Maya sky. The Moon Goddess weighed on me; Venus had become the elder Hero Twin, Hunahpu, maker of wars and difficult fortunes. The underworld, Xibalba, so full of dreadful beings, had rotated upward to take the place of the day sky. Fear dropped over me. I hoped that the omens for my journey were good, and I worried that the deities were not propitiated.

In that instant I suddenly understood for the first time how intensely populated with significant beings the night sky had been for the ancient Maya; how reciprocal had been human life and the sky's life; how *necessary*, finally, had been the arcane rituals—the self-mutilation, the sacrifice of captives, the ballgames and fasting....

Linda had said to me, "People have a religious experience out here." Now here I stood, in Palenque, under a palpable sky. The stars up north, at least where I live, are small, cold, remote; the mind acknowledges that light years separate us from them. But here in the tropics that is not what you *see*. That is not what you *feel*.

Religious experience or paradigm shift, it makes little difference: the night sky had touched me. When that cold shudder passed, I picked up my jug, which I had set down for a moment, and struggled toward the roadway.

—Richard A. Wertime, "A Maya Sky," *Archaeology*

RHODA BLECKER

* * *

Twist of Faith

Two religions are intertwined
like strands of DNA.

SEVERAL YEARS AGO AT MY SYNAGOGUE, THE RABBI RAISED THIS
question: "Why don't Jews come to services?" After listening to
"Services are boring," "We're usually very tired at the end of the
week" and the like, I hesitantly raised my hand. "I'm having a
very strange experience here," I said. "I'm wondering if it's somehow inappropriate to mention God."

Later, when I told my nun friend Mother Miriam that I would
probably be regarded as the weird one in my congregation "because I'll be the one who is always bringing God into the discussion," she said dryly, "My dear, there are worse things to be
known for."

But I'm getting ahead of my story.

There was a long period in my life when I lived very much in
my head and body, and not at all in my soul. Since I had been
brought up as a Reform Jew, in the generations in which rationality was considered only sensible and God was no longer important,
I understood religion to be largely a matter of social action. I
prided myself on my rationality, even on my skepticism. I believed
that Judaism was fully "user-friendly," in that, having been born
Jewish, I did not have to do anything, and I would still always be

Jewish. I stopped performing most rituals, as they were meaningless to me, but I continued to give money to Jewish causes, and considered myself a Jew when Israel was threatened. That was, I was convinced, Jewish enough for life in America today.

But then something inexplicable happened. Even today, in the Passover-Easter season, I fight the urge to "explicate" it when I tell the story, because I have been a rational being for so long that I want to make completely rational and accessible everything that touches me.

In mid-December of 1971, living in California, I awoke one morning with the vivid recollection of a strange dream. Remembering any dream was unusual for me, but it was the content of this dream that was haunting: My face was turning dark blue. The doctors I consulted said they could not help me. They said that I should seek help at a place in Connecticut, where nuns lived. They told me its name and sent me away. That was all the dream that I remembered.

It was a work day, and at scattered moments the memory of the dream returned, somehow more urgently each time, until about 3:30 in the afternoon. Then I closed my office door, dialed the Connecticut area code and asked the operator if they had a listing for a convent by the name I'd been told in my dream. Without hesitation, she gave me a number.

This was not the response I'd expected or desired, because it was not the rational response. I must have sat by my phone for half an hour, staring at the number and feeling icy cold. Around 4:15 p.m., I dialed the number.

When the phone was answered, I asked only, "If I were to send a contribution, to whom would I direct it?" The person on the other end gave me the name and I thanked her. I wrote a check and sent it off with a letter that read, in its entirety, "I do not know who you are. Here is a contribution. I am Jewish." And I signed it. I have been more eloquent, but I believed I was doing the right thing.

Afterward, I decided that I must have read the name of the convent somewhere. Once I had explained the dream to myself,

I was content not to think about it any longer. Then a letter arrived from one of the nuns, Mother Miriam. She thanked me for the contribution and told me about her order, which was dedicated to prayer according to the Rule of St. Benedict. And then she asked me if I had thought about why I had written.

To say to myself, "Well, because of the dream" wasn't enough, not for a rational, secular Jew. And I knew that I was not being called to Christianity. Over the next couple of days, I thought seriously about what might be lacking in my diet. Finally, I wrote back: "I seem to feel that social action isn't enough."

By the time she responded, it was early January, and she sent me a book: *The Earth is the Lord's/The Sabbath,* by Abraham Joshua Heschel. Heschel was a 20th century Jewish theologian whose books were published by Paulist Press (the publishing house of the Paulist order) because his philosophical approach to God and Judaism was widely ignored by the Jewish community.

Holding the book, I swallowed hard. I had *met* Heschel. The supervisor on my first job was his niece. I had met him at her wedding.

My habit on work nights was to fall asleep after the 11:00 o' clock news, but that night I stayed awake reading the Heschel book. As a result, I instantly smelled smoke when the baseboard of my service porch caught fire at 1:00 a.m. I ran into the kitchen, saw the flames, filled a pot repeatedly with water and put the fire out.

The men from the gas company could find nothing wrong, could not even bring themselves to turn the water heater off, since it was behaving perfectly normally. They did, however, volunteer that the baseboard certainly looked as if it would have gone up "like a flash" if I hadn't been so quick to stop it. After they left, I sat on the floor staring at the baseboard with what I can only describe as bewilderment.

The fire was a shock, because it defied not just easy explanation, but any explanation. I began to see it as instructive, as a wake-up call that something else was going on.

✳

I wanted to give something to Mother Miriam for sending me the book. I had to find a way to say, "Thank you; I believe you just saved my life."

There were blizzards that year in Connecticut and I thought— I don't know why—that I might send some birdseed, because there would probably be birds on the grounds who might find it hard going. I went to the supermarket, bought 20 pounds of birdseed and mailed it off with a note saying, "Thank you for your caring. If you have any winter birds at the convent, please give them a meal on me."

The letter I received back was a revelation to me. It began, "Now I believe you have been connected to us for some purpose." It seemed that Mother Miriam had been feeding the birds at the place for seventeen years and had run out of birdseed the day before my package arrived. The 200 pounds she had ordered had not been delivered because of bad weather, but just as she thought she would have to turn the birds away hungry, the mail got through— with the birdseed.

Such commonplace things make up the world of the spirit.

For the next four years we wrote often. I stopped being so ignorant about nuns and Catholicism, because I started reading more about them. I learned that there were sisters in convents, but that "my" nun was in a monastery, because a monastery is any religious house that is completely enclosed.

In those days, about 1976, I was miserably lonely, a workaholic. Knowing I needed something. I started trying to pray. But it took a different form than

An even more surprising feature of the quantum potential was its implications for the nature of location. At the level of our everyday lives things have very specific locations, but Bohm's interpretation of quantum physics indicated that at the subquantum level, the level in which the quantum potential operated, location ceased to exist. All points in space became equal to all other points in space, and it was meaningless to speak of anything as being separate from anything else. Physicists call this property "nonlocality."

—Michael Talbot,
The Holographic Universe

I had imagined. I began sitting in the front window of my second-floor apartment late at night, looking out over the deserted street and yelling at God. I didn't worry about such considerations as awe or fear, and I certainly didn't count my blessings. I told God that if I was really in his thoughts, the way Mother Miriam said that I was, he ought to be able to see that I needed a man to share my life with. I had spent ten years dating, and it had led me nowhere but this windowsill.

I confess that I didn't tell Mother Miriam that I was yelling at God, because I thought she would be horrified, and I valued her friendship too much to risk that.

About six months after I started yelling, I met the man I married. Honestly, I couldn't have done better if I'd picked him out myself, but I know I didn't, because I never would have picked him out myself. The other reason that I know some sort of intervention was involved in the match is that, after we had been married for more than eight years, my husband told me that before he met me, he used to sit up at night and yell at God because he was all alone.

By the time he told me that, I was no longer surprised by what rational people call "coincidences." And now when someone says, "That was a coincidence," I agree; but a "coincidence" does not mean to me what it means to them. To most people a coincidence is an accident, a bit of what Jewish people might call *mazel* (luck). But to me, the word "co-incidence" means that something that is happening on this plane reflects what is happening on another plane as well. In hundreds of small ways, my experience with the nuns is wrapped up in coincidences. One example: The first time I actually traveled the 3,000 miles to see the monastery, I discovered that—while Mother Miriam was herself unavoidably absent—I had mutual friends with two of the other people visiting that day.

As a lapsed Catholic, my husband had been unwilling to spend any time at the monastery, for fear the nuns would seek to draw him back. His youthful experiences with nuns were deep and hostile. I said, "I don't believe they would do that."

"You don't know nuns," he said.

But I thought I did. Early in our friendship, I asked Mother Miriam, "Will we reach a point in out relationship when the only way for us to continue would be for me to become a Catholic? Because I can't."

Mother Miriam said, "We Catholics have brought people to Catholicism by the point of the sword too often in the past. You and I will be friends no matter what. But I'd like you to think about something. You are a Jewish woman, and you don't know what that means. Why don't you try and find out?"

After we'd been married for three years, in 1981, my husband went with me to the monastery for the Christmas season. When I met Mother Miriam at last, we threw our arms around each other and hugged as if we were soul-mates. The whole visit was so rich that we decided to return, yet my husband was uneasy. He couldn't shake the feeling that they would try to bring him back to a faith that he had lost.

I told this to Mother Miriam, who suggested once again that I look more closely into Judaism. But I thought I understood Judaism. I was dealing with experiences that did not easily submit themselves to rational understanding—what could Judaism possibly have to say about them?

Several weeks later, early one Sunday, I was flipping through the television channels and came upon someone saying, "The problem is that Jews don't pray in the synagogue." At the end, the speaker was identified as a Los Angeles rabbi. His congregation happened to be walking distance from my house.

Soon I met him, and found myself talking to him semi-coherently about needing something, and not knowing where to find it. I did not tell him I had been sent by a nun.

We are a childless couple, and I married well into my thirties. My husband and I were strongly dependent upon each other; if something had happened to one of us, the other would have been badly adrift. We needed support that was part of the mainstream of our rather ordinary lives.

When we had been married about six years, I proposed that I re-explore my Jewish roots, and if my husband would like to re-explore his Catholic ones, I would not be adverse to going to Mass. "I treasure being in the presence of faith," I had said to Mother Miriam. "It does not have to be my faith for me to treasure it."

My husband did not want to be a Catholic, however, so I didn't push him. Instead we started attending Jewish services together, after which we would discuss what happened, what difference being Jewish might make in our lives.

Then, on the eve of Yom Kipper in 1985, the rabbi spoke about how lonely it was to be an observant Jew. My husband responded to the loneliness and asked the rabbi if he would be able to attend his classes. I felt an amazing sense of pride when my husband, who graduated from high school with a GED from the Navy, began to study Hebrew. Three-quarters of the way through the class, he told me that he wanted to become a Jew.

Mother Miriam was ecstatic. I understood that she felt that faith was far better than no faith; she told me plainly, "It is infinitely better to be a good Jew than it is to be a bad Catholic."

That Christmas, when we were invited back to the monastery, my husband was very comfortable. He had made a decision, he believed the nuns would support him and he no longer feared being pulled back into a faith in which he did not belong.

When the Christmas tree was brought into the guest house, my husband was unwilling to help decorate it; the priest understood, but asked if I would. I set up the crèche and brought some hay in from the barn to lay in the manger scene. I put holly on the candles. Returning to the guest house, the priest looked around the common room and said to me, "Thank you so much for bringing Christmas."

For a moment or two, I couldn't deal with that. Then it occurred to me that if it hadn't been for a Jewish woman, there wouldn't be Christmas, and I said quietly, "You're welcome." I wondered if more Christians would ever feel grateful to Jews for bringing them Christmas, and if more Jews would ever be given the grace to be humbled by the thanks.

Mother Miriam and her sisters have taught me a great deal about gifts. The oldest nun, well into her eighties, took my hands once, emotionally, after Mass at Christmas, and said, "You don't know what a gift you give us by being here at this time. When Reverend Mother sings the genealogy of Jesus before Midnight Mass starts, every name she's reading is a Jewish name. You are a sign of continuity and truth to us."

I hadn't set out to be any such thing. But how, I asked myself, did I get here, from where I started? When I say, "I feel like I was lucky," the rabbi nods, and the priest shakes his head and corrects me, "You were blessed." When I ask, "Why me?" the rabbi shrugs, and Mother Miriam says, "Why not you?"

That is the journey I have made, pushed, I think, by more than mere chance. I have learned to say prayers of thanks and prayers of praise, and I don't yell at God any longer (though I know it remains an option). I did not come back to Judaism because it gave me a revelation—but I know that *something* did. I did not come back because I believed in the miracles of the Bible and my tradition, but because I had been brought, after all, to believe that there are such things as miracles. All we have to do is recognize them when they happen to us. And I owe this growth to the loving kindness of Catholics.

As a rational person, I know I can prove nothing, but I no longer need to. I am far happier now than I was when the story began. I also think that I am, wonder of wonders, a better Jew than I used to be. Thank God.

Rhoda Blecker, a former Jewish co-chair of the Los Angeles Catholic-Jewish Women's Conference, is an author and lecturer in the area of interfaith relations.

*

Perhaps God lies not in the plethora of faulty symbols that men have concocted through time, but in the common reality these metaphors clumsily seek to express. Beneath it all, every faith boils down to this: there is a moral power governing the universe, a power whose primary requirements are that we return its love and treat our neighbors with kindness. As for what this power is and precisely how we can do its bidding, *that* is where the faiths diverge.

—Jonah Blank, *Arrow of the Blue-Skinned God:
Retracing the Ramayana Through India*

JUDY MAYFIELD

✦ ✦ ✦

The Guy at the End
of the Bed

The inner voyage begins at home.

THE VEIL BETWEEN THE VISIBLE AND "INVISIBLE" FOR ME HAS always been quite thin. It is not uncommon for me to see people or faces of strangers looking at me, sometimes a lot of them. They seem to look and then just wander off. Sometimes I meet them later, more often I never see them again, and I seldom understand who they are or what they want, so it wasn't unusual for me to see someone at the foot of my bed watching me one evening a few years ago.

My husband John was reading to me out loud. I looked at the foot of our bed and saw a man there. He was about 5'2" with dark skin, a brown sash over one shoulder and wrapped around his body to his knees. He was barefoot and had a staff in his left hand. He was kind of dusty, and seemed to have come from the desert. He stood watching me for about fifteen minutes then began to shift his weight slightly impatiently from one foot to the other.

I realized that I hadn't been listening to John for a while so I said, "I'm sorry dear, I just realized that I'm not listening to you. There is a man standing at the foot of the bed who has drawn my attention." I went on to describe him to John.

John said, "Well, talk to him."

I said dreamily, "Oh yeah," but I again sat for five minutes and couldn't think of a thing to say. I finally told John I didn't know what to say.

He said, "Ask him what he wants." So I clumsily did this and the man replied, "Tell me about the photo on your refrigerator."

In an aloof manner I said, "Oh, it's nothing. John and I just like it." (This was a lie!)

When the man turned and started to walk away, I quickly collected myself and began to tell him the truth of what the photo— an elderly tribal couple in the buff—really meant. It was a joke of sorts, but not really. John and I feel it is the two of us when we grow old: naked again, sitting on the earth with nothing but our connection to the universe, the earth, the trees, the wind, the creatures, the living spirit. These are our relations—our family—our Soul's "truth." All of this "stuff" around us is nothing and will be nothing but the soil another day, so here we sit on our truth, the soil, "God's kingdom." The man turned around and came back.

Again I am tongue-tied. John prompts, "Ask him what he wants."

The visitor laughs deeply and spontaneously, and calls me by a name I don't understand. It has a guttural "click" in it, and I can't repeat it so we will call me X—.

The man says, "It's good to greet people when they come to visit!" He thinks we are all so funny when we put on white skin, we don't even remember our relations! He laughs and hits

*he palm at the
end of the mind,
Beyond the last thought, rises
In the bronze distance,*

*A gold-feathered bird
Sings in the palm, without
human meaning,
Without human feeling,
a foreign song.*

*You know then that it is
not the reason
that makes us happy or unhappy.
The bird sings. Its feathers shine.*

*The palm stands on the
edge of space.
The wind moves slowly in
the branches.
The bird's fire-fangled feathers
dangle down.*

—Wallace Stevens, "Of Mere Being,"
Opus Posthumous

his stick on the ground stomping his foot joyously. "It's okay to say Hello or Good Morning! It's *good* to greet people when they come to visit. Just say, *hello, welcome!*

"I traveled all the way across the spirit world to visit and you should have felt me coming many miles away and been prepared to receive me. When you didn't greet me, I didn't know what to do—should I leave or stay or what, so I just waited." Then he realized how much we have forgotten, that we don't even remember simple courtesies, simple greetings to our relations.

He motions for me to follow him.

I say, "Oh, no, not without my hiking boots."

He laughs hysterically again and says, " Yes, yes this is good. Wear your hiking boots, and bring your air conditioning also." He finds this very, very funny and can't believe this is really how X— is in white skin! So off we go to the desert—me in my pajamas, hiking boots, with a round invisible bubble of air conditioning around me. He is barefoot. He thinks it's funny, but he also accepts this "white skin" way of being quite respectfully.

He tells me I must walk the earth and touch the mother everywhere—the leaves, the stones, the trees, the earth—and tell her out loud that I love her. Everyone used to talk to their relations. The trees and stones are lonely, they need to hear our voice. We must touch the earth everyday just like we touch our loved ones. We have lost our relationships—even to each other. All of life is tribal—the trees, the birds, the coyotes, the deer, the fish, the people—all of life is tribal. We have lost our relationships because we harbor too many lies and secrets. We shut off telepathy to house our secrets and lies and then we are lonely.

Even people who live in the same house are lonely because they can't hear each other's thoughts, there is no communication. All of creation is tribal and inter-related by nature. This is the natural way. We talk to each other. We say, "Good morning." More laughter.

John says, "Ask how I can see him too."

This brings much laughter as the man stomps his foot and stick to the ground. "You don't need to see me! I come to X— to be seen. X— sees me and tells you what I say. You are a med-

icine man, she is the seer. We are tribal, we rely on each others'
gifts. People want to be all things themselves—the healer, the
hunter, the seer, the herbalist, the food preparer, the musician.
This is too much. We are tribal. These things are meant to be
shared. It's too much to be everything. It makes people sick and
lonely. In the old days everyone talked to each other—the wind,
the rain, the wild ones. We all talked to each other. The water
came when it was needed, the clouds parted and let the sun in.
Everybody knew what to do because we communicated. Now
everybody is lonely. The plants, the trees, and the stones all com-
plain that people don't love them anymore. Nobody talks to
them. Nobody prays."

After a period of silence, John asks, "How can I help heal
the earth?"

The man laughs and jumps up and down with great joy and
amusement. "You are not so big, you are very small. You must
ask your mother what she wants you to do and then do these
things. She will tell you what her needs are. You have a very big
ego sometimes. X— has a very small one. Both of these are illusion. They are the ego trickster game. Too big, too small, they
both cripple you and make you stumble. This is all a big joke, it
doesn't exist! Too big, too small, this is a children's game. The Ego
Trickster." He laughs again and then is very serious.

"We are leaving now and very few of you are left. You must pray
higher. Pray for the thousands of people who sleep. All people used
to pray. Now those of you who remember must pray the prayers
for everyone. Stand on the mother, touch her, let her prayers come
through your feet and go a thousand directions. Let the mother
play you like a flute. Pray the mother's prayers and then all of creation, all of life, will be well loved and prayed for. You must pray
hard and big and fill this world with light so that when the skies
crack open and the earth cracks open, the prayers fill in the cracks
and darkness cannot seep in. These things are very important now.
There are not many of you left.

"When you pray high you connect with all the others who pray
high. Do not pray little small prayers. Do not pray needy prayers.

Wake up and say 'Thank you for this new day! Thank you for this sun that shines and rain that falls, for this new food and shelter. Thank you for my *new purpose this day.* Thank you for my loved ones and all of our good health. Thank you for my ancestral rela-
tionships. Bless all of these things.' Then pray *very high for the whole universe.* This is important every-day. Many people are hungry, many people suffer. *Pray for these things every day!* Do not pray on the man's face. Do not pray sick prayers, this is very bad. *Pray very high prayers.* Stand in a good place and let mother play you like an instrument. This is how it's meant to be.

> *I wished it would all last forever. But it didn't, and finally we were back to the swelling hills of home, bosky with copses and stringy streams and things with associations, leaving all the wild places behind for a while.*
>
> *But happy with a thought.*
>
> *"That the wildest places of all are deep within and there's no end to the exploration and enjoyment of their mysteries and magic."*
>
> *And that is sufficient.*
>
> *For the moment.*
>
> —David Yeadon, *The Back of Beyond: Travels to the Wildest Places of the Earth*

"X— needs to quit letting her ego trick her into being needed. X— spends too much time help-ing others when they don't need to be helped and not enough time alone to listen and make prayers. X— needs to lay her belly on the earth and spit out all the dead babies from her heart. Spit all of those dead babies and let the mother heal you. We are needed now. There is no time for the Ego Trickster to play with us.

"*Smash the talking box! It steals people's spirits and turns them into robots! There is no time for these thing now.*

"Many of my people are starving to death. Our families right now on this earth! Much prayer is needed. All of this senseless! The Ego Trickster and the talking box have taken people over and stolen their spirits. This is not good. Make your high prayers very strong. *Do not mention these evil things. Pray above them!*

"When the sky and the earth break open like a cracked egg there must be enough prayers to hold the darkness out and seal the cracks. Otherwise the darkness can seep in and the world will be very, very bad for many thousands of years if this happens.

"Ego is not a truth place, it is a big trickster—like a big joke we play on ourselves. There is no time for this play now. We need to remember our ancestral relations and welcome them. We pray for them and they pray for us. Circles of light. This is how life forms, in goodness and prayer.

"Learn to greet each other (more laughter) it's so simple…."

It was getting late and I was having a hard time staying awake. I told him, "I'm very tired."

He very sweetly said, "Yes, Dream Walker, it is time for your sleep now," and turned and walked towards his people waiting for him. They walked off together in the desert, singing the most exquisite four-part harmony, peacefully, lovingly.

Judy Mayfield is a former family therapist and director of a drug abuse crisis intervention program. Her interest in American Indian spirituality led her to the Nevada desert where she was initiated into sacred ways by a Cherokee Medicine Man. After moving to Northern California, she continued her studies with a Creek-Shawnee pipe holder who led Sweat Lodge ceremonies in the Lakota Sioux tradition. Judy has also worked in the field of parapsychology and hypnotic regression, and was the clinic director of a natural childbirth center. Now she lives and works with her husband in Grass Valley, California, where they have a chiropractic healing practice.

*

Renowned supercomputer designer Seymour Cray would do much of his computer design work on a fresh pad of engineering paper, frequently going through an entire pad in a day.

There have been many legends that have grown up around Mr. Cray's reclusive work habits which frequently went late into the night.

Mr. Rollwagen recounts one story of a customer who visited Mr. Cray's home in Chippewa Falls. When the man asked what were the secrets of his success, Mr. Cray said, "Well, we have elves here and they help me."

When the visitor, a French scientist, expressed his astonishment, Mr. Cray took him to look at a tunnel that he had dug under his home. Shored up with four-by-four cedar logs, the tunnel appeared to go in random directions, at one point going straight up into Mr. Cray's lawn. (Mr. Cray later explained to Mr. Rollwagen that the tunnel had gone straight up because one day it had collapsed while he was digging and a tree in his front yard had fallen into the tunnel.)

Mr. Cray explained to his visitor that he would work at his home on computer design problems for three hours at a stretch. When he reached a technical stumbling block, he would then retire to the tunnel where he would dig for an hour.

"While I'm digging in the tunnel the elves will often come to me with solutions to my problems," he said.

—John Markoff, "A Salute to Seymour Cray"

RICHARD GOODMAN

⋆ ⋆ ⋆

Instincts

*In the South of France, many
things are revealed.*

I RECOMMEND THAT ALL BACHELORS HAVE A GARDEN. IT WILL GIVE
them, in some small way, the experience of being a parent. I make
analogies to sex and birth and children when I talk about a garden
because they come naturally. In a garden, you put your seeds into
the earth, into the mother earth. They germinate, they grow, they
flower—like children. After they begin to grow, you worry about
them, you tend them constantly, you fret over their maladies. Some
are stronger, bigger and healthier than others. That concerns you.
And mystifies you.

I reacted to my garden strongly, and in ways I hadn't foreseen.
At various moments, I felt responsible, protective, anxious, proud. I
also felt mournful, impotent, defiant and lost. I remember once
when my tomato plants were sick. Or at least they looked sick to
me. Their leaves were withered and curled and hung limply all
down the long stems, no longer the vivid things they used to be. In
my anxiousness, I went about the village and sought the advice of
men I knew, and I also went and talked to some I hadn't met before—something I would have been too shy to do before I had a
garden. But my connection made the indulgence of shyness impossible. I had sick plants. I needed to make them well.

These men took my problem seriously, but they ended up confounding me. I'll never forget talking to them in the square in a small shaded area next to the town hall on a hot July afternoon. These men of the earth, doctors of the soil, gave me conflicting diagnoses and advice.

When I presented my situation to them, Albin Polge, the husky, near-sighted farmer who happened also to be the mayor of St. Sébastien, asked me, "Did you treat your plants, Richard?"

"Yes, yes," I said. "With sulphur."

"You mean," he said, taking off his glasses and wiping the telescope-thick lenses, "you didn't use sulphite, too?"

"*Sulphite*? Don't you mean sulphur?"

"No. No. Sulphite. You must use it." He put his glasses back on. Then he looked at me carefully. "That may be the problem. A sickness."

Several of the men nodded along with his words.

> *The author made up the name St.-Sébastien to protect the privacy of its inhabitants—but the town where he lived with his girlfriend, Iggy, is real.*
>
> —SO'R, JO'R, and TO'R

"No, no," Monsieur Massot said to Albin. "It's not that." Monsieur Massot was a short, mustached man with a soft, word-caressing voice. He was a retired railroad worker who lived at the edge of the village with his wife, and he had a large garden. I used to pass by it on my walks, and I would often talk to him about the things he was growing. His advice was to be reckoned with. He turned from Albin to me. "It's the sun, Richard. The heat has dried all the leaves. It's happened before." He raised his eyebrows upward. "The sun is much too strong this year."

Even as he spoke, the sun's great heat penetrated into our shaded area. The only place where you were safe was inside the houses, behind the thick, cooling walls of stone.

"But," I said desperately, "can't I do anything about it?"

"No. Nothing," he said, with a kind of papal finality.

I couldn't accept that. "Not even if I water a lot more?"

"No." He shook his head. "It's too late."

I groaned.

"But don't worry, Richard," he said. "It won't harm your tomatoes. They will still come."

"Are you sure?"

"Yes. Certain."

As these men disagreed—there was even a third hypothesis about the type of soil I had—I remember feeling edgy and wondering, Can't you villagers agree *for once*? We're talking about my tomato plants!

My garden brought out a stronger instinct in me. Protectiveness. Those who feel a general love of all animals, or who are against the abuse of animals, should have a garden. They might modify their views. I remember one morning—and this after my garden was quite far along and very pretty, too—I found traces of a mole, *une taupe*. His tunneling wove in and out of my lettuce plants crazily, like a drunken driver. Apparently he had eaten nothing, because all the plants were still there, sitting in a row, healthy. (As Iggy said, "Maybe he didn't realize it was a garden.") But seeing that long, narrow mound of disturbed earth next to my plants ignited me. I thought, If I ever catch him (how, in God's name?), you can forget about the ASPCA—or whatever they call it here in France—I will personally bash his brains in. He will *not* wreck my garden.

And I would have killed him, too. Without remorse. Now, I suppose there may be methods by which you can keep a mole out of your garden without resorting to murder. But I didn't care. At that moment, protecting my garden was more important to me than saving his mangy little French hide, and I wasn't going to go out of my way to insure his well-being over that of my plants. And that was what made the feeling so exciting and free of moral doubt: it was an instinct.

Sometimes my instincts not only surprised me, they made me laugh, too. On my way to the garden one morning, I spotted a pile of horse manure on the road, a product of some adventurer from the riding stable in the nearby village of Boissac. Without hesitating—without thinking, really—I stopped the car, scooped the flaky, brown lumps into my bucket and zoomed off. Had I no pride? Not when it came to my garden. This stuff was *gold*. Pure gold. I'm sure no bird of prey could have been more satisfied bringing the chewed-up carcass of a field mouse to its fledglings than I did when I arrived with my bucketful of manure. I remember saying aloud to my plants: "Have I got something special for you today. *C'est la merde*."

When you have a garden, you constantly ask yourself, like a parent, the question *why?* and *why not?* I remember one eggplant, small and emaciated—it never really was healthy—was about to give up the ghost. I slowly uprooted it; it dangled in my hand, already dead. And just down the row, eggplants I had planted at the same time, bought from the same nursery, were big and strong as American farm boys. Why? or, why *it*, and not them? Was it me? Was it the soil? Was it the weather? Disease? Insects? I never did find out. No matter how much I cared, I wasn't omnipotent. Eventually, I just had to accept.

> *We can think of no better symbol of man's earthly life than that of the seed planted in the darkness of the earth in order that it may grow into the perfect flower. The perfect flower, the archetypal flower, is created first in the mind of God, and then the seed is planted in the earth to grow to fullness. So is it with you, who are as seeds planted in physical form to grow towards the light until you become perfect sons and daughters of God—the perfect archetypal God-man which God held in His mind in the beginning.*
>
> —White Eagle, *Spiritual Unfoldment 1: How to Discover the Invisible Worlds and Find the Source of Healing*

The garden taught me that not only wasn't I all-knowing or all-powerful, but that it was a mistake to try to be. I could put the seeds into the ground. I could water. I could fertilize. I could grate. I could weed. But that was about it. The rest was up to them. Sometimes that was hard to accept. I had to be constantly doing something for, or to, my plants. I couldn't accept the idea that every bit of progress wasn't in some small measure due to me. Or to put it another way, I couldn't believe that my plants could, for long stretches at a time, do without me. And very well. I have seen meddling parents behave much the same way toward their children. Sometimes you have to let go.

All the while I felt protective toward my plants, but once they began producing their ripe fruit, my attitude changed. In a sense, my job was done. I had given and now I was ready to receive. Gardening is, in its perfect state, a true give-and-take relationship. Along with this natural shift came a different set of feelings, none of them less strong. This final hour produced moments of great glory. I remember the time when I could count on something being ripe, and ready to pick, every day. And when I could get up in the morning knowing that after I went to the garden I would have something to bring to Iggy. That was a wonderful feeling. It was primitive, and it went very deep. It wasn't stronger than the urge to defend what was mine, but in a sense it was more profound, a calm, masculine instinct, resonating from my soul.

I remember, early on in the gathering process, returning from the garden one morning with a bucketful of vegetables—lettuce, cucumber, tomatoes, zucchini, even a small melon. Driving back to the village, I glanced over at the many-colored bounty from time to time, just for pleasure. That glance was the reward of months of labor. When I came home, Iggy had a cup of coffee for me and a piece of fresh, buttered bread. I showed her the vegetables, many still caked with damp earth. "Oh, *great!*" she said, her eyes wide with excitement. She smiled her open, sunny smile and came to me, putting her arms around my sweaty shoulders. I sat down and took a sip of the coffee. I felt proud. I was a provider.

Richard Goodman lives in New York. He has apprenticed as a French chef and has been involved in writing and producing films, but his main interest now is in writing books. He is the author of French Dirt: The Story of a Garden in the South of France *from which this story was excerpted.*

✳

The greatest poverty is not to live
In a physical world, to feel that one's desire
Is too difficult to tell from despair. Perhaps,
After death, the non-physical people, in paradise,
Itself non-physical, may, by chance, observe

The green corn gleaming and experience
The minor of what we feel. The adventurer
In humanity has not conceived of a race
Completely physical in a physical world.
The green corn gleams and the metaphysicals
Lie sprawling in majors of the August heat,
The rotund emotions, paradise unknown.
This is the thesis scrivened in delight,
The reverberating psalm, the right chorale.

One might have thought of sight, but who could think
Of what it sees, for all the ill it sees?
Speech found the ear, for all the evil sound,
But the dark italics it could not propound.
And out of what one sees and hears and out
Of what one feels, who could have thought to make
So many selves, so many sensuous worlds,
As if the air, the mid-day air, was swarming
With the metaphysical changes that occur,
Merely in living as and where we live.

—Wallace Stevens, *"Esthetique du Mal"*

* * *

The Serpent

What was that about an apple?

MY JOURNEY HAD COME BACK AROUND TO THE CONGREGATION on Sand Mountain, the remnant of Glenn Summerford's flock that had left the converted service station on Wood's Cove Road in Scottsboro and then met under a brush arbor in back of J. L. Dyal's house until the weather got too cold. After worshiping for a while in the basement of an old motel, they finally found a church for sale on the mountain. It was miles from nowhere, in the middle of a hay field south of Section, Alabama, home of Tammy Little, Miss Alabama 1984. The nearest dot on the map, though, was Macedonia, a crossroads consisting of a filling station, a country store, and a junk emporium. It was not the

G lendel Buford Summerford was the pastor of The Church of Jesus with Signs Following. A man given to fighting, drinking, and philandering, he was arrested and charged with attempting to murder his wife Darlene by making her stick her hand into a cage which contained a canebrake rattlesnake. Summerford, though drunk, had the presence of mind to force his wife to write a suicide note at gunpoint. She survived. As author Dennis Covington covered the trial, he discovered the bizarre and compelling world of holiness snake handling. Summerford was later sentenced to 99 years in jail.

—SO'R, JO'R, and TO'R

kind of place you'd visit of your own accord. You'd have to be led
there. In fact, Macedonia had gotten its name from the place in the
Bible that Paul had been called to go to in a dream. Paul's first
European converts to Christianity had been in Macedonia. But
that was, you know, a long time ago and in another place.

Glenn Summerford's cousins, Billy and Jimmy, negotiated the
deal for the church. Billy was friendly and loose limbed, with a
narrow red face and buck teeth. He'd worked mostly as a carpenter, but he'd also sold coon dogs. Jimmy was less amiable but more
compact. Between them, they must have been persuasive. They
got the church for two thousand dollars. A guy down the road
had offered five thousand, Billy said, but the owner had decided
to sell it to them. "God was working in that one," he concluded.

It was called the Old Rock House Holiness Church, in spite of
the fact that it wasn't made of rock. But it was old in contrast to
the brick veneer churches out on Highway 35, the ones with green
indoor-outdoor carpet in the vestibules and blinking U-HAUL IT
signs out front.

The Old Rock House Holiness Church had been built in 1916,
a few years before Dozier Edmonds first saw people take up serpents in Jackson County, at a church in Sauty Bottom, down by
Saltpeter Cave. I'd met Dozier during the brush-arbor meetings.
A rail-thin old man with thick glasses and overalls, he was the
father-in-law of J. L. Dyal and the husband of Burma, the snake-
handling twin. Dozier said he'd seen men get bit in that church in
Sauty Bottom. They didn't go to a doctor, just swelled up a little
bit. He also remembered a Holiness boy at the one-room school
who would fall into a trance, reach into the potbellied stove, and
get himself a whole handful of hot coals. The teacher would have
to tell the boy to put them back. There was a Baptist church in
those days called Hell's Half Acre, Dozier said. They didn't take
up serpents, but they'd do just about anything else. They were
called Buckeye Baptists. They'd preach and pray till midnight, then
gamble and fight till dawn. One time a man rode a horse into the
church, right up to the pulpit. Out of meanness, Dozier said.
Everything was different then. "They used to tie the mules up to

a white mulberry bush in the square," he said. Why, he remembered when Scottsboro itself was nothing but a mud hole. When the carnival came through, the elephants were up to their bellies in mud. There wasn't even a road up Sand Mountain until Dozier helped build one. And it seemed like the Civil War had just occurred.

Dozier came from a family of sharecroppers who lived on the property of a famous Confederate veteran named Mance. He had a bullet hole through his neck. He'd built his own casket. Every Easter, Colonel Mance invited the children of the families who lived on his property to come to the big house for an egg hunt. One Easter, he wanted the children to see what he'd look like when he was dead, so he lay down in the casket and made the children march around it. Some of the grown-ups had to help get him out. It was a pine casket with metal handles on it, Dozier said. Colonel Mance eventually died, but he wasn't buried in the casket he'd made. He'd taken that thing apart years before and given the handles to the families who lived on his property, to use as knockers on the doors of their shacks.

That was the kind of place Sand Mountain had been when the Old Rock House Holiness Church was in its heyday. By the time the Summerford brothers bought it in the winter of 1993, it had fallen onto hard times. Didn't even have a back door. Paper wasps had built nests in the eaves. The green shingles on the outside were cracked, and the paint on the window sills had just about peeled off. Billy Summerford and some of the other men from the congregation repaired and restored the church as best they could. It'd be another year, though, before they could get around to putting in a bathroom. In the meantime, there would be an outhouse for the women and a bunch of trees for the men. The church happened to be sited in the very center of a grove of old oak trees. Fields of hay surrounded the grove and stretched to the horizon. As you approached the church along a dirt road during summer heat, the oak grove looked like a dark island in the middle of a shimmering sea of gold and green.

That's the way it looked to me, anyway, on a bright Sunday morning in late June, six months after the Summerfords had bought the church, when Jim and I drove up from Birmingham for their first annual homecoming. Brother Carl had invited us by phone and given us directions. He was scheduled to preach at the homecoming. Other handlers were coming from all over— from East Tennessee and South Georgia, from the mountains of Kentucky and the scrub lands of the Florida panhandle. If we hadn't had Carl's directions, we'd never have found the place. The right turn off the paved road from Macedonia was unmarked. It was one of several gravel roads that angled off into the distance. Where it crossed another paved road, there finally was a sign, made of cardboard and mounted at waist level on a wooden stake. After that, the gravel turned to dirt. Dust coated the jimson-weed. The passionflowers were in bloom, and the blackberries had begun to ripen in the heat. There were no houses on this road, and no sound except for cicadas, a steady din, like the sound of approaching rain.

For once, Jim and I were early. We stepped up on a cement block to get through the back doorway of the church. The door itself was off its hinges, and none of the windows in the church had screens. There were no cushions on the pews and no ornaments of any kind, except a portrait of Jesus etched into a mirror behind the pulpit and a vase of plastic flowers on the edge of the piano bench, where a boy with a withered hand sat staring at the keys. We took our places on a back pew and watched the handlers arrive. They greeted each other with the holy kiss, women with women, men with men, as prescribed by Paul in *Romans 16*. Among them was the legendary Punkin Brown, the evangelist who I'd been told would wipe the sweat off his brow with rattlesnakes. Jamie Coots from Kentucky and Allen Williams from Tennessee were also there. They sat beside Punkin on the deacons' bench. All three were young and heavyset, the sons of preachers, and childhood friends. Punkin and Jamie both wore scowls, as though they were waiting for somebody to cross their paths in an unhappy way. Allen Williams, though, looked serene. Allen's father had died drinking strychnine in 1973, and his brother had died of snakebite in 1991. Maybe he thought he didn't have anything more to lose. Or maybe he was just reconciled to losing everything he had. Within six months of sitting together on the deacons' bench at the Old Rock House Church, Jamie, Allen, and Punkin would all be bit.

The church continued to fill with familiar faces, many from what used to be The Church of Jesus with Signs Following in Scottsboro, and the music began without an introduction of any kind. James Hatfield of Old Straight Creek, a Trinitarian church on the mountain, was on drums. My red-haired friend Cecil Esslinder from Scottsboro was on guitar, grinning and tapping his feet. Cecil's wife, Carolyn, stood in the very middle of the congregation, facing backward, as was her habit, to see who might come in the back way. Also in the congregation were Bobbie Sue Thompson, twins Burma and Erma, J. L. Dyal and his wife and in-laws, and just about the whole Summerford clan. The only ones missing were Charles and Aline McGlocklin. Charles was still recovering from neck surgery on an old injury, but I knew from the conversation we'd had at New Hope that even if he'd been well, he wouldn't have come.

One woman I didn't recognize told me she was from Detroit, Michigan. This came as some surprise, and her story seemed equally improbable. She said her husband used to work in the casinos in Las Vegas, and when he died she moved to Alabama and started handling rattlesnakes at the same church on Lookout Mountain where the lead singer of the group Alabama used to handle. "Didn't you see the photo?" she asked. "It was in the *National Enquirer*."

I told her I'd missed that one.

Children were racing down the aisles. High foreheads. Eyes far apart. Gaps between their front teeth. They all looked like miniature Glenn Summerfords. Maybe they were. He had at least seven children by his first wife, and all of them were old enough to have children of their own. I started to wonder if there were any bad feelings among the Summerfords about the way Brother Carl Porter had refused to let them send the church offerings to Glenn in prison.

About that time, Brother Carl himself walked in with a serpent box containing the biggest rattlesnake I'd ever seen. Carl smelled of Old Spice and rattlesnake and something else underneath: a pleasant smell, like warm bread and apples. I associated it with the Holy Ghost. The handlers had told me that the Holy Ghost had a smell, a "sweet savor," and I had begun to think I could detect it on people and in churches, even in staid, respectable churches like the one I went to in Birmingham. Anyway, that was what I smelled on Brother Carl that day as he talked about the snake in the box. "I just got him today," he said. "He's never been in church before."

Carl looked over his glasses at me and smiled. He held the serpent box up to my face and tapped the screen until the snake started rattling good.

"Got your name on him," he said to me.

A shiver went up my spine, but I just shook my head and grinned.

"Come on up to the front," he said. I followed him and sat on the first pew next to J. L. Dyal, but I made a mental note to avoid Carl's eyes during the service and to stay away from that snake of his.

Billy Summerford's wife, Joyce, led the singing. She was a big woman with a voice that wouldn't quit. *"Remember how it felt, when you walked out of the wilderness, walked out of the wilderness, walked out of the wilderness. Remember how it felt, when you walked out of the wilderness…"* It was one of my favorite songs because it had a double meaning now. There was the actual wilderness in the Old Testament that the Israelites were led out of, and the spiritual wilderness that was its referent, the condition of being lost. But there was also the wilderness that the New World became for my father's people. I don't mean the mountains, I mean the America that grew up around them, that tangled thicket of the heart.

"Remember how it felt, when you walked out of the wilderness…" My throat tightened as I sang. I remembered how it had felt when I'd sobered up in 1983. It's not often you get a second chance at life like that. And I remembered the births of my girls, the children Vicki and I had thought we'd never be able to have. Looking around at the familiar faces in the congregation, I figured they were thinking about their own wildernesses and how they'd been delivered out of them. I was still coming out of mine. It was a

measure of how far I'd come, that I'd be moved nearly to tears in a rundown Holiness church on Sand Mountain. But my restless and stubborn intellect was still intact. It didn't like what it saw, a crowd of men dancing up to the serpent boxes, unclasping the lids, and taking out the poisonous snakes. Reason told me it was too early in the service. The snakes hadn't been prayed over enough. There hadn't even been any preaching yet, just Billy Summerford screaming into a microphone while the music swirled around us like a fog. But the boys from Tennessee and Kentucky had been hungry to get into the boxes. Soon, Punkin Brown was shouting at his snake, a big black-phase timber rattler that he had draped around his neck. Allen Williams was offering his copperhead up like a sacrifice, hands outstretched. But Brother Carl had the prize, and everyone seemed to know it. It was a yellow-phase timber, thick and melancholy, as big as timber rattlers come. Carl glanced at me, but I wouldn't make eye contact with him. I turned away. I walked to the back of the church and took a long drink of water from the bright yellow cooler propped up against a portrait of Jesus with his head on fire.

"Who knows what this snake is thinking?" Carl shouted. "God knows! God understands the mind of this snake!" And when I turned back around, Carl had laid the snake down and was treading barefoot on it from tail to head, as though he were walking a tightrope. Still, the snake didn't bite. I had heard about this, but never seen it before. The passage was from *Luke: Behold, I give unto you power to tread on serpents and scorpions, and over all the power of the enemy: and nothing shall by any means hurt you*. Then Carl picked the snake back up and draped it around his neck. The snake seemed to be looking for a way out of its predicament. Carl let it nuzzle into his shirt. Then the snake pulled back and cocked its head, as if in preparation to strike Carl's chest. Its head was as big as a child's hand.

Help him, Jesus! someone yelled above the din. Instead of striking, the snake started to climb Carl's sternum toward his collarbone. It went up the side of his neck and then lost interest and fell back against his chest.

The congregation was divided into two camps now, the men to the left, with the snakes, the women to the right, with each other. In front of Carl, one of the men suddenly began jumping straight up and down, as though he were on a pogo stick. Down the aisle he went and around the sanctuary. When he returned, he collapsed at Carl's feet. One of the Summerford brothers attended him there by soaking his handkerchief with olive oil and dabbing it against the man's forehead until he sat up and yelled, "Thank God!"

In the meantime, in the corner where the women had gathered, Joyce Summerford's sister, Donna, an attractive young woman in a lime green dress, was laboring in the spirit with a cataleptic friend. She circled the friend, eyeing her contortions carefully, and then, as if fitting her into an imaginary dress, she clothed her in the spirit with her hands, an invisible tuck here, an invisible pin there, making sure the spirit draped well over the flailing arms. It took her a while. Both of the women were drenched in sweat and stuttering in tongues by the time they finished.

"They say we've gone crazy!" Brother Carl shouted above the chaos. He was pacing in front of the pulpit, the enormous rattlesnake balanced now across his shoulder. "Well, they're right!" he cried. "I've gone crazy! I've gone Bible crazy! I've got the papers here to prove it!" And he waved his worn Bible in the air. "Some people say we're just a bunch of fanatics!"

Amen, Thank God.

"Well, we are! Hai-i-salemos-ah-chan-ne-hi-yee! Whew! That last one nearly took me out of here!"

It's not true that you become used to the noise and confusion of a snake-handling Holiness service. On the contrary, you

> *There is a kind of free-association with your higher self that involves speaking the first sounds that come to you. Visionary author Solara refers to this as Star Language in her book,* How to Live Large on a Small Planet. *You might look at your dog and shout,* "e komo ney aya yi" *and it is a kind of primal meaning between souls. Your dog will love and understand star language. Solara sometimes opens business meetings with this kind of utterance. Everybody loosens up in a hurry. Speaking in tongues operates on a similar principle.*
>
> —Sean O'Reilly, "Mind Jumping"

become enmeshed in it. It is theater at its most intricate—improvisational, spiritual jazz. The more you experience it, the more attentive you are to the shifts in the surface and the dark shoals underneath. For every outward sign, there is a spiritual equivalent. When somebody falls to his knees, a specific problem presents itself, and the others know exactly what to do, whether it's oil for a healing, or a prayer cloth thrown over the shoulders, or a devil that needs to be cast out. The best, of course, the simplest and cleanest, is when someone gets the Holy Ghost for the first time. The younger the worshiper, the easier it seems to be for the Holy Ghost to descend and speak—lips loosened, tongue flapping, eyes rolling backward in the head. It transcends the erotic when a thirteen-year-old girl gets the Holy Ghost. The older ones often take time. I once saw an old man whose wife had gotten the Holy Ghost at a previous service. He wanted it bad for himself, he said. Brother Charles McGlocklin started praying with him before the service even started, and all through it, the man was in one attitude or another at the front of the church—now lying spread-eagled on the floor, while a half dozen men prayed over him and laid on hands, now up and running from one end of the sanctuary to the other, now twirling, now swooning, now collapsing once again on the floor, his eyes like the eyes of a horse that smells smoke, the unknown tongue spewing from his mouth. He got the Holy Ghost at last! He got the Holy Ghost! you think, until you see him after the service eating a pimiento cheese sandwich downstairs. His legs are crossed. He's brushing the crumbs from his lap. He agrees it was a good service all right, but it sure would have been better if he'd only gotten the Holy Ghost. You can never get enough of the Holy Ghost. Maybe that's what he means. You can never exhaust the power when the Spirit comes down, not even when you take up a snake, not even when you take up a dozen of them. The more faith you expend, the more power is released. It's an inexhaustible, eternally renewable resource. It's the only power some of these people have.

So the longer you witness it, unless you just don't get into the spontaneous and unexpected, the more you become a part to it. I did, and the handlers could tell. They knew before I did what was going to happen. They saw me angling in. They were already making room for me in front of the deacons' bench. As I said, I'd always been drawn to danger. Alcohol. Psychedelics. War. If it made me feel good, I'd do it. I was always up for a little trip. I figured if I could trust my guide, I'd be all right. I'd come back to earth in one piece. I wouldn't really lose my mind. That's what I thought, anyway. I couldn't be an astronaut, but there were other things I could do and be. So I got up there in the middle of the handlers. J. L. Dyal, dark and wiry, was standing on my right; a clean-cut boy named Steve Frazier on my left. Who was it going to be? Carl's eyes were saying, you. And yes, it was the big rattler, the one with my name on it, acrid-smelling, carnal, alive. And the look in Carl's eyes seemed to change as he approached me. He was embarrassed. The snake was all he had, his eyes seemed to say. But as low as it was, as repulsive, if I took it, I'd be possessing the sacred. Nothing was required except obedience. Nothing had to be given up except my own will. This was the moment. I didn't stop to think about it. I just gave in. I stepped forward and took the snake with both hands. Carl released it to me. I turned to face the congregation and lifted the rattlesnake up toward the light. It was moving like it wanted to get up even higher, to climb out of that church and into the air. And it was exactly as the handlers had told me. I felt no fear. The snake seemed to be an extension of myself. And suddenly there seemed to be nothing in the room but me and the snake. Everything else had disappeared. Carl, the congregation, Jim—all gone, all faded to white. And I could not hear the earsplitting music. The air was silent and still and filled with that strong, even light. And I realized that I, too, was fading into the white. I was losing myself by degrees, like the incredible shrinking man. The snake would be the last to go, and all I could see was the way its scales shimmered one last time in the light, and the way its head moved from side to side, searching for a way out. I knew then why the handlers took up serpents. There is power in the act of disappearing; there is victory in the loss of self. It must be close to our conception of paradise, what it's like before you're born or after you die.

I came back in stages, first with recognition that the shouting I had begun to hear was coming from my own mouth. Then I realized I was holding a rattlesnake, and the church rushed back with all its clamor, heat, and smell. I remembered Carl and turned toward where I thought he might be. I lowered the snake to waist level. It was an enormous animal, heavy and firm. The scales on its side were as rough as calluses. I could feel its muscles rippling beneath the skin. I was aware it was not a part of me now and that I couldn't predict what it might do. I extended it toward Carl. He took it from me, stepped to the side, and gave it in turn to J. L.

"Jesus," J. L. said, "Oh, Jesus." His knees bent, his head went back. I knew it was happening to him too.

Then I looked around and saw that I was in a semicircle of handlers by the deacons' bench. Most had returned their snakes to the boxes, but Billy Summerford, Glenn's bucktoothed cousin, still had one, and he offered it to me, a medium-sized canebrake that was rattling violently. I took the snake in one hand without thinking. It was smaller than the first, but angrier, and I realized circumstances were different now. I couldn't seem to steer it away from my belt line. Fear had started to come back to me. I remembered with sudden clarity what Brother Charles had said about being careful who you took a snake from. I studied the canebrake as if I were seeing it for the first time and then gave it back to Billy Summerford. He passed it to Steve Frazier, the young man on my left. I watched Steve cradle

> *What happened? I am still not sure how to express it. It was as if a great vibrant humming curtain of molten silence descended. It did hum, but internally, sometimes near, sometimes far, a great high sound, something in between the supersonic whistle of a bat and the singing of the telegraph wires. I have read enough to know what at last I am hearing: the* Shabd, *the sound of origin, one of the sounds the* Upanishads *mention as announcing the rising of the true, divine self in the mind.*
>
> —Andrew Harvey, *Hidden Journey: A Spiritual Awakening*

it, curled and rattling furiously in his hands, and then I walked out
the side door of the church and onto the steps, where Bobbie Sue
Thompson was clutching her throat and leaning against the green
shingles of the church.

"Jesus," she said. "Jesus, Jesus."

It was a sunny, fragrant day, with high-blown clouds. I looked
into Bobbie Sue's face. Her eyes were wide and her mouth hooked
at the corner. "Jesus," she said.

I thought at first she was in terrible pain, but then I realized she
wasn't. "Yes. I know. Jesus," I said.

At the conclusion of the service, Brother Carl reminded everyone there would be dinner on the grounds. Most of the women had
already slipped out, to arrange their casseroles and platters of ham
on the butcher paper that covered the tables the men had set up
under the trees. Jim and I waited silently in line for fried chicken,
sweet potatoes, and black bottom pie, which we ate standing up
among a knot of men who were discussing the merits of various
coon dogs they'd owned. "The next time you handle a snake," Jim
whispered, "try to give me a little warning. I ran out of film."

I told him I'd try, but that it was not something I'd be likely
to do in the future, or be able to predict even if I did. There was
more I wanted to tell him, but I didn't know how, and besides, I
figured he knew. We'd lain in a ditch together thinking we were
dead men. It was pretty much the same thing, I guessed. That kind
of terror and joy.

"This one I had, it was a cur," said Gene Sherbert, a handler
with a flattop and a scar. "He treed two coons at the same time."

"Same tree?" one of the other men asked.

"Naw," Gene said. "It was two separate trees, and that fool dog
nearly run himself to death going back and forth."

The men laughed. "Was that Sport?" another man asked.

"Sport was Brother Glenn's dog," Gene said, and he turned his
attention back to his plate.

I remembered then that Gene Sherbert was the man Glenn
Summerford had accused Darlene of running with. I tried to imagine them in bed together—his flattop, her thick auburn hair. Gene

was also Brother Carl's cousin. He'd kept the church in Kingston going while Carl did drugs and chased women on the Coast. Where was Brother Carl? I found a trash bag for my paper plate and went off to find him. I still felt like I had not come back all the way from the handling. My feet were light, my head still encased in an adrenaline cocoon. The air in the oak grove was golden. A breeze moved in the leaves and sent a stack of paper plates tumbling across the grass. On the breeze I heard snatches of a sweet and gentle melody. It was coming from a circle of handlers at the edge of the grove. Some were standing, some leaning against cars, some squatting on their heels in the dirt. As I got closer, I saw that Cecil Esslinder, the redheaded guitar player from Scottsboro, was sitting in the center of the circle. He was playing a dulcimer under the trees.

I stopped and listened. I'd never heard music more beautiful. It was filled with remorse and desire. When it ended, I asked Cecil what song he'd been playing. He shrugged. A hymn about Jesus. I asked how long he'd been playing the dulcimer.

"Never played one before in my life," he said.

His wife, Carolyn, was leaning into the fender of a battered Dodge Dart behind him. "Come on, Cecil," she said. "I want to go. My head is killing me."

Cecil smiled up at me, but he was talking to Carolyn, "You ought to go up and get anointed with oil. Let 'em lay hands on you. Ask for a healing. God'll heal you."

"I know that," Carolyn said. "But you've got to have faith."

"You've *got* faith," Cecil said, still smiling at me.

"My faith's been a little poorly." She took a pill bottle from the pocket of her dress. "I'm putting my faith in here," she said.

Cecil just laughed, and so did the other men. He handed the dulcimer back to its owner and stood up from the grass. "There's something I forgot to tell you," he said to me, although I couldn't even remember the last time we'd talked.

"You have to be careful when you're casting out demons," he said. "An evil spirit can come right from that person into *you*."

That's when it washed over me, the memory of the story I'd

written when I was nineteen. "Salvation on Sand Mountain." About a church like the Old Rock House Holiness Church, and two brothers, family men, who pretend to get saved, so they can fake their own rapture, caught up like Elijah in the air, when what they're really doing in running off to live with their girlfriends in Fort Payne. I'd never been on Sand Mountain when I wrote the story, but 25 years later, I knew that this was the place. This was the church, in a grove of oak trees, surrounded on all sides by fields of hay. I don't mean it resembled the church in my story. What I mean is that this was the church *itself*.

> *Whether we know it or not, we transmit the presence of everyone we have ever known, as though by being in each other's presence we exchange our cells, pass on some of our life force, and then we go on carrying that other person in our body, not unlike springtime when certain plants in fields we walk through attach their seeds in the form of small burrs to our socks, our pants, our caps, as if to say, "Go on, take us with you, carry us to root in another place." This is how we survive long after we are dead. This is why it is important who we become, because we pass it on.*
>
> —Natalie Goldberg, *Long Quiet Highway: Waking Up in America*

At the heart of the impulse to tell stories is a mystery so profound that even as I begin to speak of it, the hairs on the back of my hand are starting to stand on end. I believe that the writer has another eye, not a literal eye, but an eye on the inside of his head. It is the eye with which he sees the imaginary, three-dimensional world where the story he is writing takes place. But it is also the eye with which the writer beholds the connectedness of things, of past, present, and future. The writer's literal eyes are like vestigial organs, useless except to record physical details. The only eye worth talking about is the eye in the middle of the writer's head, the one that casts its pale, sorrowful light backward over the past and forward into the future, taking everything in at once, the whole story, from beginning to end.

I found Brother Carl by his pickup truck. He was talking to J. L. Dyal. They'd just loaded the big yellow-phase rattler into the bed of the truck, and they were giving him one last look.

Carl hugged me when I walked up. "I sure am proud of you," he said.

I asked if he was leaving for Georgia already.

"I've got to get back to God's country," he said.

While Carl went to say goodbye to some of the others, J. L. and I stared at the snake in the back of the truck. I told J. L. I just couldn't believe that we'd taken it up.

"It's something, all right," he said.

I asked what it had been like for him.

"It's love, that's all it is," he said. "You love the Lord, you love the Word, you love your brother and sister. You're in one mind, one accord, you're all combined together. The Bible says we're each a part of the body, and when it all comes together...Hey!" He whistled through his teeth. "What was it like for you?" he asked.

I didn't know what to say.

It's hard for me to talk about myself. As a journalist, I've always tried to keep out of the story. But look what had happened to me. I loved Brother Carl, but sometimes I suspected he was crazy. Sometimes I thought he was intent on getting himself, and maybe the rest of us, killed. Half the time I walked around saying to myself, "This thing is real! This thing is real!" The other half of the time, I walked around thinking that nothing was real, and that if there really was a God, we must have been part of a dream he was having, and when he woke up...poof! Either way, I worried I'd gone off the edge, and nobody would be able to pull me back. One of my uncles by marriage was a Baptist minister, one of the kindest men I've ever known. I was fifteen, though, when he killed himself, and I didn't know the whole story. I just knew that he sent his family and friends a long, poignant, and some have said beautiful letter about how he was ready to go meet Abraham, Isaac, and Jacob. I believe he ran a high-voltage line from his basement to a ground-floor bedroom. He put "How Great Thou Art" on the record player. Then he lay down on the bed, reached up, and grabbed the live wire. He left a widow and two sons. My uncle's death confirmed a suspicion of mine that madness and religion were a hair's breadth away. My beliefs about the nature of God and man have changed over the years, but that one never has. Feeling after God is dangerous business. And Christianity without passion, danger, and mystery may not really be Christianity at all.

Dennis Covington teaches creative writing at the University of Alabama at Birmingham. He writes on the South for The New York Times *and is the author of the award-winning novel* Lizard. *He lives in Birmingham with his wife, novelist Vicki Covington, and their two daughters.*

★

I am not I.
                              I am this one
Walking beside me, whom I do not see,
Whom at times I manage to visit,
And at other times I forget.
The one who forgives, sweet, when I hate,
The one who remains silent when I talk,
The one who takes a walk when I am indoors,
The one who will remain standing when I die.

—Juan Ramon Jiménez, *Lorca and Jiménez: Selected Poems,*
edited and translated by Robert Bly

⋆ ⋆ ⋆

The Interior Landscape

Hunting takes on a different meaning.

ONE SUMMER EVENING IN A REMOTE VILLAGE IN THE BROOKS Range of Alaska, I sat among a group of men listening to hunting stories about the trapping and pursuit of animals. I was particularly interested in several incidents involving wolverine, in part because a friend of mine was studying wolverine in Canada, among the Cree, but, too, because I find this animal such an intense creature. To hear about its life is to learn more about fierceness.

Wolverines are not intentionally secretive, hiding their lives from view, but they are seldom observed. The range of their known behavior is less than that of, say, bears or wolves. Still, that evening no gratuitous details were set out. This was somewhat odd, for wolverine easily excite the imagination; they can loom suddenly in the landscape with authority, with an aura larger than their compact physical dimensions, drawing one's immediate and complete attention. Wolverine also have a deserved reputation for resoluteness in the worst winters, for ferocious strength. But neither did these attributes induce the men to embellish.

I listened carefully to these stories, taking pleasure in the sharply observed detail surrounding the dramatic thread of events. The story I remember most vividly was about a man hunting a wolverine from a snow machine in the spring. He followed the animal's tracks for several miles over rolling tundra in a certain valley. Soon he caught sight ahead of a dark spot on the crest of a hill— the wolverine pausing to look back. The hunter was catching up, but each time he came over a rise the wolverine was looking back from the next rise, just out of range. The hunter topped one more rise and met the wolverine bounding toward him. Before he could pull his rifle from its scabbard the wolverine flew across the engine cowl and the windshield, hitting him square in the chest. The hunter scrambled his arms wildly, trying to get the wolverine out of his lap, and fell over as he did so. The wolverine jumped clear as the snow machine rolled over, and fixed the man with a stare. He had not bitten, not even scratched the man. Then the wolverine walked away. The man thought of reaching for the gun, but no, he did not.

The other stories were like this, not so much making a point as evoking something about contact with wild animals that would never be completely understood.

When the stories were over, four or five of us walked out of the home of our host. The surrounding land, in the persistent light of a far northern summer, was still visible for miles—the striated, pitched massifs of the Brooks Range; the shy, willow-lined banks of the John River flowing south from Anaktuvuk Pass; and the flat tundra plain, opening with great affirmation to the north. The landscape seemed alive because of the stories. It was precisely these ocherous tones, this kind of willow, exactly this austerity that had informed the wolverine narratives. I felt exhilaration, and a deeper confirmation of the stories. The mundane tasks which awaited me I anticipated now with pleasure. The stories had renewed in me a sense of the purpose of my life.

Barry Lopez is a contributing editor to Harper's *and* North American Review, *and has received an Award in Literature from the American Academy and Institute of Arts and Letters, the American Book Award, and the John Burroughs Medal, among other honors. He is the author of* Arctic Dreams, Of Wolves and Men, *and* Crossing Open Ground, *from which this story was excerpted. He lives in rural Oregon.*

✳

Travelling as a young man through the canyon lands of Arizona, Aldo Leopold and his companions stopped one day to eat lunch on a high rimrock. Gazing into the canyon below, they suddenly caught sight of what appeared to be a doe fording the river. Only when she had crossed the river and had begun climbing toward them did they realize their error: they were watching a wolf. Following behind her were a half-dozen others, grown pups who "sprang from the willows and…joined in a welcoming melee of wagging tails and playful maulings. What was literally a pile of wolves writhed and tumbled in the center of an open flat at the foot of our rimrock." Leopold and his friends did not hesitate: "in a second we were pumping lead into the pack," bringing the old wolf down and scattering the others. He reached the old wolf in time "to watch the fierce green fire dying in her eyes. I realized then, and have known ever since, that there was something new to me in those eyes—something known only to her and to the mountain."

—Douglas Burton-Christie, "The Literature of Nature and the Quest for the Sacred," *The Way Supplement Magazine*

REDMOND O'HANLON

⋆ ⋆ ⋆

Up Your Nose

"Feed your head," said the White Rabbit, which
is just what the author does deep
in a South American jungle.

GALVIS, PERHAPS REALISING THAT HE WAS TEMPORARILY FREE OF
mosquitoes, dry, and surrounded by half-naked girls, burst into song.
In his high tenor he sang the sad songs of the Llanos, the latest
Venezuelan pop songs, and then, eventually, exhausted, he turned to
his audience and indicated that now they should sing their songs to us.

The girl with the matchstick marshalled all the young women
into a line and began a high-pitched, nasal, dissonant chant to
which the others provided a chorus. They stood quite still as they
sang their eerie song, impassive, unsmiling, without moving their
hands and feet, and after about five minutes they all sat down. We
clapped and shouted for more, but Jarivanau, shaking his head, got
up, went to his hammock, and came back bearing his *yoppo* pipe
and a small glass phial of brown powder.

He squatted in the middle of the mud floor and two other
young men joined him. Neither of them had shaved their heads;
but one was disfigured by a deep, badly-healed scar which ran from
his right shoulder down his right arm to his elbow. Jarivanau beck-
oned to me and I went and squatted in line.

"Reymono," said Chimo," don't be a fool. You don't know
what you're doing."

"Don't make more stupids," said Juan. "It damages the brain. It hurts the head."

"It's all right," I said, grinning nervously.

"How do you know?" said Juan.

"I've read about it," I said, regretting everything.

"Read about it!" said Juan, disgusted. "Read about it!"

"You take the camera," I said.

"I'll take you being sick," said Juan, "like the dogs."

Jarivanau and the two men smiled at me.

"Kadure!" said the one with the scar, thumping his chest.

"Wakamane!" said the other.

I shook hands.

"Reymono!" I said, completing things.

Jarivanau tipped a handful of powder into his thick palm. He cupped it into the open end of the *yoppo* pipe and flicked the

Like the cyclic urge to relieve sexual tension, the urge to suspend ordinary awareness arises spontaneously from within, builds to a peak, finds relief, and dissipates— all in accordance with its own intrinsic rhythm.

—Andrew Weil, *The Natural Mind*

barrel to distribute it evenly. Kadure took the nozzle, inserted it in his left nostril, and shut his eyes. Jarivanau drew in an enormous draught of air, expanding his high chest, and blew long and hard down the tube. Brown dust hissed out of the nozzle, up Kadure's nose, but also, such was the force of the blast, mushroomed out at the edges and clouded his face; he dropped the tube, put both hands to the back of his head, and sat, staring at the floor, gasping; brown slime trickled out of his nostril, down his lip, and into his mouth. Jarivanau re-loaded the pipe and waited. Kadure dribbled a long stream of saliva down his chest; he bent forward, pummelled the ground with his fists, and inserted the nozzle in his other nostril. Jarivanau blew. Kadure put his hands to the back of his neck, his face contorted. "Whoooaaa!" he said. He started to his feet, grabbed a support-post, and was horribly sick.

Jarivanau, ignoring his distress, ministered to Wakamane. At the second blast, Wakamane sat, shaking, coughing and spitting for some moments, his hands clasped at the back of his head, brown gunge glistening down his lip and chin and throat. "Whooooaaa!" he said, collecting himself and struggling, very slowly, to his feet. He began a powerful stamping to and fro, his arms bent above his head as if carrying a small planet which, but for his support, would crash to earth. His eyes unfocused, his lungs tugging for breath in desperate spasms, he called to his *hekura*, his spirits, in a deep, monosyllabic chant, pausing only to spit. After ten minutes, drained and faltering, he sat down, withdrew into himself, and became quiet.

It was, I realised, with the kind of panic that shrivels the penis, my turn.

Jarivanau blew the dust into my left nostril. Someone at once seemed to hit me just above the bridge of the nose with a small log. I put my hands to the back of my head, to stop it detaching itself. Someone else eased a burning stick down my throat. My lungs filled with hot ash. There was no water, anywhere. Jarivanau offered me his re-loaded tube. Bang. My ear, nose and throat system went into shock. I sat, unable, it seemed, to breathe, my hands pressed to the back of my head, my head between my knees. And then suddenly I was gulping oxygen through a clogging goo of ejaculating sinuses; I mouthed for air as *yoppo*-stained snot and mucus from nasal recesses whose existence I had never suspected poured out of my nostrils and on down my chin and chest.

The pain went. I realised that I was still alive; that it was all over; that I was taking the best breaths I could remember. (Well, you would, after such a clear out.) I looked up. Kadure and Wakamane, who were squatting, to my surprise, on either side of me, put their arms briefly across my shoulders. The Yanomami seemed the most welcoming, the most peaceful people on earth. I felt physically invulnerable: a mere bash on the head from a club, I thought, could not possibly do me any damage. The hut had grown larger; there was more than enough room for us all; I could sit on the mud floor, happily, forever. Given the opportunity, I could have seen across vast distances; as it was, every detail in front of me was extraordinarily clear—a long black bow and two reed-cane arrows, with notched points of a different wood bound on and stained black with curare, their flights cut from the wing feathers of a Black curassow, seemed luminously themselves, leaning between the angle of the roof and the floor, a work of art. It all seemed so safe and familiar: the frayed, red-dyed, split-vine hammocks; the worn rim of a wooden bowl; the hand-smoothed bands a third of the way up the central support-posts. Indeed, given enough *yoppo,* it occurred to me, becoming a Yanomami would be a desirable and simple matter. *Hekura,* I knew, the tutelary gods who lived in the rocks and in the mountains until summoned to live in our chests, appeared, coyly at first, as small shards of light, a migraine of spirits. I searched the periphery of my field of vision. Nothing. But in it, instead, very obviously, sat the matchstick girl.

She was really there, it seemed to me; she sat, cross-legged, no more than ten feet away. She gave me the most enormous, encouraging, kind smile; it was not simultaneous, this smile, in its spread to the left and the right across her cheeks: the matchstick tilted first one way and then the other. I smiled back, giddy, overcome with slow tenderness and deep desire. We had, after all, more time than any man and woman could possibly need: it stretched away in all directions across six million square kilometres of jungle. She appeared to be perfect in every way. I admired her, slowly. I stroked, in imagination, her cropped neck. I ran my hand through the round tuft of thick, fine black hair on her head. I kissed her stubby nose, her strong chin. I wiggled her wooden ear-ring plugs. I ran my hands over her square shoulders and short, straight back. I explored her spatulate toes and the built-in platform soles of calluses on her feet. I felt her round calves and I undid the single strand of tight vine-bonding beneath each battered knee. I kissed the old scars and newish cuts. I ran my tongue, for several night-times, up the long, soft insides of her thighs, devoid, as far as I could see, of even the downiest hairs. It seemed a sensible idea, too, at the time, the Yanomami idea that sperm comes straight from the lower abdomen, has nothing to do with the testicles, and that, in order to enjoy a week or a month of uninterrupted erections, all you have to do is constantly replenish the reservoir by eating equivalent amounts of well-chewed meat between each bout of love-making.

"Matchstick girl," I wanted, very much, to say to her, "I know I am old and hairy and that, unlike you, I sweat and I smell horrible and I happen to be filthy, whereas you are clean, and used to all this, and know what to do, and anyway have the most beautiful brown eyes of all the Siapateri—but just supposing we slipped outside together...?"

I was suddenly grabbed from behind. I tried to shake myself free, but could not. The hands pinioning my arms were large and powerful. I looked up. An enormous stomach seemed to curve away above me into the far dark of the roof.

"Get up," said Chimo, "It's time to go."

The matchstick girl grinned. She had seen it all before.

Redmond O'Hanlon is the author of Into the Heart of Borneo, Joseph Conrad and Charles Darwin: The Influence of Scientific Thought on Conrad's Fiction, *and* In Trouble Again: A Journey Between the Orinoco and the Amazon, *from which this story was excerpted. He lives in Oxford, England with his wife and two children.*

★

We are all going up to Malibu for dinner; Zhang Jie and Allen Ginsberg are sitting in the back of the van. Between them, by chance, sits an interpreter. Zhang Jie is dressed to the nines, in a severely tailored blue dress.

How did it get started between them? I witness only the climax: "Mr. Ginsberg!" Zhang Jie is leaning forward fiercely over the interpreter's knees. Her slender shoulders are squared. "You should not think only of yourself! You must live and work so as to fulfill your obligations! Have your goals firmly in your mind. You should not take drugs! Think of your responsibility to society. As for myself, my goals are always clear. My mind is *never* confused!"

Ginsberg smiles his intelligent, vulnerable smile, and tilts his head like the Chesire cat.

"My mind," he says, with the tiniest shrug, "is always confused."

—Annie Dillard, *Encounters with Chinese Writers*

⋆ ⋆ ⋆

Meera Gazing

In which the boundaries of
cynicism become fluid.

YOU ARE ABOUT TO ENCOUNTER GOD—OR, AT THE VERY LEAST, someone believed to be His front woman.

The setting is a white room bathed with light from white lamps and filled with the scent of white flowers. It is actually a sprawling addition to a split-level home in a boondocks German village called Thalheim. Hundreds of people are crammed into every inch of the room: an international hive of WASPS, Catholics, Jews, Buddhists, Hindus, and agnostics. Businessmen in French cuffs sit beside socialites in cruise wear who sit beside Bay Area spiritual buccaneers in North Face jackets. Only minutes ago, these people were speaking every imaginable language. But now, at seven p.m. on a Friday night, they are silent, reverently silent, and standing.

She walks into the room like an ancient Indian temple goddess seeking protection from a thunderstorm, a slight, black-haired, big-eyed, stately woman wearing a brilliant golden sari. Saying nothing, acknowledging no one, she sits in a white chair at the front of the white room and begins *darshan*, Sanskrit for the revelation of a transcendent being, an avatar.

One by one, the seekers kneel on an orange carpet at her feet. Eyes on the carpet, she places her dark, thin, ring-circled fingers

on each seeker's head for thirty seconds, then relaxes her hands—
the signal to stare into her eyes. Lips pursed, head moving up and
down almost imperceptibly, as if generating energy, she stares
impersonally into the seeker's eyes for thirty seconds more, then
closes her eyes and lowers her head, the signal for a new supplicant
to kneel before her.

I had embarked upon my journey a skeptic. But now I'm
tempted by the possibility of maybe. Maybe there is something to
this conventionally uneducated Indian woman called Mother
Meera, born December 26, 1960, as Kamala Reddy, the daughter
of a farming family in Andhra Pradesh, India. Maybe Meera—
whose very name means "miracle"—can truly pull down the milky
white light of *Paramatman*, the light of the absolute, and inject it
into the needy souls kneeling before her.

I have to admit, her style is inspiring. At a time when many
gurus and spiritual leaders are ensnared in earthly scandals or
accused of financial improprieties, Mother Meera has thus far
remained untainted. Seeking neither cult, ashram, television pulpit,
infomercial, twelve-part tape series, or even religious conversion of
her devotees, she imparts her *darshan* without fee—although
donations are accepted. Best yet, what could be a more welcome
reprieve from the endless babble and blasphemy of the fallen tele-
vangelists than an avatar who imparts her power in *silence*?

By all accounts, she seems an unlikely celebrity. Yet fame has
found her. With the 1991 publication of Oxford-educated Anglo-
Indian mystic Andrew Harvey's *Hidden Journey: A Spiritual
Awakening*, a fiery manifesto of the author's dream-haunted, soul-
ravaged salvation at the hands of Mother Meera, she has become a
spiritual pop star. Her followers are increasingly upscale—international film and literary bigwigs, European royals, and American
socialites now mix with the far-flung mystical masses—arriving
on everything from Birkenstocks to Lear jets, trekking into tiny
Thalheim to seek answers in her wordless sanctuary.

It is quite a scene. Controlling her congregation in silence better than most evangelists move their flocks with words, she repeats
the head-touching/eye-staring process again and again and again,

without moving, without blinking, without even gulping.

It goes on this way for more than two hours, until every seeker has received his or her kneeling minute, and the silence becomes punctured by a hundred groaning bellies and creaking bones. Sitting for a few seconds, her vacant eyes cast downward, Meera rises and, as everyone rises with her, walks out of the room.

Some people remain in their seats in deep meditation or place their faces on the cushion on which she sat or kneel upon the orange carpet, bathing in her left-over light for a half-hour more.

I do not play in the white light. When someone marvels that "she's a powerful little lady, a lot of *shakti*, a lot of energy," then rambles on about the ecstasy of

As I started to walk back to the hotel along the shore, I heard the sound around me I had often heard when Ma came down the stairs at Thalheim to give darshan—*a buzzing as if of a thousand bees, very high this time and very insistent. I looked up. The sky, from the right-hand corner, was beginning to peel. I thought of the times as a child when I had steamed stamps off letters; it was as if in front of me the sky was being steamed open. And where the sky disappeared, there shone a blinding vast white light.*

—Andrew Harvey, *Hidden Journey: A Spiritual Awakening*

surrendering one's ego and totally accepting Her light, *my* ego corners the comment like a drunk in a bar fight.

"Show me," I hear myself thinking. "If you have the power, *show it to me…*"

To witness the revelation of the divine, you must make a reservation. "So sorry, sir, you should have called much earlier," laments a voice named Bernard over the transatlantic phone line from Mother Meera's office. The voice is friendly, but peculiar: Bernard laughs after every word spoken. "We're (ha) completely (ha, ha) full (ha-ha-ha) for (ha-ha-ha) months," he says.

I beg.

It's the only time I'll ever be remotely close to Thalheim, Germany, an hour outside of Frankfurt, where Mother Meera shakes the silence four nights a week in *darshan*. I must see Mother,

I insist. I must write about Mother. I must—in the words of one otherwise grounded friend who has worshiped before Mother—"stare into her big dark eyes and bathe in the tempestuous whirlpool of her energy."

Bernard, God's maitre d', laughs. "We just had a cancellation," he says. "Come."

Those seeking the power of Mother Meera are steered toward the 28 hotels, hostels, and rooming houses recommended by Mother Meera's one-page directions sheet. My hotel is the most expensive on the list, the Nassau-Oranien in the village of Hadamar. The hotel's general manager, Ursula, hovers over an all-woman staff and a sold-out guest manifest. Most names are highlighted in blue with the words MOTHER MEERA written by their side.

The bellhop bustles in, wearing a suit and a weary disposition. "She holds your head, looks into your eyes and"—he expels air as if blowing a piece of lint off his upper lip—"that's it! It's a transfer of energy. She has a ghost in her brain. The pilgrims love it."

I look up Mother Meera's telephone number in the Wiesbaden/Limburg telephone book and find it on page 72: "Meeramma, Thalheim, Oberdorf 4a." I dial, and an Indian woman's voice lilts like a calliope. It is Adilakshimi Olati, Meera's chief devotee, guardian, and secretary.

I mutter a rambling salutation, then get down to business: "As I said in my letter. I would like an interview with Mother Meera."

"That is not possible," she says. "Mother does not give interviews."

"But first I would like to interview you," I say.

"That you can do," says Adilakshmi. "Come to see me at ten tomorrow morning. Just ring the bell."

When I hang up the phone, I hear music. The hotel Muzak. It's the perfect tune, as if some spiritual disc jockey were playing a Mother Meera-ordained hit parade:

> *How do you talk to an angel?*
> *How does your heart know where you are?*
> *How do you talk to an angel?*
> *It's like trying to catch a falling star.*

The hotel shuttle bus to Meera's *darshan* departs at six p.m. At five, I wait in the lobby, listening to half a dozen pilgrims. They have come in search of miracles—revelation, inspiration, direction—and describe "The Mother" as if she were a spiritual A&P. Bring me your empty carts and I will fill them.

"Don't think," says a South Carolina seeker, a woman on her third pilgrimage. "Just go. How can you think about something like this?"

She smiles sagely. "The power that Mother imparts is foreign to logic but completely familiar to the soul. You may not be wiped off your feet, but it'll change your life. They get in there and clean up everything right away."

Michelle from Manhattan, an artist who learned of Mother Meera from a spiritual workshop, bustles into the lobby, full of questions.

"My husband thinks I'm crazy for even coming here," she says. "Not that I told him. I told him I was coming for a painting workshop. People think you're weird when you do these things. They don't trust."

Under her breath she adds, "Maybe it *is* weird."

"It's like she looked into my heart, where I have two lights—a green light and a red light," says Rudi De Cramer, a Liam Neeson look-alike. "And she turned on the green light, the light that means, Go!"

Happily married, father of three, former professional soccer player, and now the owner of a Belgian construction firm, Rudi is a far cry from a vacant-eyed spiritual wastrel. "Normally," he explains, "I keep my feet on the ground. But after two *darshans,* I got very emotional. After two or three days back at home, I realized she'd cleaned something inside."

He opens his briefcase: spiritual leaflets are mixed with construction specifications. "I have a very busy factory. But since I came to *darshan,* decisions have become very easy for me. Once I was in a board meeting and I saw so clearly the eyes of the Mother."

A horn honks. The bus is waiting. As I walk through the lobby, the Muzak plays a song to send us into the night: "Oh, the night has a thousand eyes…"

The village of Thalheim is a metaphor for how a seeker should approach the Mother. Most villages in the area command proud status atop the mountains. But Thalheim, which means "valley home," nestles down low, prostrate, kneeling, subservient to all that stands above.

"Oh my God!" the newcomers shout as the bus enters the parking lot of the *Mehrweckhalle*, the community center. More than two hundred pilgrims await the half-mile neighborhood walk to Mother Meera's home.

The organizational mantra of Meera's *darshan* is LET IT BE. There is no registration or orientation, just a bearded devotee standing at the head of the footpath, wearing a picture of Mother Meera on his lapel and addressing the mob without the aid of megaphone or loud voice. "You should be silent," he says. "If you are new and you sit in the front rows, you shouldn't wave or shake around. Before you go to Mother, there is a waiting chair, a wooden chair. You will see how it works when you are inside…"

Near the front of the procession, Cassandra Struthers, a Jungian psychotherapist from London, is flush with the giddy excitement of following a spiritual call. Thin and pale-faced, she wears a 1920s cloche-style hat, a bright green double-breasted jacket, and bobbed hair á la Louise Brooks.

"A medium said to me, 'You're going to be visiting someone called Mother Meera,'" she says, heels clip-clopping across the footpath. "I said, 'Mother Meera?' I had never heard of her. But shortly after that, a documentary about Andrew Harvey ["The Making of a Mystic"] came on the television. Then, two days after that, I met a reflexology teacher who had all the Mother Meera photographs. Being a Scot, I'm a very down-to-earth person. But I decided I would follow the path."

The path leads past lawns where plastic gnomes and bike-riding schoolboys seem to be laughing at the procession: past street-corner shrines of Jesus and the Virgin Mary. We walk toward the divine in a disciplined line, turning up a gravel drive toward the two-story white house, then step through the doorway decorated with a wrought-iron peacock—the bird of spiritual victory.

Inside the door, the herd packs the main *darshan* room, then spills over into the gift shop and hallways, grabbing every available seat and floor space. Scrambling for a cramped spot on the floor, I notice a sign on a far door that presumably leads to Meera's quarters. PRIVATE, it says, repeating the warning in five different languages. Just before seven p.m., all talk stops and silence descends, the silence Andrew Harvey has described as "full of uncanny, wounding joy."

Led by the tall, dark-haired, fifty-something, sari-clad Adilakshmi, Mother Meera enters. She sits on a white chair with white armrests on a white marble floor. Without an audible signal, the *darshan* begins. It is a procession of needy faces: inquiring faces, weary faces, faces of pain and triumph and vacancy, all kneeling easily and naturally. Meera appraises each face with the same steady, expressionless gaze.

Then it's my turn.

I kneel at her feet, head down, feeling her fingers on my temples like tiny probes. This is to untie the knots of doubt and soul deterioration that block the inflow of the divine light, I have read. Do I feel a rush of energy? Or is it merely imagination? My head is fogged with so much doubt. Her hands remain on my temples for what seems like an eternity, then the fingers release, my head bolts up, and I stare into...what? She is supposed to be looking into my soul, drenching every corner of my being with her light. But I cannot focus on her eyes, only pools of dizzy liquid darkness, and my own feelings of foolishness.

Back at the hotel bar, the locals are partying, an egofest of *oom-pah* music and bottomless steins of beer. I seek the bonding of mortal communion, a shot of cynicism to blot out the craziness of the night. But when I enter the bar, the *oom-pah* band stops abruptly, and that devilish metaphysical Muzak starts again:

"Come along, take control of the comfort zone..."

I want to laugh about Mother Meera, to howl at the improbability of it all. So I grab a beer and hunker down with the locals at the bar, baiting them with conversation.

"I have tried to see her," says a barmaid, much too earnestly. "But I can never get a reservation!"

"A few weeks ago, [European TV and film star] Terence Hill was here," interrupts a barfly. "She must be the real thing."

That night I sleep fitfully, without dreams.

Ten a.m. on a sunny Saturday. The filigreed door with the wrought-iron peacock opens, and there stands Adilakshmi, a woman with a regal, radiant bearing and a brilliant smile. As Mother Meera's constant companion, secretary, treasurer, housekeeper, *darshan* administrator, and sergeant-at-arms, Adilakshmi also has the burden of saying "no." No to media representatives seeking interviews with the Mother. No to wealthy and celebrated devotees seeking private audiences. And today, no to me.

In the gift shop, the dark eyes of Meera flash from a bulletin board covered with sixteen different numbered photographs ($5 each) and from infinite displayed copies of Harvey's *Hidden Journey*, Meera's own *Answers*, and Adilakshmi's *De Moeder*. Adilakshmi serves instant coffee, chocolate coffee cake, and sincere apologies. "Mother never encourages any propaganda," she says. "She doesn't like publicity. She doesn't do interviews."

Adilakshmi smiles, seeking to please. She is, after all, from a very good Indian family, a rich family, an intensely spiritual family. Her politician and businessman father and religious mother opened their doors for yogis and *sadhus* as readily as they did for moguls and money men.

Adilakshmi tells me her story, with a never-ending smile. At 25, after graduating from Venkateswara University with an M.A. in philosophy, Adilakshmi took 100 rupees, caught a train, and embarked upon what she calls "a journey to find God." Her destination: the pilgrimage center for Shiridi Sai Baba of Bombay. But once she got to the train station, she blurted out a different destination: Pondicherry.

"I was alone," Adilakshmi remembers. "It was late at night. The train stopped many times. But I had no fear. I was cool and calm. I saw lions and tigers around me. I felt protected."

In 1969, Adilakshmi was accepted into the Sri Aurobindo ashram, worshiping with Aurobindo and Sweet Mother, a French woman who would become Aurobindo's partner in the work of transformation. When Sweet Mother died in 1973, Adilakshmi suffered terribly. Then she dreamed of Meera. "I saw the Sweet Mother disappear and the little mother, Mother Meera, appear. I asked her, 'How will I recognize you?' And she said, 'You will know.' There were a thousand people around her and I saw the small star-shaped mark on her nose."

Four centuries have passed since Saint Teresa of Avila, the great Spanish mystic and reformer, committed to writing the experiences which brought her to the highest degree of sanctity in the Catholic Church. Near the end of her life, she wrote, "The feeling remains that God is on the journey, too."

—P. M. H. Atwater, Lh.D., *Future Memory: How Those Who "See the Future" Shed New Light on the Workings of the Human Mind*

Then Adilakshmi met Balgur Venkat Reddy. A landowner and politician, Reddy had surrendered everything—fortune, fame, family—in his search for the Divine Mother, a dark-eyed face that had haunted him since childhood. In the early '50s, Reddy set out to find her: meditating with a female saint who lived in a cave without food or water; living for four years with a "realized being" who was reportedly forced into naked existence because clothes would burn off her body; and residing in the Sri Aurobindo ashram in Pondicherry for seventeen years with Sweet Mother. Still, his soul hungered for more.

In 1972, he returned to his village of Chandepalle to manage his property after the death of an uncle. There, in his mother-in-law's home, was Kamala Reddy, the daughter of a distant relative, a twelve-year-old girl with the face from his dreams. One night, when Kamala had left to stay in a city fifty miles away, Reddy heard her voice calling him. A few days later, he traveled to the city and asked Kamala how she had called him from such a distance. "There is another way of traveling," she replied. "*Don't you know?*"

Reddy began to care for Kamala, who was all but estranged from her biological parents, as if she were his own child. But she was clearly an extraordinary girl. "Every day she would tell me what she had seen and done on the higher planes." Reddy would later recount. In endless nights of fantastic dreams and days of extended trances, the gods conferred their powers upon her, the girl told him. Light entered her fingernails "like a procession of ants," then marched through her brain: the milky white light of the divine, the yellow light of Saraswati healing, the strong feminine red light of Durga, the blue light of transformation. Sound assaulted her senses in an endless crescendo of *Om*, and then—*silence*. It would be in silence, Meera informed her guardian, that she would impart her power to transform humanity.

Reddy did not keep his golden child a secret. With great enthusiasm, he discussed her power with the many friends dropping by his farmyard. From mouth to mouth, news of Meera's powers spread. At the age of twelve she performed her first *darshan* in the farmyard at Chandepalle.

In 1974 Reddy took Meera with him to Pondicherry. Adilakshmi smiles at the memory of first seeing the fourteen-year-old pigtailed girl bearing the mark on her nose that looked like a star. "I knew," Adilakshmi recalls. "This is my reason for being."

By the late '70s, the word-of-mouth message of Meera's power had spread throughout India. A stream of devotees arrived to receive *darshan* in the house Adilakshmi, Reddy, and Mother Meera shared in Pondicherry. The mailbox bulged with letters "begging Mother's help for every conceivable problem and difficulty," Adilakshmi remembers.

In 1981, they visited devotees in Canada, then, on the way home, stopped off to see fellow seekers in Germany, where Reddy fell ill. For four years, the German government gave Reddy kidney dialysis in Bonn. To be near her beloved guardian, Mother Meera bought the first of two houses in Thalheim. Reddy eventually died, but Meera stayed on.

Adilakshmi's story is intriguing, but time is running short. "I would like an interview with Mother," I repeat.

Once again, Adilakshmi shakes her head, negatively.

"What if I don't ask a question?" I ask.

Adilakshmi's head straightens abruptly, then bends forward, like a curious crane. "No questions?" she says, chewing on the proposition. "You mean, just…" She gropes for the right words. "A simple glance?"

"That's all," I say. "Just a simple glance."

She stands. "I will ask Mother," she says. "Only Mother is the boss."

She walks out of the gift shop. Much time passes. The eyes of Mother Meera beat down on me from a hundred different poses. Out the window I can see Meera's barn, where she sometimes works in overalls, and her garden, where carrots, it is said, burst from the earth with multiple heads.

Then Adilakshmi is standing before me. She bows from the neck and smiles. "Simple glance," she repeats.

I rise excitedly. "But," she reminds, jamming her index finger to her lips, *"don't talk!"*

The gift shop door opens, and Meera stands transformed. Body bigger. Complexion ruddier. Eyes much more mortal than the army of photographic eyes staring down upon her. She wears a purple sweater, a shiny multicolored sari, and a pearl-and-diamond necklace (a gift from an Indian jeweler devotee in London). Andrew Harvey has written that Mother Meera adopts different forms depending on her seeker's needs—from sensuous goddess to majestic queen to tigerlike burning face completely detached from her body. But today she wears the guise of a simple schoolgirl.

I stare at her in the doorway as if she were an exotic bird, my eyes washing over every inch of her before settling upon her face. My simple glance has turned into a convoluted gawk.

Then she grins, a giddy grin that grows into a giggle. Accustomed to staring at the multitudes without expression,

Mother Meera seems embarrassed by this naked attention of one-on-one.

"No talk," I say.

Adilakshmi laughs, "Well, perhaps you can talk," she says.

Mother Meera sits on a white plastic chair and kicks her right foot out from beneath the sari. I can see her Birkenstock-style sandals and purple socks. She clutches a Kleenex.

Meera nods. Permission has been granted to ask a question! But which question? My mind reels. Then I hear the music from the night before, the long-lost song conjured up by the hotel's metaphysical Muzak.

"How do you talk to an angel?" I ask.

Adilakshmi translates the question into Telugu, a language of southern India. Meera laughs—low, guttural, other-wordly giggle—then rattles off her answer for translation.

"There is no language," she says.

"Do you remember anything about last night?"

"Yes," she says. "*Yes!*"

"Do you see the faces of the devotees who kneel before you?"

"I see *all*," she says.

"What is your goal in *darshan?*"

Meera speaks a Telugu streak, a roil of choppy syllables interspersed with English phrases. Unadorned by inflection, her voice is a piano sonata played only on the black keys, a far cry from the symphony of her silence.

"I came to give *darshan* to humanity," she says. "To help people to clear themselves. To help them physically, mentally, and spiritually. There is no goal for me. The goal is only for human beings to remember the divine."

"Who is your God?"

"Different people, different Gods."

"But who is your God?"

Adilakshmi: "Mother says the one God is Paramatman. Same God, different names. He is the only one for all humanity."

"Do you feel the skepticism about your work?"

There is a curl of a crooked smile, then a flurry of Telugu. "If they want to feel, they can feel," she says. "I cannot force anybody to believe in me…But it is my duty just to do what I do, whether they believe it or not."

"How do you feel about being a celebrity?"

She grins widely, exposing a mouth full of imperfect teeth. She plays with the rings on her fingers and the bangles on her wrists, then stares down at her hands. "What is a celebrity?" she asks.

"How does it feel to have the God force?"

She shakes her head, negatively. "For me, it's normal, common," she says. "If I didn't have it, but then, suddenly, it came, then I could tell how it feels. But I have always had this force. So how can I describe the feeling?"

Meera stares out the window and shakes her head, as if shaking out memories. "When I am in the light, there is nothing to see, nothing to feel, nothing to hear, nothing," she says.

"Can your power be imparted only in silence?"

"Mother says that is the important way," says Adilakshmi.

"The only way?"

"*Nein*," says Meera. "When we are talking about Mother wholeheartedly, we can get it. It can come, speaking or not speaking. With or without my physical presence or photos of me, my power can come."

"Can you heal the sick?"

"Yes, I heal different kinds of sickness," she says.

"But if you have the power to heal, why have you gotten sick yourself?"

She smiles. "The Mother has a physical body and it functions normally, so it is possible to become sick," Adilakshmi says. "The Mother will suffer due to the sickness, but not like a human being."

"What do you see when you're looking in your devotees' eyes in *darshan*?"

"Every part of their being," Meera says. "When they have problems, I see their problems and help those problems."

"What are your thoughts about false prophets?"

Her mouth arcs upward at the question. Her fingers loosen in her lap.

"We cannot say they do not exist or they do exist," she says. "One must feel their consciousness. If you say you have the power, the people must feel it."

"How do you feel about your own disciples, the men and women who worship you like a goddess?"

"I have no such disciples," she says. "Those who believe in me believe in others also, like Ramana Maharshi, Sri Aurobindo, Sai Baba, the TM movement. They are all mixed up. It is not necessary to be devoted to me only."

"Do you watch television?" I ask.

"Yes," she grins.

"What do you like?"

She ponders the question, then says, in hesitant English, "Jokes."

"Why don't you do *darshan* on television?"

Adilakshmi jumps. *"You want Mother Meera on television?!"*

Meera smiles benevolently. "That is not my way," she says. "It would work. But that is not the Mother's way."

"Are there rules for spirituality?"

> *True happiness, we are told, consists in getting out of one's self, but the point is not only to get out—you must stay out; and to stay out you must have some absorbing errand.*
>
> —Henry James, *Roderick Hudson*

"There are no rules, but people like to make rules according to their mentality," she says. "Due to the name of the God, you should not leave your job, leave your family, or make other people unhappy. It is not necessary. For some, [spiritual devotion] is idleness. They want to escape from job and responsibility. I never encourage this. Do your job, live your normal life, help your family. When you have time, do *japa* [the repetition of divine names, mantras, or prayers] and remember the God."

"What is your philosophy about money?"

She straightens: Meera as business-woman. "There are no fixed, set rules," she says. "If they want to give, then they can give. If not, nothing."

"Is operating *darshan* expensive?"

Adilakshmi to the rescue! "Operating *darshan* is very simple. Mother gives and you take."

"But we cannot emphasize only on *darshan*," Meera interjects in urgent Telugu. "To manage the house, we need money."

For two hours, I question her, test her, search for a chink in her aura. Meera says that any problem, no matter how minute, should be presented before God. "God is always giving chances for someone to change—first chance, second chance, endless chances," she says.

She discusses her relationship with the Virgin Mary. "Some see me as the Virgin Mary; some feel I am the Virgin Mary. I cannot say I have no relation to the Virgin Mary, but at the same time I cannot say I am like the Virgin Mary."

Suddenly, she seems sad, alone. My ego longs to rescue her from the pressures of constant devotion and escort her into the Saturday night of idle pleasure. Perhaps to show her the ecstatic scream of great rock, beginning with the Beatles, then seguing through the Hit Parade. When I mention this, both Adilakshmi and Mother Meera laugh.

Arthur Koestler coined the term "holon" to refer to an entity that is itself a whole and simultaneously a part of some other whole. And if you start to look closely at the things and processes that actually exist, it soon becomes obvious that they are not merely wholes, they are also parts of something else. They are whole/parts, they are holons.

—Ken Wilber, A Brief History of Everything

"We have heard this name, but we have never heard the music of these Beatles," Adilakshmi says wryly.

Then, Meera rises, without farewell, and heads back to the hidden halls of her silent devotion.

"Mr. Seal, of coouuurrssee," says the suit-clad maitre d' holding a clipboard list of reservations for the packed Saturday night *darshan*. A snaking line of seekers swarms the door. He waves his arm grandly. "Please, go right in."

Greeting the multitudes in the entryway, Adilakshmi smiles

when she sees me, then says, "Please, sit in the chair right next to Mother."

Sitting six inches from Meera's armrest, I am suddenly very sleepy, so sleepy that when I close my eyes I can't seem to open them. When I finally pry them apart, staring at the circus of silent faces, I want to laugh, then cry, then scream. A growing ball of emotion rises in my throat, making me want to bolt, to escape, to return to the comfort zone of my ego.

When Mother Meera enters, beginning *darshan,* I cannot watch the procession. Some strange energy is playing with me, teasing me, seducing me. It seems to flow through my body, bulging out my shoulders, then bubbling up in the middle of my forehead, making my brain feel like it is going to burst. I close my eyes, and my mind seems to expand to the size of a watermelon, then a giant balloon, then as big as the expansive open skies over Thalheim.

A movie rolls in my brain. A plume of white smoke paints the distant sky. It's a train, India's famous Palace on Wheels, every inch of its exterior decorated with the holy Hindu symbol for *Om.* Smiling from a window is the nut-brown face of Adilakshmi, not as a middle-aged woman but as a beautiful young girl, surrounded by lions and tigers, on her journey to find God. Suddenly, an MGM-style lion leaps from the train and begins chasing me, hunting me, nipping at my sprinting Reeboks. The chase is both frightening and exhilarating.

Then the vision breaks, and I open my eyes; the *darshan* hall is pulsating with a blizzard of white light.

I kneel before Mother Meera, who wears a virginal snow-white sari that explodes at her shoulders in a thousand magenta threads and a flock of golden peacocks. She holds my head for an eternity, then stares into my eyes until the millennium. When I return to my seat my soul is swimming toward heaven, but my ego retains a slippery grip on the ground. I cannot—will not—make the mental leap to proclaim this woman a god force! But how can I doubt the energy with which she's tossed my consciousness like a football?

When the *darshan* is over, I step into the night, babbling.

Nick, a California yoga instructor, listens analytically to my experience. "That's classic," he says. "That's her *shakti* energy working on you. They set you up. She knew where you were sitting. She knew your vibrations."

Back at the hotel, I wolf down a big dinner as fellow pilgrims speak reverently of wonders witnessed.

"I feel like I'm falling in love with her," swoons Aida of Santa Fe. She touches her breast and smiles. "Like the way your heart feels at the start of a new love affair."

I would rather not peek into the verticals of my own fluttering heart. Not now; not here. So I escape to the bar, to drown this feeling of "maybe" with stout drafts of German beer and American ego. But alcohol won't work tonight; neither will raucous conversation. Heading off to bed, I stumble through the lobby, and there, blasting through the speakers, is the perfect coda. It is, of course, the Beatles, crying for "Help!"

"Won't you please, please, help me, help me, help me-eeeee! *Ommmmmm.*"

Mark Seal is a freelance writer living in Dallas, Texas.

*

It's eternity in a person that turns the crank handle.

—Franz Kafka

PART FOUR

THE PROBLEM OF EVIL

BILL BUFORD

$\star \; {}^{\star}_{\star}$

Slouching Towards Turin

*An American journalist recounts his experience traveling
in Italy with British "football hooligans."*

THE FIRST PERSON TO GREET THE GROUP IN TURIN, THERE AT THE
foot of the ramp, was a man named Michael Wicks. Mr. Wicks was
the Acting British Consul. He was about fifty—a tweed jacket, a
Foreign Office accent, educated—and relentlessly friendly. Mr.
Wicks was almost always smiling, and he continued smiling even
when he met the first one off the plane, an extremely fat boy
called Clayton.

Clayton had a number of troubles but his greatest one was his
trousers. In all likelihood Clayton will have trouble with his trousers
for the rest of his life. His stomach was so soft and large—no adjec-
tive seems big enough to describe its girth—that his trousers, of impressive dimensions to begin with, were not quite large enough to
be pulled up high enough to prevent them from slipping down again.
Clayton emerged from the airplane and waddled down the ramp,
clasping his belt buckle, wrestling with it, trying to wiggle it over his
considerable bulk. He was singing, "We're so proud to be British." His
eyes were closed, and his face was red, and he repeated his refrain
over and over again, although nobody else was singing with him.

Mick was not far behind. He had finished his bottle of vodka
and was drinking a can of Carlsberg Special Brew that he had

snapped up from the drinks trolley as he bumped past it on his way out. On reaching the end of the ramp, Mick was greeted by Mr. Wicks. Mick was confused. Mr. Wicks did not look Italian. Mick paused, started to utter something, in the puffy, considered way that characterizes the speech of a man who has consumed a litre of spirits in the span of ninety minutes. And then Mick belched. It was a spectacular belch, long and terrible, a brutal, slow bursting of innumerable noxious gastric bubbles. It was a belch that invited speculation: about the beverages, the foods and the possible quantities that had contributed to a spray so powerful that it seemed to rise endlessly from deep within Mick's tortured torso. But Mr. Wicks was unflappable. He was happy to view Mick as no different from any other tourist who had found the excitement of air travel a bit much to contain comfortably. Clearly a diplomat through and through, Mr. Wicks was not offended. I don't think it was possible to offend Mr. Wicks. He just smiled.

The others followed. They were also singing—on their own or arm in arm with friends—and their songs, like Clayton's were all about being English and what a fine thing that was. Something had happened to the group shortly after landing; there had been a definitive change. As the plane approached the terminal, someone had spotted the army: it was waiting for them, standing in formation.

The army!

This was not going to be an ordinary passage through passport control: the plane was about to be surrounded, not by the police—you could see them clustered near the loading ramp—but by a troop of Italian soldiers. The soldiers were funny-looking, according to Mick, who was sitting next to me. Actually the phrase he used was "fuckin' poofters." They wore strange uniforms and brightly-coloured berets; the soldiers were not English—that was the point; the soldiers were *foreign*.

The effect was immediate: these were no longer supporters of Manchester United; they were now defenders of the English nation. They had ceased to be Mancunians; in an instant, their origins had, blotter-like, spread from one dot on the map of the country to the entire map itself. They were now English: English *and,* apparently, dangerous. People stood up, while the plane was taxiing, amid protests from a stewardess to sit down again, and, as if on cue, began changing their clothes, switching their urban, weekday dress for a costume whose principal design was the Union Jack. All at once, heads and limbs began poking through Union Jack t-shirts and Union Jack swimming suits and one pair (worn unusually around the forehead) of Union Jack boxer shorts. The moment seemed curiously prepared for, as if it had been rehearsed. Meanwhile, everyone had started singing "Rule Britannia"— sharp, loud, spontaneous—and they sung it again, louder and louder, until finally, as the terminal grew near, it was not being sung but shouted:

> *Rule, Britannia! Britannia, rule the waves!*
> *Britons never, never, never shall be slaves.*
> *When Britain first, at Heaven's command,*
> *Arose from out the azure main,*
> *When Britain first arose from out the azure main,*
> *This was the charter, the charter of the land,*
> *And heavenly angels sung the strain:*
> *Rule, Britannia! Britannia, rule the waves!*
> *Britons never, never, never shall be slaves!*
> *Rule, Britannia! Britannia, rule the waves!*
> *Britons never, never, never shall be slaves!*

The Italians, too, had changed their identity. They had ceased to be Italians: they were now "Eyeties" and "wops."

This was what Mr. Wicks greeted, a man whose friendly relationship with reality I found to be intriguing. After all, here he was, having decided to meet an airplane full of supporters who, having been banned from the match that they were about to attend, were about to wreak crime and mayhem upon the city of Turin. What could he have done? It is easy to say after the event: he should have informed the civil aviation authorities that this particular charter flight must not be allowed to land and that everyone on it should be returned to Britain. *That* was what he should have done. But on what pretext could he have done such a thing? Mr. Wick's alternative—the only one—was to declare his faith in the humanity of what came out of the airplane, even though such a declaration meant overlooking so many things—like Clayton or Mick or the Union Jack boxer shorts worn as a tribal head-dress or the expression of unequivocal terror on the eight flight attendants' faces or the fact that by eleven-thirty in the morning 257 litres of 80-proof spirits that had been purchased an hour and a half beforehand had already been consumed. "Everybody," Mr. Wicks said, still smiling, as everybody came zig-zagging down the loading ramp, "everybody is here to have a good time."

Everybody *was* here to have a good time, and everybody agreed. But where was the man in charge? Mr. Wicks asked after Mr. Robert Boss of the Bobby Boss Travel Agency, but no one could help. No one knew his whereabouts. For that matter, no one knew where we'd be staying or where we might find our tickets for the match. In fact, most people, including myself, were so grateful to have found a plane waiting for us at Manchester airport and so surprised that it had conveyed us to Italy that we weren't in a great rush to ask more questions, fearing that by look-

> *A mob is a strange phenomenon. It is a gathering of heterogeneous elements, unknown to one another (except on some essential points such as nationality, religion, social class); but as soon as a spark of passion, having flashed out from one of these elements, electrifies this confused mass, there takes place a sort of sudden organization, a spontaneous generation. This incoherence becomes cohesion, this noise becomes a voice, and these thousands of men crowded together soon form but a single animal, a wild beast without a name, which marches to its goal with an irresistible finality. The majority of these men would have assembled out of pure curiosity, but the fever of some of them soon reaches the minds of all, and in all of them there arises a delirium. The very man who came running to oppose the murder of an innocent person is the first to be seized with the homicidal contagion, and moreover, it does not occur to him to be astonished at this.*
>
> —Gabriel Tarde,
> *The Penal Philosophy* (1912)

ing too closely at what we had it might all fall apart. It was better—
and, after so much drink drunk so fast, easier—to believe that
somehow it would all work out.

Then from the back of the plane emerged an attractive, chirpy
woman with the bouncy cheerfulness of an American cheerleader.
She introduced herself—"Hi, I'm Jackie"—and announced that
she was in charge and that everything was going to be fine. Jackie
turned out to be a police cadet who had abandoned her training
because she decided that she wanted to travel and see the world
instead. She had met Bobby Boss at a party. He offered her the
world—and this job. This trip to Turin, in the company of
257 football supporters, was her first time abroad. Jackie was 22
years old.

Mr. Wicks was concerned.

What do you do, I wondered, when your instinct is telling you
to arrest everyone, and your sense of justice is telling you that you
can't, and your mind, thoroughly confused, is telling you to smile
a lot, and then you discover that in place of the person responsible
for your predicament you have instead a 22-year-old police drop-
out surrounded by 257 drunken boys on her first time abroad?

What would you do?

What Mr. Wicks did was this: still smiling, he confiscated everyone's passport (the appearance of an American one, I would learn,
raising the momentary fear that the CIA was involved). Mr. Wicks
appeared to be thinking that he might want to control who was
allowed to leave. He wouldn't—Mr. Wicks would simply want
everyone to leave—but that was later. At the time, Mr. Wicks was
trying to limit the consequences of what, in his heart of hearts, he
must have known he could not prevent. He had prepared an information sheet of useful phone numbers arranged with an omi-
nous sense of priorities. The number of the British Consulate was
first, followed by the numbers of the police, the hospital, the ambulance service and, finally, the airport. Another sheet was filled
with a number of damage-limiting phrases in Italian ("Will you get
a doctor quickly, please?"), and it closed with the wishful imperative that, now in a foreign country, each member of the group

was to conduct himself as an ambassador for Britain, not something that the Claytons and the Micks or anyone else needed to be encouraged to do: their sense of Britishness, irrevocably intact, was verging on imperial. Mr. Wicks led everyone in a schoolmasterly manner through passport control and then gathered them together for an old fashioned locker-room pep talk—they were all to be on their best behaviour—concluding with the disclosure that he had arranged a police escort. It consisted of four motorcycles and two squad cars for each of the four buses that were waiting outside. All this intelligent and careful work revealed a man of great forethought. Yet you could see in Mr. Wicks' eyes—as he stood in the shade of the terminal awning, all that tweed and education waving to us, as one by one each bus pulled out for the noisy drive into the city—that he had failed. Something very terrible was about to happen, and it would somehow be his fault. There was the realization—his face seemed to convey the pain and the regret of it—that he had just granted freedom to a body of unusual beings, beings who should be treated in a humane fashion (fed, viewed, appreciated with affection) but who should never have been allowed to enter the city of Turin. Never. Not even on a leash. Or in a cage. And yet, optimist to the end, Mr. Wicks was still smiling.

A police escort is an exhilarating thing. I felt it to be exhilarating. I didn't particularly like the idea that I did, but I couldn't deny that I was sharing something of the experience of those around me, who, their shouting momentarily muted by the deafening sound, now felt themselves to be special people. After all, who is given a police escort? Prime ministers, presidents, the Pope—and English football supporters. By the time the buses reached the city—although there was little traffic, the sirens had been turned on the moment we left the parking lot—the status of their occupants had been enlarged immeasurably. Each intersection we passed was blocked with cars and onlookers. People had gathered on every street, wondering what all the fuss was about, wanting to get a look, and several blocks ahead you could see more people, bigger crowds, more congestion. The sound of twenty sirens is hard to miss. Who in the city of Turin could not have known that the English had arrived?

The English themselves, moved by the effect they were having, started to sing, which they managed to do more loudly than the brain-penetrating sirens that heralded their entrance into the city. To sing so powerfully was no small achievement, although to describe the noise that emerged from the bus as singing is to misrepresent it. One song was "England." This was repeated over and over again. There were no more words.

Another, more sophisticated, was based on the tune of "The Battle Hymn of the Republic." Its words were:

> *Glory, glory, Man United*
> *Glory, glory, Man United*
> *Glory, glory, Man United*
> *Yours troops are marching on! on! on!*

Each "on" was grunted a bit more emphatically than the one before, accompanied by a gesture involving the familiar upturned two fingers. There was an especially simple tune, "Fuck the Pope"—simple because the words consisted exclusively of the following: *Fuck the Pope.* "Fuck the Pope" was particularly popular, and, despite the sirens and speed, at least two buses (the one I was in and the one behind us) succeeded in chanting "Fuck the Pope" in some kind of unison.

I noticed Clayton. He was several rows in front. Somehow Clayton, like an unwieldy lorry, had reversed himself into a position in which the opened window by his seat was filled by his suddenly exposed and very large buttocks—his trousers, this time, deliberately gathered round his knees, the cheeks of his suddenly exposed and very large buttocks clasped firmly in each hand and spread apart. Just behind him was a fellow who was urinating through his window. People were standing on the seats, jerking their fists up and down, while screaming profanities at pedestrians, police, children—any and all Italians.

Then someone lobbed a bottle.

It was bound to happen. There were bottles rolling around on the floor or being passed from person to person, and it was inevitable that, having tried everything else—obscene chants, abuse, peeing—someone would go that much further and pick up one of the empty bottles and hurl it at an Italian. Even so, the use of missiles of any kind was a significant escalation, and there was the sense, initially at least, that bottle-throwing was "out of order."

"What the fuck did you do that for?" someone shouted, angry, but not without a sense of humour. "What are you, some kind of hooligan?"

A meaningful threshold had been crossed. Moments later there was the sound of another bottle breaking. And a second, and a third, and then bottles started flying out of most windows—of each of the four buses.

I wondered: if I had been a citizen of Turin, what would I have made of all this?

After all, here I'd be, at the foot of the Alps, in one of the most northern regions of Italy, surrounded by an exquisite, historic brick architecture, a city of churches and squares and arcades and cafés, a civilized city, an intellectual city, the heart of the Communist Party, the home of Primo Levi and other writers and painters, and, during my lunch hour, when perhaps I, a Juventus supporter like everyone else, had gone out to pick up my ticket for the match that evening, I heard this powerful sound, the undulating whines of multiple sirens. Were they ambulances? Had there been a disaster? All around me people would have stopped and would be craning their necks, shielding their eyes from the sun, until finally, in the distance we would have spotted the oscillating blue and white lights of the approaching police. And when they passed—one, two, three, four buses—would my response be nothing more than one of fascination, as in the window of each bus, I would see faces of such terrible aggression—remarkable aggression, intense, inexplicably vicious? Perhaps my face would be splattered by the spray of someone's urine. Perhaps I would have to jump out of the way of a bottle being hurled at my head. And perhaps, finally, I would have responded in the manner

chosen by one Italian lad, who, suddenly the target of an unfore-
seen missile, simply answered in kind: he hurled a stone back.

The effect on those inside the buses was immediate. To be, suddenly, the target came as a terrible shock. The incredulity was
immense: "Those bastards," one of the supporters exclaimed, "are
throwing stones at the window," and the look on his face conveyed such urgent dismay that you could only agree that a stone-
throwing Italian was a very bad person indeed. The presumption—
after all a window could get broken and someone might get
hurt—was deeply offensive, and everyone became very, very,
angry. Looking around me, I realized that I was no longer surrounded by raving, hysterically nationalistic social deviants; I was
now surrounded by raving, hysterically nationalistic social deviants
in a frenzy. They were wild, and anything that came to hand—
bottles, jars of peanuts, fruit, cartons of juice, anything—was sum-
marily hurled through the win-
dows. "Those bastards," the lad
next to me said, teeth clenched,
lobbing an unopened beer can at
a cluster of elderly men in dark
jackets. "Those bastards."

> *It is so dark
> inside the wolf.*
> —The Brothers Grimm

Everyone was now very excited. But no one was more excited
than our bus driver. Amid all this, few people had noticed that
our bus driver had been rendered insane.

I had been nervous about the bus driver for some time. Since
entering the city, he had been trying to bring everyone to order.
He could see what was going on in the large rear-view mirror
above his head. He tried dealing with his passengers diplomatically:
he had no reason to believe that they were, in any fundamental
sense, different from others he had driven before. But his request
for order was ignored. And so he remonstrated. He appealed with
his hands, his face, his whole body, as if to say, "Please, there are
laws and we must obey them." This time, he was not ignored, but
the response was not the desired one. The entire bus, which had
been singing something about the Falklands or Britannia or the
Queen, started chanting in unison that the driver should fuck

himself. They then changed languages and said the same, more or less, in Italian.

I did not think this was a good idea. I cannot begin to convey the strength of my feeling. After all, the driver was just trying to do his job. Our lives were in his hands. In fact, our lives were *literally* in his hands. And it was with those hands that he expressed his unhappiness.

What he wanted, I suspect, was to stop the bus and order everyone off. He'd had enough. But he couldn't stop because he had three other coaches hurtling at top speed behind him. Nor could he go any faster because he had two motorcycle policemen in front. Unable to go forwards or backwards, he expressed his rage by going sideways: by swinging the steering wheel violently to the left, to the right and then back again. Those lads perched atop the seats found that they were not perched atop anything at all. Very few of us were: so violent were the drivers' movements that most of the slippery vinyl seats were emptied. Jackie, our 22-year-old caretaker, had stood up and turned, with school-matronly authority, to reprimand her unruly following, but when she opened her mouth a strange, incomprehensible gurgling came out and then she, like everyone else, was catapulted off her feet. The interesting thing about the driver's rage was that the act of venting it seemed to increase it, as if expressing his anger showed him how really angry he was. His face started changing colour—it was now a very deep red—when he swung the steering wheel again, and we lurched to the left, and then again swung it to the right, and back we tumbled. I feared, watching the terrible chromatic display across his features, that something was about to burst. I feared that his heart would seize up and, midway through another lurching swing of the steering wheel, he would clutch his chest, leaving the bus to spin into the oncoming traffic.

And then: a rainbow. The streets, which had been getting tighter and tighter, opened, at last, on to a square: Piazza San Carlo. Light, air, the sky, and the bus slowly, undeniably coming to rest. We had arrived.

More to the point: we were not dead, or, rather, *I* was not dead.

We had survived the drive from the airport. As we were disembarking, the supporter ahead of me turned, just before stepping off the bus, and shouted at the driver that he had been completely out of order. And then, drawing deep from within his sinuses, he spat into the driver's face, and missed, leaving a drooping wet, elastic ball dripping from his shoulder....

When finally we were ushered through a tunnel that led to the [playing field], police in front and police behind, it became apparent that, while the English supporters may have been accommodated, their accommodation wasn't in the most salubrious part of the stadium. We were heading for the bottom steps of the terraces, directly beneath the very people who had been hurling missiles at us while we waited outside.

I did not like the look of this.

I kept thinking of the journalist from the *Daily Star*, the one who ran off when things got violent. He emerged in my mind now as an unequivocally sympathetic figure. He had, the supporters said, shit himself, and it was worth noting that this phrase had now entered my vocabulary.

I was not, I found myself muttering, going to shit myself.

One by one, we walked from out of the darkness of the tunnel into the blinding light of the ground—the sun, though setting, was at an angle and still shining bright—and it was hard to make out the figures around us. There were not many police—I could see that—and it appeared that Italians had spilled on to the pitch in front of the terraces where we were meant to stand, separated only by a chain-link perimeter fence. Once again things were coming at us from the air: not just bottles and pieces of fruit but also long sticks—the staffs of Juventus flags—firecrackers and smoke bombs. The first one out of the tunnel, drunk and arrogant and singing about his English pride, was hit on the back of the head by an eight-foot flag pole and he dropped to the concrete terrace. Out of the corner of my eye I saw a Union Jack had been set alight, its flames fanned as it was swirled in the air. I saw this only out of the corner of my eye because I was determined not to look up at the Italians above me who were hurling things down, or down to the Italians below who were hurling things up. I had the suspicion that if I happened to make eye-contact with anybody I would be rewarded with a knock on the head. Also I didn't want to lose my concentration. Looking straight ahead, I was concentrating very hard on chanting my new refrain.

I will not shit myself, I will not shit myself.

As we arrived at the patch of concrete allocated for us, television cameramen appeared along the edges of the pitch. They looked Italian (thin, not beer-drinking) and were squatting between the missile-throwing Juventus fans. There was also a number of newspaper photographers. They looked English (fat, clearly beer-drinking). The curious thing about both the television and newspaper men was this: they were only a couple of feet away from the masked, missile-throwing Juventus fans.

They could see that the English supporters were being felled—several people were on their knees holding their heads. I couldn't help thinking: it wouldn't take much effort to grab someone's arm, just as it was pulled back to hurl another pole or flare or smoke bomb or beer bottle; it would take virtually no effort at all to say a word or two urging these masked terrorists of the terraces to stop behaving in this way. Nobody did a thing. And while there is the old argument that to have done so would have been considered interventionist—participating in the event that they were meant to be reporting—for me, as one of the targets, such an argument was not very persuasive. They were not worried about getting in the way of the event. They were trying to create it: not only were they not stopping the masked, missile-throwing Juventus fans, but they were also not photographing them. It was images of the English they wanted.

They wanted the English tattoos; their sweaty torsos, stripped to the waist; their two fingers jabbing the air; the vicious expressions on their faces as they hurled back the objects that had been thrown at them. Italians behaving like hooligans? Unheard of. English behaving like English? *That* was interesting! I remember thinking: if the day becomes more violent, who do you blame?

The English, whose behaviour on the square could be said to have been so provocative that they deserved whatever they got? The Italians, whose welcome consisted in inflicting injuries upon their visitors? Or can you place some of the blame on these men with their television equipment and their cameras, whose misrepresentative images served only to reinforce what everyone had come to expect?

Somehow the match started, was played, ended. And, while it could be said that there was no single serious incident, it could also be said that there was no moment without one. Several people were hurt, and one supporter was taken away to hospital. During the half-time, when yet another Manchester lad was felled by a beer bottle, the English supporters, with a sudden roar, rushed to the top of the terraces, trying to climb the wall that separated them from the Italians. The wall was too high to scale, and the supporters ended up jumping up and down, trying to grab the Italians by their shoes until the police arrived to pull them away.

Crime represents a choice based upon a certain lack of optimism, the absence of the feeling of infinite potentiality.

—Colin Wilson,
Poetry and Mysticism

Police kept pouring through the tunnel, now wearing riot gear—moon helmets and blue uniforms instead of green—with obvious instructions to place themselves between each English supporter and everybody else. It was evident that the police continued to regard the English supporters as the problem, and they probably were simply by the fact that they were there. But they were not the only problem, which the police discovered after surrounding every English supporter and ignoring the Italians above them, who, in that uninhibited way that has come to characterize the Mediterranean temperament, continued to express their strong feelings: by the end it appeared to me that the police were being struck down more frequently than the English.

It was a peculiar setting for watching a sporting event, although, oddly, it didn't seem so at the time. The day had consisted of such a strange succession of events that, by this point in the evening, it was the most natural thing in the world to be watching a football game surrounded by policemen: there was one on my left, another on my right, two directly behind me and five in front. It didn't bother me; it certainly didn't bother the supporters, who, despite the distractions, were watching the match with complete attentiveness. And when Manchester United equalized, the goal was witnessed, as it unfolded, by everyone there (except me; I was looking over my shoulder for missiles), and jubilation shot through them, their cheers and songs suddenly tinny and small in that great cavity of the Juventus football ground, its 70,000 Italians now comprehensively silent. The United supporters jumped up and down, fell over each other, embraced.

But the euphoria was brief. In the final two minutes Juventus scored again. The exhilaration felt but minutes before by that small band of United supporters was now felt—magnified many times—by the 70,000 Italians fans who, previously humiliated, directed their powerful glee in our corner. The roar was deafening, invading the senses like a bomb.

And with that explosive roar, the mood changed.

What happened next is confusing to recall. Everything started moving at great speed. Everything would continue to move at great speed for many hours. I remember that riot police started kicking one of the supporters who had fallen down. I remember hearing that Sammy had arrived and then coming upon him. He was big, well-dressed, with heavy horn-rimmed glasses that made him look like a physics student, standing underneath the bleachers, his back to the match, an expensive leather bag and camera (Nikon) hanging over his shoulder, having just come from France by taxi. I remember watching Ricky and Micky, the improbable pair I had met on my early-morning minibus in London, scooting underneath the stands, exploiting the moment in which the Italians were embracing, crushing together in their celebrations, to come away with an handful of wallets, three purses and a watch, got by reaching up from below the seats. And I remember some screaming: there had been a stabbing (I didn't see it) and, with the screaming, everyone bolted—animal speed, instinct speed—and pushed past the police and rushed for the exit. But the gate into the tunnel was locked, and the United supporters slammed into it.

It was impossible to get out.

Throughout this last period of the match, I had been hearing a new phrase: "It's going to go off."

It's going to go off, someone said, and his eyes were glassy, as though he had taken a drug.

If this keeps up, I heard another say, then it's going to go off. And the phrase recurred—it's going to go off, it's going to go off—spoken softly, but each time it was repeated it gained authority.

Everyone was pressed against the locked gate, and the police arrived moments later. The police pulled and pushed in one direction, and the supporters pushed in another, wanting to get out. It was shove and counter-shove. It was crushing, uncomfortable. The supporters were humourless and determined.

It's going to go off.

People were whispering.

I heard: "Watch out for knives. Zip up your coat."

I heard: "Fill up your pockets."

I heard: "It's going to go off. Stay together. It's going to go off."

I was growing nervous and slipped my notebook into my shirt, up against my chest, and buttoned up my jacket. A chant had started: "United. United. United." The chant was clipped and sure. "United. United. United." The word was repeated, *United*, and, through the repetition, its meaning started changing, pertaining less to a sporting event or a football club and sounding instead like a chant of unity—something political. It had become the chant of a mob.

"United. United. United. United. United. United…"

And then it stopped.

Minds, my mind and yours, are run by the same principles. We are not unique. We mirror what is around us. If we walk into a red room, we become red. If we are always in a group of angry people, it is hard not to become angry. If we are with someone who is clear, our mind reflects that back and we become clearer.

—Natalie Goldberg, *Long Quiet Highway: Waking Up in America*

There was a terrible screaming, a loud screaming, loud enough to have risen above the chant. The sound was out of place; it was a woman's screaming.

Someone said that it was the mother of the stabbed boy.

Someone said that it was no such thing, just a "fucking Eyetie."

The screaming went on. It appeared that a woman had been caught by the rush to get away and swept along by it. I spotted her: she was hemmed in and thrashing about, trying to find some space, some air. She couldn't move towards the exit and couldn't move away from it, and she wasn't going to be able to: the crush was too great, and it wouldn't stay still, surging back and forth by its volition, beyond the control of anyone in it. She was very frightened. Her scream, piercing and high-pitched, wouldn't stop. She started hyperventilating, taking in giant gulps of air, and her screams undulated with the relentless rhythm of her over-breathing: it was as if she were drowning in her own high-pitched oxygen, swinging her head from side to side, her eyes wild. I thought: Why hasn't she passed out? I was waiting for her to lose consciousness, for her muscles to give up, but she didn't pass out. The scream went on. Nobody around me was saying a word. I could tell that they were thinking what I was thinking, that she was going to have a fit, that she was going to die, there, now, pressed up against them. It went on, desperate and unintelligible and urgent.

And then someone had the sense to lift her up and raise her above his shoulders—it was so obvious—and he passed her to the person in front of him. And he passed her to the person in front of him. And in this way, she was passed, hand to hand, above everyone's heads, still screaming, still flailing, slowly making her way to the exit, and then, once there, the gate was opened to let her out.

And it was all that was needed. Once the gate had been opened, the English supporters surged forwards, pushing her heavily to one side.

I was familiar with the practice of keeping visiting supporters locked inside at the end of a match until everyone had left, and of using long lines of police, with horses and dogs, to direct the visitors to their coaches. The plan in Turin had been the same, and the police were there, outside the gate, in full riot regalia, waiting for the United supporters. But they weren't ready for what came charging out of the tunnel.

For a start, owing to the trapped woman, the supporters came out earlier than expected—the streets were filled with Juventus supporters—and when they emerged, they came out very fast, with police trailing behind, trying to keep up. They came as a mob, with everyone pressed together, hands on the shoulders of the person in front, moving quickly, almost at a sprint, racing down the line of police, helmets and shields and truncheons a peripheral blur. The line of police led to the coaches, but just before the coach door someone in the front veered sharply and the mob followed. The police had anticipated this and were waiting. The group turned again, veering in another direction, and rushed out into the space between two of the coaches. It came to a sudden stop, and I slammed into the person in front of me, and people slammed into me from the behind: the police had been there as well. Everyone turned round. I don't know who was in front—I was trying only to keep up—and nothing was being said. There were about two hundred people crushed together, but they seemed able to move in unison, like some giant, strangely-coordinated insect. A third direction was tried. The police were not there. I looked to the left and the right: there was no police anywhere.

What was the duration of what followed? It might have been twenty minutes; it seemed longer. It was windy and dark, and the trees, blowing back and forth in front of the street lamps, cast long, moving shadows. I was never able to see clearly.

I knew to follow Sammy. The moment the group broke free, he had handed his bag and camera to someone, telling him to give them back later at the hotel. Sammy then turned and started running backwards. He appeared to be measuring the group, taking in size.

The energy, he said, still running backwards, speaking to no one in particular, the energy is very high. He was alert, vital, moving constantly, looking in all directions. He was holding out his hands, with his fingers outstretched.

Feel the energy, he said.

There were six or seven younger supporters jogging beside him, and it would be some time before I realized that there were always six or seven younger supporters jogging beside him. When he turned in one direction, they turned with him. When he ran backwards, they ran backwards. No doubt if Sammy had suddenly become airborne there would have been the sight of six or seven younger supporters desperately flapping their arms trying to do the same. The younger supporters were in fact very young. At first I put their age at around sixteen, but they might have been younger. The might have been fourteen. They might have been nine: I take pleasure, even now, in thinking of them as nothing more than overgrown nine-year-olds. They were nasty little nine-year-olds who, in some kind of pre-pubescent confusion, regarded Sammy as their dad. The one nearest me had a raw, skinny face with a greasy texture that suggested an order of fish'n'chips. He was the one who turned on me.

Who the fuck are you?

I said nothing, and Fish'n'chips repeated his question—Who the fuck are you?—and then Sammy said something, and Fish'n'chips forgot about me. But it was a warning: the nine-year-old didn't like me.

Sammy had stopped running backwards and had developed a kind of walk-run, which involved moving as quickly as possible without breaking into an outright sprint. Everybody else did the same: the idea, it seemed, was to be inconspicuous—not to be seen to be actually running, thus attracting the attention of the police—but nevertheless to jet along as fast as you could. The effect was ridiculous: two hundred English supporters, tattooed torsos tilted slightly forwards, arms straight, hurtling stifling down the pavement, believing that nobody was noticing them.

Everyone crossed the street, decisively, without a word spoken. A chant broke out—"United, United, United"—and Sammy waved his hands up and down, as if trying to bat down

the flames of a fire, urging people to be quiet. A little later there
was another one-word chant: this time it was "England." They
couldn't help themselves. They wanted so badly to act like normal football supporters—they wanted to sing and behave drunk-
enly and carry on doing the same rude things that they had been
doing all day long—and they had to be reminded that they
couldn't. Why this pretense of being invisible? There was Sammy
again, whispering, insistent: no singing, no singing, waving his
hands up and down. The nine-year-olds made a shushing sound
to enforce the message.

Sammy said to cross the street again—he had seen something—
and his greasy little companions went off in different directions,
fanning out, as if to hold the group in place, and then returned to
their positions beside him. It was only then that I appreciated fully
what I was witnessing: Sammy had taken charge of the group—
moment by moment giving it specific instructions—and was using
his obsequious little lads to ensure that his commands were being
carried out.

I remembered, on my first night with Mick, hearing that leaders had their little lieutenants and sergeants. I had heard and I had
noted, it, but I hadn't thought much of it: it sounded too much
like toyland, like a war game played by schoolboys. But here, now,
I could see that everything Sammy said was being enforced by his
entourage of little supporters. Fish'n'chips and the other nine-
year-olds made sure that no one ran, that no one sang, that no
one strayed far from the group, that everyone stayed together. At
one moment, a cluster of police came rushing towards us, and
Sammy, having spotted them, whispered a new command, hissing
that we were to disperse, and the members of the group split up—
some crossing the street, some carrying on down the centre of it,
some falling behind—until they had got past the policemen,
whereupon Sammy turned round, running backwards again, and
ordered everyone to regroup: and the little ones, like trained dogs,
herded the members of the group back together.

I trotted along. Everyone was moving at such a speed that, to
ensure I didn't miss anything, I concentrated on keeping up with

Sammy. I could see that this was starting to irritate him. He kept having to notice me.

What are you doing here? He asked me, after he had turned round again, running backwards, doing a quick head-count after everyone had regrouped.

He knew precisely what I was doing there, and he had made a point of asking his question loudly enough that the others had to hear it as well.

Just the thing, I thought.

Fuck off, one of his runts said suddenly, peering into my face. He had a knife.

Didja hear what he said, mate? Fish'n'chips had joined the interrogation. He said fuck off. What the fuck are you doing here anyway, eh? Fuck off.

It was not the time or the occasion to explain to Fish'n'chips why I was there, and, having got this far, I wasn't about to turn around now.

I dropped back a bit, just outside of striking range. I looked about me. I didn't recognize anyone. I was surrounded by people I hadn't met; worse, I was surrounded by people who kept telling me to fuck off. I felt I had understood the drunkenness I had seen earlier in the day. But this was different. If anyone here was drunk, he was not acting as if he was. Everyone was purposeful and precise, and there was a strong quality of aggression about them, like some kind of animal scent. Nobody was saying a word. There was a muted grunting and the sound of their feet on the pavement; every now and then, Sammy would whisper one of his commands. In fact the loudest sound had been Sammy's asking me what I was doing there, and the words of the exchange rang round in my head.

What the fuck are you doing here anyway, eh? Fuck off.

What the fuck are you doing here anyway, eh? Fuck off.

I remember thinking in the clearest possible terms: I don't want to get beaten up.

I had no idea where we were, but, thinking about it now, I see that Sammy must have been leading his group around the stadium, hoping to find Italian supporters along the way. When he turned to run backwards, he must have been watching the effect his of two hundred walk-running Frankensteins was having on the Italian lads, who spotted the English rushing by and started following them, curious, attracted by the prospect of a fight or simply by the charisma of the group itself, unable to resist tagging along to see what might happen.

And then Sammy, having judged the moment to be right, suddenly stopped, and, abandoning all pretense of invisibility, shouted: "Stop."

Everyone stopped.

"Turn."

Everyone turned. They knew what to expect. I didn't. It was only then that I saw the Italians who had been following us. In the half-light, street-light darkness I couldn't tell how many there were, but there were enough for me to realize—holy shit!—that I was now unexpectedly in the middle of a very big fight: having dropped back to get out of the reach of Sammy and his lieutenants I was in the rear, which, as the group turned, had suddenly become the front.

Adrenalin is one of the body's more powerful chemicals. Seeing the English on one side of me and the Italians on the other, I remember seeming quickly to take on the properties of a small helicopter, rising several feet in the air and moving out of every-

Richard Dawkins, in exploring the nature of the selfish gene, made what I believe to be one of the most radical and useful suggestions in the history of ideas. It is one which concerns ideas themselves as the carriers of human culture. Suppose, he says, that we have given birth to a new and more rapid kind of evolution that involves culture rather than chemicals; then the process will need pieces on which to operate. Genetics has genes, so culture must have its own units of transmission—and Dawkins calls these memes.

Memes are tunes, catchy phrases, fashions, ways of making pots or playing games. "Just as genes propagate themselves in the gene pool by leaping from body to body…so memes propagate themselves in the meme pool by leaping from brain to brain." Viewed in this light, memes become living structures capable of implanting themselves in another mind like viruses which parasitize the genetic mechanism of a host cell.

—Lyall Watson, *Dark Nature: A Natural History of Evil*

body's way. There was a roar, everybody roaring, and the English supporters charged into the Italians.

In the next second I went down. A dark blur and then smack: I got hit on the side of the head by a beer can—a full one—thrown powerfully enough to knock me over. As I got up, two policemen, the only two I saw, came rushing past, and one of them clubbed me on the back of the head. Back down I went. I got up again, and most of the Italians had already run off, scattering in all directions. But many had been tripped up before they got away.

Directly in front of me—so close I could almost reach out to touch his face—a young Italian, a boy really, had been knocked down. As he was getting up, an English supporter pushed the boy down again, ramming his flat hand against the boy's face. He fell back and his head hit the pavement, the back of it bouncing slightly.

Two other Manchester United supporters appeared. One kicked the boy in the ribs. It was a soft sound, which surprised me. You could hear the impact of the shoe on the fabric of the boy's clothing. He was kicked again—this time very hard—and the sound was still soft, muted. The boy reached down to protect himself, to guard his ribs, and the other English supporter then kicked him in the face. This was a soft sound as well, but it was different: you could tell that it was his face that had been kicked and not his body and not something protected by clothing. It sounded gritty. The boy tried to get up and he was pushed back down—sloppily, without much force. Another Manchester United supporter appeared and another and then a third. There were now six, and they all started kicking the boy on the ground. The boy covered his face. I was surprised that I could tell, from the sound, when someone's shoe missed or when it struck the fingers and not the forehead or the nose.

I was transfixed. I suppose, thinking about this incident now, I was close enough to have stopped the kicking. Everyone there was off-balance—with one leg swinging back and forth—and it wouldn't have taken much to have saved the boy. But I didn't. I don't think the thought occurred to me. It was as if time had dramatically slowed down, and each second had a distinct beginning and end, like a sequence of images on a roll of film, and I was mesmerized by each image I saw. Two more Manchester United supporters appeared—there must have been eight by now. It was getting crowded and difficult to get at the boy: they were bumping into each other, tussling slightly. It was hard for me to get a clear view or to say where exactly the boy was now being kicked, but it looked like there were three people kicking him in the head, and the other were kicking him in the body—mainly the ribs but I couldn't be sure. I am astonished by the detail I can recall. For instance, there was no speech, only that soft, yielding sound—although sometimes it was a gravelly, scraping one—of the blows, one after another. The moments between the kicks seemed to increase in duration, to stretch elastically, as each person's leg was retracted and then released for another blow.

The thought of it: eight people kicking the boy at once. At what point is the job completed?

It went on.

The boy continued to try to cushion the blows, moving his hands around to cover the spot were he had just been struck, but he was being hit in too many places to be able to protect himself. His face was now covered with blood, which came from his nose and his mouth, and his hair was matted and wet. Blood was all over his clothing. The kicking went on. On and on and on, that terrible soft sound, with the boy saying nothing, only wriggling on the ground.

A policeman appeared, but only one. Where were the other police? There had been so many

Moral values have the character of indispensability. It is a pity if people have poor intelligence or are lacking in appreciation of art or of poetry; but it is far more than a pity if they are unjust or untruthful— they are simply failing in their basic human vocation. Furthermore, it is natural that human beings may not be endowed with every single intellectual gift, but they can, they ought, they should, possess all moral values. Thus the element of "ought" is exclusively predicated of moral values. All moral values are demanded of everyone insofar as they are human.

—Sean O'Reilly, M.D., *Bioethics and the Limits of Science*

before. The policeman came running hard and knocked over two of the supporters, and the others fled, and then time accelerated, no longer slow-motion time, but time moving very fast.

We ran off. I don't know what happened to the boy. I then noticed that all around me there were others like him, others who had been tripped up and had their faces kicked; I had to side-step a body on the ground to avoid running on top of it.

In the vernacular of the supporters, it had now "gone off." With that first violent exchange, some kind of threshold had been crossed, some notional boundary: on one side of that boundary had been a sense of limits, an ordinary understanding—even among this lot—of what you didn't do; we were now someplace where there would be few limits, where the sense that there were things you didn't do had ceased to exist. It became very violent.

A boy came rushing towards me, holding his head, bleeding badly from somewhere on his face, watching the ground, not knowing where he was going, and looked up just before he would have run into me. The fact of me frightened him. He thought I was English. He thought I was going to hit him. He screamed, pleading, and spun round backwards to get away and ran off in another direction.

I caught up with Sammy. Sammy was transported. He was snapping his fingers and jogging in place, his legs pumping up and down, and he was repeating the phrase, It's going off, it's going off. Everyone around him was excited. It was an excitement that verged on being something greater, an emotion more transcendent—joy at the very least, but more like ecstasy. There was an intense energy about it; it was impossible not to feel some of the thrill. Somebody near me said that he was happy. He said that he was very, very happy, that he could not remember ever being so happy, and I looked hard at him, wanting to memorize his face so that I might find him later and ask him what it was that made for this happiness, what it was like. It was a strange thought: here was someone who believed that, at this precise moment, following a street scuffle, he had succeeded in capturing one of life's most elusive qualities. But then he, dazed, babbling away about his happiness, disappeared into the crowd and the darkness.

There was more going on than I could assimilate: there were violent noises constantly—something breaking or crashing—and I could never tell where they were coming from. In every direction something was happening. I have no sense of sequence.

I remember the man with his family. Everyone had regrouped, brought together by the little lieutenants, and was jogging along in that peculiar walk-run, and I noticed that in front of us was a man with his family, a wife

Neither necessity nor desire, but the love of power is the demon of mankind. You may give men everything possible—health, food, shelter, enjoyment—but they are and remain unhappy and capricious, for the demon waits and waits; and must be satisfied. Let everything else be taken away from men, and let this demon be satisfied, and then they will nearly be happy—as happy as men and demons can be.

—Friedrich Nietzsche,
The Dawn of the Day

and two sons. He was shooing them along, trying to make them hurry, while looking repeatedly over his shoulder at us. He was anxious, but no one seemed to notice him: everyone just carried on, trotting at the same speed, following him not because they wanted to follow him but only because he happened to be running in front of us. When the man reached his car, a little off to the side of the path we were following, he threw open the door and shoved the members of his family inside, panicking slightly and badly bumping the head of one of his sons. And then, just as he was about to get inside himself, he looked back over his shoulder—just as the group was catching up to him—and he was struck with such force that he was lifted into the air and carried over his car door on to the ground on the other side. Why him, I thought? What had he done except make himself conspicuous by trying to get his family out of the way? I turned, as we jogged past him, and the supporters behind me had rammed into the open car door, bending it backwards on its hinges. The others followed, running on top of the man on the ground, sometimes slowing down to kick him—the head, the spine, the ass, the ribs, anywhere. I couldn't see his wife and children, but knew they were inside, watching from the back seat.

There was an Italian boy, eleven or twelve years old, alone, who had got confused and ran straight into the middle of the group and past me. I looked behind me and saw that the boy was already on the ground. I couldn't tell who had knocked him down, because by the time I looked back six or seven English supporters had already set upon him, swarming over his body, frenzied.

There was a row of tables where programmes were sold, along with flags, t-shirts, souvenirs, and as the group went by each table was lifted up and overturned. There were scuffles. Two English supporters grabbed an Italian and smashed his face into one of the tables. They grabbed him by the hair on the back of his head and slammed his face into the table again. They lifted his head up a third time, pulling it higher, holding it there—his face was messy and crushed—and slammed it into the table again. Once again the terrible slow motion of it all, the time, not the clock-time, that elapsed between one moment of violence and the next one, as they lifted his head up—were they really going to do it again?—and smashed it into the table. The English supporters were methodical and serious; no one spoke.

An ambulance drove past. Its siren made me realize that there was still no police.

The group crossed a street, a major intersection. It had long abandoned the pretence of invisibility and had reverted to the arrogant identity of the violent crowd, walking, without hesitation, straight into the congested traffic, across the bonnets of the cars, knowing that they would stop. At the head of the traffic was a bus, and one of the supporters stepped up to the front of it, and from about six feet, hurled something with great force—it wasn't a stone; it was big and made of a metal, like the manifold of a car engine—straight into the driver's windscreen. I was just behind the one who threw this thing. I don't know where he got it from, because it was too heavy to have been carried for any distance, but no one had helped him with it; he had stepped out of the flow of the group and in those moments between throwing his heavy object and turning back to his mates he had a peculiar look on his face. He knew he had done something that no one else had done yet, that it had escalated the violence, that the act had crossed another boundary of what was permissible. He had thrown a missile that was certain to cause serious physical injury. He had done something bad—extremely bad—and his face, while acknowledging the badness of it, was actually saying something more complex. It was saying that what he had done wasn't that extreme, was it? What his face expressed, I realized—his eyes seemed to twinkle—was no more than this: I have just been naughty.

He had been naughty and he knew it and was pleased about it. He was happy. Another happy one. He was a runt, I thought. He was a little shit, I thought. I wanted to hurt him.

The sound of the shattering windscreen—I realize now—was a powerful stimulant, physical and intrusive, and it had been the range of sounds, of things breaking and crashing, coming from somewhere in the darkness, unidentifiable, that was increasing steadily the strength of feeling of everyone around me. It was also what was making me so uneasy. The evening had been a series of stimulants, assaults on the senses, that succeeded, each time, in raising the pitch of excitement.

vil has two faces. There is the banal face that Hanna Arendt wrote about in her classic book Eichmann in Jerusalem, *which chronicled the life and trial of a senior Nazi official sentenced to death in Jerusalem for crimes against humanity. Arendt wrote that Adolf Eichmann was a dull man, neither intelligent nor venal, a bureaucrat whose hands were bloodied only by paper cuts. He personified the "banality of evil." If you want to pursue an evil policy, you need people like Eichmann. The leaders are a different breed. They are deranged geniuses, the vulgar face of evil, the Hitlers and Stalins, the ones who come up with final solutions. In Bosnia, they were the ones who resurrected the notion of ethnic cleansing and fired the first shots or committed the first rapes. In the disturbed universe of evil, they are the "brave" ones who shout the unspeakable and perform the undoable and snap everyone else into line.*

—Peter Maass, *Love Thy Neighbor: A Story of War*

And now, crossing this intersection, traffic coming from four directions, supporters trotting on top of cars, the sound of this thing going through the windscreen, the crash following its impact, had the effect of increasing the heat of the feeling: I can't describe it any other way; it was almost literally a matter of temperature. There was another moment of disorientation—the milliseconds between the sensation of the sound and knowing what accounted for it, an adrenalin moment, a chemical moment—and then there was the roar again, and someone came rushing at the bus with a pole (taken from one of the souvenir tables?) and smashed a passenger's window. A second crashing sound. Others came running over and started throwing stones and bottles with great ferocity. They were, again, in a frenzy. The stones bounced off the glass with a shuddering thud, but then a window shattered, and another shattered, and there was screaming from inside. The bus was full, and the passengers were not lads like the ones attacking them but ordinary family supporters, dads, and sons and wives heading home after the match, on their way to the suburbs or a village outside the city. Everyone inside must have been covered with glass. They were shielding their faces, ducking in their seats. There were glass splinters everywhere: they would cut across your vision suddenly. All around me people were throwing stones and bottles, and I felt afraid for my own eyes.

We moved on.

I felt weightless. I felt nothing would happen to me. I felt that anything might happen to me. I was looking straight ahead, running, trying to keep up, and things were occurring along the dark peripheries of my vision: there would be a bright light and then darkness again and the sound, constantly, of something else breaking, and of movement, of objects being thrown and of people falling.

A group of Italians appeared, suddenly stepping forward into the glare of a street lamp. They were different from the others, clearly intending to fight, full of pride and affronted dignity. They wanted confrontation and stood there waiting for it. Someone came towards us swinging a pool cue or a flag-pole, and then, confounding all sense, it was actually grabbed from out his hands—it was Roy; Roy had appeared out of nowhere and had taken the pole out of the Italian's hands—and broken it over his head. It was flamboyantly timed, and the next moment the other English supporters followed, that roar again, quickly overcoming the Italians on the ground, wriggling helplessly while English supporters rushed up to them, clustering around their heads, kicking them over and over again.

Is it possible that there was simply no police?

Again we moved on. A bin was thrown through a car showroom window, and there was another loud crashing sound. A shop: its door was smashed. A clothing shop: its window was smashed, and one or two English supporters lingered to loot from the display.

I looked behind me and I saw that a large vehicle had been overturned, and that further down the street flames were issuing from a building. I hadn't seen any of that happen: I realized that there had been more than I had been able to take in. There was now the sound of sirens, many sirens, different kinds, coming from several directions.

The city is ours, Sammy said, and he repeated the possessive, each time with greater intensity: It is *ours, ours, ours.*

A police car appeared, its siren on—the first police car I had seen—and it stopped in front of the group, trying to cut it off. There was only one car. The officer threw open his door, but by the time he had got out the group had crossed the street. The officer shouted after us, helpless and angry, and then dropped back inside his car and chased us down, again cutting us off. Once again, the group, in the most civilized manner possible, crossed the street: well-behaved football supporters on their way back to their hotel, flames receding behind us. The officer returned to his car and drove after us, this time accelerating dangerously, once again cutting off the group, trying, it seemed to me, to knock down one of the supporters, who had to jump out of the way and who was then grabbed by the police officer and hurled against the bonnet, held there by his throat. The officer was very frustrated. He knew that this group was responsible for the damage he had seen; he knew, beyond all reasonable doubt, that the very lad whose throat was now in his grip had been personally responsible for mayhem of some categorically illegal kind; but the officer had not personally seen him do anything. He had not seen anyone commit a crime. He saw only the results. He kept the supporter pinned there, holding him by the throat, and then in disgust he let him go.

A fire engine passed, an ambulance and finally the police—many police. They came from two directions. And once they started arriving, it seemed that they would never stop. There were vans and cars and motorcycles and paddy wagons. And still they came. The buildings were illuminated by their flashing blue lights. But the group of supporters from Manchester, governed by Sammy's whispered commands, simply kept moving, slipping past the cars, dispersing when needing to disperse and then regrouping, reversing, with Sammy's greasy little lieutenants bringing up the rear, keeping everyone together. They were well-behaved fans of the sport of football. They were once again the law-abiding supporters they had always insisted to me that they were. And, thus, they snaked through the streets of the ancient city of Turin, making their orderly way back to their hotels, the police following behind, trying to keep up.

"We did it," Sammy declared, as the group reached the railway station. "We took the city."...

I got back to London at about eight o'clock at night, feeling tired and mean and nasty. I was gritty and hungover, and my mind was full of images from the night before. I was in a hurry to get home.

The escalator at the Marble Arch Underground station was not working. My train left in minutes. I bolted down the steps of the station; the stairs were long and steep. There was an old man and woman in front of me. The old woman was helping the man, but they were having trouble negotiating the stairs, taking one gentle step at a time. Both had canes. But together they were also taking up the width of the staircase. I was in a hurry. I started muttering underneath my breath: "Get on with it." And still they proceeded,

step by step, frail and careful. I said it again: "Get on with it."
And then something snapped and I shoved them forcefully aside,
pushing them sideways with the flat part of my hand. I shot past
and then looked back up at them.

"Fuck off," I said. "Fuck off, you old cunts."

*Bill Buford was born in Baton Rouge, Louisiana, in 1954. He lived for
many years in England, where he was the founder and editor of the literary
magazine,* Granta. *He is now the literary and fiction editor of* The New
Yorker. *This story was excerpted from his book,* Among the Thugs.

✳

If you spend much time in Bosnia, even it its wrecked state, you learn
very quickly that it was a relatively sophisticated place before the war.
The living standard in Yugoslavia was similar to poorer regions of Western
Europe and America. The country had an open socialist economy that delivered a decent standard of living, including Levi's jeans and Madonna
records. Yugoslavia broke from the Soviet orbit in 1948, so its citizens
enjoyed unheard-of freedoms for a socialist country, such as the ability to
travel where they wanted. Yugoslavia was not America, but neither was
it Africa. Many of the cleansers in Bosnia were lawyers and engineers
who, in peacetime, wore ties to work and had Sony televisions in their
living room.

I couldn't figure it out. My journey into the depths of human spirit
had just begun, and I could not yet make sense of the things I was seeing.
I was still too curious about them to be repulsed; all I knew at the time
was that the Muslims of Visegrad had been mistaken to think that everything was okay and that barbarism was behind them because they had university diplomas and poetry readings and skiing vacations in the Alps. They
forgot Andric's warning, that when the call of the wild comes, the bonds
of civilization turn out to be surprisingly weak, professors turn into
nutcases and everything that a generation built up can be destroyed in a
day or two, often by the generation that built it. The wild beast had not
died. It proved itself a patient survivor, waiting in the long grass of history
for the right moment to pounce.

—Peter Maass, *Love Thy Neighbor: A Story of War*

PETER MAASS

⋆ * ⋆

Ground Zero

The Dark Force continues
to be busy.

WE DROVE INTO THE COUNTRYSIDE AND WITHIN FIFTEEN MINUTES arrived at a former elementary school that had an English-language banner draped over its entrance: "Trnopolje Open Reception Center." When the first journalists had arrived there a few days earlier, barbed wire surrounded the place and there was no welcoming banner. But Trnopolje had changed only superficially since then; it was fundamentally the same place. A few thousand Bosnians were penned in, not by barbed wire but by the roaming presence of armed guards and the knowledge that they had nowhere to flee to. The entire countryside was in the hands of Serbs, so the inmates could not run, they could not hide, they could only stay put and hope for deliverance.

I never thought that one day I would talk to a skeleton. That's what I did at Trnopolje. I walked through the gates and couldn't quite believe what I saw. There, right in front of me, were men who looked like survivors of Auschwitz. I remember thinking that they walked surprisingly well for people without muscle or flesh. I was surprised at the mere fact that they could still talk. Imagine, talking skeletons! As I spoke to one of them, I looked at his arm and realized that I could grab hold of it and snap it into two pieces like a brittle twig. I could do the same with his legs. I saw dozens of other walking skeletons of the sort. I could break all of their arms, all of their legs. Snap. Snap. Snap.

I have visited America many times since my reporting in Bosnia, and I often face the same question: Did you visit those camps? Were they really so bad? I still find it hard to believe that Americans and West Europeans are confused about Bosnia and, in particular, confused about the camps. Yes, I visited them, and yes, they were as bad as you could imagine. Didn't you see the images on television? Don't you believe what you see? Do you give any credence to the word of Radovan Karadzic, the Bosnian Serb leader, who said the pictures were fakes? Chico Marx had a great line in *Duck Soup* as he tried to fool an unsuspecting woman (Margaret Dumont) into believing a preposterous put-on: "Well, who you gonna believe, me or your own eyes?" It was like that with Karadzic and the camps.

Trnopolje was the repository for men who had been released from the hard-core concentration camps of Omarska and Keraterm. That's where the skeletons came from. Also, women and children who had been cleansed from nearby villages came to Trnopolje voluntarily. Yes, voluntarily. It was one of the strangest situations in Bosnia—people seeking safety at a prison camp. Trnopolje was no picnic, but the known brutalities dished out there were preferable to the fates awaiting Bosnians who tried to stay in their homes. Women might be raped at Trnopolje but probably not gang-raped. They might be beaten but probably not killed. Ironically, the first television images that shocked the world came from Trnopolje, the "best" camp. No one ever saw the worst camps when they were at their worst.

The luckiest prisoners at Trnopolje had found a spot on the floor in the school building, which stank of urine and unwashed humanity. You could not walk inside without tripping over someone. The less fortunate inmates lived outside, baking in the August sun and shivering in the cool nights. The latrine was an outhouse over a ditch; people camped out within a few feet of it. Drljaca gave us fifteen minutes to wander around, and technically speaking, we were free to talk with whomever we wished. But guards with Kalashnikov assault rifles and Ray-Ban sunglasses sauntered through the grounds, and I could talk for no more than a minute or so before one of them would creep up behind me and start listening to the conversation. A few guards had slung their rifles across their backs and started snapping pictures of us as we talked with prisoners. They were not subtle; they were in charge, and they wanted us to know it. If there's one thing that all bullies have in common, it's the fact that they want you to know they are bullies. One skeletal prisoner had just enough time to unbutton his shirt, showing off a mutilated chest with a few dozen fresh scars from God-knows-what torture, before a look of horror came over his face. He was staring, like a deer caught in a car's headlights, at a spot just above the top of my head. I looked around. A guard stood behind me.

I walked on. A prisoner tugged at my sleeve. *Follow me.* I followed, trying to pretend as though I wasn't following. He led me to the side of the school building and, after glancing around, darted through a door. I followed. Where was he taking me? Why? I feared not only the trouble that I might be getting into, but the trouble that he might be getting into. The door closed behind me. The room was small, dark. My eyes took a moment to adjust. People were whispering beside me. I looked at the floor. Two bodies on the ground. Corpses? Not yet. I was in the infirmary, the sorriest infirmary you could imagine. No medicine, no beds. I was not supposed to be there.

The doctor, also a prisoner, motioned for me to crouch down so that guards could not see me through the window. He began peeling off a filthy bandage from the leg of one of the two men. Puss oozed out. The man had an infected hole the size of a baseball just under his knee. A bone-crushing blow from a rifle butt. In a few days, the leg would turn gangrenous, and the man would die. The doctor whispered his explanations to Vlatka, my interpreter, who whispered them to me. I handed my notebook and pen to her. Ask the questions, write down the answers, I told her, we don't have time for translation. Vlatka had worked for me and other journalists long enough to know the right questions. She was the best.

I looked at the other body, barely alive. The man seemed to be in his late thirties or early forties. It was hard to tell. His face was cut and bruised, colored black and red, and swollen, as though I was looking at the kind of grossly expanded reflection you get from a trick mirror at a circus. I looked at his naked torso—more bruises, more swelling, more open wounds. He didn't move, and I doubted that he was still alive. I didn't need to ask questions about what had happened to this poor man, or what was going to happen to him. His agony would be over soon, for if his wounds didn't finish him off in the next twenty-four hours, then the guards would. As I learned later, guards routinely killed prisoners who could not recover quickly from the beatings. Prisoners who could neither talk nor walk were of no use.

We slipped out after a few minutes, Vlatka first, me a few seconds later. An eighteen-year-old youth came up to us. He had just arrived at Trnopolje after two months at Omarska, the worst camp of all. His skin was

I heard her say:
Now I will show you the twentieth century.
Gaze with all your courage into its darkness.

I saw writhing bodies, burning, flayed, spattered with blood. I saw bombs flowering, the faces of mad dictators as they cut open the eyes of living children, torturers masturbating over the women they had just electrocuted. I saw all these nightmares arising out of the darkness and returning to it.

Then, just as I thought I would faint because I could not bear the sight and smell of so much horror, I realized, with a clarity and certainty beyond my power to express, that this terrible, unparalleled filth and depravity, this unspeakable desolation spread out over every continent and enacted in every culture, was feeding the New Light.

The spiral of light rises out of the darkness.

—Andrew Harvey, *Hidden Journey: A Spiritual Awakening*

stretched like a transparent scarf over his ribs and shoulder bones. "It was horrible," he whispered. "Just look at me. For beatings, the guards used hands, bars, whips, belts, chains, anything. A normal person cannot imagine the methods they used. I am sorry to say that it was good when new prisoners came. The guards beat them instead of us."

I slipped into his hand a sandwich from my shoulder bag. It was a ham sandwich.

"I'm sorry, it's all I have," I said. "Will you eat it?"

He stared at me, as though I was a naked fool. Of course he would eat it. It was food. Allah would look the other way as he devoured the forbidden pork.

I approached another skeleton, this one too afraid to talk, turning away after whispering a single word, "Dachau."

It was time to go. The guards started rounding up the journalists. We boarded the van. There were about six of us: a reporter from *Newsweek*, myself, a French photographer. We were staying at the same hotel in Banja Luka and, thrown into a hard situation together, we had quickly become friends, chatting all the time. But the van was silent as we pulled away from Trnopolje. We were thinking the same thing. "Fucking hell, I can't believe this."

> "*Nature, Mister Allnutt, is what we are put in this world to rise above.*"
>
> —Katherine Hepburn
> to Humphrey Bogart,
> *The African Queen*

I forget my parting words as I broke off my conversation with the last prisoner. What do you say in a situation like that? See you later? Good luck? You are leaving the condemned, the half-dead, and the fact that you spoke to them probably puts them into greater peril than they already were. You had a good breakfast that morning, a couple of eggs, some toast, lots of jam. He had half a slice of stale bread, if he was lucky. Your money belt contains five thousand dollars, and there is always more where it came from. He has nothing. You have an American passport that allows you to walk into the camp and walk out unmolested. He has no passport, only two eyes that watch you perform this miracle of getting out alive. You have a home somewhere that has not been dynamited. You have a girlfriend who has not been raped. You have a father who has not been killed in front of your eyes.

Whenever I returned to a normal place after an assignment in Bosnia friends would ask me what it was like to suddenly leave a war zone and then be in a place where bombs are not falling. I would say that it was no big deal, which was the truth. Going from Sarajevo to London in a day is a piece of cake in psychological terms. I would feel relief, splendid relief. It didn't compare to the experience of mixing with death camp inmates and then walking away, a free man with a future. The misery of Bosnia is not half a world away at places like a prison camp; it is staring right at you, less than a foot away, watching you as you get into a van and drive away, and it notices that you don't look back.

Peter Maass was a foreign correspondent based in Asia and Europe. His articles have appeared in the Washington Post, The New York Times, The Wall Street Journal, *and* The New Republic. *He is currently a staff writer for the* Washington Post *and lives in Maryland. This story was excerpted from his book* Love Thy Neighbor: A Story of War.

✶

"Doug?" Selene asked. "Do you really believe in witches like you told Dwayne last night?"

"Yes," I said slowly. "I do."

"Really? Get *out* of here."

"Well," I said, "I don't mean to say that I literally believe a man can put on a wolf skin and run sixty miles an hour. But there's no doubt in my mind that there are skinwalkers like Dwayne said. There are always people who want to take what's good, like the Navajo healing ceremonies, and turn them around. Witchcraft is a very real force."

"But the red eyes? And the corpse powder?"

"Who's to say those things can't possibly exist? Maybe they exist for real, or maybe they exist because people believe in them. All societies have something like witchcraft. An ultimate perversion of their values."

"What's perversion?"

"Something strange and unnatural."

"Witchcraft," Christine said, "is just another way of describing evil. It exists everywhere."

"So what's our witchcraft?" Selene asked.

"It's the same thing Dwayne talked about," I said. "The same old desire for money, power, and control over other people. When I lived in New York City, I met plenty of people who were sort of like Navajo skinwalkers. Only they wore suits. There's not much difference between digging up the dead to get their jewelry and making a business deal that ruins a thousand people's lives."

"Well," Selene said firmly, "I hope *I* never meet a skinwalker."

"I think," I said, "that there's a little bit of skinwalker in each one of us. There's a part that craves power and money. There comes a time in everyone's life when they have to face that skinwalker inside."

—Douglas J. Preston, *Talking to the Ground: One Family's Journey on Horseback Across the Sacred Land of the Navajo*

KATIE HICKMAN

* * *

Parade of Demons

Some cultures have formal rituals for
dealing with the Dark Side.

MUCH LATER, AFTER WE HAD LEFT THE CIRCUS FINALLY, I OFTEN
used to think of Mundo's theories about clowns and how the circus functioned as a kind of fiesta, releasing people from their everyday selves.

Of all the countries I have travelled through, I have never
been anywhere the fiesta is taken as seriously as it is in Mexico.
We came across fiestas everywhere, in all the forms and disguises
which the Mexican exuberance could devise: saints' days and village feasts, pilgrimages and processions, bullfights, flower and
music festivals, beauty pageants, parades and candle-lit vigils;
even the circus itself. It was as if the Mexican's need to escape
from behind the mask of their machismo, from their Indian fatalism, and from all the violence and fear and corruption of their
lives, built up to such a pitch that finally it was torn from them,
like a rocket or a burst of silver stars, transformed into a thousand celebrations.

And the poorer and more disenfranchised the community,
particularly among the Indian peoples, the greater the detail, the
intensity—to the point of *ekstasis* sometimes—with which their
fiestas were conducted.

★

The first time I saw the demon army we were sitting in the corner cafeteria in Jesús-María. At first they were no more than a reverberation, a distant rumble coming from far off, from the very belly of the earth. On our table, glasses and bottles shook, and the tables around us rattled—a demonic presence felt long before it came into sight.

Apart from a loincloth at their waists, the men were naked. The entire surface of their bodies, their limbs, their smooth naked chests and backs, were striped over with black and white paint. I guessed that they were mostly young men, aged between about fifteen and twenty, although it was impossible to tell with any particular accuracy. Each man wore an animal mask over his face, a white mask to match the white body paint. I saw coyotes, deer, bulls, baboons, owls, and others impossible to identify; monstrous, snouted faces with teeth and sharpened fangs, a faint lapidary glitter just visible behind the eye-slits.

At their approach there was an involuntary movement. Everyone in the cafeteria drew back from the porch and we stood pressed together, as though for protection, just inside the door.

In silence the army marched past us at a steady trot into the dirt plaza beyond the café. Four captains, recognizable by their white *képis,* marched at their head, while the rest were arranged into two parallel phalanxes behind them. Because of the press of people I could not see down the road in the direction from which the army were coming, and so first I could not tell how many of them there were. As they passed us I counted ten, twenty, fifty rows of men, but still they kept coming at that same inexorable slow run.

In their hands the demon army carried flat-edged swords, their tips painted white. Seventy, a hundred rows went by. Outside in the silent street the sun burnt down onto baked adobe roofs. Ninety degrees in the shade, but the army never altered their pace. Everyone was indoors: doors slammed, shutters scraped across windows. Little whirlpools of dust, like avenging spirits, eddied through the deserted streets. I was still counting. A hundred and twenty, a hundred and fifty rows at least. They ran and ran, and there was no end to them.

In their dazzling white masks, the army looked neither to left nor to right. At their waists they each wore a river tortoise shell, filled with seeds which rattled as they ran. Fine white dust licked at their naked ankles and the ground trembled beneath their feet.

Two hundred rows went past us in all. Four hundred men. They crossed the little plaza in front of the church, turned up a street behind the *ayuntamiento*, and were gone.

"The demon army," Juan said, when the last of the dust had died down. "The *Judea*, as they are known here. The Jews. From now on, all civil authority is suspended and the town is under their control. Even if we wanted to, we cannot leave here now."

I knew then that we had passed into a time which is known among the Cora people as the *días prohibidos*, or forbidden days: a sacred time which seeks to recreate the beginning of the world, the time before the creation of Tayan, the deity known to the Cora as Our Father the Sun. The infernal army which we had just seen represented the inhabitants of this pre-Creation world, all the deer, the owls, the iguanas and other monsters who inhabited the dark caves and caverns before Our Father the Sun came into being.

We sat down at our table again and the owner of the café, a stout mestizo woman in a flowered pinny, brought us some more *refrescos*.

"Haven't you got any beer?" Victor looked glum.

"Plenty of beer, but not until Saturday. Not until all this is over." The woman gestured into the somnolent street, to where the dust had been churned by the demon feet. "It's one of the forbidden things. No alcohol, no music, no cars circulating, not even any washing in the river is allowed by the *Judea* while they control the town."

"And definitely no photograph." Pancho grinned at Tom through a mouthful of crooked gold-capped teeth.

"Photography! *Ni hablar!*" The woman rolled her eyes heavenward. "If they even see you holding a camera they'll confiscate it, or worse. If you want to take pictures, Señor, you've come to the wrong place. Take it from me, I'm a Mexican but I'm married to a Cora. I know their ways."

Behind her on the wall of the café hung a picture of the Virgin of Guadalupe. Beneath it a tiny revolving fan whirred a thin stream of hot air into our faces.

"At least we've been allowed to stay in Jesús-María, Señora," Juan passed a handkerchief over his face. "We were already late when we picked these two up on the road," he indicated Tom and myself. "Their truck had broken down. We wanted to stay in Mesa del Nayar for the night, the village just before here, but they wouldn't have us."

"It was already nearly dark." Victor rubbed a hand over his heavy jowls. "But no sooner had we driven in when we were surrounded by all these men carrying sticks. Their bodies were all painted over with black, so that only the whites of their eyes were showing."

"They made us pay a fine just for the privilege of being able to pass through their village at all. '*Cooperación*' they called it," Pancho said.

"And they said that if we stayed they would shut us up in the church for three whole days, until the forbidden days were over…"

"They were going to keep us there and not let us sleep or anything, but prod us with sticks all night long to make sure that we had no rest…"

"It was only because we had

We all remember that childhood game and rhyme using linked and folded fingers:

*This is the church
   And this is the steeple.
Open the doors
   And here are the people.*

Every child peers inside the hands, suddenly made mysterious by the chant. Almost all children discover that they too can make mystery for themselves by the magic of a new perspective on the familiar world. We go, in foreign places, to look at castles, places of worship, city streets, country roadways, squares, cafés and people, our eyes made available to their mysteries and secrets. We even learn to open ourselves to the pleasures and pains of others. The French have a word, disponible, *which refers to an emotional availability, openness, willingness to be moved.*

—Herbert Gold, "Comfort in the Strangest Places," *Travel & Leisure* been giving a lift to some other Cora that they let us get away so lightly."

"It was an assault, Señora." Even Juan, the most senior of our three companions, sounded aggrieved. "An assault, nothing less. I wouldn't have minded giving them something, but [thousands of] pesos! I am a Mexican, am I not? I should be able to go anywhere I like in my own country without having to pay for the privilege."

"Don't tell me about it." The woman sighed. "It's lucky you came on here. Jesús-María is a bigger place, so things are a little more relaxed. But it didn't always used to be this way, I can tell you. The *Judea* used to be much stricter. Ay, they were terrible. *No dejaron a la gente reir*...they wouldn't even let people laugh, I tell you. Nothing. If you had a child who was sick and you needed to fetch water for him, you had to go out in the middle of the night to get it and hope that no one saw. And woe betide you if they did."

Juan, Victor and Pancho, from the Boneteria Britannia, Mexico City, had picked us up, as Juan said, the day before on the dirt road where we had broken down in our truck exactly four hours up the eight-hour track which led into the desiccated hills of the northwestern Mexican state of Nayarit.

With his gold chains and his baseball cap, his smooth-skinned belly just beginning to spill over his waistband, Juan, at forty-ish, was the oldest of the three. He had an avuncular, slightly bullying relationship with the two other boys, who fetched his cigarettes, queued up to buy his *refrescos*, pulled and pushed our car, and carried out as many other small errands as he, in the kindest possible way, could devise for them.

The two boys, it has to be said, were not prepossessing. In his early twenties, Victor was large and stolid-looking, with a pale, unhealthy complexion; while Pancho, his friend, was tiny, wiry and dark.

As a travelling salesman, the sock, knicker and pantyhose business had sent Juan to many parts of Mexico, where he had conceived—for a Mexican, at least—an unusual passion for all things which were both native and Indian. He had been to the Tzotzile and Tzeltal villages of Chiapas at Carnival, he had visited the Otomies, the Tarahumaras, the Tarascans, and even been as far as the great Maya ceremonial sites of the Yucatán. Now, like us, he was trying to reach the Cora, who at this time of year were the least hospitable of the Mexican indigenous tribes, for their "Easter" celebrations.

This part of the Nayarit sierra is one of the remotest places in Mexico. We had arrived in Jesús-María, an impoverished settlement of single-storeyed adobe houses, late the night before and had been invited to stay in the house of Melesio Valentín, a Cora Indian, to whose family the good-natured Juan had also given a lift the day before.

Melesio's house was very simple. There were only two rooms and no windows. We slept in a row on sacking on the floor, with the door open to the moon and the stars to let in the breeze. Very early the next morning, before there was a danger of the *Judea* being about, I went down with the women to the river to wash.

The river had all the beauty of the early morning. In the midday heat these hills have the disturbing energy of mirages; now the slopes above us were desiccated and barren still, but somehow quieter, sapped of their usual strength. Their colours were quieter too, alternately pink and mouse-coloured, except for the banks of the river itself which were stitched along with reeds and with cactus and with the spiny, acid-green trees known as guamuchils.

Boys brought their animals down to drink. Women in little groups were washing, their clothes spread out to dry on the rocks like the petals of tropical plants, lime green and ochre and turquoise. The water was cold against my skin, and afterwards I sat alone on a rock in the pale sun, with my skin smelling of river water, watching the women and the boys downstream and wondering what it would be like to stay here for a time, as we had done with the circus, to seek out the rhythms and textures of ordinary life, and how long it would take me to find out their true patterns.

But this was not ordinary life. For the Cora, the *días prohibidos* are magical time, a time when the rules of ordinary life are suspended. Already there was a fever in the air, and the *Judea,* as yet unseen, were on the move.

My second sighting of the *Judea* was from Melesio's house. I was sitting with his daughter-in-law, Paula, a beautiful Cora girl with high cheek bones and skin like spun silk, eating the pods of the guamuchil tree, a sweet white fruit with a shiny black pip, about the size of a pea. It was still early, but already the sun was too hot to sit in. As we sat there, there came a thundering sound and all at once the baking street, with its dust and picking chickens and sleepy brown adobe houses, was full of noise and confusion.

The demon army had metamorphosed during the night.

Instead of black and white body paint they had daubed themselves in every conceivable colour: legs and torsos and chests were daubed with psychedelic swirls of fluorescent oranges, purples and yellows; bright pink tiger stripes were offset with startling green leopard spots, navy blue zebra dashes against crimson hyena crescents, bars of cerulean boa criss-crossed with deep-sea amethyst scales and fins. The masks, pure white the day before, were now painted spring greens, scarlets, vermilions, ochres and lilacs.

When she saw the *Judea,* Paula's lapful of guamuchil pods fell to the floor. Plucking at my arm for me to do likewise, she shrank back out of sight into the shadows. For these were no longer the silent and organized army they had been the day before, running in perfect formation behind the four captains. Down the dusty street they came, whirling and chattering like desert ghouls. When they spoke, the noise that came from beneath their masks was incomprehensible to me, at once guttural and distant, as if they were speaking from the bottom of the sea.

Two mestizo men came walking down the street towards them. One of the *Judea* challenged them, asking for cigarettes. The first man offered him one willingly enough, but as he held the packet out the demon plucked the whole thing from his hand and ran off gibbering. I watched as he ran back to the rest of the army with his booty; a self-satisfied shriek went up as he shared the cigarettes round.

The demons were approaching Melesio's house now. Paula was still flattened to the wall in the darkest corner of the room, but I could see nothing to worry about. The doorways and windows of many of the neighbouring houses had filled up with people watching the show. They were laughing as the demons capered and skipped, licensed fools in their fantastic animal motley. So far the atmosphere was lighthearted, or so I thought. Somewhere at the back of my mind I remember registering how few women there were about, and that those who were in evidence were mostly old grandmothers, but Indian women are almost always more retiring than men on these occasions, and so at the time I did not think much about it. Tom and Juan came out of the next-door room and were immediately rounded on by two of the demons. One wore a coyote mask painted yellow and green, the other a deer head, with real antlers fixed to the papier mâché frame. Juan surrendered the rest of his packet of Rothmans, but when Tom was discovered to have nothing on him to take, the demons growled at him angrily. The crowd laughed. As a *gringo,* the only one in town, Tom was bound to be a particular object of the devils' buffoonery. One of them raised his sword and with the flat hit him across the arm. But this was a show, and it was only a jesting blow—or was it? I saw Tom hesitate. Beneath the mask, the glint of the man's eyes gave nothing away.

Now three of the demons appeared in Melesio's doorway. I could not understand what they were saying, but by their point-ing gestures I guessed they must be making the same request—cigarettes. "*No fumo,* I don't smoke," I explained, thinking we would have to buy a few packets, if only to have something to give away. But the three men only shook their heads, babbling at me, louder now, in their strange gibber-language.

I thought how strange it was: not that I could not understand them but that, hidden beneath their masks, I could not read the expressions on their faces. All of a sudden I was unsure. Was this in jest or for real? It was impossible to tell. I turned to see if Juan might have a new packet of cigarettes which I could give them, and as I did so I felt one of them starting to lift up my skirt with the point of his sword. As I pulled the material away from him another made a grab for my breast, but before he could touch me I had darted back inside the house and slammed shut the door. Outside in the street I heard the sound of fingernails scratching against the wood and then the crowd laughing again; but after a few more minutes they went away and I was left alone with Paula, the frightened whites of her eyes glowing opposite me in the dark.

The process of demonization, like the process of arriving at the divine, is a slow and complicated one. During the "forbidden days" in Jesús-María the Cora experience both. Neither is arrived at easily.

The demon army, the *Judea,* make their first appearance on the Tuesday of Holy Week, but they do not become infernal beings immediately. In order to pass without danger from ordinary time into sacred time, from the real world into the magical world of their mythic origins, in their first metamorphosis the *Judea* are merely ghosts. They march the streets silently, their bodies painted over in pure white, powerless to do anything but survey the streets where, much later, when they are fully awakened, their great battle will take place.

A friend, driving across the high windswept plateau north of Mexico City, looks curiously at a group of people standing behind a large truck. As she approaches she begins braking, sensing something interesting. She passes them slowly, just enough time to get a good look at the huge, bloody severed head of an elephant being wrestled into the back of the truck. There is nothing else in sight but miles of dry grassy slopes and an occasional foraging goat.

—Carl Franz, *The People's Guide to Mexico*

But as the week progresses so does the metamorphosis of the *Judea,* who gain in both strength and colour, as though gradually being pulled into focus. By the Thursday, the day we arrived, they are strident and bold in black and white; by Friday they have erupted into fantastic colour. It is then that their strength is at its most terrifying.

Having made their magical transition, the *Judea* are now compelled to carry out the consequences of their metamorphosis to their ultimate conclusion. They have won their first battle, which is for control over the community of Jesús-María itself. During the *días prohibidos* all civil authority is suspended, and the *Judea* alone rule. All the rules of the real world are turned on their heads. Everything which symbolizes real life is forbidden; everything which is forbidden in real life is courted, magnified, driven to its most extreme limits. *Novios* may not walk hand in hand; women may not knit nor sew nor chastise their children; there is to be no bathing in the river; nor are beasts of burden to work in the fields. There is no music, no alcohol, no driving of vehicles. The *Judea* themselves must speak backwards and, despite the intense heat and the physical demands of their task, may not eat or drink until the afternoon. To give them energy under these gruelling conditions many take peyote, the hallucinogenic cactus bulb which grows in the northern deserts and is sacred to many of its Indian tribes.

All day the demon army cavorted through the town, appearing and disappearing out of the dust like a fantastic mirage from the hills. Sometimes they marched in strict formation under the discipline of their captains; at other times they roamed in small bands, mischievous and free as they had been outside Melesio's house. They ran in and out of the crowd at will, nicking cigarettes, *refrescos* and lighters, knocking off the men's *sombreros;* doing anything, in fact, which took their pixie-like fancy. They threw water and urine and burning straw; they ran races and staged mock fights with their swords. Their movements were gleeful, Puck-like; and they made strange little crowing sounds as they pounced.

It was not dangerous to be around them but it was never exactly safe, either. Everything they did was apparently playful, but their playfulness had a wild, bacchanalian quality which was only ever a whisper away from real menace.

With Juan, Pancho and Victor, we went back to the cafeteria from which we had first seen the *Judea* marching the day before. It was on the plaza—if that was what the empty, beaten mud space in front of the church could be termed—and therefore had the best view. I also hoped that we might be less visible there among other mestizos than in a purely Cora district.

As well as the animal-demons and their captains, other figures now came drifting into the plaza to join them, men with masked faces and outsized Mexican *sombreros* carrying drums and flutes.

With them were their "women," young boys cross-dressed in frocks or skirts, with well-padded breasts and long, blonde wigs.

"They are dancing troupes"—Juan adjusted his baseball cap so that his eyes were shaded from the glare—"but comic ones. Sort of like clowns. We saw some last night, Pancho and me, after you had gone to bed."

With his luxuriant handlebar moustache, the gold chains jangling at his neck and the buttons of his shirt straining over his nascent paunch, ever since he had rescued us on the road the day before, Juan had seemed to me like the archetypal Mexican. And yet now, amongst these Cora, I was struck by how foreign, almost European, he seemed in comparison.

"How do you see yourself amongst all this?" The three of them seemed so out of place here, almost as much so as we were ourselves. "Don't you ever feel Spanish at all?"

"Spanish! *Ni hablar!*" I knew I had uttered a terrible heresy by even suggesting it. "No, *hombre*," Juan shrugged his shoulders with feeling, "the Spanish were the oppressors of our people, the destroyers of our civilization."

The conventional response, just as I had expected.

"Indian then?" Juan looked over into the packed and dusty plaza.

"You mean, am I proud to be descended from Moctezuma and all that shit?" He shook his head. "No, *hombre,* not that either. People say we're a mixture of Spanish and Indian, but quite frankly I don't feel part of either. Us Mexicans, you could call us a *pueblo huérfano,* an orphan nation. And as for me…" he shrugged again, "well, I'm just me, I guess." He laughed, scratched at his spilling belly. "Just your average son-of-a-bitch Mexican."

We watched as the dancing troupes capered beneath the three-foot brims of their hats, piping reedily.

"But look at these Cora, though, they're something else, aren't they?" Juan spoke indulgently, in the manner that more enlightened mestizos often use to talk about the indigenous population. "They like to—how do you say?—take the piss out of us Mexicans…" The smile froze on his face. "*¡Dios mio!*"

One of the musicians had grabbed the "woman" in the long blonde wig, pulled down his trousers, and was proceeding to mount her from behind. I could see his penis, brown and flaccid, rubbing between his partner's proffered buttocks. They fell to the floor, writhing in the dust in simulated ecstasy.

"Ah!" The crowd lining the street outside, in the ironmonger's shop opposite us, and beneath the café porch, drew in their breath. "Oh!"

Some people were laughing; others had turned away, too shocked to watch. A group of young mestizo girls, their hair braided into neat schoolgirl plaits, hid their faces, giggling helplessly into each other's shoulders.

Two other members of the dancing troupe came up. Unlike the others these were not wearing outsized Mexican *sombreros;* instead one had on a plastic mask of the Mexican president, and the other a strange headpiece which I saw now was in the shape of an erect penis. Two swollen balls hung down on either side of his cheeks. When the man in the hat had finished, the President and the Penis took over, falling over themselves in their efforts.

"Ay!" The crowd sighed again, horrified, titillated. Pancho and Victor's mouths hung slightly open. Juan had sunk down into his seat and pulled his baseball cap down still further over his eyes until I could not see his expression at all.

I felt a tap on my shoulder. It was Carmen, the proprietor, the one who was married to a Cora Indian. She was beckoning to me.

"I have a better place for you." She glanced towards the thrashing bodies, and then back at me. "Come with me, all of you, up to my roof." She put her hand on my shoulder. "No one will see you there."

I did not have to ask why she was doing this. I had found these scenes more disturbing than I would ever have imagined. Not because of the sex, which was

> *Do not go around the edges or else you'll fall. No good that place or else you slip.*
>
> —Daisy Utemorrah, "Do Not Go Around the Edges," *Dreamkeepers: A Spirit-Journey into Aboriginal Australia* by Harvey Arden

pure burlesque, so much as the sight of its main recipient: a blonde, and therefore foreign, woman. I was used to the idea that in almost all parts of Mexico blonde hair is extremely rare; but in Jesús-María that day, amongst a predominantly dark-skinned Indian crowd, even to me that wig, peroxide white and hanging to the boy's waist, was shocking in its impact. It sung out like a clarion call, like a roll of drums. A clap of thunder. I looked at that blonde figure, fucking so merrily now with the president of Mexico—and I saw myself.

For the audience, most of whom would never have been to a theatre or any other kind of live performance, here was the greatest spectacle of their lives. This was the circus, I realized, carried to its wildest excess. Here was both release and recognition. The Cora had come together—many such as Melesio and his family travelling many days to be here—not just to celebrate their version of the Resurrection, but also to celebrate the fact that they were Cora. During the rest of the year they might be reviled and humiliated as one of the poorest and most diminished of Mexico's indigenous peoples, but for this brief, magical space, this reign of the demon army, they were restored to their truest and purest selves.

But there was something else, too. Even at its crudest and most burlesque, I was struck by the seriousness of this spectacle. Even at its most basic level, that of pure entertainment, every part of this elaborate masque was imbued with meaning. The Cora's idea of the sacred was not limited to our narrow Sunday School perspective. For them the sacred encompassed not only the forces for good, but also—in the shape of the demon army—their dark face, and the seeds of their destruction. Everything else, the clowning and buffoonery, the orgiastic ritual and self-parody, were simply extensions of this mystical vision.

That afternoon was never-ending, stretched out on elastic. On Carmencita's roof the sun glanced down on us with ferocious multiple slanting blows. From our hiding place the five of us watched as the demon army began to reassemble itself under the direction of the captains, forming up into two parallel lines in front of the church. Up until now Christian Easter rites and Cora ritual had remained separate, but now the two were beginning to come closer, encircling one another until finally they would merge. The *Judea's* last and greatest battle was about to begin.

As we watched, a child dressed in a yellow robe with a crown of leaves about his head was brought running out of the church. He was led by the hand by one man, while two others ran in front of him, lashing at him with cords. At the rear came two more young boys, their bodies painted all over in black.

At the sight of the child a great howl went up among the demon army. They did not move, even when the child was led running between their ranks, but beneath their masks their strange subterranean backwards-language reached fever pitch. Some bayed and gibbered, while others crouched down on their haunches, pawing and sniffing at the ground as if any minute they would spring forwards and devour him.

Led by his entourage, the Jesus-child vanished into the dusty back streets. The demon army waited for about five minutes and then started to run after them. Jesus would not be crucified that day, but hunted down, like the Deer God of the ancient Cora legends. All through the baking adobe streets of Jesús-María the demon army gave chase to the Jesus-child. It was hotter than ever that afternoon, but sustained by the peyote their pace never faltered. In their two parallel flanks, the coyotes and the deer, the owls, the iguanas and the baboons moved with that same remorseless tread that we had seen on our first day. As they ran tiny whirlpools of dust kicked up from beneath their feet, mingling with their daubed and smeared and chequered bodies, until, like a hallucination, the streets were running with rivers of pure colour.

On and on they went, tracking the child from house to house. At their head was a *marakame,* a witch doctor with turkey feathers in his hat. At each cross-roads he knelt down like a hunter to examine the dust for signs of the child's footprints. Each time the demons came to a house where he was hiding they would try to break in, beating the door with their fists, digging in the ground around it with their bare hands, scratching, snuffling, howling for blood. And each time the doors were thrust open, and the child was dragged running past them and out on to the next stage of his weary run, they would crouch down on their haunches, spitting with wordless fury.

In the extraordinary heat of that afternoon, with all the colour and the dust and the glancing light, and with the taste of the sacred peyote still on their lips, I wondered how the world looked to them just then. How, exactly, was it altered?

Watching the demon army as they crouched down on their haunches, hissing and hooping and sniffing the ground, it seemed to me that their metamorphosis was complete. This was not a masque after all. This was real. These were no longer just men in papier mâché masks, but real coyotes, real wolves, real demons from the mythological past. This was the circus *reductio ad absurdum*. After nearly a week of this existence they had finally crossed the point at which fantasy and reality meet, passed over into some magic realm that the rest of us would only ever dimly guess at.

Katie Hickman has lived in Europe, the Far East, and South America and was educated at Oxford. She is the author of Dreams of the Peaceful Dragon *and* A Trip to the Light Fantastic: Travels with a Mexican Circus *from which this story was excerpted. She lives in London with her husband, photographer Tom Owen Edmunds.*

✳

I got a glimpse of the pantheistic unity of the cosmos that yogis attempt to reach at a little village in Mahyua Pradesh. It was during the festival of Holi that I saw, clear as a reflection in a cold stream, the God inside us all.

On Holi, straight-faced farmhands and dour *dhobis* become as playful as kindergartners. Throughout the north it is a celebration to mark the end of winter and the return of balmy days. Gray-haired aunts and white-haired grandmothers, fathers who barely know how to smile, giggling sisters, sniggling cousins, uncles almost too fat to move—all observe the holiday by dousing each other with brightly colored water.

Some throw water balloons, some shoot water pistols, most toss buckets of water tinged with dye or glittering with slivers of ground mica. Some even hurl cans of unadulterated paint. Friends, relatives, and total strangers stalk each other through calculating fields of fire, shrieking with glee as they splash each other with all the colors known to man.

By midday I'd been hit enough times not to care anymore. I joined the gang of teenage boys who ruled the town's streets. They quickly showered me with blue and green dye and, once I was completely stained, welcomed me wholeheartedly into their band. Every boy's face and hands were already masked with color. We pelted all the cars, houses, and pedestrians we could find, and every victim accepted the bath with good humor. That, after all, is what the rite is all about.

For the week after Holi, most of the population of northern India goes about its business spattered with indelible splotches of paint. Clothes can be changed, but it takes many washings to rinse all the dye from one's skin and hair. Every town's walls are streaked with rainbow smudges. Even the animals are not safe—goats, cows, and dogs walk about with hides stained red, yellow, and purple, sometimes until the monsoon rains come to wash it all away.

When I got back to my room at the end of the day, I looked in the mirror and saw God staring back at me: my skin, just like the skin of Lord Rama himself, was a delicate shade of blue.

—Jonah Blank, *Arrow of the Blue-Skinned God: Retracing the Ramayana Through India*

MIKKEL AALAND

⋆ ⋆ ⋆

Sword of Heaven

Did a Shinto priest save the world?

IT WAS MY LAST SHINTO GOD. I WAS ABOARD THE *MARREIRO II*, A
weathered jungle boat, as it struggled against the merging currents
of the Rio Negro and the Rio Solimoes just outside the Brazilian
town of Manaus.

This god, like the one I had placed two weeks earlier in South
Africa, like all the others I had spent the last six years placing
around the world, was wrapped in white prayer cloth and im-
printed with the ancient Japanese symbols *Ten* (heaven) and *Ken*
(sword). I leaned carefully over the wooden railing, weak from a
fever that had gripped me since the day I placed the god at the
Cape of Good Hope and which had become worse as I spent days
in the jungle trying to find the proper place for this last god.

Below me were two rivers—the Negro, full of minerals and
humus and as dark as a bat's cave, and the Solimoes, full of light
Andean silt. They mixed like oil and water, just like me and
everything else about this confusing project. I looked away from
the primordial gumbo, through the moist air, only to see where
huge patches of the verdant jungle had been ripped from the earth
to make room for factories made of concrete.

"This place isn't beautiful," I thought, "but it's got to be here,
now." I removed the white cloth to uncover another familiar

barrier (always another barrier), this one of plain white paper. Just before the boat burst free of the mottled mess and entered the Negro proper, I heaved the heavy stone overboard. A pink dolphin, which the natives call "devil fish," swam by.

I felt better the instant the hollowed stone, filled with its precious contents, splashed into the water. I watched with tears in my eyes as the impact blended the tan and black stew, creating a third distinct color, one richer and more beautiful than before. Patience, I told myself. In time, even oil and water become one. The mixed water, now called the mighty Amazon, moved leisurely downstream toward the distant sea.

A grueling but marvelous journey was over. Perhaps, I thought, tonight I can sleep in peace—my nightmare, and the wall around my heart, gone forever.

I first heard about the Sword of Heaven in the early fall of 1982 at a dinner party in San Francisco. It was the height of the Cold War and our conversation had turned to the end of the world. I was 30 years old, single, and like many of the other dinner guests—baby boomers who had grown up with their share of duck-and-cover drills—found such apocalyptic talk not only interesting but normal.

Sometime during this frightful discussion one of the dinner guests—Juan Li was his name—told us a remarkable story he had heard while traveling in Asia. He told us that many years ago, shortly after the bombing of Hiroshima, a Shinto priest had a horrific vision of the end of the world. His spirit was crushed. He became despondent. But then the priest had another vision, a vision of how to save the world.

The priest was instructed by God to break an ancient Shinto relic—the Sword of Heaven—into 108 pieces and then encase each piece in stone. The stones—which became *kamis,* or gods—would take on magical properties and become capable of battling the evil that was engulfing the world.

No one at the table knew very much about Shinto, but Juan explained that a Shintoist believes that evil results when nature and one's ancestors are not properly worshipped. Shintoists also believe that gods or spirits dwell inside inanimate objects. A stone, a sword, a jewel, a rainbow—anything that evokes or inspires awe or the divine—can possess power and become a *kami,* or god. And like the ancient Greeks, the Shintoists have a pantheon of mythical gods to whom they pray.

Followers of the priest, Juan told us, began to place the stones in a protective ring around the world. After each stone was placed, special ceremonies were held during which the priest and his followers left their physical bodies and joined the heavenly gods in the ensuing battle. But the battle was going slowly. Only 30 of the 108 stone gods had been placed.

"Who told you all this?" someone asked.

"One of the teacher's disciples, a young Japanese named Kazz Tagami," Juan replied. Juan's answer satisfied the questioner, but I still had my doubts.

Spirits? Out-of-body travel? Wizards? I liked Juan, and I wanted to believe him, but this was the stuff of fiction, not fact.

> *The mind is a portion of the absolute; and if it can draw upon all the absolute's celestial armoury, it can also draw upon all the absolute's infernal engines. In the absolute, both good and evil descend to fathomless depths; and both can be tapped at will by the conscious mind; for the back of the conscious mind is a strange No Man's Land, whereof all the borders melt into the absolute.*
>
> —John Cowper Powys, *The Meaning of Culture*

"How do you know the story is true?" I asked.

"Well, I just placed a god," he answered matter-of-factly. "In Taiwan."

With this revelation of his involvement, my skepticism turned to curiosity. "What makes them think their ambitious plan will succeed?" I thought. "What exactly does it mean to worship a tree?" I wasn't raised religiously—my father was a man of science—but I was drawn to this Oriental religion that seemed to emphasize the organic relationship between man and nature, and that had spawned such an intriguing project.

As the evening ended and guests said their good-byes, something compelled me to give Juan my address and to offer my help, even though I really didn't expect anything to come of it.

I still marvel at how the simple act of offering to help that long-ago evening in San Francisco led me on a six-year odyssey to five continents, from Africa to Europe, from South America to Asia, plus three trips to Japan—each visit stranger than the next. During those years I encountered many wondrous things which challenged my Western rational mind.

In Florida a tornado appeared just after I placed a god. In Japan I saw the old teacher, in a trance, move his spirit to the Kremlin and back, reporting that he had seen the fortress dismantled and turned into a giant shrine. Just outside of Hiroshima, atop Mt. Iwakiyama, I participated in the sacred, week-long Fire Ceremony—the first Westerner to do so. I watched in amazement as the completion of the project and the placing of the gods coincided with the fall of the Berlin Wall and the end of the Cold War. Coincidence? Perhaps. But who knows.... As time went on I gained an appreciation for Shinto's ancient spiritual belief that man and nature are one and that evil occurs when these basic connections are forgotten.

My journey didn't only take me to faraway places and to a culture that believes the placing of stone gods can change the course of human history. My road also led me literally underground to a place I had long buried and forgotten. It led me to my father's bomb shelter, buried in front of our suburban home in Livermore, California, home of the Livermore Laboratory, one of the cornerstones of the U.S. nuclear weapon's program and my father's employer. We stayed in the bomb shelter during the Cuban missile crisis.

After the crisis had passed, when the rest of the family had returned upstairs, I made it my bedroom. I loved almost everything about the bomb shelter. It was cold in the summer, warm in the winter. It protected me and I felt safe. I loved everything except the nightmare.

The nightmare always started the same. I was in the bomb shelter, alone, lying on my metal cot. Suddenly there was a loud noise. It came from the escape hatch, which I had painted fluorescent orange. Wham! Someone or something was knocking. I reached for the light switch, but my arm was heavy as lead. I tried to move a leg, but I couldn't. In the blackness I sensed something truly evil outside. If I opened the heavy metal door, whatever was on the other side would rush in. It would kill me, then kill my family sleeping peacefully upstairs. The pounding became more insistent. I wanted to run, but I was frozen with fear. And worse, I knew the only way out was through the escape hatch—right past the evil itself. My mind and my body seemed disconnected. I tried to scream. Nothing.

Do something! Anything! Open the door! No, I can't!

The nightmare always ended the same way. I'd awaken, drenched in sweat, silently screaming.

The nightmare stopped when I moved away to attend college, but not long after I placed the first Shinto god the nightmare returned. The Shinto project, in confronting the possibility of nuclear war, had brought back an unresolved memory that begged for attention. The nightmare clearly represented my fear of

> *It is not power that corrupts but fear.*
> —Aung San Suu Kyi,
> 1991 Nobel Peace Prize Winner

nuclear annihilation—a fear that I shared with many of my generation. As I struggled with placing Shinto gods over the years I began to understand how fear had come to control me, to stop me from fully engaging in life, and in love. But how to overcome my fear? After many years, in South Africa I got the answer I so desperately sought and needed.

My last trip began on the 28th of February, 1988, the first day of the Chinese New Year. (It was the year of the Dragon, the same legendary animal under which I was born.) In my excitement about the trip I imagined a dramatic ending to the project. I would be arrested as a danger to the state by a South African goon squad:

"No, no, don't take him away," a voice would cry from a crowd that had gathered to give me a hero's welcome. "He was only doing it for our good. For the world. Don't punish him!"

Finally, after a world-wide outcry I would be released. "No, not the Nobel Peace Prize!" I'd say humbly. "I really don't deserve it. But my Japanese teacher, it was his idea."

Or, or perhaps a romantic ending: I'd meet a beautiful woman who'd think that placing Shinto gods was heroic, that I was a warrior fighting for peace. I wasn't clear what would happen after I met her, after we fell in love. Maybe the ending should take place at an airport, like the final scene in *Casablanca*. A kiss good-bye? Hello?

It was all good fantasy. In real life, the closure I craved would come—but not as I fantasized.

For a few moments, after I arrived at the Johannesburg airport, I thought to find a guide book on South Africa in the States.

Her name was Pascale and—so much for the romantic fantasy—she was married. She was a medical doctor, from Paris, but lived with her husband, a surgeon, and their child in Tahiti. They were tired of Tahiti, but didn't want to move back to France.

"In France, we are stuck. If we want to switch fields in medicine, even if we go back to school, we are not allowed. If we moved here, we could."

"But why South Africa?" I asked incredulously. "This country is a mess."

"You can't believe everything you read," answered Pascale. "I want to see for myself."

At dinner that night we learned that our itineraries were nearly identical. We agreed to share the cost of a rental car and explore the country together.

Everywhere we went I saw incredible wealth, clean modern cities, and the most developed highway system in all of Africa. It was not only human wealth: the countryside burst with fertility and power. But I also sensed powerful fear. The fear wasn't only among the blacks and "colored" who daily faced oppression and violence. It was also among the fortified communities of the privileged whites. Fear hung over the country like a dense smog. One day I went to an Afrikaaner bank to cash a traveler's check, and before I opened my bag or mouth the teller addressed me in English.

"How did you know?" I asked.

"You look so relaxed, you have to be a foreigner," she answered.

Just after Krueger Park, I told Pascale about the Shinto project. Telling stories is like giving away something precious, and I hoped that she'd appreciate what I was giving her. Instead she listened without comment, and her indifference made my words seem empty. "She thinks I'm a crazy Californian," I thought. "I'd better shut up."

But later, when I brought up my love life, I realized that she had been listening. I told her about Donna, my artist girlfriend, about our difficulties, and about our eventual split, which I suspected was partially caused by my commitment to the Shinto project.

"You choose this project—putting simple stones around the world—over her?" she asked incredulously. "This is what you think? There was something else, no? She was ugly? Stupid? You didn't like her?"

"It's more complicated than that. She wanted to live in New York."

"That doesn't matter. You can make things work if you want," Pascale said quickly. "Didn't she help you?"

"Yes," I said reluctantly. "She was very helpful."

"Did she believe this, this peace project would actually work?"

In the classical Chinese model, spatial forms—or "things"—are temporal flows. "Things" and "events" are mutually shaping and being shaped, and exist as a dynamic calculus of contrasting foci emerging in tension with each other. Changing at varying degrees of speed and intensity, the tensions constitutive of things reveal a site-specific regularity and pattern, like currents in the water, sound waves in the air, or weather systems in the sky. Etymologically, the character ch'i—"the stuff of existence"—is probably acoustic, making "resonance" and "tensions" a particularly appropriate way of describing the relations that obtain among things.

—Sun-tzu, *The Art of War*, translated by Roger T. Ames

"I'm not sure. But, you know, I never asked her directly what she thought of the project. I know she saw it as a kind of huge art project, a performance piece."

"She knew you had to do it alone, right?"

"Well, yes, actually she did say that she understood that it was my project. That's why she didn't want to interfere."

"The hero. I know men like you. They are out to save the world. You think you have to do this, to prove yourself. I wouldn't have been so patient."

"She wasn't all that patient."

"Do you really think being a hero makes that much difference to a woman?"

"You don't understand."

"Yes, I don't understand," she said. "But you don't either. You haven't figured out where Donna—or any woman—belongs in your life."

"Maybe. But this story isn't about Donna and me."

"Of course it is. All stories are about love. What else is there?"

I was quiet for a long time.

After nearly three weeks in South Africa I still carried the Shinto god. It wasn't for lack of opportunity. There was the fantastic beauty of the Transvaal, Krueger Park, and the dramatic Indian Ocean coast. Of course, I could always point to some tangible reason for not placing the god—lack of water, simple privacy, or convenience. But mostly I just felt not now. Relax. Have faith.

By the time we arrived in Durban, on the southern coast, I was tired and irritable. It didn't help when I saw a white woman yank her three-year-old from a freshwater pool at a playground near the beach. The child was playing with two black children her age and the mother had a fit. The child reached sadly back to her play-mates. It was a pitiful sight, worse even than the signs on the beach designating "whites only" areas. "Why the hell can't they get it together," I thought. "Stupid people! They have so much, why don't they just share?" Pascale, who witnessed the scene, was also shocked.

That night in our hotel we returned to our separate rooms. A refrigerator motor kicked in and I turned on the television to drown out the noise. *Dallas,* the American soap, was playing and I turned the TV off. I stuffed plugs into my ears. Before I fell into an anxious sleep I wondered what I would do if Cape Town—our final destination—wasn't right. Where would I place the god? I couldn't stay in South Africa forever.

When the nightmare began I was at the top of the stairs leading out of the bomb shelter, rather than inside. The violent noise, which usually came from behind the escape hatch, now came from behind the door, which I had slammed shut after running up the stairs. I was terrified as usual. But this time I looked around me and saw Kazz, my Japanese friend, and the teacher dressed in white robes. As they waved swords above their heads, they chanted.

I turned back to the door and cried the words, *Amaterasuomikami,* repeating the Japanese incantation to the sun goddess over and over. I reached for the doorknob. Suddenly the door flung open. An evil stench slammed into me. Then something horrible, without form, gripped me. I struggled and turned back to Kazz and the teacher, but they had disappeared. I was alone.

"Go away! Go away!" I screamed. Never had I been so close to the creature who guarded the door. I felt nauseous and overwhelmed. The more I struggled, the more I became entwined with the creature. I reached for the doorknob and grabbed it for support.

> *I have lived on the lip of insanity, wanting to know reasons, knocking on a door. It opens. I've been knocking from the inside.*
>
> —Rumi

I don't know where the voices came from. Surely they were my own. They were soft and tender and not at all filled with terror. I was suddenly aware of my heart beating furiously. For the first time since Kazz and the teacher disappeared I felt the presence of others—powerful others, who, like the evil one, were formless. I had the vague feeling that these were the great savants of the world: Buddha, Mohammed, Confucius, and Christ, the great teachers who preached the universal lesson of love. They were all talking to me. Now it was Christ's voice I heard.

"You?!" I cried.

"Who did you expect?" The voice answered calmly.

"Help me!"

"Let go. Relax. Open your heart. Now!"

I began to pray. It was a very simple prayer. It wasn't for me; it was for the people of South Africa, so full of fear and hate. Then I took a deep breath, and as I released the air I imagined myself pliant like a willow tree. All the while the evil swept past me in spasms, buffeting me with unimaginable force. This went on for a long time, but I kept breathing deeper and deeper, imagining that my heart was opening wider and wider until it encompassed the very evil itself. Then I let go of my grip on the doorknob, and suddenly I was on the other side feeling porous and floating happily above the stairs. There was no sign of the beast or the door.

When I awoke I was clutching the tiny sword Kazz had given me for protection. I turned to my side and placed it carefully on the dresser, and fell into an easy sleep.

The next morning I was relieved when Pascale offered to drive. I pushed my seat back, so exhausted from my night of revelation that I hardly noticed the fantastic speeds she was hitting. I stared at the green hills, then at the well-tended vineyards that bordered the road. Far away, lightning struck a mountain range. Huge bolts shattered the air and I watched the show with amazement. After a while I dozed.

"Cape Town!" cried Pascale, slapping my leg. "It's beautiful."

The sky cleared, except for one small cloud which spouted a rainbow that dropped to a cluster of elegant buildings. Pascale stopped the car so I could snap a picture.

As we drove to the center we both felt an immediate change. This town was unlike anything we had seen in the rest of South Africa. If Johannesburg felt like Los Angeles, with its impersonal highrises and suburbs sprawling out from no apparent center, Cape Town was like San Francisco. The air was sweet and fresh from the two oceans that engulf the Cape. People seemed much more relaxed. I felt at home.

I envisioned that when the time came for me to place the god, I would go alone. I couldn't imagine Pascale would be interested. But when I told her my plans, she wanted to come along.

"At first, I was sure you didn't know what you were doing," she said. "But you are so persistent."

"You thought it was stupid."

"It might be. It might not. Now I am not sure."

At the Cape of Good Hope there were hordes of German and British tourists posing on the ledge overlooking the Indian and Atlantic oceans. It was foggy with intermittent blue.

I found a ledge about 100-200 meters up and watched the two seas join together between puffs of wind and fog. Pascale placed herself on a ledge above me and snapped pictures as I steadied myself in preparation for tossing the god.

"Careful," she yelled down at me. "Don't get so close to the edge."

There was no need for worry. I wasn't going to slip or jump. I had been on the edge for the last six years and I wasn't going to fall now. There would be no such dramatic ending to this story. The finale—and this would take me years to fully understand—had already occurred. It was that moment in my nightmare when I finally had the power to face my worst fears and open the escape hatch door. The Sword of Heaven had helped push me toward the door and given me the means to open it; the receptiveness of my heart had ultimately protected and saved me from the evil.

And what did I find on the other side of the door, on the other side of fear?

I found a place that poets speak of, a place that has simply been called love, God, or the infinite. In it my mind was at peace and my body one with that which surrounded it. All barriers were gone and I felt totally engaged with the world. It is a place that I learned is always near but a place I had to travel far to find.

The god left my hand and flew through the air. It splashed just off the rocky beach, into the crashing surf.

Pascale cried for me to hurry—she was flying back to Johannesburg, while I planned to return to Brazil to place my last Shinto god. I stared across the two oceans for a long time before scrambling up the cliff.

Mikkel Aaland is an author and photographer currently living in Washington, D.C., with his wife, Rebecca, and daughter, Miranda Kristina.

＊

The prevailing world of thought is like some frozen sea heaving and cracking, with a trickle of shy life rushing beneath its surface, carrying fragrant memories of what has long been forgotten, a world beyond the world of matter. Human beings will always need to interpret themselves in ancient and familiar terms, the intentional circle enlarging but never breaking; they will never find an explanation for the way things are so complete and so compelling as to make their transcendental urges irrelevant. Something is going, and something is gone, some aspect of conviction broken. In return, there is something familiar, and something recaptured. *For lo, the winter is past. The rain is over and gone; the flowers appear on the Earth; the time of singing is come, And the voice of the turtle is heard in our land.*

—David Berlinski, "As Elvis Said"

PART FIVE

SIMPLE GIFTS

Encounter with a Stranger

You never know who you'll
meet on the road.

THREE MONTHS LATER I FOUND MYSELF IN THE SOUTH OF INDIA,
in Pondicherry, a former French colonial town on the sea, visiting
the ashram of Aurobindo. I had not heard of Aurobindo or
Pondicherry before I came back to India; I had no intentions of
visiting any ashrams (four years' experience at an Oxford college
had cured me of any fascination with "monasticism"). I went there
on a whim, on a chance remark from a fellow traveler who had
found me thin and depressed in a fleapit in Tanjore and said, "Go
to Pondy and get yourself a supply of good English beer, French
bread, and a clean room."

My first days in Pondicherry—despite the English beer, French
bread, and clean room—were disgruntled. The city itself unnerved
me with its long, straight, empty avenues baking in unwaveringly
harsh sun. I disliked the ashram with its pompous colonial buildings and air of goody-goody white-washed piety. What little I
gleaned of Aurobindo's philosophy of evolution struck me as
ridiculous. I wrote to a friend in England who had been afraid I
would "get religion" in India that Aurobindo was obviously an
escapee from reality, a fantasist of the most grandiose proportions.
How could anyone but a fantasist believe at this moment that

humankind had any hope of saving itself, let alone "leaping into Divine Being," or some such rubbish, after the Gulags, the First and Second World Wars? After Hiroshima and Auschwitz, Kampuchea and Vietnam? As for sweet Mother, his Shakti, the half-French half-Turkish sibyl who had accompanied him on his "adventure," I wrote: "I see nothing in the so-called Mother of the Universe and Co-creator of the coming transformation of human beings into divine infants but an ancient Jewess with an appalling taste in clothes." I ended the letter: "I am leaving this incense-scented morgue tomorrow for the beach (*any* beach *anywhere*) and a little sensual sanity. I'd rather die drunk in a Calcutta ditch than spend another day here."

In fact, I went on to spend four more months.

That evening I met Jean-Marc Frechette and began a friendship that would change my life.

He was standing in front of me in the ashram food queue, frail, stooped, with balding light chestnut hair and large, slightly protruding eyes, reading Jaccottet's translations of Hopkins. I was so relieved to see someone reading and not wandering in the usual ashram daze that I moved close to him and craned over his shoulder. We started talking and continued most of the night. He was from Montreal and lived in a guest house near the ashram. He loved Rilke, Piero della Francesca, and Callas, as I did; we had a whole culture in common, and that bound us immediately. But he had made a transition into the Eastern world that I had not managed.

"Why are you here?" I asked him.

"To change my life."

"You believe in Aurobindo's philosophy?"

"I experience his philosophy."

That made me furious. As we walked by the sea I launched into a denunciation of the escapism of ashrams in general and the uselessness of Eastern Wisdom in the face of the problems of the world.

"The world is in its last nightmare, and sweet old clichés like 'peace of mind' and 'the power of meditation' and 'evolution into divine being' aren't going to wake it up. So-called Eastern wisdom is as bankrupt and helpless as that of the West—more so, in fact, because its claims are so much more grandiloquent."

Jean-Marc heard me out with barely suppressed amusement.

"Why don't you just let go of it?" he said.

"Let go of what?"

"The toy you are holding."

"Don't be cryptic."

"You are holding on to horror and tragedy like a child on to its last toy. It is all you have left, the last rags of a costume you do not want to give up."

His certainty exploded me into another tirade. "I'd rather

Many people today are having spiritual or transmental experiences— experiences from the higher or deeper stages of consciousness evolution. But they don't know how to interpret them. They have these extraordinary intuitions, but they unpack the intuitions in a very inadequate fashion. And these inadequate interpretations abort further transformation, derail it, sabotage it.

—Ken Wilber, *The Brief History of Everything*

die than be calm. I'd rather die of the horror I see everywhere than hide from it in some snug yogic catatonia."

Jean-Marc dropped to the sand laughing.

"Oh, my god," he said, wiping his eyes. "No wonder you like Callas so much."

He imitated my indignant face and flailing arms.

"You see the world as one long grim nineteenth-century opera with nothing in it but pain and loss. You refuse to imagine anything but catastrophe."

He started laughing again. "How conventional."

"Stop laughing, damn you!"

"I don't have to stop laughing. *You* have to start. Don't you see how absurd you are being? Look around you. Feel this night, its sweetness, the softness of the sand where we are walking. You've been running from your spirit for years. You must stop. You must sit down, shut up, open, listen, and wait. Give your soul a chance to breathe. Never in my life have I seen a performance such as the one you have just given. The only thing you *didn't* do is cut open a vein."

He stood up and put his arm around me. "The room next to mine in the guest house is vacant tomorrow. Why don't you take it? We could go on talking and walking by the sea. I could introduce you to my poetic genius, and we could drink tea in the garden in the afternoon like old British colonels."

Undoing a year's careful planning, I accepted.

I see everywhere in the world the inevitable expression of the concept of infinity.... The idea of God is nothing more than one form of the idea of infinity. So long as the mystery of the infinite weighs on the human mind, so long will temples be raised to the cult of the infinite, whether it be called Brahmah, Allah, Jehovah or Jesus.... The Greeks understood the mysterious power of the hidden side of things. They bequeathed to us one of the most beautiful words in our language—the word 'enthusiasm'—en theos—a god within. The grandeur of human actions is measured by the inspiration from which they spring. Happy is he who bears a god within, and who obeys it. The ideals of art, or science, are lighted by reflection from the infinite.

—Louis Pasteur

Jean-Marc's gift to me—for which I will always be grateful— was to live the spiritual life before my eyes with such a happy simplicity I could not deny its truth. Jean-Marc had given up all "normal" life for a small room with a badly working fan by the sea in South India. He had almost no money, no job to go to, no ring of friends to sustain his choice— nothing, in fact, but his faith, his few books of Claudel, Rene Char, and Aurobindo, and the sound of the sea. Yet he was the clearest man I had ever known, spare, joyful, delightfully eccentric, like his room with its narrow, lopsided wooden bed, its desk with one leg propped up by an old copy of the *Upanishad,* its cracked blue china bowl kept always full of flowers. Nothing interested him less than preaching his mystic insights; he lived them, writing them down in huge swirling letters in the garden swept by sea wind, reading Meister Eckhart and John of the Cross, swigging tea from a flask, walking up and down the beach in his loping zigzag gait, his eyes brilliant with mischief and hilarity.

Jean-Marc never talked about renunciation or expiation; although he had been brought up a Quebecois Catholic in a country village, he detested all notions of guilt and original sin—"how vulgar to imagine that God cannot forgive anything," "this world is divine," he would repeat again and again, leaning down to stroke the beach like an old dog or ruffling the long grass with closed eyes. "Hopkins was right: 'There lives the dearest freshness deep down in things.' You just have to go deep enough to find it and to stay with it."

"Your problem," he would say, lowering his voice conspiratorially, "is that, like so many post-romantics, you find suffering glorious. Pain has become your substitute for religion. But pain is not glorious, it is boring. Joy is glorious. Praise is glorious. Because they are hard. You have to work at them with your whole being. Your other problem is that you want—like almost every other intellectual Westerner I have ever met—to do everything yourself. You think there is something "unmanly" in asking anyone else for help, let alone looking for a Master who could guide you. Meister Eckhart said: 'A fly in God is greater that an angel in himself.' You are a vain angel."

Slowly Jean-Marc persuaded me to go with him to the ashram, to visit Aurobindo's tomb, to examine my earlier dismissal of meditation. One day he said, "Why don't you just sit by Aurobindo's tomb and see what happens?" I sat day after day with the other silent meditators by the white slab heaped with lotuses and jasmine. Nothing happened; I just felt hot, sad, and angry at the confusion in my mind.

Then, one afternoon, just as I decided to leave and get some tea, the thoughts that had been racing through my brain were suddenly silenced. I felt my entire being gasp for joy, a kind of joy I had never before experienced. I did not tell Jean-Marc for fear that if I talked about the experience it would vanish—but it repeated with more or less the same intensity for days afterward.

At last I told him.

"Well..." Jean-Marc smiled. "Now you know that the power

of meditation is not a 'sweet old cliché.' Your new life is starting."

We went to the Hôtel de Ville on the seafront and celebrated with one tepid bottle of beer each. Later, as we sat on the beach under a nearly full moon, he wrote out one of his poems for me in the sand:

> O moon
> Mingle our quiet tears
> With the tail of comets…
> For so the soul begins.

Now Jean-Marc began to lay before me the visionary treasures of his inner life. I listened astonished as he told me of a vision he had had in Duino Castle when Aurobindo had appeared to him in the middle of a lotus of fire; a week before I would have been tempted to dismiss this as fantasy, but now each detail seemed essential, a key to a new possibility.

"Mystics are not special human beings," Jean-Marc said. "Each human being is a special kind of mystic. Not everyone, however, wants to know this or to find out what it means. Those who do, and who become conscious of their inner power, see and know as clearly as you and I see this rose or the sea outside the window."

I still had no real idea what he was talking about. Experiences of the next few weeks would sweep that ignorance away.

The Baael Shem Tov, a Hasidic master who lived 200 years ago in Poland, once compared the moment of his awakening to turning and stepping out the back door of his own mind.

—Mark Matousek, *Sex, Death, Enlightenment*

Every day I meditated before sleep and soon began to hear a low hum coming from all around me, the walls, the flowers, the sound of the sea itself. If I tried too hard to concentrate on it, it would go away. When I let my mind rest, it would surround me. I told Jean-Marc.

"Good," he said. "So that is beginning."

I pressed him.

"Creation has a sound. You are hearing it, or part of it."

One night, about a week after I had been hearing the sound, I had the first vision of my life, which overturned everything I had known up until then.

I fell asleep but I did not feel it like sleep at all. I was simply at peace, detached from my body, which I could see lying beneath me. Rapidly, as if in a great wind, I found myself taken to a white room, open to sounds of the afternoon, in which Aurobindo himself was sitting, white-haired, calm, surrounded by a group of silent disciples. The room was not his room in Pondicherry, which I had seen, but one more ancient. I felt as if I were in ancient India. Nothing was said; I moved toward Aurobindo naturally, as if to a long-lost father. I put my head in his lap, and he rested one hand on it.

Then I entered a cloud of swirling light. The Light was filled with thousands and thousands of voices, all singing in rapture. Some of the words I could make out, some were in languages I knew, some in languages I had never heard before. I heard my own voice singing with them, mingling with theirs, singing the words "I hate to leave you, but it is your will and I must go down." I did not know what the words meant, but my heart was filled with an immense love for the Light I was mingled with. Having to leave it filled me with grief; my voice burned and rose and fell with the others.

The music stopped. I found myself bound, almost choking, in a dark chute hurtling down what seemed like a long slide. Then, with a bump, I hit ground and woke up.

I heard the words distinctly, spoken in a calm male voice: "Remember who you are. Remember where you come from."

My body was flooded with waves of blissful energy that

The river of life struggles through all obstacles and conditions to reach the vast and infinite ocean of existence who is God. It knows no rest, no freedom and no peace until it mingles with the waters of immortality and delights in the visions of infinity.

—Swami Ramdas, *In Quest of God: The Saga of an Extraordinary Pilgrimage* swept up and down into the pulse and rhythm of the music I had heard.

As soon as I could collect myself, I went out into the morning, lay in the long grass of the garden, and wept with gratitude.

Then fear began. Was I going mad? What would I *do* with this new, overwhelming knowledge? How would I always remember who I am and where I came from? I knew I had been graced with a great insight, but what would I *do* with it?

"What do you *do*?" Jean-Marc laughed. "You get down on your knees and say a hundred thousand thank-yous for a start. Then you wait."

"*Wait?*" I exploded.

Jean-Marc broke into wild laughter. "Two weeks ago you denied enlightenment existed. Now you want to be enlightened instantly. Some people work and wait years for what you have just been given, and here you are already demanding everything. Go on meditating; be calm. And, for God's sake, enjoy yourself."

Even after my vision I avoided reading Aurobindo seriously. I had an intuition that I would have to be taught inwardly how to read him, that if I read him too soon and with an unripe, defensive, or merely curious mind, I would miss the immediacy of his vision. All my life I had thought myself intelligent enough to understand anything: now I realized how limited my understanding of intelligence had been. Nothing in my Western training could help me explore what I had begun to see; now I knew only enough to know I would have to trust and be led forward by whatever Power was educating me.

In the following weeks of quiet talks with Jean-Marc and meditation by Aurobindo's tomb, I began to see how much of my inner life my mind had been repressing or denying. A thousand memories of my Indian childhood returned in their old wide happiness: I began to connect the joys I had known in music and friendship and in a few moments of lovemaking with the greater joy that was dawning in my spirit. I began to see how my fascination with the drama of my emotional life and my too-great faith in the powers of my intellect had withered my spirit. Jean-Marc had a dream of me in black, sitting at the end of a long, dark corridor, surrounded by books. "You have become imprisoned in the knowledge you acquired in order to 'become' yourself," he said to me. "Now you must let it go so another knowledge can arrive."

About a week after the first vision I was given another one in sleep, although it was more vivid than any dream.

I was sitting on one of the beaches of my childhood, the beach at Cannanore, where I had often gone in the summer holidays with my mother. In the distance I could see fishermen on their primitive boats, and the sight of their lean, tough bodies in the sun comforted me.

Something told me to look to my right. Far down the beach a figure in white was walking in my direction. As it came closer I saw the figure had a face of blinding beauty—oval, golden with large, tender eyes. I had no idea whether the figure was male or female or both, but a love for it and a kind of high, refined desire began in me. With a shock I realized the figure was coming toward me, had, in fact, walked the length of the beach to come to me. The figure approached, sat down so close by me in the sand that I could smell its sandalwood fragrance.

I had no idea what to do. I sat with my head turned away from the figure. It said, in a soft voice, "Look at me." I turned and saw its face irradiated by a golden light that was not the light of the afternoon dancing around us on the sand but a light emanating from its eyes and skin. It put out a hand and touched my face and then cradled it.

Leaning against its breast, I experienced the most complete love for any other being I had ever felt, a love in which there was desire, but a desire so fiery and clear it filled my whole self and was focused nowhere.

Still embraced, I asked the figure, "Who are you?"

The voice came back, amused and gentle: "Who am I? Who do you think I am? I am *you.*"

I fainted, and awoke.

Andrew Harvey is the author of A Journey to Ladakh, Burning Houses, The Web, *and* Hidden Journey: A Spiritual Awakening, *from which this story was excerpted. He was the youngest fellow ever elected to Oxford, and has written several books of poetry and works of translation.*

★

I was privileged to visit the Atomic Energy Testing Station near Arco, Idaho, four times during the late fifties and early sixties.... Although the atomic plane project was scrapped as impractical, I use the word "privileged" to convey how touring the nuclear facility affected me. I loved the place.

Not as much was known then about atomic energy and fission as is known now; hence, visitors such as myself had quite a bit of latitude. Yes, we were required to wear radiation badges while on tour, and yes, we were checked regularly by having to walk through doorlike detector frames. Yet reactors were off-line (shut down) for only a few hours before the crowds came, and always there was one, namely me, who took advantage of that. Since part of each tour included the opportunity to climb stairs to the top of a still-somewhat-active nuclear reactor with its cap opened and peer inside, people like myself, if clever, could easily outwit on-duty technicians. And this I did, consistently, for three years running.

I couldn't get enough of it. When my turn would come to peer inside the reactor core, I'd stick my whole head in there and stay as long as possible. I'd drink it up, smell it, taste it, bliss out on the energy. I could even see it, the vibration of the core's radiation, and to me it was a fresh, sparkly bright, piercingly wondrous radiance so utterly pure and powerful that it was ecstasy itself even to be near the stuff. As I walked around the reactors, I would caress them, kiss them. Even when I stood over pools of irradiated matter, I could still feel the vibrations, and I could see, smell, and taste them as well. I would devise ways of avoiding detector checks so that I could go back and absorb more of that energy, and absorb I did, like a sponge. I called it LOVE, that feeling the energy gave me, LOVE in capital letters because it was a feeling beyond any frame of reference I had at the time. When public tours of the facility ceased I was crushed. This cancellation meant to me that I would forever be denied the most incredible source of love I had ever known.

—P. M. H. Atwater, Lh.D., *Future Memory: How Those Who "See the Future" Shed New Light on the Workings of the Human Mind*

DAVID BERLINSKI

✳

Prague Interlude

A mathematician channels a monk.

SEVEN HUNDRED MILES TO THE EAST OF PARIS, THERE IS PRAGUE at dusk, a full moon over the Karluv Most—the Charles Bridge—the river glossy below, swans paddling slowly, Hradcany Castle and the gentle stone buildings of the Mala Strana in the background. It is there, as a mist rises from the river, that Bernhardt Bolzano, dressed in the coarse woolen cloth of a Franciscan friar and dead officially since 1848, walks late at night, and where he can be heard muttering to himself, and I mention this queer implausible fact because for the whole of the time I was in Prague, there *he* was, a gentle, tubby, spectral form.

I had come to Prague to deliver a lecture at Prague University, where in 1796 Bolzano had entered the faculty to attend courses in theology and philosophy; I found myself lodged in an ancient building attached to the main part of the university by a common wall. My quarters were palatial, a living room, separate bedroom, bathroom, and foyer. The ceilings were at least fifteen feet high and timbered, the huge wooden beams decorated in what looked like pastels, an effect made unnerving because of the contrast between the solidity of the timber and the fragility of the colors. Later, someone told me that these quarters had been reserved for the daytime use of high party officials. I could imagine a pretty woman sitting in this apartment, braiding her hair, waiting.

Bolzano's spirit flowed freely through the walls, where on occasion it took up residence in the concierge, a mild, inoffensive, middle-aged man; he spent most of his time watching television.

"You lif in California, *tak?*" he asked me one day.

"*Tak.*"

He opened his ledger and began to rifle through the pages. "Ve had here in April zomvon else from California. Here is. Professor Jacobson. You know?"

It was no one that I knew.

"*Tak*, here he go out in morning, come back for lunch."

Continuity is an aspect of things as rooted in reality as the fact that material objects occupy space; it is the contrast between the continuous and the discrete that is the great generating engine by which the real numbers are constructed and the calculus created. The concept of continuity is, like so many profound concepts, both simple and elusive, elementary and divinely enigmatic. A process is continuous if it has no gaps, no place where the process itself falls into abeyance. The flight of an eagle is an example. The great bird gathers its shoulders, pushes off from a rotted tree stump, lifts into the wind, its wings beating, soars upward on a thermal current, and then, its neck curved downward, folds its wings together and dives toward the stream below. Although in the course of flight the bird does different things, there is no moment when what it does simply lapses so that it *jumps* from one part of its aerial repertoire to another.

We live in disorderly times. Things seem often discontinuous and almost always chaotic. Quantum theory suggests, especially to those who have not studied it, that on some level of analysis, quanta bounce around for no good reason whatsoever. It is worth remembering, if only for the sense of calm that it provides, that the calculus was created by men who looked out on a different world, one in which the great panorama of natural processes were all of them clearly continuous.

In its representation of the real world, the calculus subordinates processes to functions—that is its most compelling impulse—and so a definition of continuity must have as its aim a statement to the effect that a function is continuous just in case—and there follows, of course, a moment of confusion in which the familiar fog rearranges itself. Just in case what? A first essay at a definition proceeds by imitation. A real valued function *f* is continuous if in its behavior it has no gaps. It is here that the imagination endeavors to evoke within a purely mathematical mirror that essential seamlessness so plainly a part of the physical world. And here inevitably the mirror becomes cloudy, returning for the world's bright images something turbid and unclean.

odern attempts to create a mathematical Theory of Everything accept an evolutionary cosmology, but at the same time accept the traditional faith in eternal laws of nature and the invariance of the fundamental constants. The laws were in some sense already there before the initial singularity; or rather they transcend time and space together. But the question remains: Why should the laws be as they are? And why should the fundamental constants have the particular values they have?

—Rupert Sheldrake, *Seven Experiments That Could Change the World: A Do-It-Yourself Guide to Revolutionary Science*

I mention this to my hosts, Professor Swoboda, who is a mathematician, and Professor Schweik, who is a philosopher. We have been walking toward the Vltava River. Both men appear to me to be in late middle age, perhaps sixty or so. They have very similar round, almost globular heads, thinning hair, very sallow skin, and shockingly bad teeth. They are dressed in shabby suits, and their bodies have a defensive weariness.

Swoboda is extraordinarily intelligent. He speaks English in an odd way, appearing to fetch each word he utters from a great distance. Nonetheless, his grasp of English grammar is perfect, and very often he expresses himself not only with precision but with an eerie economy of effect.

We reach the Karluv Most. I am struck by the extraordinary light, in which blue, blue gray, and gray are offset by a kind of smokiness. I wonder if it might be pollution, but there are few cars in Prague and almost none in the central quarter. "The smokiness," says Swoboda, "is the atmospheric effect of the decomposition of the sandstone that has gone into the construction of the bridge itself, an interesting example of an artistic entity making possible the unique conditions under which it may best be appreciated."

"*Tak,*" says Schweik.

"It is the same," Swoboda says, "with mathematics."

That afternoon I walk through the oldest quarter in Prague. The streets are narrow and the houses timbered. It is here that Bolzano was born in 1781. There is everywhere a mood of moral earnestness, as palpable as the lowering color of the sky. Reading a biography of Bolzano published in German, I am not surprised that he proposed to order his life by a principle of *benevolence.* By and by, I wander back to the university to meet with the director of the institute, Ivan Havel. He is a small, energetic, merry man, with gray hair worn in thick curls, gray eyes, and a trim compact body. He is dressed in a well-cut English suit and wears a shirt with French cuffs. He speaks English, which he has acquired at Berkeley, with a considerable Czech accent and lisps as he talks, spraying saliva in every direction; at lunch he is a menace. Presently Sir Arnold Bergen enters the room. He is an immensely distinguished British pharmacologist, in Prague to deliver a lecture to the Academy of Science. He is perhaps in his mid-sixties, lean, vulpine, his hair covering the top of his head in strands drawn up from one ear; he has a large powerful nose, the thing like a flügelhorn.

We go to lunch at a club said to be frequented by Czech reporters. The food is mystifying. I order dumplings and Bergen, carp. Steins of foaming pilsner all around.

Later, I give my talk in a room with a strange glass blackboard. When I am introduced, Havel says that I am a writer as well as a scientist. This elicits a murmur of approval. There are twenty or so people in the audience. The room quickly grows stuffy, but everyone listens intently.

I speak slowly and distinctly, in the way one does to an audience that treats English as a second language; I am supposed to talk about Tychonoff's theorem, but to my surprise I find myself explaining the elementary calculus to a roomful of mathematicians, re-creating in my own mind the steps that Bolzano took in order to define continuity. For some reason I feel it absolutely crucial to explain how the concept of a limit is applied to functions. No one seems to mind or even notice.

"A function indicates a relationship in progress, arguments going to values. Given any real number, the function $f(x)=x2$ returns its square, *tak?*"

The solemn serious men nod their heavy heads.

"The image of a machine, something like a device making sausages, is irresistible," I say decisively.

I walk over to the blackboard and with quick strokes of chalk draw a sausage-making machine, or what I imagine looks like one.

"*In* go the arguments 1,2,3, *out* come the values, 1,4,9."

There is a snicker from one of the men sitting on the rough wooden pew in front of the class. "Vulgar?" I say. "*Tak*, vulgar." I wipe the palms of my hands on my suit, a gesture that I realize I have never made before. And then I resume.

Physicist Roger Penrose has said that the chance of an ordered universe happening at random is 10 to the 10 to the 30th against—a number so large that if you programmed a computer to write a million zeros per second, it would take a million times the age of the universe just to write the number down.

Ultimately, one has to wonder how scientists who assume the profound presence of patterns in nature in order to practice their very art can also assume that those patterns developed randomly, from nothingness. Patterns imply intelligence, and an ordered creation implies an orderer.

—Andy Fletcher, Letter to the Editor, *Harper's*

"As the arguments of f get larger and larger, its values get larger and larger in turn."

Sir Arnold Bergen and Ivan Havel seem fascinated, and I receive the impression that this is material that they have never heard before. Swoboda and Schweik are looking at me intently.

"Now imagine," I say, "arguments coming closer and closer to the number 3, *tak?*"

I walk back to the blackboard and show the men in my audience what I mean, writing, 2, 2.1, 2.2, 2.3, 2.4, 2.5, 2.6…, before the function.

"What then happens to the function? How does it behave?" I ask, realizing with a sense of wonder somewhat at odds with the hard-boiled pose I usually affect, that a function is among the things in the world that *behaves*—it has a life of its own and so in its own way participates in the drama of things that are animate.

"I mean," I say, "what happens to the values of *f* as its arguments approach 3?"

I look out toward my audience. Swoboda and Schweik are looking at me intently, their faces serene, without irony. It is plain to me that they do not know the answer yet.

> *The steps [one] takes from the day of birth until that of death trace in time an inconceivable figure…. This figure (perhaps) has its given function in the economy of the universe.*
>
> —Jorge Luis Borges,
> *The Mirror of Enigmas*

"They approach, those values, the number 9, so that the function is now seen as running up against a limit, a boundary beyond which it does not go."

Swoboda leans back and sighs audibly, as if for the first time he had grasped a difficult principle. The room, with its wooden pews and narrow blackboard, is getting close.

I say, "The concept of a limit, as it is applied to functions, is forged in the fire of these remarks."

I step back to the blackboard and write:

As x approaches 3, f(x) approaches 9.

Or again:

As x gets closer and closer to 3, f(x) gets closer and closer to 9.

Or yet again:

As x gets closer and closer to 3, f(x) approaches 9 as a limit.

"You see," I say, "the function $f(x)$ has a limit at L if, as x approaches some number C, $f(x)$ gets closer and closer to L."

Sir Arnold Bergen mouths the words *closer* and *closer*.

"The analysis," I say professorially, "proceeds as it has proceeded in the case of sequences; *f(x)* is getting closer and closer to the limit L if the differences between $f(x)$ and L are getting smaller and smaller, if they may be made small without end—arbitrarily small."

Sir Arnold allows the accumulated tension in his body to collapse. I am tremendously pleased that I have made my point, even though it is a point with which every mathematician in the modern world is familiar.

And then I say something that astonishes *me*: "It is when functions are seen in *this* context that the poignancy of the process becomes for the first time palpable."

Several of the men cross themselves.

"In the example of $f(x)=x2,$ the function achieves a moment of blessed release at the number 3 itself; *there $f(x)$ is 9,* the process of getting closer and closer over and done with."

"Yes," says Sir Arnold.

Then I write the symbols $f(x)=(x2-1)/(x-1)$ on the blackboard and rap the board with my knuckles.

"Here," I say, "is another story."

Ivan Havel has let his attention wander, but Swoboda and Schweik are looking at me raptly.

"As x approaches ever more closely the number 1," I say, "*f(x),* as a few examples will reveal, gets closer and closer to the number 2. It *approaches* 2 as a limit."

I say this dramatically, wiping my hands again on my suit in the same gesture that I find so strange.

"But *at* 1 itself—I pause dramatically and allow a heavy, meaningful silence to invade the room—"*f(x)* lapses into nothingness, *tak?*"

Sir Arnold Bergen is frowning again in concentration.

"The function *f(x)* lapses into nothingness *because*"—I say this word very deliberately—"(1-1)/(1-1) is simply 0/0. At its limit, this function is *undefined*. The behavior of a function at an inaccessible point is expressed or explained by its behavior in a *neighborhood* of that point."

There is another puzzled look from Sir Arnold. I see suddenly what I really wish to say: "The function gets closer and closer to its limit, but, you see, it never *reaches* that limit."

Tak, says someone in my audience, *like man to God*.

I say good-bye to Swoboda and Schweik at the metro station. I watch for a moment as they trudge down the street. Their tread is heavy and tired; I notice that they barely lift their feet from the ground.

David Berlinski received a B.A. degree from Columbia College and a Ph.D. from Princeton University. Having a tendency to lose academic positions with what he himself describes as an embarrassing urgency, Berlinski now devotes himself entirely to writing. His books include Black Mischief: Language, Life, Logic and Luck, Less Than Meets the Eye, The Body Shop *and* A Tour of the Calculus, *from which this story was excerpted. He lives in San Francisco.*

★

When Einstein—this piece of the Milky Way—was asked what he sought, he answered: "I want to know how the Old One thinks. The rest is detail." This creature wearing worn-out shoes, this mustachioed member of the notochord phylum, this living flesh with its creases from a lifetime of laughter, this lumpy concentration of molecules, this soul searing with wonder burned to know how the Old One thinks. How the Old One is shaping great vaults of the heavens. How the Old One is casting a billion stars in their circlings. How the Old One is fastening the baryons together, how the Old One is releasing electromagnetism throughout the cellular membranes.

—Brian Swimme, *The Hidden Heart of the Cosmos:*
Humanity and the New Story

JOHN KRICH

✦ ✦ ✦

Allah Hit Me

The oneness of humanity
is inescapable.

WE FILED INTO A VILLAGE TAVERN WHERE THE FOOD SIMMERED forever in giant pots. Each of the passengers pointed at the stew of their choice. While we ate, half-dazed, we saw the dim outlines of peasants lingering in the town's one cobblestone square. Hands jammed down their pockets, watch-chains showing from their vest pockets, pancake-shaped caps overhanging flesh-buried eyes, the men were submerged in silence. They seemed to be holding a tortuous vigil, waiting for a drawing of lots that would determine the next one to lose his crop, his land, his best mule or his wife. Or the next man to sneak away in the night for America.

Before reboarding the bus, while Iris searched out a toilet. I wandered off into the square. The night offered a sweet sheep-herding darkness, though it was lit by stars plentiful as prophets' oaths. The villagers smoked strong cigarettes; they fiddled in syncopation with strings of sorrow-polished worry beads. I did nothing but drift, circle and watch. From the way their wide-brimmed caps shielded their weary faces, from their formidable recalcitrance, they could have been Sicilian Mafiosi. Any of them could have been my grandfather, a guarded and suspicious greenhorn, getting off the boat at Ellis Island. And I realized *I* was wearing my Mao cap from Hong Kong to the same effect; slung over same eyes, same anxieties, same gratitude for night. Hunched over, in their black vests, the Turks were coughing and whinnying and worrying. They carried the burden of the stars. In my homespun white vest, I whinnied and worried and hunched over, too. When I tried to turn away from my likeness with them, I noticed how all of them seemed to turn away doggedly from their common likeness. The turning away was part of the likeness itself.

Then Allah hit *me*. A genetic chill struck, more strongly than it had with the yiddisher mommas of businessmen on the bus. I knew that I was getting as close to my beginnings as I was ever likely to get. In silence, I communed with these brethren of mine, with a peasant's legacy of grieving and furtive strength that I carried in my bones. What difference did it make if I moved up and down these well-traveled routes from one hiding place to another? The planet spun and held me to it along with these crumbling walls and broken men. I would always be found in the village square.

Together, under the stars, under our thinking caps and our planning caps and our working caps and our yearning caps, clinging to our glorious separation, my colleagues and I brooded over the unyielding terrain we'd been placed on and over our identity,

> "*Turk men keep word. All Turks Muslims.*"
>
> He announced that like none of us could possibly know.
>
> "*Very religious, good Muslims. Must be good. Keep Muslim rules.*" And what about keeping schedules? "*If I bad Muslim, when I die, go to heaven, Allah hit me.*"
>
> Iris and I couldn't help laughing. The hierarchy of fisticuffs rose into the sky. There was only one bully and his name was Allah!
>
> "*Yes! Yes! That true!*" Kemil was encouraged by our laughter and sought to sustain it. "*If I no good, Allah hit me good. Give me one right across here.*" To illustrate, he socked another of the kids in the jaw. "*Allah strong man. Just like Muhammed Ali Clay.*"
>
> —John Krich, *Music in Every Room: Around the World in a Bad Mood*

which came hard, which also had to be sown and reaped, all of us pondering long journeys, and what purpose we might serve on this earth.

Award-winning writer John Krich is the author of a novel about the private life of Fidel Castro, A Totally Free Man, *as well as three non-fiction books,* Why is This Country Dancing?: A One-Man Samba to the Beat of Brazil, El Beisbol: Travels Through the Pan-American Pastime *and* Music in Every Room: Around the World in a Bad Mood, *from which this story was excerpted. His travel and sports writing, reportage and fiction, have appeared in* Mother Jones, Vogue, Sports Illustrated, *the* Village Voice, The New York Times, *and many other publications. He lives in San Francisco.*

*

You could not discover the frontiers of the soul, even if you traveled every road to do so; such is the depth of its meaning.

—Heraclitus of Ephesus

WILLIAM ELLIOTT

⋆ ⋆ ⋆

Everything for God

Who will minister to a saint?

THE BUS RIDE FROM DHARAMSALA TO NEW DELHI TOOK ALMOST a day. We traveled a winding road through mountains that were both breath-taking and deadly. It wasn't unusual to see the remains of a poorly driven bus at the bottom of a ravine or cliff.

In New Delhi, I hopped on a train to Calcutta. I've always enjoyed the rustic barrenness of Indian trains, especially third class, where the seats and sleepers are plain wooden boards, hanging by chains. Third class is an austere experience that connects a person to the simplicity and salt-of-the-earth, day-to-day existence of Indian life. Years before I had traveled third class and loved being among the common people. This time I again opted for third class, and although I paid for a sleeper for myself, there were other people sharing the space with me. The train was packed. We sat shoulder to shoulder in a car without air-conditioning, and everyone sweated together. After a day of intense heat, my romanticism melted away. I slipped off the train anonymously, paid extra, and boarded the second-class air-conditioned car.

I was given a sleeper across from a wealthy Indian businessman. I tried to make small talk, but he didn't say much. He had an air of superiority and seemed distant. The only thing we seemed to have in common was our balding heads. "So," I asked, "when did you start losing you hair?"

He looked at me, and his face softened. It was the first time he had smiled. We spoke for the next few hours about baldness cures and politics.

"Would you take a pill if it cured baldness?" I asked.

"Most definitely," the man replied without hesitation. We laughed together and lay awake in our sleepers till deep into the night, talking like two brothers.

When the train arrived in Calcutta, I asked an Indian man for directions to my hotel. He showed me the line for taxis and waited with me. After thirty minutes, a taxi came. When I asked if he wanted to share the taxi, he said no, that he waited in line only to make sure I continued my journey safely.

Within the first few minutes of arriving in Calcutta, I got sick. I stayed inside my hotel the entire day. The next morning I felt better and went outside, but within minutes, I was sick again. I was sick for three days.

The night of the first day, I was delirious. I was so sick that before I went to sleep and while waiting for a doctor, I wrote my Last Will and Testament. That night, I dreamt that my mind had broken into clear, small cubes. In each cube, there was an electrical charge that was pulsating on and off. When I awoke, I wasn't sure I could even speak.

The first mass at Mother Teresa's mission started at 5:45. As soon as I stepped out of the taxi, beggars surrounded me. "Are you a Christian?" they asked.

I nodded in affirmation.

"Me, too. Let me show you her door."

The mission's door was halfway down the alley; there, the beggars held out their hands, expecting payment. It was hard to refuse a beggar in Mother Teresa's doorway.

The chapel inside the mission was very simple. There were few chairs; most people sat on the cement floor. Mother Teresa sat near the back wall deep in prayer and looked as though she had been sitting there for a hundred years. She seemed so normal, so ordinary. How did a person of her simplicity ever become famous? Even at her age, she sat on the same cement floor everyone else at Mass sat on, except me—I cheated and brought a blanket.

After a while, Mother Teresa got up and walked to the altar. She wore a blue and white habit, and her walk was like that of a bride about to be married. There were no necessary distractions in her walk. It was simple and deliberate.

Perhaps in Mother Teresa's walk was the secret of her life. Mother Teresa didn't appear to be a visionary with grand ideas and the need to complete them. Instead, her life was a series of steps; with each step, she accomplished what God presented to her. And because her Beloved was here in the midst of life and not in the future or some heavenly realm, Mother Teresa was also here, in this present moment. For Mother Teresa, each step on her way to the altar was done in God's presence. Each step was a communion.

After the Mass, I lost Mother Teresa in the crowd of people who gathered around her. When the people dispersed, I told a nun I was there to see Mother Teresa.

"Oh," she said, motioning to her right. "She is right here." I was surprised to see that Mother Teresa had been standing only a few feet away. If you didn't know she was a "saint," you probably wouldn't look twice at her.

arallel with the natural philosophy of alchemy and strongly influencing it are ideas of Jewish mysticism. I refer to the Cabalistic idea of tsim tsum, *or retreat, withdrawal. The Cabalistic argument follows this line of reasoning: Since God is everywhere, "the existence of the universe is made possible by a process of shrinking in God." To create, to produce, room must be made for the things of this world. God, so omnipresent, so omnipotent, crowds out all other kinds of existence. So he must pull back for the creation to come into being. Only by withdrawal does God allow the world. The ruling principle at the top must not be omnipresent (being everywhere) and omniscient (knowing everything). Productivity happens by God's getting out of the way. He ignores; becomes an ignorant God; rules by benign neglect. He puts himself into exile.*

—James Hillman, *Kinds of Power: A Guide to Intelligent Uses*

I told her why I had come. "I don't do interviews anymore," she said, waving her hand. "So many interviews."

My excitement suddenly turned to disappointment. Without Mother Teresa's interview, I felt that the book [I was writing] would be incomplete. It wouldn't be the way I planned.

I wanted to ask her again—to use my traveling such a distance and to use my suffering and the suffering of the world in order to persuade her to do the interview. I wanted to beg her, because I didn't want to go home feeling I had failed myself and anyone who might read my book.

I handed her the letter she sent me. Perhaps she didn't realize she had already consented to do an interview. She glanced at the letter and gave it back to me. Then she took my hand and held it lovingly in both her hands and pulled me close to her. Her gray eyes looked into mine.

"I'm not feeling well," she said. "And I'm tired."

When she said that, it was as though God was telling me she was going to die. My concern for myself suddenly shifted to her. And by looking into those eyes, I saw it and took it in as though it were a gift. It was suffering. In some strange way, I felt the vast *suffering* Mother Teresa had witnessed. It was a suffering I had experienced before but rejected, because it had been too much for me. Now, years later, the suffering had returned. It had come full circle; only now I had grown enough to accept it.

"Do everything for God..." Mother Teresa continued. "God has given you many gifts—use them for the greater glory of God and the good of the people. Then you will make your life something beautiful for God; for this you have been created. Keep the joy of loving God ever burning in your heart, and share this joy with others. That's all."

I barely heard her; there was something deeper overwhelming me. I had come all this way with my mind set on interviewing Mother Teresa, but now that all changed because she was asking for something from me. Her eyes conveyed this. After having understood so many, I realized that Mother Teresa also needed understanding.

There was a line of people outside waiting to see Mother Teresa. A line that never ends. What will they do when she dies? Who will be our Mother Teresa then?

I tried to forget the thought of Mother Teresa dying, because dying was something our society didn't talk about—especially when talking about Mother Teresa. But I couldn't get away from it. And the moment seemed to take on a timeless element. Everything seemed to be happening quite slowly. Looking down, I could see Mother Teresa's hand in mine. Looking back up at her, I saw her eyes. She was such a small, simple person, perhaps not even five feet tall, and yet there was something else in our interaction that was making itself known. I was being stretched further and further.

It was a feeling I had had before when my mother was dying. It was utter disappointment, a disappointment from which no one could save me. And this disappointment stemmed from the fear that I was being abandoned in this world.

The child in me had once wondered, What will I do without my mother? Now, as an adult, I wondered what I would do without Mother Teresa. What would the human race do without a Mother Teresa? Who would be our Mother after she was gone? All this passed before me in a moment—a moment that ran the length of my life.

Mother Teresa in all her wonderful loving presence now appeared to me in a different way. She was no longer a saint; she was more than that. She was a human being. She was what we, as human beings, were meant to be all along. She was so deeply human and ordinary that she had touched that part of humanity that touched God, a humanity that can suffer, cry, laugh, and even die while staying connected with that essence that infuses us.

There was a bittersweet quality to this moment. A year earlier when I met Brother David, he said. "The difference between you and me is that you are young and expanding and I am old and contracting." He had said this with a genuine smile, but the shadow of sadness had framed the moment.

"Anyway," Mother Teresa continued, and I suddenly became

aware again of her presence, "You have the Dalai Lama. He's enough!"

As she said that, she waved her hand in the air as though to say, "Go on. It's going to be all right; you've got everything you need."

She turned and walked slowly back to her room. Her walk was just as it was the first time I saw her—nothing special. In some ways, her presence was also nothing special. It was a presence of utter simplicity. I doubt whether there has ever been a human being as ordinary as Mother Teresa, but it is precisely this quality that has made her so extraordinary.

Out in the hallway, people sat on benches that lined the walls. They waited to get a glimpse of Mother Teresa and smiled at me when they realized I had met the person they came to see. Today, I was proud to be a human being—because Mother Teresa was one.

Back in the street the beggars besieged me. Though I gave them money, they pressed me for more. In my frustration I waved them away because I was overwhelmed and even Mother Teresa was tired.

The next day, I went to see Mother Teresa again. I wanted her to bless the *malas,* which are prayer beads similar to Christian rosaries. I figured it would be a nice gift for my friends—prayer beads blessed by the Dalai Lama and Mother Teresa.

In the end, God manifests not as some kind of super floor show, but as a human being.

—George Simon, *Notebooks*

I met with the nun who was Mother Teresa's assistant. I asked her to give the *malas* to Mother Teresa to bless. "Oh, no," she replied, "I can't do that."

When I asked why, the nun said they were Hindu and not Christian rosaries. I tried to tell her that they were Christian to me, but she didn't seem convinced.

"Can you take them to her anyway?" I asked. But she refused again, until I told her that I didn't think Mother Teresa would mind. She relented and begrudgingly took the prayer beads to Mother Teresa.

I sat in the dimly lit waiting room. I found it hard to believe that one of Mother Teresa's nuns would make this distinction. If here, in such a place as this, people still believed in the illusion that religions are so different, what could we expect of the outside world?

Just then, the nun returned, smiling. She said Mother Teresa had blessed the prayer beds without hesitation.

William Elliot spent almost a decade traveling and interviewing for his book Tying Rocks to Clouds, *from which this story was excerpted. He currently works as a mental health professional at night while writing and pursuing a master's degree in counseling psychology during the day.*

⋆

I must remember
to go down to the heart cave
& sweep it clean; make it warm
with a fire on the hearth,
& the candles in their niches,
the pictures on the walls
        glowing with a quiet light

                    I must remember
to go down to the heart cave
            & make the bed
with the quilt from home,
strew
            rushes on the floor
                    & hang
lavendar and sage
            from the corners

        I must go down
to the heart cave & be there
        when you come
                    —Geoffrey Brown, "The Heart Cave,"
                    Road of the Heart Cave

JULIAN GREEN
TRANSLATED BY J. A. UNDERWOOD

✦ ✦ ✦

The Palais-Royal

In our father's house there
are many mansions.

ONE SPRING DAY WHEN ERRANDS HAD BROUGHT ME TO THE
vicinity of the Louvre, I was driven by the noise of the streets as far
as the north entrance of the Palais-Royal, in the rue de Beaujolais.
This is one of those places where there lurks a certain quality of
mystery more easily divined than defined. Walking in under the
dark vault, between columns whose symmetry, by some quirk of
visual perception, was not apparent to me, I had the feeling that
I was entering an enchanted forest, leaving everyday life behind
me, because one of the privileges of Paris, one of its rarest graces,
bestowed only on those who know how to waste time there, is
suddenly to show itself in unusual guises, arousing both the pleasure of the unexpected and a subtle anxiety that could easily tip
over into fear. Where am I? Shall I, when I come to retrace my
steps, find myself back in the world I know? Such questions tend
to cross the mind of the stroller who is given, as I am, to certain
forms of day-dreaming, and for the space of a second or two I
experienced the faint distress that comes from thinking you have
lost your way. Was it the light of that stormy afternoon, or the
fortuitous loneliness of the spot, or the silence after the tumult of
the streets and squares? I felt I was on the threshold of a new

country whose names figured in no book and where everything we think of as belonging to the material world was by some elusive mechanism becoming, as it were, the tangible aspect of the inner world; or rather I had the feeling of suddenly slipping behind the scenes of reality and coming upon a secret, except what secret could be more futile than one whose meaning escapes you! The fact is, I could not have said what it was that made everything seem different to me: was there a spot in all Paris with which I was more familiar than that space bounded on one side by a wrought-iron gate and on the other by dark shops that might have been shops for ghosts? My hand brushed against one of the white columns, and I took a few paces forward. I was advancing not so much in space as in memory, and not so much in the memory of my own life as in the scattered recollections of a whole race of men.

Like someone experiencing a hallucination, I went over and placed my face between the bars of the gate, the gilded tips of which shone brightly against a threatening sky. It was towards that sombre sky, now turning from grey to lilac, that my gaze was drawn. I could glimpse it between the tiny leaves, still shy in their greenness, that shivered in the first gusts of the storm. One by one the birds fell silent and the nannies dragged away their spade-waving charges. Soon I was the only one left observing the inky clouds as they unfurled above the rooftops amid the solemn murmur of the wind. Suddenly, in that moment that precedes the first clap of thunder, when everything seems to be listening attentively for the initial roll, I was taken out of myself, as it were, and handed over to an invisible crowd. Countless thoughts went flooding through my mind, like a wave crashing on the shore with a sort of violent tenderness. The soul of an entire city entered into the cries, sighs, and guffaws of the storm gathering above my head, and my heart began to beat in unison with that great joy so full of anger and alarm. It was as if the dull rumble of the sky was being answered by a distant voice issuing from the depths of time. I listened, motionless; then a long line of fire split the sky from end to end, and amid the din that almost immediately ensued the rain came lashing down on the ancient garden.

I heard it with delight, that intricate sound whose muffled tones are so aptly tuned to the melancholy of old memories; and soon there rose up from the ground, restoring me to myself with that immense benediction of the universe that we all sense at some time in our lives, the most exquisite smell in the world, at once the freshest and the most immemorial, the most mysterious and the most innocent, the closest to the origins of our planet and the most recent, the smell that moves the heart of man to the greatest sadness and the greatest gladness, the odour of damp earth.

Born in 1900 of American parents living in Paris, Julian Green has spent most of his literary career there, writing in French for a wide and enthusiastic European readership. He has published over sixty-five books in France; novels, essays, plays, and fourteen volumes of his Journal. *This story was excerpted from his book,* Paris.

✳

Recommended Reading

We hope *Travelers' Tales: The Road Within* has inspired you to read on. A good place to start is the books from which we've made selections, and these are listed below along with other books that we have found to be valuable. Some of these may be out of print but are well worth hunting down.

Arden, Harvey. *Dreamkeepers: A Spirit Journey into Aboriginal Australia.* New York: Harper Perennial, 1994.

Atwater, P.M.H. Lh.D., *Future Memory: How Those Who "See the Future" Shed New Light on the Workings of the Human Mind.* New York: Birch Lane Press, 1996.

Berlinski, David. *A Tour of the Calculus.* New York: Pantheon, 1995.

Blank, Jonah. *Arrow of the Blue-Skinned God: Retracing the Ramayana Through India.* New York: Image Books, 1993.

Bly, Robert. *Iron John: A Book About Men.* 15th ed. New York: Addison-Wesley, 1991.

Brown, Geoffrey. *Road of the Heart Cave.* Newton, Massachusetts: Thrown to the Winds Press, 1984.

Brown, Tom Jr. *The Way of Scout.* New York: Berkeley, 1995.

Buford, Bill. *Among the Thugs: The Experience, and the Seduction, of Crowd Violence.* London: Martin, Secker & Warburg, 1990.

Bullitt, Stimson. *River Dark and Bright.* Seattle: Willows Press, 1995.

Chaudhuri, Haridas. *Sri Aurobindo: The Prophet of Life Divine.* India: Sri Aurobindo Ashram Press, 1951.

Chopra, Deepak. *The Seven Spiritual Laws of Success: A Practical Guide to the Fulfillment of Your Dreams.* San Rafael, California: Amber-Allen Publishing, 1994.

Cooper, David A. *Entering the Sacred Mountain: Exploring the Mystical Practices of Judaism, Buddhism, and Sufism.* New York: Bell Tower, 1994.

Covington, Dennis. *Salvation on Sand Mountain: Snake Handling and Redemption in Southern Appalachia*. New York: Addison–Wesley, 1994.

Dillard, Annie. *Encounters with Chinese Writers*. Connecticut: Wesleyan University Press, 1984.

Dillard, Annie. *Pilgrim at Tinker Creek*. New York: Harper Perennial, 1988.

Donner, Florinda. *Being-in-Dreaming*. San Francisco: HarperSan Francisco, 1991.

Ehrlich, Gretel. *A Match to the Heart*. New York: Pantheon, 1994.

Elliott, William. *Tying Rocks to Clouds: Meetings and Conversations with Wise and Spiritual People*. Wheaton, Illinois: Quest Books, 1995.

Franz, Carl. *The People's Guide to Mexico* (8th ed.). Santa Fe, New Mexico: John Muir Publications, 1992.

Gattuso, John. *A Circle of Nations: Voices and Visions of American Indians*. Hillsboro, Oregon: BeyondWords Publishing, 1993.

Goldberg, Natalie. *Long Quiet Highway: Waking Up in America*. New York: Bantam Books, 1993.

Goodman, Richard. *French Dirt: The Story of a Garden in the South of France*. North Carolina: Algonquin Books of Chapel Hill, 1991.

Green, Julian. J. A. Underwood, trans. *Paris*. New York: Marion Boyars Publishers, 1991.

Hall, James. *Sangoma: My Odyssey into the Spirit World of Africa*. New York: Touchstone, 1994.

Harvey, Andrew. *Hidden Journey: A Spiritual Awakening*. New York: Arkana, 1992.

Harvey, Andrew. *A Jounrey in Ladakh*. London: Jonathan Cape, 1983.

Hickman, Katie. *A Trip to the Light Fantastic: Travels with a Mexican Circus*. London: Flamingo, 1994.

Hillman, James. *Kinds of Power: A Guide to Intelligent Uses*. New York: Currency/Doublday, 1995.

Hodgson, Michael, ed. *No Shit! There I Was…Wild Stories from Wild People*. Merrillville, Indiana: ICS Books, Inc., 1994.

Kaku, Michio. *Hyperspace: A Scientific Odyssey Through Parallel Universes, Time Warps, and The Tenth Dimension*. New York: Oxford University Press, 1994.

Kingsolver, Barbara. *High Tide in Tuscon: Essays from Now or Never*. New York: HarperPerennial, 1996

Krich, John. *Music in Every Room: Around the World in a Bad Mood.* New York: Bantam Books, 1984.

Lopez, Barry. *Crossing Open Ground.* New York: Random House, 1988.

Maass, Peter. *Love Thy Neighbor: The Story of War.* New York: Borzoi, 1996. London: Picador, 1996.

Matousek, Mark. *Sex, Death, Enlightenment.* New York: Riverhead Books, 1996.

McIntyre, Mark. *The Kindness of Strangers: Penniless Across America.* New York: Berkley Books, 1996.

Mehta, Ved. *Mahatma Gandhi and His Apostles.* New York: Viking Press, 1976.

Newton, Michael. *Journey of Souls: Case Studies of Life Between Lives.* Minnesota: Llewelleyn Publications, 1994.

O'Hanlon, Redmond. *In Trouble Again: A Journey Between the Orinoco and the Amazon.* New York: Vintage Departures, 1990. New York: Atlantic Monthly Press, 1988.

Powys, John Cowper. *The Meaning of Culture.* New York: W.W. Norton & Co., 1929.

Preston, Douglas. *Talking to the Ground: One Family's Journey on Horseback Across the Sacred Land of the Navajo.* New York: Simon & Schuster, 1995.

Ramdas, Swami. *In Quest of God: The Saga of an Extraordinary Pilgimage.* San Diego: Blue Dove Press, 1994.

Raymo, Chet. *Honey from Stone: A Naturalist's Search for God.* New York: Penguin Books, 1989.

Roberts, Paul William. *River in the Desert: Modern Travels in Ancient Egypt.* New York: Random House, 1993.

Roberts, Paul William. *In Search of the Birth of Jesus: The Real Journey of the Magi.* New York: Riverhead Books, 1996.

Rogers, Susan Fox, ed. *Another Wilderness: New Outdoor Writing by Women.* Seattle: Seal Press, 1994.

Salzman, Mark. *Iron & Silk.* New York: Vintage Departures, 1990.

Sheldrake, Rupert. *Seven Experiments That Could Change the World: A Do-It-Yourself Guide to Revolutionary Science.* New York: Riverhead Books, 1995.

Swimme, Briane. *The Hidden Heart of the Cosmos: Humanity and the New Story.* Maryknoll, New York: Orbis Books, 1996.

Tagore, Rabindranath. *Gitanjali*. New York: Scribner, 1997.

Talbot, Michael. *The Holographic Universe*. New York: HarperPerennial, 1991.

Thomsen, Moritz. *The Saddest Pleasure: A Journey on Two Rivers*. St. Paul, Minnesota: Graywolf Press, 1990.

Trench, Richard. *Forbidden Sands*. Chicago: Academy Chicago Ltd., 1980.

van der Post, Laurens. *About Blady: A Pattern Out of Time*. Orlando, Floriday: Harvest/HBJ Books, 1993.

Ward, Tim. *What the Buddha Never Taught*. Berkeley, California: Celestial Arts, 1993.

Ward, Tim. *Arousing the Goddess*. Toronto: Somerville House Books, 1996. New York: Random House, 1997.

Watson, Lyall. *Gifts of Unknown Things: A True Story of Nature, Healing, and Intiation from Indonesia's Dancing Island*. Rochester, Vermont: Destiny Books, 1991.

Watson, Lyall. *Dark Nature: A Natural History of Evil*. New York: HarperCollins Publishers, 1995.

Weil, Andrew. *The Natural Mind*. New York: Houghton Mifflin Company, 1972, 1986.

Wilber, Ken. *A Brief History of Everything*. Boston: Shambala, 1996.

Wilson, Colin. *Poetry and Mysticism*. San Francisco: City Lights Books, 1969.

Yeadon, David. *The Back of Beyond: Travels to the Wild Places of the Earth*. New York: HarperPerennial, 1992.

Zukav, Gary. *The Seat of the Soul*. New York: Fireside, 1990.

Index

Africa 91, 220
Alabama 275
Alaska 291
Albuquerque, New Mexico 9
Arizona 293
Assisi 186
Aurobindo 387
Australia 236
Ayers Rock 236

Banda Sea 19
Barcelona 3
Beijing 73
Bodh Gaya 52, 53
Bosnia 349, 350
Buckminster Fuller 136
Buddha 123, 139
Buddhism 53, 139, 232, 235

Cairo 59, 178
Calcutta 409
California 127, 180, 262
Cape of Good Hope 383
Cape Town 382
Catholicism 164
Cerro de la Neblina, Venezuela 34
China 73, 211
Czech Republic 397

Darshan 300
Deepavali 108
Diwali 108
Dreamtime 236, 240, 243
Durban 380

Ecological research 36
Egypt 58, 178

Fishing 144
France 150, 244, 269, 415

Gardening 269
Germany 299
Great Imambara 204

Hiking 159
Himalayas 44
Hinduism 52, 108, 206
Hípana 36
Holi 371
Horseback riding 178
Humboldt County 129

India 52, 105, 204, 387, 408
Initiation ceremony 220
Islam 58
Israel 78
Italy 163, 186, 319

Japan 232
Jerusalem 78, 84
Jesús-María 358
Johannesburg 378
Judaism 78, 254, 410
Jungle expedition 34

Kali Gandaki gorge 41
Kayaking 191
Kyoto 232

Labyrinth 204
Lake Superior 156
Lama Foundation 16
Lucknow 204

Mahyua Pradesh 371
Malaysia 199
Malibu 180
Mexico 252, 357
Minnesota 155, 191
Mother Meera 300
Mother Teresa 409

Nepal 41, 44
Nilajan River 55

Palais-Royal 415
Paris 150, 415
Patna 113
Philippines 167
Pondicherry 387
Prague 397
Puget Sound 191

Quantum physics 257
Quantum theory 398

Rio Baría 35
Rio Mawarinuma 36
Rio Negro 373
Rio Solimoes 373
Rome 163

Sangoma 220
Sea voyage 167
Skinwalkers 355
Snake handling 276
Snoqualmie River 145
Snorkeling 194
Sorcery 231
Soul 138, 203
South Africa 378
South China Sea 167

Sri Lanka 194
St. Peter's Basilica 163
St. Victor la Coste 244
Star Language 282
Sufism 58
Sukkot 87
Surabaja 19
Surfing 180
Swaziland 220
Swimming 192
Tai Chi 101, 102
Tantric experience 121, 147
Taos 16
Tembeling River 199
Thalheim 299
Trekking 41, 44
Trnopolje 350
Turin 319
Turkey 405

USA 249, 254

Varanasi 106
Venezuela 294
Vision quest 249

Washington 144, 191
Western Wall 83, 84
Witchcraft 355
Wushu 211

Yugoslavia 349

Zambezi River 198
Zen 232
Zuma Beach 180

Index of Contributors

Aaland, Mikkel 373–384
Arden, Harvey 243
Atwater, P.M H. Lh.D. 149, 307, 394

Barone, Jeanine 244–248
Berlinski, David 384, 397–404
Blank, Jonah 204–208, 261, 371–372
Blecker, Rhoda 254–261
Bly, Robert 12, 290
Bonaparte, Napoleon 206
Borges, Jorge Luis 402
Brown, Geoffrey 174, 414
Brown, Tom Jr. 214
Buford, Bill 319–349
Bullitt, Stimson 217
Burton–Christie, Douglas 293

Camus, Albert 1 29
Carey-Astrakhan, Claudia 180–184
Chaudhuri, Haridas 30
Chesterton, G.K. 133
Cooper, Rabbi David A. 78–89
Covington, Dennis 275–290
Cox, Lynne 84

David-Neel, Alexandra 212
Dillard, Annie 51, 73–77, 101, 298
Donner, Florinda 70, 231, 241
Dresser, Marianne 52–56

Ehrlich, Gretel 226, 228
Elkjer, Thom 3–8
Elliott, William 408–414
Erickson, Scott 155–161

Fletcher, Andy 401
Fontaine, Gary Ph.D. 22, 248

Franz, Carl 365

Gold, Herbert 360
Goldberg, Natalie 9–18, 113, 288, 333
Goodman, Richard 269–273
Green, Julian 415–417
Grimm, The Brothers 327

Habegger, Larry 191–202
Hall, James 220–230
Harvey, Andrew 123, 235, 285, 301, 353, 387–395
Hawk, Steve 185
Heraclitus of Ephesus 407
Hickman, Katie 357–371
Hillman, James 410
Hope, Francis 151
Howe, John R. 44–50
Huth, Tom 89–90

Inge, Dean William R. 159

James, Henry 312
Jaspers, Karl 250
Jimenez, Juan Ramon 290
Johnson, Marael 186–189
Jones, Gladys Montgomery 139–142

Kafka, Franz 315
Kaku, Michio 103–4
Kaplan, Robert D. 194
Khadka, Rajendra S. 41, 53, 108
Kingsolver, Barbara 17–18
Krich, John 208, 405–407
Kyi, Aung San Suu 377

Lopez, Barry 291–292

Maass, Peter 345, 349, 350–355
Markoff, John 267–268
Matousek, Mark 193, 392
Mayfield, Judith 262–267
McHugh, Paul 94–103
McIntyre, Mike 127–137
McKiernan, Dennis L. 164
Mehta, Ved Parkash 201
Merton, Thomas 14
Morris, Holly 144–149

Newton, Michael Ph.D. 153–154
Nietzsche, Friedrich 343

O'Hanlon, Redmond 294–298
O'Reilly, James 182
O'Reilly, Sean 163–165, 282
O'Reilly, Sean M.D. 341
O'Reilly, Tim 165

Pasteur, Louis 390
Powys, John Cowper 375
Preston, Douglas J. 356

Ramdas, Swami 393
Raymo, Chet 16, 93
Rilke, Rainer Maria 143, 291
Roberts, Paul William 48, 58–72,
    178–179
Robinson, Joe 175
Roze, Janis 34–42
Rumi 381
Russell, Bertrand 77

Salzman, Mark 99, 211–218
Sandburg, Carl 171
Sansone, Barbara 8

Seal, Mark 299–315
Sheldrake, Rupert 42–43, 399
Silha, Otto 136
Silha, Stephen 136
Simon, George 32–33, 413
Smith, Huston 232–234
Stark, Margaret P. 38
Sterling, Richard 167–178
Stevens, Wallace 263, 273–274
Sun-tzu 379
Swimme, Brian 404

Talbot, Michael 56–57, 122, 257
Tammaro, Thom 166
Tarde, Gabriel 322
Teilhard de Chardin, Pierre 117
Thomas, Dylan 168
Thomsen, Moritz 72
Trench, Richard 162
Tzu, Chuang 189
Tzu, Lao 152, 177
Utemorrah, Daisy 368

van der Post, Laurens 91–93, 238

Ward, Tim 68, 190, 105–123
Watson, Lyall 19–32, 339
Weil, Andrew 295
Wertime, Richard A. 253
White Deer of Autumn (Gabriel
    Horn) 249–252
White Eagle 272
Wilber Ken 147, 233, 313, 389
Wilson, Colin 100, 156, 331
Wozek, Gerard 150–153

Yeadon, David 236–243, 266

Zukav, Gary 138, 202–203

Acknowledgements

Many, many thanks to Judy Anderson, Peg Balka, Susan and Jeff Brady, Geoff Brown, Harriet Bullitt and Alexander Voronin, Kathleen Clark, Toby Clark, Cindy Collins, Bridget Davis, Deborah Greco, Beatrice and Bert Hernady, Chris Hince, Patty Holden, Faith Hornbacher, Michelle and Noel James, Priscilla Kapel, Raj Khadka, Hans King, Kerry and Maureen Kravitz, Jennifer Leo, Greg and Sharon Lunz, Judy and John Mayfield, Paula Mc Cabe, John McLean, Kevin O'Brien, Paul O'Leary, Brenda, Clement, Seumas, Liam, and Tobias O'Reilly, Christina, Arwen, and Meara O'Reilly, Fr. David O'Reilly, O.F.M., Noelle, Anna, Mariele, and Wenda O'Reilly, Sean and Anne O'Reilly, the staff of the periodical department of the Phoenix Central Library and the Luke Air Force Base library, Luis Pistener, Ron and Joan Rochon, Trisha Schwartz, Jack Schwarz, George and Mildred Simon, Solara, Jana Soriano, Curtis and Neise Turchin, George V. Wright, and David Yeadon.

"No Distance in the Heart" by Thom Elkjer published by permission of the author. Copyright © 1997 by Thom Elkjer.

"Garden of Paradise" by Natalie Goldberg excerpted from *Long Quiet Highway: Waking Up in America* by Natalie Goldberg. Copyright © 1993 by Natalie Goldberg. Used by permission of Bantam Books, a division of Bantam Doubleday Dell Publishing Group, Inc.

"Out of the Depths" by Lyall Watson excerpted from *Gifts of Unknown Things: A True Story of Nature, Healing, and Intiation from Indonesia's Dancing Island* by Lyall Watson, published by Destiny Books, an imprint of Inner Traditions International. Copyright © 1991 by Lyall Watson.

"Call of the Jungle" by Janis Roze originally appeared as "Journey to the Mountains of Mists" in Issue #3, 1996, of *Lapis*. Reprinted by permission of *Lapis*. Copyright © 1993 by *Lapis*.

"The Green Halo" by John R. Howe published by permission of the author. Copyright © 1997 by John R. Howe.

"Passing Through" by Marianne Dresser published by permission of the author. Copyright © 1997 by Marianne Dresser.

"Hearts with Wings" by Paul William Roberts excerpted from *River in the Desert: Modern Travels in Ancient Egypt* by Paul William Roberts. Copyright ©

"Treading Water" by Larry Habegger published by permission of the author. Copyright © 1997 by Larry Habegger.

"The Labyrinth" by Jonah Blank excerpted from *Arrow of the Blue-Skinned God: Retracing the Ramayana Through India* by Jonah Blank. Copyright © 1992 by Jonah Blank. Reprinted by permission of Houghton Mifflin Co. All rights reserved.

"The Master" by Mark Salzman excerpted from *Iron & Silk* by Mark Salzman. Copyright © 1986 by Mark Salzman. Reprinted by permission of Vintage Books, a division of Random House, Inc.

"The Vomiting Game" by James Hall excerpted from *Sangoma: My Odyssey into the Spirit World of Africa* by James Hall. Reprinted by permission of The Putnam Publishing Group. Copyright © 1994 by James Hall.

"A Taste of *Satori*" by Huston Smith published by permission of the author. Copyright © 1997 by Huston Smith.

"Dreamtime Odyssey" by David Yeadon published by permission of author. Copyright © 1997 by David Yeadon.

"Stone by Stone" by Jeanine Barone published by permission of the author. Copyright © 1997 by Jeanine Barone.

"The Great Holy Mystery" by White Deer of Autumn (Gabriel Horn) excerpted from *A Circle of Nations: Voices and Visions of American Indians* edited by John Gattuso. Reprinted by permission of Beyond Words Publishing. Copyright © 1993.

"Twist of Faith" by Rhoda Blecker originally appeared in the Aprill 11, 1993 issue of *The Washington Post*. Reprinted by permission of the author. Copyright © 1993 by Rhoda Blecker.

"The Guy at the End of the Bed" by Judy Mayfield published by permission | of the author. Copyright © 1997 by Judy Mayfield.

"Instincts" by Richard Goodman excerpted from *French Dirt: The Story of a Garden in the South of France* by Richard Goodman. Copyright © 1991 by Richard Goodman. Reprinted by permission of Algonquin Books of Chapel Hill, a division of Workman Publishing, and Darhansoff & Verrill.

"The Serpent" by Dennis Covington excerpted from *Salvation on Sand Mountain: Snake Handling and Redemption in Southern Appalachia* (pages 156-177) by Dennis Covington. Text copyright © 1995 by Dennis Covington. Reprinted by permission of Addison-Wesley Longman, Inc.

"The Interior Landscape" by Barry Lopez excerpted from "Landscape and Narrative" from *Crossing Open Ground* by Barry Lopez. Reprinted by permission of Sterling Lord Literistic. Copyright © 1984, 1988 by Barry Halstun Lopez.

"Up Your Nose" by Redmond O' Hanlon excerpted from *In Trouble Again: A Journey Between the Orinoco and the Amazon* by Redmond O'Hanlon. Copyright © 1988 by Redmond O'Hanlon. Used by permission of Grove/Atlantic, Inc. and Peters, Fraser & Dunlop Group, Ltd.

"Meera Gazing" by Mark Seal reprinted from the July/August 1994 issue of *New Age Journal*. Reprinted by permission of Mark Seal. Copyright © 1994 by Mark Seal.

Selection from *The Back of Beyond: Travels to the Wild Places of the Earth* by David Yeadon reprinted by permission of the author. Copyright © 1991 by David Yeadon.

Selections from *Being-in-Dreaming* by Florinda Donner copyright © 1991 by Florinda Donner. Published by HarperCollins.

Selection from *Bioethics and the Limits of Science* by Sean O'Reilly, M.D. reprinted by permission. Copyright © Sean O'Reilly, M.D.

Selections from *A Brief History of Everything* by Ken Wilber copyright © 1996 by Ken Wilber. Reprinted by arrangement with Shambala Publications, Inc.

Selection from "A Church in Italy" by Thom Tammaro excerpted from *When the Italians Came to My Home Town* by Thom Tammaro. Reprinted by permission of the author. Copyright © 1995 by Thom Tammaro.

Selection from *Dark Nature: A Natural History of Evil* by Lyall Watson copyright © 1995 by Lyall Watson. Reprinted by permission of HarperCollins Publishers and David Higham Associates.

Selection from "Diwali, Deepvali, Tihar" by Rajendra S. Khadka published by permission of the author. Copyright © 1997 by Rajendra S. Khadka.

Selection from *Do Not Go Around the Edges* by Daisy Utemorrah, illustrated by Pat Torres, copyright © 1990 by Daisy Utemorrah. Reprinted by permission of Magabala Books, Broome Australia.

Selection from *Dreamkeepers: A Spirit Journey into Aboriginal Australia* by Harvey Arden copyright © 1994 by Harvey Arden. Reprinted by permission of HarperCollins Publishers, Inc.

Selection from "Einstein, Moondoggie and Me" by Steve Hawk reprinted from the July 1996 issue of *Surfer* magazine. Reprinted by permission of the author. Copyright © 1996 by Steve Hawk.

Selection from *Encounters with Chinese Writers* by Annie Dillard copyright © 1984 by Annie Dillard. Reprinted by permission of Wesleyan University Press.

Selection from *Forbidden Sands* by Richard Trench copyright © 1978 by Richard Trench. Reprinted by permission of Academy Chicago Ltd.

Selections from *Future Memory: How Those Who "See the Future" Shed New Light on the Workings of the Human Mind* by P. M. H. Atwater copyright © 1996 by P. M. H. Atwater. Reprinted by permission of Carol Publishing Group.

Selection from *Gitanjali* by Rabindranath Tagore reprinted with the permission of Scribner, a Division of Simon & Schuster and Macmillan Ltd (UK). Copyright © 1913.

Selection from "Gliding Across the Kali Gandaki" by Rajendra S. Khadka published by permission of the author. Copyright © 1997 by Rajendra S. Khadka.

Selection from *The Hidden Heart of the Cosmos: Humanity and the New Story* by Brian Swimme copyright © 1996 by Brian Swimme. Reprinted by permission of Orbis Books.

Selections from *Hidden Journey: A Spiritual Awakening* by Andrew Harvey copyright © 1991 by Andrew Harvey. Reprinted by permission of Henry Holt & Co., Inc. and Aitken & Stone Ltd.

Reprinted by permission of the editors, Heythrop College, Kensington Square, London. Copyright © 1994.

Selections from *Long Quiet Highway: Waking Up in America* by Natalie Goldberg copyright © 1993 by Natalie Goldberg. Used by permission of Bantam Doubleday Dell Publishing Group, Inc.

Selection by Juan Ramon Jimenez from *Lorca and Jimenez: Selected Poems,* edited and translated by Robert Bly, Beacon Press, Boston, 1997. Copyright © 1973, 1997 by Robert Bly. Reprinted by permission of Robert Bly.

Selections from *Love Thy Neighbor: The Story of War* by Peter Maass copyright © 1996 by Peter Maass. Reprinted by permission of Alfred A. Knopf, Inc. and MacMillan Ltd. (UK).

Selection from *Mahatma Gandhi and his Apostles* by Ved Mehta reprinted by permission of the author. Copyright © 1976 by Ved Mehta.

Selection from "The Man Watching"/"Archaic Torso of Apollo" excerpted from *Selected Poems of Rainer Maria Rilke* by Rainer Maria Rilke, edited and translated by Robert Bly copyright © 1981. Reprinted by permission of HarperCollins Publishers, Inc.

Selection from "The Man Who Levitates Hotels" by Tom Huth reprinted from the April 1988 issue of *California*. Copyright © 1988 by Tom Huth.

Selections from *A Match to the Heart* by Gretel Ehrlich copyright © 1994 by Gretel Ehrlich. Reprinted by permission of Random House, Inc.

Selection from "A Maya Sky" by Richard Wertime reprinted from the January/February issue of *Archaeology Magazine,* Vol. 44, No. 1. Reprinted by permission. Copyright © 1991 by the Archaeological Institute of America.

Selection from *The Meaning of Culture* by John Cowper Powys reprinted by permission of Laurence Pollinger Limited and the Estate of John Cowper Powys. Copyright © 1929 by John Cowper Powys.

Selection from "Mind Jumping" by Sean O'Reilly published by permission of the author. Copyright © 1997 by Sean O'Reilly.

Selections from *Music in Every Room: Around the World in a Bad Mood* by John Krich reprinted by permission of the author. Copyright © 1984 by John Krich.

Selection from *The Natural Mind* by Andrew Weil copyright © 1972, 1986 by Andrew Weil. Reprinted by permission of Houghton Mifflin Company. All rights reserved.

Selection from "Of Mere Being" by Wallace Stevens excerpted from *Opus Posthumous* by Wallace Stevens. Copyright © 1957 by Elsie Stevens and Holly Stevens. Reprinted by permission of Alfred A. Knopf, Inc. and Faber & Faber, Ltd.

Selection from *The People's Guide to Mexico* by Carl Franz, published by John Muir Publications, Santa Fe, NM 87505. Reprinted by permission. Copyright © 1972, 1974, 1975, 1976, 1979, 1982, 1986, 1988, 1990 by Carl Franz.

Selections from *Pilgrim at Tinker Creek* by Annie Dillard copyright © 1974 by Annie Dillard. Reprinted by permission of HarperCollins Publishers, Inc.

Selection from *Sri Aurobindo: The Prophet of Life Divine* by Haridas Chaudhuri copyright © 1951. Reprinted by permission of Sri Aurobindo Ashram Press.

Selection from *Talking to the Ground: One Family's Journey on Horseback Across the Sacred Land of the Navajo* by Douglas Preston copyright © 1995 by Douglas Preston. Reprinted by permission of Simon & Schuster, Inc. and Janklow & Nesbitt Associates.

Selection from "To Aqaba" by Lynne Cox published by permission of the author. Copyright © 1997 by Lynne Cox.

Selection from "Under the Mango Tree" by Barbara Sansone published by permission of the author. Copyright © 1997 by Barbara Sansone.

Selection from *The Way of Scout* by Tom Brown Jr. copyright © 1995 by Tom Brown Jr. Permission granted by The Berkley Publishing Group. All rights reserved.

Selection from *Way to Wisdom* by Karl Jaspers, translated by Ralph Manheim published by Yale University Press. Copyright © 1954.

Selections from *What the Buddha Never Taught* by Tim Ward reprinted by permission of the author. Copyright © 1990, 1993 by Tim Ward.

Selection from "Wilderness" by Laurens van der Post reprinted from Edition #2, 1995 of *Lapis*. Reprinted by permission of *Lapis*. Copyright © 1995 by *Lapis*.

About the Editors

The O'Reilly brothers grew up in San Francisco, attending St. Cecilia's Grammar School and St. Ignatius High School. At an early age they took a strong interest in world religions and the metaphysical, doing hatha yoga as youngsters, studying at the California Institute of Asian Studies as teens, and always reading, from Aquinas and Aurobindo to Wittgenstein and Colin Wilson. Early influences were also Tarzan of the Apes and John Carter of Mars.

Sean O'Reilly is a former seminarian, stockbroker, and prison instructor who lives in Arizona with his wife Brenda and their four small boys. He's had a life-long interest in consciousness and theology, and is at work on a book called *How to Manage Your Dick: A Guide for Men and Women*, which makes the proposition that classic Greek, Roman, and Christian moral philosophies, allied with post-quantum physics, form the building blocks of a new ethics and psychology. Widely traveled, Sean is Editor-at-Large and Director of International Sales for Travelers' Tales.

James O'Reilly, President and Editor-in-Chief of Travelers' Tales, wrote mystery serials before becoming a travel writer in the early 1980s. In 1985 he and co-author Larry Habegger began a syndicated newspaper column, "World Travel Watch," which still appears monthly throughout the USA. He's visited more than forty countries, along the way meditating with monks in Tibet, participating in West African voodoo rituals, and hanging out the laundry with nuns in Florence. He travels extensively with his wife Wenda and their three daughters. They live in Palo Alto, California when they're not in Leavenworth, Washington.

Tim O'Reilly is the founder and president of O'Reilly & Associates, a company that is recognized worldwide for innovations in publishing, software, and the Internet. He gives much of the credit for his business success to ideas and techniques for enhancing human potential and creativity that he first encountered growing up in San Francisco in the sixties. Before founding his company, Tim taught with the late George Simon, a pioneering researcher in altered states of consciousness, at Esalen and other centers around the U.S., and after his death in 1973, was the editor and publisher of his journals. Tim lives with his wife Christina and their two daughters in Sebastopol, California.

TRAVELERS' TALES

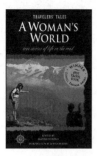

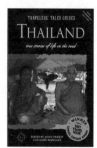

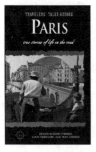